SpringBoard®
English
Language Arts

STUDENT EDITION   GRADE 8

About The College Board

The College Board is a mission-driven not-for-profit organization that connects students to college success and opportunity. Founded in 1900, the College Board was created to expand access to higher education. Today, the membership association is made up of over 6,000 of the world's leading educational institutions and is dedicated to promoting excellence and equity in education. Each year, the College Board helps more than seven million students prepare for a successful transition to college through programs and services in college readiness and college success—including the SAT® and the Advanced Placement Program®. The organization also serves the education community through research and advocacy on behalf of students, educators, and schools. For further information, visit collegeboard.org.

ISBN: 978-1-4573-1294-6

4 5 6 7 8   22 23 24 25 26

Printed in the United States of America

Acknowledgements

The College Board gratefully acknowledges the outstanding work of the classroom teachers who have been integral to the development of this program. The end product is testimony to their expertise, understanding of student learning needs, and dedication to rigorous and accessible English Language Arts instruction.

Lance Balla
Everett School District
Everett, Washington

Christina Bartholet
Goodman Middle
School, Gig Harbor,
Washington

Carisa Barnes
San Diego Unified
School District
San Diego, California

Leia Bell
Hillsborough County
Public Schools
Tampa, Florida

Alysa Broussard
Lafayette Parish
School System
Lafayette, Louisiana

Robert J. Caughey
San Dieguito Union
High School District
San Diego, California

Susie Challancin
Bellevue School District 405
Bellevue, Washington

Amanda Connell
Lisle, Illinois

Paul De Maret
Poudre School District
Fort Collins, Colorado

Michael Gragert
Plano Independent
School District
Plano, Texas

Nancy Gray
Brevard County Schools
Viera, Florida

Charles F. Hall
Peninsula School District
Gig Harbor, Washington

Charise Hallberg
Bellevue School District 405
Bellevue, Washington

T.J. Hanify
Bellevue School District 405
Bellevue, Washington

Cheryl Harris
Hurst-Euless-Bedford
Independent School District
Bedford, Texas

Karen Kampschmidt
Fort Thomas Independent
School District
Fort Thomas, Kentucky

Kerstin Karlsoon
Hillsborough County
Public Schools
Tampa, Florida

LeAnn Klepzig
Bradley County Schools
Cleveland, Tennessee

Michelle Lewis
Spokane Public School
Spokane, Washington

Susie Lowry
Volusia County
School District
Deland, Florida

John Marshall
Mead School District
Mead, Washington

Kristie Messer
Burnet Consolidated
Independent School
District Burnet, Texas

Missy Miles
Carmel Christian School
Charlotte, North Carolina

Glenn Morgan
San Diego Unified
School District
San Diego, California

Amanda Olinger
Harrisburg School District
Harrisburg, South Dakota

Kristin Oliver
Rio Rancho Public
School District
Rio Rancho, New Mexico

Molly Olmstead
Peninsula School District
Gig Harbor, Washington

Julie Pennabaker
Quakertown Community
School District
Quakertown, Pennsylvania

Bryan Sandala
School District of
Palm Beach County
West Palm Beach, Florida

Amanda Shackelford
Lafayette Parish
School System
Lafayette, Louisiana

Angela Shuttles
Hillsborough County Public
Schools Tampa, Florida

Kimberlyn Slagle
Lafayette Parish
School System
Lafayette, Louisiana

Holly Talley
Hillsborough County
Public Schools
Ruskin, Florida

Maria Torres-Crosby
Hillsborough County
Public Schools
Tampa, Florida

Susan Van Doren
Zephyr Cove, Nevada

JoEllen Victoreen
San Jose Unified
School District
San Jose, California

Aimee Welshans
San Diego Unified
School District
San Diego, California

Rebecca Wenrich
Peninsula School District
Gig Harbor, Washington

Research and Planning Advisors

We also wish to thank the members of our SpringBoard Advisory Council and the many educators who gave generously of their time and their ideas as we conducted research for both the print and online programs. Your suggestions and reactions to ideas helped immeasurably as we created this edition. We gratefully acknowledge the teachers and administrators in the following districts.

ABC Unified School District
Cerritos, California

Allen Independent School District
Allen, Texas

Bellevue, School District 405
Bellevue, Washington

Burnet Consolidated Independent School District
Burnet, Texas

Community Unit School District 308
Oswego, Illinois

Fresno Unified School District
Fresno, California

Frisco Independent School District
Frisco, Texas

Garland Independent School District
Garland, Texas

Grapevine-Colleyville Independent School District
Grapevine, Texas

Hamilton County Schools
Chattanooga, Tennessee

Hesperia Unified School District
Hesperia, California

Hillsborough County Public Schools
Tampa, Florida

ICEF Public Schools
Los Angeles, California

IDEA Public Schools
Weslaco, Texas

Irving Independent School District
Irving, Texas

Keller Independent School District
Keller, Texas

KIPP Houston
Houston, Texas

Lafayette Parish Schools
Lafayette Parish, Louisiana

Los Angeles Unified School District
Los Angeles, California

Lubbock Independent School District
Lubbock, Texas

Mansfield Independent School District
Mansfield, Texas

Midland Independent School District
Midland, Texas

Milwaukee Public Schools
Milwaukee, Wisconsin

New Haven School District
New Haven, Connecticut

Ogden School District
Ogden, Utah

Rio Rancho Public Schools
Rio Rancho, New Mexico

San José Unified School District
San José, California

Scottsdale Unified School District
Scottsdale, Arizona

Spokane Public Schools
Spokane, Washington

Tacoma Public Schools
Tacoma, Washington

SpringBoard English Language Arts

Lori O'Dea
Executive Director
Content Development

Natasha Vasavada
Executive Director
Pre-AP & SpringBoard

Doug Waugh
Vice President
SpringBoard & Pre-AP Programs

Sarah Balistreri
Senior Director
ELA Content Development

Florencia Duran Wald
Senior Director
ELA Content Development

Julie Manley
Senior Director
Professional Learning

Joely Negedly
Senior Director
Pre-AP Humanities

Jessica Brockman
Product Manager
English Language Arts

Suzie Doss
Director
SpringBoard Implementation

Jennifer Duva
Director
English Language Arts

Spencer Gonçalves
Director
Digital Content Development

Rebecca Grudzina
Senior Editor
English Language Arts

Georgia Scurletis
Senior Instructional Writer
Pre-AP English Language Arts

Abigail Johnson
Editor
English Language Arts

Casseia Lewis
Assistant Editor
English Language Arts

Natalie Hansford
Editorial Assistant
English Language Arts

Table of Contents

ACTIVITY	Unit 1: The Challenge of Heroism

CONTENTS

CONTENTS

Resources

*Texts not included in these materials.

Introduction to SpringBoard English Language Arts

About SpringBoard ELA

SpringBoard was built around a simple belief: if you give students and teachers the best materials, engaging methods, and ongoing support, then student success will surely follow. Developed by teachers, SpringBoard brings your classroom to life with materials that help you practice the skills and learn the knowledge you need to excel in middle school, high school, and beyond. Read on to find out how SpringBoard will support your learning.

Instructional Materials

SpringBoard English Language Arts supplies a Student Edition and Teacher Edition, in print and digital form, for grades 6–12. In addition to using the English Language Arts curriculum, you can sharpen your reading, writing, and language skills with materials including Language Workshop, Close Reading Workshop, and Writing Workshop.

Design that Begins with the End in Mind

- Based on the Understanding by Design model, SpringBoard teaches the skills and knowledge that matter most to meet AP and college and career readiness standards.

- You will start each unit by unpacking the assessment, so you know where you're heading and why the skills you're developing matter.

- Each activity starts with clear, standards-aligned learning targets.

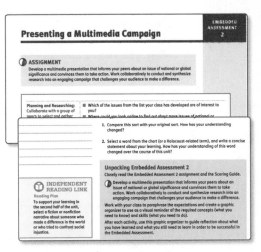

UNIT 2

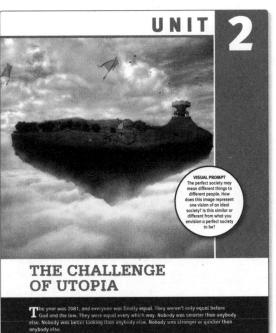

VISUAL PROMPT
The perfect society may mean different things to different people. How does this image represent one vision of an ideal society? Is this similar or different from what you envision a perfect society to be?

THE CHALLENGE OF UTOPIA

The year was 2081, and everyone was finally equal. They weren't only equal before God and the law. They were equal every which way. Nobody was smarter than anybody else. Nobody was better looking than anybody else. Nobody was stronger or quicker than anybody else.

The Practice of Reading Closely

- SpringBoard puts a special focus on close reading, giving you strategies and structure for developing this key skill.

- You will encounter compelling texts—fiction, nonfiction, poetry, drama, visuals, and film.

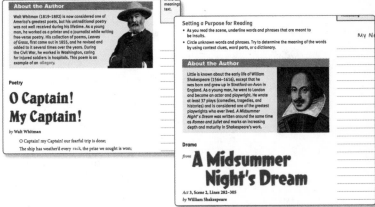

A Living System of Learning

- SpringBoard puts you and your classmates in charge of your learning to create a more dynamic classroom experience.

- With a flexible design and rich library of tools and resources, SpringBoard helps your teacher personalize instruction for your class.

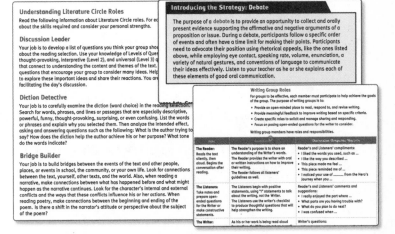

Bringing the Classroom to Life

When you enter a SpringBoard classroom you don't hear a teacher talking in the front of the room. You hear a buzz of excitement, with students working together and taking charge of how they learn. That's what the teachers who designed SpringBoard wanted for their classrooms, so they created a curriculum and materials that are focused on real classroom needs, encouraging teacher and student involvement.

SpringBoard translates the expectations of state standards into engaging daily lessons. We believe that reading, writing, speaking, and listening should all be learned together. You'll see examples of our integrated approach throughout our materials. And we put a special focus on close reading, giving you strategies and structure for developing this key skill.

Our Approach to Reading

In SpringBoard ELA, we move right into compelling texts—fiction, nonfiction, poetry, drama, visuals, and film—and offer the tools, supports, and approaches that will help you get the most out of every reading.

The Practice of Reading Closely

Texts take center stage in the SpringBoard ELA classroom, where you will prepare for close, critical reading of a wide range of materials. With guidance from your teacher, you will develop the habits of close reading that will serve you for a lifetime.

- **Setting a Purpose for Reading:** You ask questions, make predictions, observe genre characteristics and text structures, and prepare to annotate the text.

- **First Reading:** You read on your own, with a partner, in a group, or with the class. You annotate the text as you begin to uncover its meaning.

- **Making Observations:** Your teacher guides you to pause during or right after the first reading to observe the small details within a text in order to arrive at a deeper understanding of the whole.

- **Returning to the Text:** You continue to deepen your understanding of the text by responding to a series of text-dependent questions. You will use text evidence, speak with new vocabulary words, reflect on your classmates' ideas, and make connections among texts, ideas, and experiences.

- **Working from the Text:** You use the text as a source as you move from reading and analysis to productive work, including academic discussion and writing.

Reading Independently

As a SpringBoard student, you'll practice good reading habits in class so that you can read challenging texts in other classes and on your own. Independent reading is an integral part of every SpringBoard English Language Arts unit. At the beginning of the year, you will learn how to make a plan for independent reading. **Independent Reading Lists** for each unit give you a jump-start on selecting texts by offering a list of suggested titles, including a number of Spanish-language titles, that connect to the themes, genres, and concepts of the SpringBoard unit.

While you work your way through each unit, you will respond to **Independent Reading Links** that lead you to make connections between the reading you're doing on your own and the skills and knowledge you're developing in class. Twice per unit, **Independent Reading Checkpoints** give you a chance to reflect on and synthesize your independent reading in an informal writing assignment or discussion.

Reading to Build Knowledge

SpringBoard units are designed so that you can delve deeply into an overarching topic, theme, or idea. Each unit will pose essential questions that relate to the ideas and texts within the unit, and you will return to these questions again and again, each time refining your responses with new understanding and new evidence to support your point of view. You will also deepen your knowledge of key topics by conducting both on-the-spot and extended research, asking and answering questions, evaluating multiple sources, and synthesizing your findings.

Twice a unit you will go on a **Knowledge Quest**. Each Knowledge Quest begins with a Knowledge Question and supporting questions to focus your reading. After reading several texts that explore a topic, theme, or idea, you will get to return to the Knowledge Question and show your growing understanding of the topic by responding to a writing prompt or engaging in a discussion.

At the end of a Knowledge Quest, you will be encouraged to continue building your knowledge of the topic by going to **Zinc Reading Labs** and finding related texts to read. Zinc Reading Labs offers a variety of informational and literary texts that you can choose based on your interests. Vocabulary sets for each text let you learn new words and practice using them.

Your independent reading can also enhance your understanding of the topics you are studying in class if you want it to. SpringBoard's **Independent Reading Lists** include suggested books that relate to the topics and themes from each unit. By choosing those books you can see a different side of the topic, learn new words, and find other topics you want to learn more about.

Reading to Gain Perspectives

Gaining Perspectives features use a text as a jumping off point for examining an issue relevant to you. You will be asked to consider the perspectives of others and to empathize with others who have different points of view. You will also be asked to think about social and ethical norms and to recognize the family, school, and community resources available to you. Each Gaining Perspectives feature concludes with a writing task in which you will summarize the discussion you have with your classmates.

Our Approach to Writing

SpringBoard English Language Arts provides you with the support you need to write in all the major modes, emphasizing argumentative, informational, and narrative. You will write often, and you will learn to become a critical reviewer of your own and your peers' work through frequent opportunities for revision and editing. You will learn to plan with purpose, audience, topic, and context in mind; develop drafts with engaging ideas, examples, facts and commentary; revise for clarity, development, organization, style, and diction; and edit using the conventions of the English language.

The Craft of Writing

As you read texts by skilled authors, you will observe the many choices those authors make. You'll tune in to the ways authors purposefully use words, sentences, and structures to convey meaning. After analyzing and critiquing others' work, you will learn to apply your understanding of author's craft to your own writing. A few SpringBoard features help you do just that:

- **Writing prompts** lead up to the Embedded Assessments and give you practice with writing texts in multiple genres, including personal narratives, argumentative essays, letters, research papers, and more. Writing to Sources writing prompts drive you back to texts you have read or viewed to mine for evidence.

- **Focus on the Sentence** tasks help you process content while also practicing the craft of writing powerful sentences.

- **Grammar & Usage** features highlight interesting grammar or usage concepts that appear in a text, both to improve your reading comprehension and to help you attend to these concepts as you craft your own texts.

- **Language & Writer's Craft** features address topics in writing such as style, word choice, and sentence construction.

- **Language Checkpoints** offer in-depth practice with standard English conventions and guide you to develop an editor's checklist to use as a reference each time you check your own or a peer's written work.

Modes of Writing

SpringBoard helps you become a better academic writer by giving you authentic prompts that require you to use sources, and showing you how to work through the writing process. Over the course of the year you will have the chance to write narratives, arguments, and informational texts, and you will develop a wide range of writing skills:

- Consider task, audience, and purpose when structuring and organizing your writing.

- Incorporate details, reasons, and textual evidence to support your ideas.

- Generate research questions, evaluate sources, gather relevant evidence, and report and cite your findings accurately.

- Use research-based strategies that will guide you through the writing process.

Writing with a Focus on the Sentence

SpringBoard English Language Arts leverages sentence writing strategies that were developed by The Writing Revolution. These evidence-based strategies are part of the Hochman Method, the Writing Revolution's system for helping students learn to write across all content areas and grades. The Writing Revolution emphasizes the importance of embedding writing and grammar instruction into content. That's why SpringBoard's **Focus on the Sentence** tasks integrate sentence-level writing into the curriculum. These tasks not only help you learn and practice important grammar concepts and sentence forms, but they also provide a chance for you to process and demonstrate your understanding of texts, images, class discussions, and other content.

Our Approach to Vocabulary

Vocabulary is threaded throughout each unit and developed over the course of the SpringBoard English Language Arts year. You will have ample opportunities to read and hear new words, explore their meanings, origins, and connotations, and use them in written and oral responses.

- Important academic and literary terms that you will need to actively participate in classroom discussions are called out in your book.

- Challenging vocabulary terms found in reading passages are glossed at the point of use.

- Periodic Word Connections boxes guide you through the process of exploring a word with multiple meanings and nuances, an interesting etymology, a telling root or affix, a helpful Spanish cognate, a relationship to another word, or a connection to another content area.

Zinc Reading Labs

Zinc Reading Labs combines the best features of a typical vocabulary program with those of a typical reading program and makes reading and learning new words a game. Zinc offers a variety of nonfiction and fiction texts that you can choose from based on individual needs and interest. Each article has a corresponding vocabulary set that pre-teaches challenging words through spaced repetition, to help you genuinely learn and internalize the vocabulary. Additional vocabulary games focus on SAT/ACT power words and foundational words for English language learners.

Pre-AP Connections

SpringBoard shares Pre-AP's core principles and encourages you to build skills that you will use in high school and beyond. These principles are evident in every SpringBoard activity.

 ### Close Observation and Analysis
... to notice and consider

When reading, your teacher will guide you to pause to make observations and notice details in the text before analyzing or explaining. Only after you have noticed and enjoyed elements of the text do you then return to the text for deeper analysis and inferential thinking. This close reading sequence helps you interact and engage with the text in increasingly meaningful ways.

 ### Evidence-Based Writing
... with a focus on the sentence

SpringBoard challenges you to write increasingly complex, sophisticated, and precise sentences over the course of the year through regular practice with sentence-level writing. Instead of being isolated from reading, sentence-level grammar and writing exercises are integrated into the curriculum to enhance your comprehension and your ability to compose a variety of texts.

 ### Higher-Order Questioning
... to spark productive lingering

Each unit opens with two essential questions that relate to the topics, themes, and texts within that unit. You return to these questions throughout the unit and refine your answers as new evidence is presented. SpringBoard also encourages you to craft your own questions, and to dig deeply into the texts you read. After each reading passage, you evaluate the meaning of the text and examine the choices that the author made when writing it.

 ### Academic Conversations
... to support peer-to-peer dialogue

SpringBoard classrooms are places where students like you engage in collaborative learning. You will participate in discussion groups, writing groups, debates, Socratic seminars, literature circles, and oral interpretations and performances. These activities create an environment where you can share, compare, critique, debate, and build on others' ideas to advance your learning.

PSAT/SAT Connections

We want students to be rewarded for the hard work you do in your English Language Arts courses, including when you sit down to take important assessments. Therefore, SpringBoard English Language Arts focuses on the same essential knowledge and skills that are the center of the Evidence-Based Reading and Writing sections of the SAT Suite of Assessments (SAT, PSAT/NMSQT, PSAT™ 10, and PSAT™ 8/9). To be sure of our alignment, we conducted a research study, the results of which showed strong to exemplary alignment between the SpringBoard ELA courses and the corresponding SAT Suite tests. This means that you are getting ready for the SAT, PSAT/NMSQT, PSAT™ 10, and PSAT™ 8/9 in the classroom every day.

Tools and Supports

SpringBoard Digital

SpringBoard puts you in charge of what you learn and gives students and teachers the flexibility and support they need. SpringBoard Digital is an interactive program that provides always-available online content that's accessible from any device—desktop computer, laptop, tablet, or interactive whiteboard. The student edition allows you to interact with the text, respond to prompts, take assessments, and engage with a suite of tools, all in the digital space. Teachers get access to a correlations viewer that embeds correlations at point of use, a lesson planner, progress reports, grading, messaging, and more.

Zinc Reading Labs

All SpringBoard users have access to Zinc Reading Labs, where you can find a huge library of reading material chosen specifically to align with the SpringBoard English Language Arts curriculum.

Zinc offers:

- Fresh and engaging nonfiction and fiction content for independent reading.
- Interactive games, quizzes, and tasks that build skills and confidence.
- Freedom of choice: Zinc's massive and ever-growing library means that all students should find texts they want to read.

Turnitin Revision Assistant

When you develop drafts of an available Embedded Assessment through SpringBoard Digital, you can use a tool called Turnitin Revision Assistant. This online tool gives instant feedback to students as they write so they can polish their drafts and practice their revision skills. The feedback model Revision Assistant uses is based on scoring by SpringBoard teachers, and it's trained to assess the same rubric areas that they assess.

Revision Assistant offers:

- A template to help you create an outline.
- Actionable, instant feedback in specific areas such as structure, use of language, and ideas.
- Identification of strengths and weakness in your writing.

A Letter to the Student

Dear Student,

Welcome to the SpringBoard program! We created this program with you in mind: it puts you and your classmates at the center of your learning and equips you with the skills and knowledge you need to excel in middle school, high school, and beyond.

The energy and excitement you bring to class helps you and your classmates learn. You will explore compelling themes through readings, classroom discussions, and projects. You will dive into fascinating texts—some of which you'll choose on your own—from different genres including myths, poems, biographies, plays, and films. You will engage in lively discussions, debates, and performances so that you become confident sharing and presenting your ideas. You will write frequently to sharpen your ability to craft effective sentences, paragraphs, and longer texts. And you'll start each unit with a clear understanding of where you're headed by unpacking the skills and knowledge you'll need to do well on the assessment at the end.

SpringBoard helps you make connections between the concepts you're reading and writing about in class and the real world. Instead of just memorizing how to do things, you'll draw on your own and your classmates' experiences and knowledge to come to new and deeper understandings. When questions arise from the materials you're studying in class, you'll learn how to do both quick and longer-term research to find answers. Plus, you'll have access to tools and resources that are built right into the program, including powerful learning strategies, independent reading lists to help you select texts to read outside of class, and digital tools that you can access any time from any device—desktop computer, laptop, or tablet.

We want students to be rewarded for the hard work they do in their English Language Arts course. That's why the SpringBoard program focuses on the essential knowledge and skills that will prepare you for the challenging work you'll do in your high school classes, in AP courses, and in college.

Students from around the country are talking about how much they like the SpringBoard approach to learning. We hope you enjoy learning with SpringBoard, too.

Sincerely,

The SpringBoard Team

VISUAL PROMPT
What do you picture when you hear the word *hero*? What words and images immediately come to mind?

THE CHALLENGE OF HEROISM

As you set out for Ithaka
hope your road is a long one,
full of adventure, full of discovery.
Laistrygonians, Cyclops,
angry Poseidon—don't be afraid of them;
you'll never find things like that on your way
as long as you keep your thoughts raised high …

–from "Ithaka" by C. P. Cavafy

GOALS

- To create and present an original illustrated narrative based on the Hero's Journey archetype
- To analyze and synthesize a variety of texts to develop an original definition of *hero*
- To analyze and evaluate informational and narrative texts for ideas, structure, and language
- To compose texts that convey information about a topic using strategies of definition

VOCABULARY

ACADEMIC
concise
nuance
function
negation
coherence

LITERARY
archetype
pacing
mood
point of view
epic
mnemonic devices
tone
diction
denotation
connotation
allegory

Texts not included in these materials.

My Independent Reading List

Learning Strategies

Think-Pair-Share
QHT
Close Reading
Marking the Text
Paraphrasing
Graphic Organizer
Note-taking

VOCABULARY

LITERARY
An archetype is a character, symbol, story pattern, or other element that is common to human experience across cultures and that occurs frequently in literature, myth, and folklore.

My Notes

Learning Targets

- Discuss the big ideas and vocabulary for the unit.
- Demonstrate an understanding of the skills and knowledge needed to complete Embedded Assessment 1 successfully.

Preview

In this activity, you will begin thinking about the skills and knowledge needed to write a Hero's Journey narrative.

Making Connections

This unit focuses on the challenge of *heroism*. Because this word is used every day—in television shows, movies, video games, books, the news, and school—we rarely take time to actually think about what it means. You will be introduced to the archetype of the Hero's Journey and study various examples of heroes and how their journeys fit the archetype. You will also have the opportunity to practice informational writing and write a definition essay about heroism.

Essential Questions

Based on your current thinking, how would you answer these questions?

1. What defines a hero?

2. How does the Hero's Journey archetype appear in stories throughout time?

Developing Vocabulary

Begin your vocabulary study by creating a chart to use the QHT strategy to sort the terms on the Contents page. Use print or digital resources to learn more about the terms you sorted into the "Q" and "H" columns. Keep in mind that there is more to knowing a new word than just learning the definition. Truly knowing a word also involves an understanding of its syllables, pronunciation, word origin, and part of speech.

Unpacking Embedded Assessment 1

Closely read the assignment for Embedded Assessment 1: Writing a Hero's Journey Narrative.

 Think about all the heroes you have encountered in fiction and in real life. What type of hero appeals to you? Write and create an illustrated narrative about an original hero. Use the Hero's Journey archetype to develop and structure your ideas. Orally present your narrative to your classmates.

Find the Scoring Guide and work with your class to paraphrase the expectations for the assignment. Create a graphic organizer to use as a visual reminder of the required skills and concepts. Copy the graphic organizer into your Reader/Writer Notebook and revisit it after each activity to check your progress.

Understanding Challenges

Learning Targets

- Analyze and collaborate to discuss quotes and identify connections between the concepts of *challenges* and *heroism*.
- Follow complex oral instructions to complete a group task.

Preview

In this activity, you will work in groups to analyze a quote on the subject of challenges and present your analysis to the class.

The Concept of Challenge

1. **Quickwrite:** When you hear the word *challenges*, what comes to mind? Is the word positive or negative? Based on your prior experiences, how can challenges be helpful to an individual? How can they be harmful?

2. Follow your teacher's directions to form groups of four to analyze a quote in the table that follows. As needed, ask your teacher or peers clarifying questions to make sure that you understand the task.

Quotes
A. "The true measure of a man is not how he behaves in moments of comfort and convenience, but how he stands at times of controversy and challenges." —Rev. Dr. Martin Luther King, Jr. (clergyman, activist)
B. "Accept the challenges so that you can feel the exhilaration of victory." —George S. Patton (U.S. Army officer)
C. "The block of granite which was an obstacle in the pathway of the weak became a stepping-stone in the pathway of the strong." —Thomas Carlyle (writer, essayist, historian)
D. "Life's challenges are not supposed to paralyze you; they're supposed to help you discover who you are." —Bernice Johnson Reagon (singer, composer, scholar, activist)

My Notes

_____

3. Circle the corresponding letter for the quote that your group is assigned. A B C D

Paraphrase	Examples	Challenge Category

4. Write your group's summary sentence in the following space.

5. Assign speaking parts for the presentation.

Element of Presentation	Speaker
(a) Fluently read the quote and explain the meaning.	
(b) Provide specific examples from life or literature.	
(c) Explain the group's categorization of the quote.	
(d) Explain how the quote connects to the concept of heroism.	

6. Present using appropriate eye contact, adequate volume, and clear pronunciation.

7. As other groups present, listen to them, try to comprehend their main points, and take notes in your Reader/Writer Notebook.

☑ Check Your Understanding

Think about the content of all four quotes. How does the concept of *challenge* connect to the concept of *heroism*?

Understanding the Hero's Journey Archetype

- Identify the archetype of the Hero's Journey within the genre of the adventure story or myth.
- Identify the stages of the Hero's Journey within a film.

Preview

In this activity, you will learn the stages of the Hero's Journey. Then you will watch a film and think about how it fits into the archetype of the Hero's Journey.

Genre Study: The Archetype of the Hero's Journey

In literature, an archetype is a character, symbol, story pattern, or other element that is common to human experience across cultures. It refers to a common plot pattern or to a character type, such as the Innocent, the Mother Figure, or the Hero, or to images that occur in the literature of all cultures.

The archetype of the Hero's Journey describes a plot pattern that most often occurs within the genre of adventure story or myth. It shows the development of a hero.

Joseph Campbell, an American anthropologist, writer, and lecturer, studied the myths and stories of multiple cultures and began to notice common plot patterns. In *The Hero with a Thousand Faces*, Campbell defines common elements of the Hero's Journey. Campbell found that most journey myths have three parts:

Departure: The hero leaves home to venture into the unknown on some sort of quest.

Initiation: The hero faces a series of problems.

Return: With the help of a friend, the hero returns home successfully.

Although these elements may be referred to as the stages of the Hero's Journey, they are not presented in the exact same order, and some stories do not contain every element of the journey.

Setting a Purpose for Viewing

1. As you study the stages of the Hero's Journey archetype in the graphic organizer that follows, use metacognitive markers to indicate your level of understanding and to guide future discussion:
   ? = questions, ! = connections, and * = comments.

After you review the stages of the Hero's Journey archetype as a class, you will use the last column of the graphic organizer to record details from the film that align to each stage. For now, leave it blank.

Learning Strategies

Metacognitive Markers
Close Reading
Graphic Organizer
Note-taking
Collaborative Discussion

WORD CONNECTIONS

Etymology

Etymology is the study of the origin of words. Many English words come from other languages, including Latin, German, and Greek. Knowing a word's etymology can help you determine its meaning. The Greek prefix *arch-* in **archetype** means "first," and the root *type* means "model." When first used in the 14th century, the word meant "original pattern from which copies are made." Today it is used to denote a common story element or a perfect example of something.

Knowing the meanings of *arch-* and *type* can help you determine the meanings of other words, such as *archbishop* and *prototype*.

Hero's Journey Archetype		
Steps	**Explanation**	**Example**
Stage 1: Departure		
1. **The Call to Adventure** The future hero is first given notice that his or her life is going to change.	The story's exposition introduces the hero, and soon the hero's normal life is disrupted. Something changes; the hero faces a problem, obstacle, or challenge.	
2. **Refusal of the Call** The future hero often refuses to accept the Call to Adventure. The refusal may stem from a sense of duty, an obligation, a fear, or insecurity.	At first the hero is reluctant to accept the change. Usually this reluctance presents itself as second thoughts or personal doubt. Hesitation, whether brief or lengthy, humanizes the hero for the reader.	
3. **The Beginning of the Adventure** The hero begins the adventure, leaving the known limits of his or her world to venture into an unknown and dangerous realm where the rules and limits are unknown.	The hero finally accepts the call and begins a physical, spiritual, and/or emotional journey to achieve a boon, something that is helpful or beneficial.	
Stage 2: Initiation		
4. **The Road of Trials** The hero experiences and is transformed by a series of tests, tasks, or challenges. The hero usually fails one or more of these tests, which often occur in threes.	The story develops rising action as the hero faces a series of challenges that become increasingly difficult as the story unfolds.	
5. **The Experience with Unconditional Love** During the Road of Trials, the hero experiences support (physical and/or mental) from a friend, family member, mentor, and so on.	This love often drives the hero to continue on the journey, even when the hero doubts him/herself.	

Hero's Journey Archetype		
6. The Ultimate Boon The goal of the quest is achieved. The boon can be a physical object or an intangible item, such as knowledge, courage, or love. The Road of Trials makes the hero strong enough to achieve this goal.	The story reaches the climax as the hero gains what he or she set out to achieve. The Call to Adventure (what the hero is asked to do), the Beginning of the Adventure (what the hero sets out to do), and the Ultimate Boon (what the hero achieves) must connect.	
Stage 3: Return		
7. Refusal of the Return When the goal of the adventure is accomplished, the hero may refuse to return with the boon or gift, either because the hero doubts the return will bring change or because the hero prefers to stay in a better place rather than return to a normal life of pain and trouble.	The falling action begins as the hero begins to think about the Return. Sometimes the hero does not want to look back after achieving the boon. Sometimes the hero likes the "new world" better. This step is similar to the Refusal of the Call (in both cases, the hero does not take action right away).	
8. The Magic Flight The hero experiences adventure and perhaps danger as he or she **returns** to life as it was before the Call to Adventure.	For some heroes, the journey "home" (psychological or physical) can be just as dangerous as the journey out. Forces (sometimes magical or supernatural) may keep the hero from returning. This step is similar to the Road of Trials.	
9. Rescue from Without Just as the hero may need guides and assistance on the quest, oftentimes he or she must have powerful guides and rescuers to bring him or her back to everyday life. Sometimes the hero does not realize that it is time to return, that he or she can return, or that others are relying on him or her to return.	Just as it looks as if the hero will not make it home with the boon, the hero is "rescued." The rescuer is sometimes the same person who provided love or support throughout the journey.	
10. The Crossing or Return Threshold At this final point in the adventure, the hero must retain the wisdom gained on the quest, integrate that wisdom into his or her previous life, and perhaps decide how to share the wisdom with the rest of the world.	The final step is the story's resolution, when the hero returns with the boon. The theme is typically revealed at this point. To determine theme, think about the hero's struggles, transformation, and achievement. The reader is expected to learn a lesson about life through the hero's experience.	

My Notes

_____

_____

_____

_____

_____

_____

_____

_____

_____

VOCABULARY

LITERARY

Pacing is a narrative technique that refers to the amount of time a writer gives to describing each event and the amount of time a writer takes to develop each stage in the plot. Some events and stages are shorter or longer than others.

A **theme** is a main idea that runs through a text or literary work. A writer develops a theme through events, characters, setting, and plot. A text may have more than one theme, but usually there is one underlying main theme that drives the narrative.

Working from the Film

Embedded Assessment 1 requires you to use the Hero's Journey to sequence and structure events in your narrative. You already know the basic elements of plot development. All plot development includes:

Exposition: Events that set the context for the story; the setting (time and place), characters, and central conflict are introduced.

Rising Action: Events that develop the plot and lead to the climax.

Climax: The main event; the turning point, or highest point of tension in the story.

Falling Action: The events that lead to the resolution.

Resolution: Conflict is completely resolved, and the lesson has been learned.

2. Create a plot diagram in your Reader/Writer Notebook and label each step. Then provide examples of each step from the film you just watched. Use your notes from the film for guidance.

3. **Discussion:** One narrative technique that writers use is **pacing**. Notice how the plot diagram gives an idea of how rising action is paced in contrast to falling action. How does a writer effectively pace plot events?

4. **Discussion:** Determining a story's **theme** is important to understanding an author's message. Read the Literary Terms box to learn more about theme. What is a theme of *Big Hero 6*? Review the labels you created for each stage of the plot diagram. How do each of these events show the development of the theme?

5. In your Reader/Writer Notebook, write a summary of *Big Hero 6*, using your completed plot diagram. Include the main theme of *Big Hero 6* in your summary. Use details you recorded from each stage to tell how events, characters, setting, and plot help determine the main theme of the story.

☑ Focus on the Sentence

Write "S" if the words form a complete sentence. Capitalize and punctuate the sentences. Write "F" if the words are a sentence fragment. Change the fragments into complete sentences using what you learned about the Hero's Journey archetype.

_____ the call to adventure

_____

_____ transformed by a series of tests, tasks, or challenges

_____

_____ the ultimate boon occurs when the goal of the quest is achieved

_____

_____ the falling action

_____

Planning for Independent Reading

Learning Targets

- Select criteria for a reading text.
- Set goals for an independent reading plan.

Preview

In this activity, you will preview a self-selected book that contains a Hero's Journey and set goals for your independent reading.

My Notes

📖 Planning Independent Reading

The focus of this unit is the Hero's Journey archetype. For Embedded Assessment 1, you will be writing your own Hero's Journey narrative with accompanying visuals. In the previous activity, you were able to preview the stages of the Hero's Journey using a film. Now, in your Independent Reading, you have the opportunity to read a full-length Hero's Journey story. Reading a full-length story will help you with creating your Embedded Assessment, and it will expose you to how authors create a Hero's Journey narrative. In the back of your SpringBoard book, you'll find a list of suggested Hero's Journey narratives. To help you choose the right book, use the following questions as a guide.

1. What have you enjoyed reading in the past? What is your favorite book or favorite type of book? Who is your favorite author?

2. Preview the book you have selected. What do the front and back covers show you? What type of visual is shown? What types of fonts and colors are used? Are there awards or brags that tell you about the book?

3. Read the first few pages. Are they interesting? How does the author try to hook you to keep reading? What can you tell about the characters and setting (location and time) so far? Does this seem too hard, too easy, or just right?

Reading Discussion Groups

Follow your teacher's oral guidance through a book pass. Practice previewing each book by looking at the covers and reading the first few pages.

1. In your Reader/Writer Notebook, record each book's title and author, something from your previewing that stands out to you, and your rating of the book.

2. After previewing each book and thinking about the goals of this unit, do you want to continue reading the book you brought to the group or choose something else?

3. Create an Independent Reading Plan to help you set personal reading goals. Keep this plan in your Reader/Writer Notebook.

I have chosen to read _____

by (author) _____

because (reason from previewing) _____

_____

I will set aside time to read at (time, place) _____

I should finish this text by (date) _____

4. Record your daily reading progress in your Independent Reading Log. Write a brief daily report in your log responding to what you have read. Include in your report questions, personal connections, or inferences about what you have read.

5. As you identify new titles to read for your independent reading, add them to the My Independent Reading List on the Table of Contents pages of this unit.

6. Use this graphic organizer to record each stage of the Hero's Journey from your Independent Reading book.

Text: _____

Stage 1: Departure

1. **The Call to Adventure:**

2. **Refusal of the Call:**

3. **The Beginning of the Adventure:**

Stage 2: Initiation

4. **The Road of Trials:**
   (a)
   (b)
   (c)

5. **The Experience with Unconditional Love:**

6. **The Ultimate Boon:**

Stage 3: Return

7. **Refusal of the Return:**

8. **The Magic Flight:**

9. **Rescue from Without:**

10. **The Crossing or Return Threshold:**
    (Theme Statement)

The Onset of Adventure

Learning Targets

- Analyze the imagery in a poem and describe how it achieves specific ideas, themes, and moods.

Preview

In this activity, you will explain the author's message in a poem by analyzing imagery and how it contributes to the mood.

Setting a Purpose for Reading

- As you read, underline figurative language and descriptive words and phrases that help to create an image in your mind.
- Circle unknown words and phrases. Try to determine the meaning of the words by using context clues, word parts, or a dictionary.

About the Author

Constantine P. Cavafy (1863–1933) was born to Greek parents in 1863, in the Egyptian city of Alexandria. His poetry was obscure throughout much of his life and shared mostly with close friends. Much of his work was personal, and most of his poems were not published until after his death in 1933. His "Ithaka" was inspired by the return of Odysseus to his home island, as described by Homer in the *Odyssey*.

Learning Strategies

Marking the Text
Discussion Groups
Rereading
Summarizing
Sketching
Visualizing

VOCABULARY

LITERARY
Figurative language is language that is used to convey meaning beyond the literal definition of a word. Examples of figurative language are similes, metaphors, allusions, and personification.

My Notes

Poem

Ithaka

by **C. P. Cavafy**
translated by Edmund Keeley and Philip Sherrard

As you set out for Ithaka
hope your road is a long one,
full of adventure, full of discovery.
Laistrygonians, Cyclops,
5 angry Poseidon—don't be afraid of them;
you'll never find things like that on your way
as long as you keep your thoughts raised high,
as long as a rare excitement
stirs your spirit and your body.

My Notes

10   Laistrygonians, Cyclops,
     wild Poseidon—you won't encounter them
     unless you bring them along inside your soul,
     unless your soul sets them up in front of you.
     Hope your road is a long one.
15   May there be many summer mornings when,
     with what pleasure, what joy,
     you enter harbors you're seeing for the first time;
     may you stop at Phoenician trading stations
     to buy fine things,
20   **mother of pearl** and coral, **amber** and **ebony**,
     sensual perfume of every kind—
     as many sensual perfumes as you can;
     and may you visit many Egyptian cities
     to learn and go on learning from their scholars.
25   Keep Ithaka always in your mind.
     Arriving there is what you're destined for.
     But don't hurry the journey at all.
     Better if it lasts for years,
     so you're old by the time you reach the island,
30   wealthy with all you've gained on the way,
     not expecting Ithaka to make you rich.
     Ithaka gave you the marvelous journey.
     Without her you wouldn't have set out.
     She has nothing left to give you now.
35   And if you find her poor, Ithaka won't have fooled you.
     Wise as you will have become, so full of experience,
     you'll have understood by then what these Ithakas mean.

mother of pearl: the shiny interior of some seashells, used to make jewelry

amber: fossilized, transparent, tree sap

ebony: a valuable black wood, taken from various tropical trees

sensual: appealing to the physical senses

VOCABULARY

Making Observations

- What captures your attention?
- What emotions might someone feel while reading the poem?
- What do you notice about the journey described in the poem?

LITERARY

Mood is the overall emotion of a text, which is created by the author's language and tone and the subject matter.

Returning to the Text

- Return to the text as you respond to the following questions. Use text evidence to support your responses.
- Write any additional questions you have about the poem in your Reader/ Writer Notebook.

1. Look at stanza 3. What are some synonyms for the word *destined*?

_____

_____

_____

_____

2. What is the **mood** of this poem? How do you feel after reading it? Explain how the author's use of language contributes to the mood.

_____

_____

_____

_____

3. Remember that personification is a technique that writers use when they give human characteristics to something nonhuman. Reread lines 32–34 of the poem, and explain how Cavafy is using this technique.

_____

_____

_____

_____

4. What might the journey to Ithaka be a metaphor for? Provide evidence from the text to support your interpretation.

_____

_____

_____

_____

INDEPENDENT READING LINK

Read and Connect

Examine the opening chapter of your independent reading book and write about how it sets the context for the hero's challenges. What mood does the author set in the opening of your book? How is it similar to or different from the mood that is set in the poem in this activity? Analyze the language that the author uses to create the mood.

My Notes

5. **Craft and Structure:** Go back to the classical allusions to the *Odyssey* you underlined in the poem. How does Cavafy's use of the classical allusions impact the overall mood and tone of the poem?

_____

_____

_____

_____

Working from the Text

6. As you hear the poem read aloud, make mental visualizations of images created by the author's word choice and use of figurative language.

7. Make a list of images you pictured while you listened to the poem in the My Notes alongside the poem.

8. Return to the poem. Highlight the parts of the text that inspired the images you pictured.

9. **Discussion Groups:** Form small groups. Look at the words you highlighted in the poem. Then look at the context of those words. What imagery is the author using in that part of the poem to create mood? Draw a visual in the margin to help illustrate your meaning.

10. Focus on the words you highlighted in "Ithaka" and think about the imagery that the poet uses. What is the message about life that he is trying to tell his readers? Write a statement about the poem's theme in your Reader/Writer Notebook.

☑ Focus on the Sentence

Change the sentence fragments into complete sentences, using what you learned about the poem, "Ithaka," by Cavafy. Use correct capitalization and punctuation.

"ithaka" by cavafy uses

_____

_____

on your journey

_____

_____

imagery in the poem

_____

_____

The Departure

Learning Strategies

Marking the Text
Close Reading
Diffusing
Rereading
Summarizing

Learning Targets

- Analyze a story for structure and narrative techniques.
- Draft the opening for an original Hero's Journey narrative.

Preview

In this activity, you will read a short story about a hero's departure and begin creating a hero of your own.

The Departure

Joseph Campbell describes the first stage of the Hero's Journey as the hero's departure or separation. The Departure Stage consists of three steps: the Call to Adventure, Refusal of the Call, and the Beginning of the Adventure.

Setting a Purpose for Reading

- As you read, underline and label events relating to a Hero's Journey.
- Circle unknown words and phrases. Try to determine the meaning of the words by using context clues, word parts, or a dictionary.

About the Author

Ray Bradbury (1920–2012) is remembered mostly as a fantasy writer, although "The Drummer Boy of Shiloh" is set firmly in the real world. His most famous novel, *Fahrenheit 451*, was published in 1953. Other famous fantasy works include 1950's *The Martian Chronicles* and 1962's *Something Wicked This Way Comes*. "The Drummer Boy of Shiloh" first appeared in Bradbury's 1964 short story collection, *The Machineries of Joy*.

Short Story

The Drummer Boy of Shiloh

by **Ray Bradbury**

1   In the April night, more than once, blossoms fell from the orchard trees and lit with rustling taps on the drumskin. At midnight a peach stone left miraculously on a branch through winter, flicked by a bird, fell swift and unseen, struck once, like panic, which jerked the boy upright. In silence he listened to his own heart **ruffle** away away—at last gone from his ears and back in his chest again.

My Notes

ruffle: to flutter or move in a slow, wavy pattern

My Notes

WORD CONNECTIONS

Etymology
In the past, people would test the quality of gold or silver by rubbing a stone across it and analyzing the color of the streak it left. The 15th-century Middle English word *touch* meant "to test," so this stone became known as a **touchstone**. This term is now a metaphor for any method used to test the quality or effectiveness of something else.

romantic: fondly imaginary

helter-skelter: in a confused or disorderly way

benediction: a prayer or blessing

bindled: held together in a sack

immortality: the ability to live forever

2   After that, he turned the drum on its side, where its great lunar face peered at him whenever he opened his eyes.

3   His face, alert or at rest, was solemn. It was indeed a solemn night for a boy just turned fourteen in the peach field near the Owl Creek not far from the church at Shiloh.[1]

4   " ... thirty-one, thirty-two, thirty-three ... "

5   Unable to see, he stopped counting.

6   Beyond the thirty-three familiar shadows, forty thousand men, exhausted by nervous expectation, unable to sleep for **romantic** dreams of battles yet unfought, lay crazily askew in their uniforms. A mile yet farther on, another army was strewn **helter-skelter**, turning slow, basting themselves with the thought of what they would do when the time came: a leap, a yell, a blind plunge their strategy, raw youth their protection and **benediction**.

7   Now and again the boy heard a vast wind come up, that gently stirred the air. But he knew what it was—the army here, the army there, whispering to itself in the dark. Some men talking to others, others murmuring to themselves, and all so quiet it was like a natural element arisen from South or North with the motion of the earth toward dawn.

8   What the men whispered the boy could only guess, and he guessed that it was: "Me, I'm the one, I'm the one of all the rest who won't die. I'll live through it. I'll go home. The band will play. And I'll be there to hear it."

9   Yes, thought the boy, that's all very well for them, they can give as good as they get!

10   For with the careless bones of the young men harvested by the night and **bindled** around campfires were the similarly strewn steel bones of their rifles, with bayonets fixed like eternal lightning lost in the orchard grass.

11   Me, thought the boy, I got only a drum, two sticks to beat it and no shield.

12   There wasn't a man-boy on the ground tonight who did not have a shield he cast, riveted or carved himself on his way to his first attack, compounded of remote but nonetheless firm and fiery family devotion, flag-blown patriotism and cocksure **immortality** strengthened by the touchstone of very real gunpowder; ramrod, Minié ball[2] and flint. But without these last the boy felt his family move yet farther off away in the dark, as if one of those great prairie-burning trains had chanted them away never to return—leaving him with this drum which was worse than a toy in the game to be played tomorrow or some day much too soon.

13   The boy turned on his side. A moth brushed his face, but it was peach blossom. A peach blossom flicked him, but it was a moth. Nothing stayed put. Nothing had a name. Nothing was as it once was.

---

[1] Shiloh is the site of a Civil War battle in 1862; now a national military park in southwest Tennessee

[2] Minié ball is a type of rifle bullet that became prominent during the Civil War

14 If he lay very still when the dawn came up and the soldiers put on their bravery with their caps, perhaps they might go away, the war with them, and not notice him lying small here, no more than a toy himself.

15 "Well … now," said a voice.

16 The boy shut up his eyes to hide inside himself, but it was too late. Someone, walking by in the night, stood over him.

17 "Well," said the voice quietly, "here's a soldier crying before the fight. Good. Get it over. Won't be time once it all starts."

18 And the voice was about to move on when the boy, startled, touched the drum at his elbow. The man above, hearing this, stopped. The boy could feel his eyes, sense him slowly bending near. A hand must have come down out of the night, for there was a little rat-tat as the fingernails brushed and the man's breath fanned his face.

19 "Why, it's the drummer boy, isn't it?"

20 The boy nodded not knowing if his nod was seen. "Sir, is that you?" he said.

21 "I assume it is." The man's knees cracked as he bent still closer.

22 He smelled as all fathers should smell, of salt sweat, ginger, tobacco, horse, and boot leather, and the earth he walked upon. He had many eyes. No, not eyes—brass buttons that watched the boy.

23 He could only be, and was, the general.

24 "What's your name, boy?" he asked.

25 "Joby," whispered the boy, starting to sit up.

26 "All right Joby, don't stir." A hand pressed his chest gently and the boy relaxed. "How long you been with us, Joby?"

27 "Three weeks, sir."

28 "Run off from home or joined legitimately, boy?"

29 Silence.

30 " … Fool question," said the general. "Do you shave yet, boy? Even more of a … fool. There's your cheek, fell right off the tree overhead. And the others here not much older. Raw, raw, the lot of you. You ready for tomorrow or the next day, Joby?"

31 "I think so, sir."

32 "You want to cry some more, go on ahead. I did the same last night."

33 "You, sir?"

34 "It's the truth. Thinking of everything ahead. Both sides figuring the other side will just give up, and soon, and the war done in weeks, and us all home. Well, that's not how it's going to be. And maybe that's why I cried."

35 "Yes, sir," said Joby.

My Notes

36 The general must have taken out a cigar now, for the dark was suddenly filled with the smell of tobacco unlit as yet, but chewed as the man thought what next to say.

37 "It's going to be a crazy time," said the general. "Counting both sides, there's a hundred thousand men, give or take a few thousand out there tonight, not one as can spit a sparrow off a tree, or knows a horse clod from a Minié ball. Stand up, bare the breast, ask to be a target, thank them and sit down, that's us, that's them. We should turn tail and train four months, they should do the same. But here we are, taken with spring fever and thinking it blood lust, taking our sulfur with cannons instead of with molasses, as it should be, going to be a hero, going to live forever. And I can see all of them over there nodding agreement, save the other way around. It's wrong, boy, it's wrong as a head put on hindside front and a man marching backward through life… More innocents will get shot out of pure … enthusiasm than ever got shot before. Owl Creek was full of boys splashing around in the noonday sun just a few hours ago. I fear it will be full of boys again, just floating, at sundown tomorrow, not caring where the tide takes them."

38 The general stopped and made a little pile of winter leaves and twigs in the darkness, as if he might at any moment strike fire to them to see his way through the coming days when the sun might not show its face because of what was happening here and just beyond.

39 The boy watched the hand stirring the leaves and opened his lips to say something, but did not say it. The general heard the boy's breath and spoke himself.

40 "Why am I telling you this? That's what you wanted to ask, eh? Well, when you got a bunch of wild horses on a loose rein somewhere somehow you got to bring order, rein them in. These lads, fresh out of the milkshed, don't know what I know, and I can't tell them: men actually die in war. So each is his own army. I got to make one army of them. And for that, boy, I need you.

41 "Me!" The boy's lips barely twitched.

42 "Now, boy," said the general quietly, "you are the heart of the army. Think of that. You're the heart of the army. Listen, now."

43 And, lying there, Joby listened. And the general spoke on.

44 If he, Joby, beat slow tomorrow, the heart would beat slow in the men. They would lag by the wayside. They would drowse in the fields on their muskets. They would sleep forever, after that, in those same fields—their hearts slowed by a drummer boy and stopped by enemy lead.

45 But if he beat a sure, steady, ever faster rhythm, then, then their knees would come up in a long line down over that hill, one knee after the other, like a wave on the ocean shore! Had he seen the ocean ever? Seen the waves rolling in like a well-ordered cavalry charge to the sand? Well, that was it that's what he wanted, that's what was needed! Joby was his right hand and his left. He gave the orders, but Joby set the pace!

46 So bring the right knee up and the right foot out and the left knee up and the left foot out. One following the other in good time, in brisk time. Move the blood up the body and made the head proud and the spine stiff and the jaw **resolute**. Focus the eye and set the teeth, flare the nostrils and tighten the hands, put steel armor all over the men, for blood moving fast in them does indeed make men feel as if they'd put on steel. He must keep at it, at it! Long and steady, steady and long! The men, even though shot or torn, those wounds got in hot blood—in blood he'd helped stir—would feel less pain. If their blood was cold, it would be more than slaughter, it would be murderous nightmare and pain best not told and no one to guess.

47 The general spoke and stopped, letting his breath **slack** off. Then after a moment, he said, "So there you are, that's it. Will you do that, boy? Do you know now you're general of the army when the general's left behind?"

48 The boy nodded mutely.

49 "You'll run them through for me then boy?"

50 "Yes, sir."

51 "Good. And maybe, many nights from tonight, many years from now, when you're as old or far much older than me, when they ask you what you did in this awful time, you will tell them—one part humble and one part proud—'I was the drummer boy at the battle of Owl Creek,' or the Tennessee River, or maybe they'll just name it after the church there. 'I was the drummer boy at Shiloh.' Who will ever hear those words and not know you, boy, or what you thought this night, or what you'll think tomorrow or the next day when we must get up on our legs and move!"

52 The general stood up. "Well then ... Bless you, boy. Good night."

53 "Good night, sir." And tobacco, brass, boot polish, salt sweat and leather, the man moved away through the grass.

54 Joby lay for a moment, staring but unable to see where the man had gone. He swallowed. He wiped his eyes. He cleared his throat. He settled himself. Then, at last, very slowly and firmly, he turned the drum so that it faced up toward the sky.

55 He lay next to it, his arm around it, feeling the tremor, the touch, the muted thunder as, all the rest of the April night in the year 1862, near the Tennessee River, not far from the Owl Creek, very close to the church named Shiloh, the peach blossoms fell on the drum.

Making Observations
- What characters do we meet in the story?
- Which events relate to a Hero's Journey?

resolute: determined
slack: to diminish or fade away

☑ Focus on the Sentence

Use details from the story to complete the following sentences.

Joby is afraid of the imminent battle because _____

_____

Joby is afraid of the imminent battle, so _____

_____

Joby is afraid of the imminent battle, but _____

_____

Returning to the Text

• Return to the text as you respond to the following questions. Use text evidence to support your responses.

• Write any additional questions you have about the short story in your Reader/Writer Notebook.

1. What textual evidence in the beginning of the story shows that the boy is afraid?

_____

_____

_____

_____

2. The word *harvested* is used figuratively in paragraph 10. How do you know it is used figuratively, and why did the author choose this word?

_____

_____

_____

3. Consult reference materials to find the meanings of *ramrod* and *flint*. Relate these words to the meaning of the first sentence in paragraph 12. How does the sentence convey the boy's mood?

_____

_____

_____

_____

_____

_____

_____

4. How did Joby join the army? What is significant about that?

_____

_____

_____

_____

5. Consult reference materials to find the meaning of the word *drowse*. How does that word create a contrast in paragraph 44?

_____

_____

_____

_____

6. What shift happens in paragraphs 44, 45, and 46? Use textual evidence in your answer.

_____

_____

_____

_____

7. How does the general's comment, "Do you know now you're general of the army when the general's left behind?" prove to be a decisive moment in the conversation between him and Joby? What theme is developed through their interaction?

_____

_____

_____

_____

Working from the Text

8. Examine the first 10 paragraphs of "The Drummer Boy of Shiloh." How does the author establish the story's setting and **point of view**? Use evidence from the text to support your response.

LITERARY

VOCABULARY

Point of view is the perspective from which a story is told. In first-person point of view, a character tells the story from his or her own perspective. In third-person point of view, a narrator (not a character) tells the story.

9. Return to the text and put a star next to parts of the story that show the stages of Joby's journey. Which stages of the Hero's Journey has Joby passed through by the time the story draws to a close?

10. Reread a chunk of the text to identify and evaluate the narrative elements listed in the graphic organizer.

Structure: Exposition	What descriptive detail does the author provide?	What is the effect of the description?
Setting		
Character		
Conflict		
Point of View		

11. Now that you have identified and evaluated the narrative elements of the story, determine its central idea. In your Reader/Writer Notebook, write a summary of the central idea, supporting your interpretation using evidence from the text. Explain how the author communicates the idea that Joby is now ready to start his journey.

12. Use your imagination to create an original hero. In your Reader/Writer Notebook, sketch your image of a hero. Label unique characteristics and give him or her a meaningful name. In the right column, use the prompting questions to brainstorm ideas for a story.

The Hero: _____ (name)	The Story Exposition
Use these questions to spark ideas. Is the hero male or female? Young or old? Well liked or misunderstood? Conspicuous (obvious) or nondescript (ordinary)?	**Setting:** (In what kind of place does your hero live? Does he or she live in the past, present, or future?) **Character:** (What are the hero's strengths and weaknesses? Who are the hero's family and friends? What does the hero do every day? What does the hero want in life? What do others want from the hero?) **Conflicts:** (What challenges might the hero experience? How might the hero transform into someone stronger?)

The Hook

Nobody wants to read a dull story or one that goes on for several paragraphs before it starts becoming interesting. That's what makes the **hook** important. A hook is the opening sentence or sentences that capture the reader's interest. Hooks come in many forms. In a narrative, hooks often introduce a character or setting.

Introducing a Character: "Late in the winter of my seventeenth year, my mother decided I was depressed, presumably because I rarely left the house, spent quite a lot of time in bed, read the same book over and over, ate infrequently, and devoted quite a bit of my abundant free time to thinking about death." (Green, *The Fault in Our Stars*) or "I know I'm not an ordinary ten-year-old kid." (Palacio, *Wonder*)

Introducing a Setting: "In the April night, more than once, blossoms fell from the orchard trees and lit with rustling taps on the drumskin." ("The Drummer Boy of Shiloh") or "It was one of those super-duper-cold Saturdays." (Curtis, *The Watsons Go to Birmingham*)

Think about possible hooks for your Hero's Journey narrative as you proceed.

🖉 Drafting the Embedded Assessment

Now, think about the hero you just envisioned. What might the hero experience in the Departure Stage of his or her journey? Draft the beginning of a narrative using the three steps in this stage (The Call, The Refusal, and The Beginning) to guide your structure and development. Be sure to:

- Begin with a hook that helps establish a context and point of view (first-person or third-person).
- Use narrative techniques such as dialogue, pacing, and description to develop experiences, events, and/or characters.
- Make use of complete complex and compound-complex sentences.
- Use details and imagery to create mood.

🗋 INDEPENDENT READING LINK

Read and Recommend

Prepare a short persuasive written presentation. In it, describe a text you have independently read or are reading that incorporates the Hero's Journey archetype. Include an active recommendation of the text and provide clear reasons for that recommendation. Include relevant vocabulary from your activities so far. Present your presentation orally.

The Initiation

Genre Study: Epic Poetry

An **epic** poem is a very long poetic work that usually tells a story (often about a journey) of a hero's incredible adventures. Epic poetry is distinguished from other types of poetry by its length (from tens of thousands of words to over a million), as well as its descriptive narration of myth-like adventures.

Before the development of writing, the oldest epic poetry was passed along orally, with several individuals responsible for remembering different parts of a work. Breaking an epic poem into episodes made it easier for individuals to remember. So did breaking episodes into stanzas and poetically crafted lines that include **mnemonic devices**. An epithet is an example of a mnemonic device used by poets to help performers remember the poem. An epithet is a term or phrase used to characterize the nature of a character, an object, or an event. For example, "rosy-fingered" is an epithet often used to describe the dawn in the *Odyssey*, the epic you are about to read.

Look out for epithets and other characteristics of this genre while you read. Additionally, when you read, you'll see that the first six books of the *Odyssey* have been translated into prose, and the final book is a poetic translation. Consider how each translation depicts the initiation stage in Odysseus' heroic journey.

Setting a Purpose for Reading

- As you read, underline evidence of Odysseus' actions or words that influence key events.
- Circle unknown words and phrases. Try to determine the meaning of the words by using context clues, word parts, or a dictionary.

About the Author

Homer was an ancient Greek poet, but beyond that little is known about him. He is thought to have lived sometime between the 12th and 8th centuries BCE. Most scholars believe that he authored two famous epic poems: the *Iliad* and the *Odyssey*. Both illustrate the Hero's Journey archetype. The excerpt from the *Odyssey* that you will read in this activity tells the tale of Odysseus' return home to Ithaca after the Trojan War. Odysseus meets many obstacles on his voyage.

🧭 KNOWLEDGE QUEST

Knowledge Question:

What are some outstanding ways heroes overcome challenges?

You have been reading about heroes in literature. In Activity 1.7, you will read about challenges faced by a classical heroic figure, Odysseus. While you read, build knowledge about the theme of heroes overcoming challenges, and think about your answer to the Knowledge Question.

Epic Poetry

from The Odyssey

by **Homer**
prose translation by **Tony Kline,** *poetic translation by* **Allen Mandelbaum**

Book IX: 152–192
Odysseus Tells His Tale: The Cyclops's Cave

1   Looking across to the land of the neighboring Cyclops,[1] we could see smoke and hear their voices, and the sound of their sheep and goats. Sun set and darkness fell, and we settled to our rest on the shore.

2   As soon as rosy-fingered Dawn appeared, I gathered my men together, saying: "The rest of you loyal friends stay here, while I and my crew take ship and try and find out who these men are, whether they are cruel, savage and lawless, or good to strangers, and in their hearts fear the gods."

3   With this I went aboard and ordered my crew to follow and loose the cables. They boarded swiftly and took their place on the benches then sitting in their rows struck the grey water with their oars. When we had reached the nearby shore, we saw a deep cave overhung with laurels at the cliff's edge close to the sea. Large herds of sheep and goats were penned there at night and round it was a raised yard walled by deep-set stones, tall pines and high-crowned oaks. There a giant spent the night, one that grazed his herds far off, alone, and keeping clear of others, lived in lawless solitude. He was born a monster and a wonder, not like any ordinary human, but like some wooded peak of the high mountains, that stands there isolated to our gaze.

---

[1] **Cyclops:** one-eyed giants

Book IX: 193–255
Odysseus Tells His Tale: Polyphemus Returns

4 Then I ordered the rest of my loyal friends to stay there and guard the ship, while I selected the twelve best men and went forward. I took with me a goatskin filled with dark sweet wine that Maron, son of Euanthes, priest of Apollo, guardian god of Ismarus, had given me, because out of respect we protected him, his wife and child. He offered me splendid gifts, seven **talents** of well-wrought gold, and a silver mixing-bowl: and wine, twelve jars in all, sweet unmixed wine, a divine **draught**. None of his serving-men and maids knew of this store, only he and his loyal wife, and one housekeeper. When they drank that honeyed red wine, he would pour a full cup into twenty of water, and the bouquet that rose from the mixing bowl was wonderfully sweet: in truth no one could hold back. I filled a large goatskin with the wine, and took it along, with some food in a bag, since my instincts told me the giant would come at us quickly, a savage being with huge strength, knowing nothing of right or law.

5 Soon we came to the cave, and found him absent; he was grazing his well-fed flocks in the fields. So we went inside and marveled at its contents. There were baskets full of cheeses, and pens crowded with lambs and kids, each flock with its firstlings, later ones, and newborn separated. The pails and bowls for milking, all solidly made, were swimming with **whey**. At first my men begged me to take some cheeses and go, then to drive the lambs and kids from the pens down to the swift ship and set sail. But I would not listen, though it would have been best, wishing to see the giant himself, and test his hospitality. When he did appear he proved no joy to my men.

6 So we lit a fire and made an offering, and helped ourselves to the cheese, and sat in the cave eating, waiting for him to return, shepherding his flocks. He arrived bearing a huge weight of dry wood to burn at suppertime, and he flung it down inside the cave with a crash. Gripped by terror we shrank back into a deep corner. He drove his well-fed flocks into the wide cave, the ones he milked, leaving the rams and he-goats outside in the broad courtyard. Then he lifted his door, a huge stone, and set it in place. Twenty-two four-wheeled wagons could not have carried it, yet such was the great rocky mass he used for a door. Then he sat and milked the ewes, and bleating goats in order, putting her young to each. Next he **curdled** half of the white milk, and stored the whey in wicker baskets, leaving the rest in pails for him to drink for his supper. When he had busied himself at his tasks, and kindled a fire, he suddenly saw us, and said: "Strangers, who are you? Where do you sail from over the sea-roads? Are you on business, or do you roam at random, like pirates who chance their lives to bring evil to others?"

Book IX: 256–306
Odysseus Tells His Tale: Trapped

7 Our spirits fell at his words, in terror at his loud voice and monstrous size. Nevertheless I answered him, saying: "We are Achaeans, returning from Troy, driven over the ocean depths by every wind that blows. Heading for home

WORD CONNECTIONS

Etymology
The English word **bouquet** comes from a French word of the same spelling meaning "little wood." The term derives from the Medieval Latin word *boscus*, which means "grove."

My Notes

talents: ancient coins

draught: a liquid that one drinks

whey: the watery part of milk

curdled: separated the solid parts out of milk

we were forced to take another route, a different course, as Zeus,[2] I suppose, intended. We are followers of Agamemnon, Atreus' son, whose fame spreads widest on earth, so great was that city he **sacked** and host he **slew**. But we, for our part, come as suppliants to your knees, hoping for hospitality, and the kindness that is due to strangers. Good sir, do not refuse us: respect the gods. We are **suppliants** and Zeus protects visitors and suppliants, Zeus the god of guests, who follows the steps of sacred travelers."

8   His answer was **devoid** of pity. "Stranger, you are a foreigner or a fool, telling me to fear and **revere** the gods, since the Cyclopes care nothing for **aegis**-bearing Zeus: we are greater than they. I would spare neither you nor your friends, to evade Zeus' anger, but only as my own heart prompted. But tell me, now, where you moored your fine ship, when you landed. Was it somewhere nearby, or further off? I'd like to know."

9   His words were designed to fool me, but failed. I was too wise for that, and answered him with cunning words: "Poseidon,[3] Earth-Shaker, smashed my ship to pieces, wrecking her on the rocks that edge your island, driving her close to the headland so the wind threw her onshore. But I and my men here escaped destruction."

10   Devoid of pity, he was silent in response, but leaping up laid hands on my crew. Two he seized and dashed to the ground like **whelps**, and their brains ran out and stained the earth. He tore them limb from limb for his supper, eating the flesh and entrails, bone and marrow, like a mountain lion, leaving nothing. Helplessly we watched these cruel acts, raising our hands to heaven and weeping. When the Cyclops had filled his huge stomach with human flesh, and had drunk pure milk, he lay down in the cave, stretched out among his flocks. Then I formed a courageous plan to steal up to him, draw my sharp sword, and feeling for the place where the midriff supports the liver, stab him there. But the next thought checked me. Trapped in the cave we would certainly die, since we'd have no way to move the great stone from the wide entrance. So, sighing, we waited for bright day.

Book IX: 307–359
Odysseus Tells His Tale: Offering the Cyclops Wine

11   As soon as rosy-fingered Dawn appeared, Cyclops relit the fire. Then he milked the ewes, and bleating goats in order, putting her young to each. When he had busied himself at his tasks, he again seized two of my men and began to eat them. When he had finished he drove his well-fed flocks from the cave, effortlessly lifting the huge door stone, and replacing it again like the cap on a quiver. Then whistling loudly he turned his flocks out on to the mountain slopes, leaving me with murder in my heart searching for a way to take vengeance on him, if Athene[4] would grant me inspiration. The best plan seemed to be this:

sacked: attacked a city and stole from it

slew: killed

suppliants: people who beg

devoid: absent

revere: to regard with devotion and awe

aegis: protection

whelps: young children or animals

---

[2] **Zeus:** the king of the gods

[3] **Poseidon:** god of the sea and of earthquakes

[4] **Athene:** goddess of wisdom, the arts, and war

12 The Cyclops' huge club, a trunk of green olive wood he had cut to take with him as soon as it was seasoned, lay next to a sheep pen. It was so large and thick that it looked to us like the mast of a twenty-oared black ship, a broad-beamed merchant vessel that sails the deep ocean. Approaching it, I cut off a six-foot length, gave it to my men and told them to smooth the wood. Then standing by it I sharpened the end to a point, and hardened the point in the blazing fire, after which I hid it carefully in a one of the heaps of dung that lay around the cave. I ordered the men to **cast lots** as to which of them should dare to help me raise the stake and twist it into the Cyclops' eye when sweet sleep took him. The lot fell on the very ones I would have chosen, four of them, with myself making a fifth.

13 He returned at evening, shepherding his well-fed flocks. He herded them swiftly, every one, into the deep cave, leaving none in the broad yard, commanded to do so by a god, or because of some **premonition**. Then he lifted the huge door stone and set it in place, and sat down to milk the ewes and bleating goats in order, putting her young to each. But when he had busied himself at his tasks, he again seized two of my men and began to eat them. That was when I went up to him, holding an ivy-wood bowl full of dark wine, and said: "Here, Cyclops, have some wine to follow your meal of human flesh, so you can taste the sort of drink we carried in our ship. I was bringing the drink to you as a gift, hoping you might pity me and help me on my homeward path: but your savagery is past bearing. Cruel man, why would anyone on earth ever visit you again, when you behave so badly?"

14 At this, he took the cup and drained it, and found the sweet drink so delightful he asked for another draught: "Give me more, freely, then quickly tell me your name so I may give you a guest gift, one that will please you. Among us Cyclopes the fertile earth produces rich grape clusters, and Zeus' rain swells them: but this is a taste from a stream of **ambrosia and nectar**."

Book IX: 360–412
Odysseus Tells His Tale: Blinding the Cyclops

15 As he finished speaking I handed him the bright wine. Three times I poured and gave it to him, and three times, foolishly, he drained it. When the wine had **fuddled** his wits I tried him with **subtle** words: "Cyclops, you asked my name, and I will tell it: give me afterwards a guest gift as you promised. My name is Nobody. Nobody, my father, mother, and friends call me."

16 Those were my words, and this his cruel answer: "Then, my gift is this. I will eat Nobody last of all his company, and all the others before him."

17 As he spoke, he reeled and toppled over on his back, his thick neck twisted to one side, and all-conquering sleep overpowered him. In his drunken slumber he vomited wine and pieces of human flesh. Then I thrust the stake into the depth of the ashes to heat it, and inspired my men with encouraging words, so none would hang back from fear. When the olivewood stake was glowing hot, and ready to catch fire despite its greenness, I drew it from the coals, then my men stood round me, and a god breathed courage into us. They held the sharpened olivewood stake, and thrust it into his eye, while I threw my

My Notes

___

cast lots: to throw a set of objects in order to impartially decide something

premonition: a vision of the future

ambrosia and nectar: the food and drink of the gods

fuddled: made confusing

subtle: not obvious

My Notes

weight on the end, and twisted it round and round, as a man bores the timbers of a ship with a drill that others twirl lower down with a strap held at both ends, and so keep the drill continuously moving. We took the red-hot stake and twisted it round and round like that in his eye, and the blood poured out despite the heat. His lids and brows were scorched by flame from the burning eyeball, and its roots crackled with fire. As a great axe or adze causes a vast hissing when the smith dips it in cool water to temper it, strengthening the iron, so his eye hissed against the olivewood stake. Then he screamed, terribly, and the rock echoed. Seized by terror we shrank back, as he wrenched the stake, wet with blood, from his eye. He flung it away in frenzy, and called to the Cyclopes, his neighbors who lived in caves on the windy heights. They heard his cry, and crowding in from every side they stood by the cave mouth and asked what was wrong: "Polyphemus, what terrible pain is this that makes you call through deathless night, and wake us? Is a mortal stealing your flocks, or trying to kill you by violence or treachery?"

18 Out of the cave came mighty Polyphemus' voice: "Nobody, my friends, is trying to kill me by violence or treachery."

19 To this they replied with winged words: "If you are alone, and nobody does you violence, it's an inescapable sickness that comes from Zeus: pray to the Lord Poseidon, our father."

Book IX: 413–479
Odysseus Tells His Tale: Escape

20 Off they went, while I laughed to myself at how the name and the clever scheme had deceived him. Meanwhile the Cyclops, groaning and in pain, groped around and labored to lift the stone from the door. Then he sat in the entrance, arms outstretched, to catch anyone stealing past among his sheep. That was how foolish he must have thought I was. I considered the best way of escaping, and saving myself, and my men from death. I dreamed up all sorts of tricks and schemes, as a man will in a life or death matter: it was an evil situation. This was the plan that seemed best. The rams were fat with thick fleeces, fine large beasts with deep black wool. These I silently tied together in threes, with twists of willow on which that lawless monster, Polyphemus, slept. The middle one was to carry one of my men, with the other two on either side to protect him. So there was a man to every three sheep. As for me I took the pick of the flock, and curled below his shaggy belly, gripped his back and lay there face upwards, patiently gripping his fine fleece tight in my hands. Then, sighing, we waited for the light.

21 As soon as rosy-fingered Dawn appeared, the males rushed out to graze, while the un-milked females udders bursting bleated in the pens. Their master, tormented by agonies of pain, felt the backs of the sheep as they passed him, but foolishly failed to see my men tied under the rams' bellies. My ram went last, burdened by the weight of his fleece, and me and my teeming thoughts. And as he felt its back, mighty Polyphemus spoke to him:

22 "My fine ram, why leave the cave like this last of the flock? You have never lagged behind before, always the first to step out proudly and graze on the tender grass shoots, always first to reach the flowing river, and first to

treachery: a betrayal of trust

fleeces: the coats of wool on sheep

show your wish to return at evening to the fold. Today you are last of all. You must surely be grieving over your master's eye, blinded by an evil man and his wicked friends, when my wits were fuddled with wine: Nobody, I say, has not yet escaped death. If you only had senses like me, and the power of speech to tell me where he hides himself from my anger, then I'd strike him down, his brains would be sprinkled all over the floor of the cave, and my heart would be eased of the pain that nothing, Nobody, has brought me."

23 With this he drove the ram away from him out of doors, and I loosed myself when the ram was a little way from the cave, then untied my men. Swiftly, keeping an eye behind us, we shepherded those long-limbed sheep, rich and fat, down to the ship. And a welcome sight, indeed, to our dear friends were we, escapees from death, though they wept and sighed for the others we lost. I would not let them weep though, but stopped them all with a nod and a frown. I told them to haul the host of fine-fleeced sheep on board and put to sea. They boarded swiftly and took their place on the benches then sitting in their rows struck the grey water with their oars. When we were almost out of earshot, I shouted to the Cyclops, mocking him:

24 "'Cyclops, the men you snatched with brutal force
and ate within your cave were surely not
the comrades of a coward. You have caused
much grief; and it returns to haunt you now;
you did not hesitate; hard heart, you ate
your guests within your house; therefore lord Zeus
has joined with other gods to batter you.'

25 "My words incensed him more. He ripped the top
of a huge peak, then hurled a chunk at us;
that mass fell just beyond our ship's dark prow.
The sea surged as the mass dropped; and the wash
thrust our ship backward, closer to the coast.
But grabbing a long pole, I pushed us off
and signaled with my head: I spurred my men
to fall hard on the oars, to fend against
shipwreck; and they rowed hard—they strained, they bent.
When we were twice as distant as we'd been,
I shouted to the Cyclops, though my men
on all sides curbed me with these cautious words:

26 "'Why must you goad that savage so? Just now,
that mass that monster cast into the sea
drove back our ship to shore: we thought we'd reached
our end. And if he'd heard us breathe or speak
even the slightest word, he would have hurled
one more rough rock and smashed our heads and hull.
That brute has force to spare: he can throw far.'

27 "These were their words. But my firm heart was not
Convinced. Again my anger had to taunt:

'Cyclops, if any mortal man should ask
about the shameful blinding of your eye,
then tell him that the man who gouged you was
Odysseus, ravager of cities: one
who lives in Ithaca—Laértës' son.'

As Odysseus and his men escape on their ship, Polyphemus reveals that long ago he heard prophecy that one day Odysseus would blind him. He tries to coerce Odysseus and his men to return, promising that Poseidon will safely see Odysseus home, but Odysseus rebukes Polyphemus and continues on his way.

⌀ Knowledge Quest

- What classic traits of a hero does Odysseus possess?
- What challenges did Odysseus face?
- How did Odysseus overcome the challenges he faced?

Returning to the Text

- Return to the text as you respond to the following questions. Use text evidence to support your responses.
- Write any additional questions you have about the epic poem in your Reader/Writer Notebook.

1. What motivates Odysseus to go to the land of the Cyclops? What evidence in the first two paragraphs tells you this?

   _____

   _____

   _____

   _____

2. What does the following quote from paragraph 5 reveal about Odysseus' character? "But I would not listen, though it would have been best, wishing to see the giant himself, and test his hospitality. When he did appear he proved no joy to my men." How does Odysseus' behavior influence the events that follow?

   _____

   _____

   _____

   _____

3. Based on the words and actions of the Cyclops, how would you describe his character? How does this influence the events that follow?

   _____

   _____

   _____

   _____

4. KQ In paragraph 9, Odysseus says he "answered [the Cyclops] with cunning words." What does the word *cunning* tell you about Odysseus' special abilities?

_____

_____

_____

_____

5. List the verbs used in the blinding of the Cyclops. What effect do these verbs have on the pacing of this event?

_____

_____

_____

_____

6. Summarize paragraphs 21 and 22, maintaining meaning and logical order. How do Odysseus and his men escape? What makes paragraph 22 dramatic? How does Odysseus' behavior influence the resolution to the conflict?

_____

_____

_____

_____

7. Why do some lines in the poetic translation of the *Odyssey* end with a period and others with a comma? What is different about what those two graphical elements convey?

_____

_____

_____

_____

8. The adventure on the Road of Trials concludes with Odysseus having the last word of dialogue. Is this an effective way to end? Why or why not?

_____

_____

_____

_____

9. KQ Why is Odysseus' success so remarkable? What does his defeat of the Cyclops tell you about heroes?

_____

_____

_____

_____

Working from the Text

10. Return to the epic poem and make observations and inferences about Odysseus' character. Use the My Notes to annotate descriptions of his own words, actions, motivations, and behaviors. Also note how others react to him.

11. Use the evidence you gathered to express your understanding about Odysseus' character. In one or two sentences, describe Odysseus.

12. Use the following chart to organize your notes about Odysseus. Fill in the description column with your notes, and then analyze what this information means about Odysseus and how his character affects the plot, meaning the events and resolution of the conflict.

Character Analysis of Odysseus		
Character Development	**Description**	**Effect on the Plot**
Words		
Actions		
Motivations		
Behaviors		
Others' Reactions		

13. **Quickwrite:** Write an explanation of how Odysseus' character influences the events and resolution of the *Odyssey* excerpt. Include at least two examples of text evidence to support your response.

☑ Check Your Understanding

Reread paragraph 21 and write a statement explaining a heroic trait demonstrated by Odysseus and his men. Refer directly to the content of the paragraph.

14. Analyze the structure of the narrative and summarize the events. Then map out the sequence of events on a plot diagram in your Reader/ Writer Notebook.

_____

_____

_____

_____

_____

_____

_____

_____

_____

_____

_____

_____

_____

_____

_____

_____

_____

Setting a Purpose for Viewing

- As you look at the pictures, think about the mood the artist was trying to create.
- Think about this question: Why are the images effective?

KNOWLEDGE QUEST

What are some outstanding ways heroes overcome challenges?

1. The Cyclops lies sleeping. Illustration by comic book artist Gino D'Antonio, published in the 20th Century in *The Wanderings of Ulysses*.

2. Odysseus cunningly escapes the cave. Illustration by Charles Edmund Brock, published in *The Children's Hour: Stories from the Classics*, 1907.

3. Polyphemus tosses rocks at the fleeing Odysseus and his crew. Illustration by Louis Frédéric Schützenberger, 1887.

⊘ Knowledge Quest

- What emotions do you feel or sense while looking at the pictures?
- How did Odysseus face the challenges depicted in each image?

Returning to the Images

- Return to the images as you respond to the following questions. Use evidence to support your answers.
- Write any additional questions you have about the images in your Reader/Writer Notebook.

15. **KQ** Image 2 shows how "Odysseus cunningly escapes the cave." Why does the caption use the word *cunningly* to describe the escape?

_____

_____

_____

16. Choose one image. How does the depiction of the event in your chosen picture compare with the description in the text?

_____

_____

_____

17. **KQ** How do the three images help you understand Odysseus' ingenious plan to defeat the Cyclops?

_____

_____

_____

Knowledge Quest

Use what you have learned so far about heroes and your knowledge from reading the *Odyssey* about the ways that Odysseus overcame challenges. Write an informational essay that responds to the question: What are some outstanding ways heroes overcome challenges?

Be sure to:

- Clearly introduce the topic.
- Develop the topic with well-chosen evidence from the text.
- Provide a conclusion that supports the information.

INDEPENDENT READING LINK

You can continue to build your knowledge about this theme by reading related poetry and fiction at ZINC Reading Labs.

Select the **poetry** and **fiction** filters and type keywords such as *heroes* or *challenges* in the **Search all ZINC articles** field.

 ZINC

Working from the Images

18. Use the graphic organizer to analyze the mood each image creates. First, locate the text evidence used to illustrate the scene depicted in the image. Then, analyze the artist's interpretation. How does the image represent the text? Does the image accurately reflect the text? Did the artist take any liberties? Finally note the mood created in the image.

Image	Text Evidence	Artist's Interpretation	Mood
Image 1			
Image 2			
Image 3			

📝 Drafting the Embedded Assessment

Think about the hero you created in the previous activity. What might the hero experience in the Initiation Stage of his or her journey? Draft an event using your understanding of the Road of Trials to guide your structure and development. Be sure to:

- Use narrative techniques such as dialogue, pacing, and description and develop experiences, events, and/or characters.
- Use diction, detail, and imagery to create tone and mood.
- Sequence the event logically and naturally and use transitions to connect ideas.

Think about the shapes, shading, and expressions used in the visual depictions of the *Odyssey* and how the artist uses these devices to evoke a certain mood. What scene from your narrative would make a good visual?

The Return

Learning Targets

- Analyze a novel excerpt for archetype and narrative techniques.
- Draft and illustrate the final event in a narrative.

Preview

In this activity, you will see how the Return stage of the Hero's Journey archetype is presented in a novel excerpt.

The Return

While some stories end after the hero has achieved the Ultimate Boon (the goal he or she set out to achieve), most stories continue into the final stage: The Return.

Using Evidence to Support Understanding

To understand how Meg's journey is an example of a Hero's Journey archetype, you will need to read closely and make inferences about the characters and the conflict. You will need to keep track of **evidence** in the text that supports your understanding of events and characters, and then you **connect this evidence with what you know** about the Hero's Journey archetype to make an **inference**. These inferences will help you come to a greater understanding about the text as a whole. One strategy for keeping track of evidence is **annotation**. Use the Setting a Purpose for Reading instructions to help you annotate the text and gather evidence.

Setting a Purpose for Reading

- As you read, underline and label evidence of a Hero's Journey.
- Circle unknown words and phrases. Try to determine the meaning of the words by using context clues, word parts, or a dictionary.

WORD CONNECTIONS

Roots and Affixes

The prefix *re-*, as in **return**, is a very common and useful Latin prefix that means "again" or "back." You can use it to determine the meaning of many English words, such as *replay, rewrite, replace, regenerate, reproduce, recall, recreate,* and so on.

My Notes

About the Author

Madeleine L'Engle (1918–2007) submitted her best-known work, *A Wrinkle in Time*, to 27 publishers before it was accepted and published. It went on to win the 1963 Newbery Award for best children's book. *A Wrinkle in Time* is the first book in a series that follows the lives of Meg Murry, her youngest brother Charles Wallace, their friend Calvin O'Keefe, and twin brothers Sandy and Dennys. Beginning with A Wrinkle in Time, each novel features the characters encountering otherworldly beings and evil forces they have to defeat in order to save the world.

GRAMMAR & USAGE

Prepositions and Prepositional Phrases

Writers use **prepositions** and **prepositional phrases** to add details. Prepositional phrases show relationships of time, direction, or location. Prepositional phrases function as adjectives or adverbs. Look at paragraph 1 in the excerpt from *A Wrinkle in Time*. In the first sentence, the author uses three prepositional phrases beginning with the preposition *into: into darkness, into nothingness,* and *into the icy devouring cold.* These three prepositional phrases function as adverbs, describing where Meg went. In that same sentence, the author uses the prepositional phrase *of the Black Thing* as an adjective, describing the noun *cold.* Notice how the author's use of these prepositional phrases adds vivid details to describe what is happening to Meg.

As you read *A Wrinkle in Time,* pay attention to how the author uses prepositional phrases to paint a more vivid picture for readers.

eerie: spooky; inspiring fear

Novel

from # A Wrinkle in Time

by **Madeleine L'Engle**
excerpt from Chapter 12, "The Foolish and the Weak"

This excerpt comes near the end of Meg Murry's journey. She has found her father with the help of Mrs. Whatsit, Mrs. Who, and Mrs. Which. They have escaped Camazotz, but they were forced to leave behind her younger brother Charles Wallace in the grip of the "Black Thing." Now Meg must return to Camazotz to get her brother.

1   Immediately Meg was swept into darkness, into nothingness, and then into the icy devouring cold of the Black Thing. *Mrs Which won't let it get me,* she thought over and over while the cold of the Black Thing seemed to crunch at her bones.

2   Then they were through it, and she was standing breathlessly on her feet on the same hill on which they had first landed on Camazotz. She was cold and a little numb, but no worse than she had often been in the winter in the country when she had spent an afternoon skating on the pond. She looked around. She was completely alone. Her heart began to pound.

3   Then, seeming to echo from all around her, came Mrs Which's unforgettable voice, "I hhave nnott ggivenn yyou mmyy ggifftt. *Yyou hhave ssomethinngg thatt ITT hhass nnott.* Thiss ssomethinngg iss yyourr onlly wweapponn. Bbutt yyou mmusstt ffinnddd itt fforr yyourrssellff." Then the voice ceased, and Meg knew that she was alone.

4   She walked slowly down the hill, her heart thumping painfully against her ribs. There below her was the same row of identical houses they had seen before, and beyond these the linear buildings of the city. She walked along the quiet street. It was dark and the street was deserted. No children playing ball or skipping rope. No mother figures at the doors. No father figures returning from work. In the same window of each house was a light, and as Meg walked down the street all the lights were extinguished simultaneously. Was it because of her presence, or was it simply that it was time for lights out?

5   She felt numb, beyond rage or disappointment or even fear. She put one foot ahead of the other with precise regularity, not allowing her pace to lag. She was not thinking; she was not planning; she was simply walking slowly but steadily toward the city and the domed building where IT lay.

6   Now she approached the outlying buildings of the city. In each of them was a vertical line of light, but it was a dim, **eerie** light, not the warm light of stairways in cities at home. And there were no isolated brightly lit windows where someone was working late, or an office was being cleaned. Out of each

building came one man, perhaps a watchman, and each man started walking the width of the building. They appeared not to see her. At any rate they paid no attention to her whatsoever, and she went on past them.

7   What have I got that IT hasn't got? she thought suddenly. What have I possibly got?

8   Now she was walking by the tallest of the business buildings. More dim vertical lines of light. The walls glowed slightly to give a faint illumination to the streets. CENTRAL Central Intelligence was ahead of her. Was the man with red eyes still sitting there? Or was he allowed to go to bed? But this was not where she must go, though the man with red eyes seemed the kind old gentleman he claimed to be when compared with IT. But he was no longer of any **consequence** in the search for Charles Wallace. She must go directly to IT.

9   IT isn't used to being resisted. Father said that's how he managed, and how Calvin and I managed as long as we did. Father saved me then. There's nobody here to save me now. I have to do it myself. I have to resist IT by myself. Is that what I have that IT hasn't got? No, I'm sure IT can resist. IT just isn't used to having *other* people resist.

10   CENTRAL Central Intelligence blocked with its huge rectangle the end of the square. She turned to walk around it, and almost **imperceptibly** her steps slowed.

11   It was not far to the great dome which housed IT.

12   I'm going to Charles Wallace. That's what's important. That's what I have to think of. I wish I could feel numb again the way I did at first. Suppose IT has him somewhere else? Suppose he isn't there?

13   I have to go there first, anyhow. That's the only way I can find out.

14   Her steps got slower and slower as she passed the great bronzed doors, the huge slabs of the CENTRAL Central Intelligence building, as she finally saw ahead of her the strange, light, pulsing dome of IT.

15   Father said it was all right for me to be afraid. He said to go ahead and be afraid. And Mrs Who said—I don't understand what she said but I think it was meant to make me not hate being only me, and me being the way I am. And Mrs Whatsit said to remember that she loves me. That's what I have to think about. Not about being afraid. Or not as smart as IT. Mrs Whatsit loves me. That's quite something, to be loved by someone like Mrs Whatsit.

16   She was there.

17   No matter how slowly her feet had taken her at the end, they had taken her there.

18   Directly ahead of her was the circular building, its walls glowing with **violet** flame, its silvery roof pulsing with a light that seemed to Meg to be insane. Again she could feel the light, neither warm nor cold, but reaching out to touch her, pulling her toward IT.

---

consequence: importance
imperceptibly: in a manner that is hardly noticeable
violet: a purplish-blue color

WORD CONNECTIONS

Roots and Affixes
In the word **inexorable**, the prefix *in-* means "not." It has the same meaning in *ineffective* and *inexperienced*. The suffix *-able* means "capable or worthy of," as in *debatable* and *laughable*. The root *exor* comes from Latin and means "to plead for."

19 There was a sudden sucking, and she was within.

20 It was as though the wind had been knocked out of her. She gasped for breath, for breath in her own rhythm, not the **permeating** pulsing of IT. She could feel the inexorable beat within her body, controlling her heart, her lungs.

21 But not herself. Not Meg. It did not quite have her.

22 She blinked her eyes rapidly and against the rhythm until the redness before them cleared and she could see. There was the brain, there was IT, lying pulsing and quivering on the dais, soft and exposed and **nauseating**. Charles Wallace was crouched beside IT, his eyes still slowly twirling, his jaw still slack, as she had seen him before, with a tic in his forehead **reiterating** the revolting rhythm of IT.

23 As she saw him it was again as though she had been punched in the stomach, for she had to realize afresh that she was seeing Charles, and yet it was not Charles at all. Where was Charles Wallace, her own beloved Charles Wallace?

24 What is it I have got that IT hasn't got?

25 "You have nothing that IT hasn't got," Charles Wallace said coldly. "How nice to have you back, dear sister. We have been waiting for you. We knew that Mrs Whatsit would send you. She is our friend, you know."

26 For an appalling moment Meg believed, and in that moment she felt her brain being gathered up into IT.

27 "No!" she screamed at the top of her lungs. "No! You lie!"

28 For a moment she was free from ITs clutches again.

29 As long as I can stay angry enough IT can't get me.

30 Is that what I have that IT doesn't have?

31 "Nonsense," Charles Wallace said. "You have nothing that IT doesn't have."

32 "You're lying," she replied, and she felt only anger toward this boy who was not Charles Wallace at all. No, it was not anger, it was loathing; it was hatred, sheer and unadulterated, and as she became lost in hatred she also began to be lost in IT. The red miasma swam before her eyes; her stomach churned in ITs rhythm. Her body trembled with the strength of her hatred and the strength of IT.

33 With the last **vestige** of consciousness she jerked her mind and body. Hate was nothing that IT didn't have. IT knew all about hate.

34 "You are lying about that, and you were lying about Mrs Whatsit!" she screamed.

35 "Mrs Whatsit hates you," Charles Wallace said.

WORD CONNECTIONS

Etymology
The word **miasma** appeared in the 1660s as a Modern Latin word meaning "noxious vapors." It derives from the same Greek word that means "stain" or "pollution." Now it is used to mean a poisonous atmosphere.

permeating: spreading everywhere
nauseating: making feel ill
reiterating: repeating
vestige: a bit or trace of something

36 And that was where IT made ITs fatal mistake, for as Meg said, automatically, "Mrs Whatsit loves me; that's what she told me, that she loves me," suddenly she knew.

37 She knew!

38 Love.

39 That was what she had that IT did not have.

40 She had Mrs Whatsit's love, and her father's, and her mother's, and the real Charles Wallace's love, and the twins', and Aunt Beast's.

41 And she had her love for them.

42 But how could she use it? What was she meant to do?

43 If she could give love to IT perhaps it would shrivel up and die, for she was sure that IT could not withstand love. But she, in all her weakness and foolishness and baseness and nothingness, was incapable of loving IT. Perhaps it was not too much to ask of her, but she could not do it.

44 But she could love Charles Wallace.

45 She could stand there and she could love Charles Wallace.

46 Her own Charles Wallace, the real Charles Wallace, the child for whom she had come back to Camazotz, to IT, the baby who was so much more than she was, and who was yet so utterly **vulnerable**.

47 She could love Charles Wallace.

48 Charles. Charles, I love you. My baby brother who always takes care of me. Come back to me, Charles Wallace, come away from IT, come back, come home. I love you, Charles. Oh, Charles Wallace, I love you.

49 Tears were streaming down her cheeks, but she was unaware of them.

50 Now she was even able to look at him, at this animated thing that was not her own Charles Wallace at all. She was able to look and love.

51 I love you. Charles Wallace, you are my darling and my dear and the light of my life and the treasure of my heart, I love you. I love you. I love you.

52 Slowly his mouth closed. Slowly his eyes stopped their twirling. The tic in the forehead ceased its revolting twitch. Slowly he advanced toward her.

53 "I love you!" she cried. "I love you, Charles! I love you!"

54 Then suddenly he was running, pelting, he was in her arms, he was shrieking with sobs. "Meg! Meg! Meg!"

55 "I love you, Charles!" she cried again, her sobs almost as loud as his, her tears mingling with his. "I love you! I love you! I love you!"

vulnerable: susceptible to danger

My Notes

56 A whirl of darkness. An icy cold blast. An angry, resentful howl that seemed to tear through her. Darkness again. Through the darkness to save her came a sense of Mrs Whatsit's presence, so that she knew it could not be IT who now had her in its clutches.

57 And then the feel of earth beneath her, of something in her arms, and she was rolling over on the sweet-smelling **autumnal** earth, and Charles Wallace was crying out, "Meg! Oh, Meg!"

58 Now she was hugging him close to her, and his little arms were clasped tightly about her neck. "Meg, you saved me! You saved me!" he said over and over.

59 "Meg!" came a call, and there were her father and Calvin hurrying through the darkness toward them.

60 Still holding Charles she struggled to stand up and look around. "Father! Cal! Where are we?"

61 Charles Wallace, holding her hand tightly, was looking around, too, and suddenly he laughed, his own, sweet, **contagious** laugh. "In the twins' vegetable garden! And we landed in the broccoli!"

62 Meg began to laugh, too, at the same time that she was trying to hug her father, to hug Calvin, and not to let go of Charles Wallace for one second.

63 "Meg, you did it!" Calvin shouted. "You saved Charles!"

64 "I'm very proud of you, my daughter." Mr. Murry kissed her **gravely**, then turned toward the house. "Now I must go in to Mother." Meg could tell that he was trying to control his anxiety and eagerness.

65 "Look!" she pointed to the house, and there were the twins and Mrs. Murry walking toward them through the long, wet grass.

66 "First thing tomorrow I must get some new glasses," Mr. Murry said, squinting in the moonlight, and then starting to run toward his wife.

67 Dennys's voice came crossly over the lawn. "Hey, Meg, it's bedtime."

68 Sandy suddenly yelled, "Father!"

69 Mr. Murry was running across the lawn, Mrs. Murry running toward him, and they were in each other's arms, and then there was a tremendous happy jumble of arms and legs and hugging, the older Murrys and Meg and Charles Wallace and the twins, and Calvin grinning by them until Meg reached out and pulled him in and Mrs. Murry gave him a special hug all of his own. They were talking and laughing all at once, when they were startled by a crash, and Fortinbras, who could bear being left out of the happiness not one second longer, catapulted his sleek black body right through the screened door to the kitchen. He dashed across the lawn to join in the joy, and almost knocked them all over with the exuberance of his greeting.

70 Meg knew all at once that Mrs Whatsit, Mrs Who, and Mrs Which must be near, because all through her she felt a flooding of joy and of love that was even greater and deeper than the joy and love which were already there.

WORD CONNECTIONS

Cognates
The English word **tangible** (in paragraph 72) is spelled the same as, but pronounced differently than, its Spanish cognate with the same meaning. The Spanish word *catapultar* is a cognate of the English verb **catapult** (in paragraph 69).

autumnal: related to autumn
contagious: passed from one person to another
gravely: seriously

71 She stopped laughing and listened, and Charles listened, too. "Hush."

72 Then there was a whirring, and Mrs Whatsit, Mrs Who, and Mrs Which were standing in front of them, and the joy and love were so tangible that Meg felt that if she only knew where to reach she could touch it with her bare hands.

73 Mrs Whatsit said breathlessly, "Oh, my darlings, I'm sorry we don't have time to say good-by to you properly. You see, we have to—"

74 But they never learned what it was that Mrs Whatsit, Mrs Who, and Mrs Which had to do, for there was a gust of wind, and they were gone.

Making Observations

- Who do we meet in the excerpt?
- What is a detail you noticed that someone else might miss?

Returning to the Text

- Return to the text as you respond to the following questions. Use text evidence to support your responses.
- Write any additional questions you have about the novel excerpt in your Reader/Writer Notebook.

1. The word "devouring" is used in paragraph 1. What is the effect of this word choice on the mood of the opening?

_____

_____

_____

_____

2. Why does the author use mathematical terms such as "linear" and "vertical" to describe the scene?

_____

_____

_____

_____

3. What can you infer about IT as a character in the novel? Provide textual evidence to support your inferences.

_____

_____

_____

_____

4. Throughout the story, how do others assist Meg in her quest to rescue her brother?

_____

_____

_____

_____

5. Use context clues to determine the meaning of the word "loathing" in paragraph 32. What other word(s) helped you?

_____

_____

_____

_____

6. What is the power of "the Black Thing," of IT, that Meg must battle against? Choose a line that best expresses IT's power and explain your choice.

_____

_____

_____

_____

7. How does Meg use "the Ultimate Boon" to conquer the power of IT?

_____

_____

_____

_____

8. What is the meaning of the word "animated" in paragraph 50? Use context clues to help you, and cite textual evidence in your response.

_____

_____

_____

_____

Working from the Text

9. Use the following graphic organizer to analyze how *A Wrinkle in Time* demonstrates the Return Stage of a Hero's Journey. Return to the text to find evidence to fill in the graphic organizer.

Return Stages	Evidence from the Text
The Magic Flight (the adventure "home")	
Rescue from Without (the guide)	
The Crossing or Return Threshold—The Theme Statement (integrating wisdom into previous life)	

✅ Check Your Understanding

Write 3–4 sentences explaining how Meg represents the Hero in the Hero's Journey archetype. Use text evidence from the excerpt to support your claim.

LANGUAGE & WRITER'S CRAFT: Verbs and Mood

Writers form and use verbs in the correct mood. The list below shows the moods of English verbs.

Indicative Mood: verbs that indicate a fact or opinion

> *I am too ill to go to school today.*

Imperative Mood: verbs that express a command or request

> *Go to school. Please get up and get dressed.*

Interrogative Mood: verbs that ask a question

> *Are you going to school? Do you feel ill?*

Conditional Mood: verbs that express something that hasn't happened or something that can happen if a certain condition is met

> *I would have gone to school yesterday if I had felt well.*
> *Your teacher might want you to complete the assignments you missed.*

Subjunctive Mood: Verbs that describe a state that is uncertain or contrary to fact; when using the verb "to be" in the subjunctive, always use *were* rather than *was*.

> *I wish my cold were better today.*
> *If you were to go to school, what would you learn?*

PRACTICE Look over the excerpt from *A Wrinkle in Time* again. Find an example of a sentence to illustrate each of the moods above. Write and label these examples in your Reader/Writer Notebook. If you have time, create a few more examples on your own and add those to your Reader/Writer Notebook.

My Notes

Reading Graphic Novels

To continue thinking about how to illustrate your narrative, you will take a look at a graphic novel adaptation of the *A Wrinkle in Time* excerpt that you just read. Graphic novels use a combination of images and words to tell real or fictional stories. As you explore the graphic novel, you should note the distinct graphic features that characterize this type of storytelling. Following is a list of graphic features and their uses. These terms can help you speak and write about graphic novels with precision.

Panel—squares or rectangles that contain a single image

Gutter—space between panels

Dialogue Balloon—circular shape that contains communication between/among characters

Thought Bubbles—shape that contains a character's thoughts shared only with the reader

Caption—box that provides background information about the scene or character

Sound Effect—visual clue about sounds in the scene

Long Shot—image that shows a character or object from the distance so you can see its entirety

Extreme Long Shot—image that shows objects or characters in very small scale, often showing a landscape or crowd of characters

Close-up—image that is shown in a large view taking up at least 80 percent of the panel

Extreme Close-up—image that is shown in very large view, often focusing on a small portion of a larger object or character

Setting a Purpose for Reading

- As you read, underline and label evidence of a Hero's Journey.
- Circle unknown words and phrases. Try to determine the meaning of the words by using the images, context clues, word parts, or a dictionary.

About the Author

Hope Larson (b. 1982) is the *New York Times* best-selling author of six graphic novels. In 2007 she won an Eisner Award, the highest honor for a comic artist, for her adapted and illustrated edition of *A Wrinkle in Time: The Graphic Novel.* Some of her other graphic novels include *Who is AC?*, *Mercury*, and *Chiggers.* Currently, she writes DC Comics' *Batgirl* series and lives in Los Angeles.

Graphic Novel

from # A Wrinkle in Time: The Graphic Novel

adapted and illustrated by **Hope Larsen**

No! You're lying!

Hate's not what IT doesn't have! IT knows all about hate!

You're lying about that and you were lying about Mrs Whatsit!

Mrs Whatsit hates you.

Mrs Whatsit loves me.

That's what she told me—that she loves me.

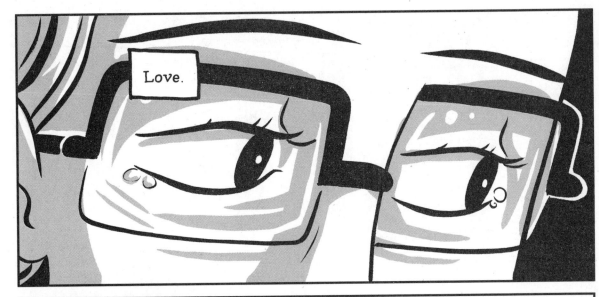

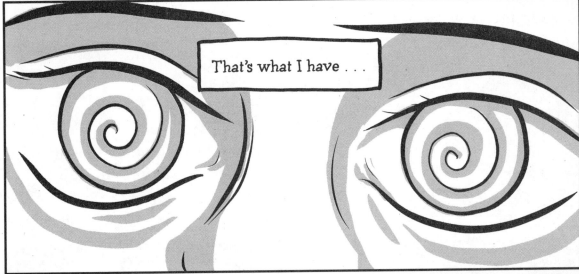

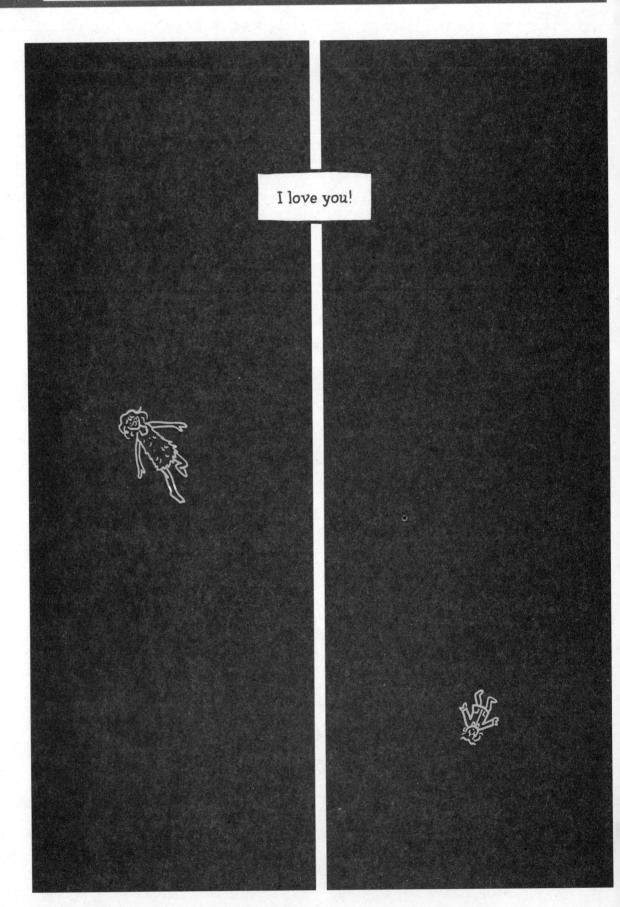

Working from the Text

10. Return to the graphic novel. Use the graphic organizer that follows to tell where each Return Stage of a Hero's Journey of *A Wrinkle in Time* is illustrated in the graphic novel. In the second column, list the visual effects the illustrator uses to communicate the ideas of each stage. In the third column, tell what mood is created by the use of these effects.

Return Stages	Visual Effects	Mood Created
The Magic Flight (the adventure "home")		
Rescue from Without (the guide)		
The Crossing or Return Threshold—The Theme Statement (integrating wisdom into previous life)		

11. By using illustrations, what did the graphic novel help you to understand about the story that the text did not?

12. Explain why the illustrator might have wanted to create a visual version of *A Wrinkle in Time*.

☑ Drafting the Embedded Assessment

Revisit your hero narrative. What might your hero learn by the end of the Return Stage in his or her journey? Draft an ending to your narrative using your understanding of the Crossing/Return Threshold to guide your development. Be sure to:

• Make sure the ending to your story follows the previous events logically and naturally.
• Include some reflection in the ending and answer the question: *What does the hero learn?*
• Use narrative techniques such as dialogue, pacing, and description.
• Incorporate sentences that use the different verb moods you have learned about in this lesson.

Language Checkpoint:
Understanding Sentence Boundaries

- Understand complete sentences, sentence fragments, and run-on sentences, including comma splices.
- Revise writing to correct sentence fragments and run-on sentences.

Preview

In this activity, you will learn to recognize complete sentences and to revise your writing to correct sentence fragments and run-on sentences.Understanding Sentence Boundaries

Skilled writers use complete sentences to express complete thoughts. A sentence fragment is less than a complete sentence; that is, it is missing one or more elements that make it complete. A run-on is more than a complete sentence; that is, it runs two or more complete sentences together as if they were one.

Recognizing Complete Sentences and Sentence Fragments

Knowing the differences between complete sentences and sentence fragments is an important part of becoming a strong writer and self-editor.

A **sentence** includes at least one independent clause. An **independent clause** includes a subject and a verb and expresses a complete thought.

Look at these sentences from *A Wrinkle in Time*:

> She (looked) around. She (was) completely alone. Her heart (began) to pound.

Each one has a subject (underlined) and a verb (circled). Each one expresses a complete thought.

A **sentence fragment** may be missing a subject and/or a verb, or it may not express a complete thought.

> **Fragment (missing a subject):** Beginning to pound.

> **Fragment (missing a verb):** Her heart in her throat.

> **Fragment (not a complete thought):** When she realized her situation.

Writers usually use complete sentences to express their meaning. Sometimes, though, a writer chooses to use sentence fragments to produce a specific effect in his or her writing.

This excerpt from *A Wrinkle in Time* includes two fragments:

> Mrs. Whatsit said to remember that she loves me. That's what I have to think about. Not about being afraid. Or not as smart as IT.

1. Which two word groups above are complete sentences? Which two are fragments?

2. Explain how you identified the fragments.

3. Quickwrite: Why might Madeleine L'Engle have chosen to use sentence fragments? What effect do the fragments create?

Recognizing Run-on Sentences

Sometimes two or more complete sentences run together as if they are a single sentence. This creates a **run-on sentence**. Like sentence fragments, run-ons are usually avoided, though some writers may use them for effect. For example, using run-ons can show rambling dialogue.

Run-ons can be confusing because they make it a hard to see where one thought ends and another begins. Alternatively, the connection between the sentences might not be clear.

Look at this run-on:

> Madeleine L'Engle wrote many acclaimed books for children and adults her best-known work, *A Wrinkle in Time*, won the 1963 Newbery Medal.

This word group contains two whole sentences (independent clauses) and two whole complete thoughts. With no punctuation between them, the sentences are not clear.

A run-on can be revised in several ways.

It can be made into two separate sentences:

> Madeleine L'Engle wrote many acclaimed books for children and adults. **H**er best-known work, *A Wrinkle in Time*, won the 1963 Newbery Medal.

A comma and coordinating conjunction (such as *and, but, or, so,* or *yet*) can be added, making a compound sentence:

> Madeleine L'Engle wrote many acclaimed books for children and adults, **and** her best-known work, *A Wrinkle in Time*, won the 1963 Newbery Medal.

In some cases, the clauses can be joined by a semicolon—if the clauses are closely connected in meaning.

> Madeleine L'Engle wrote many acclaimed books for children and adults; her best-known work, *A Wrinkle in Time*, won the 1963 Newbery Medal.

Run-ons can also be reworded so that one of the independent clauses becomes a phrase or dependent clause.

> Madeleine L'Engle wrote many acclaimed books for children and adults, **including** her best-known work, *A Wrinkle in Time*, **which** won the 1963 Newbery Medal.

Recognizing Comma Splices

One specific kind of run-on sentence is called a **comma splice**. A comma splice occurs when two sentences are run together with only a comma between them:

> Madeleine L'Engle wrote many acclaimed books for children and adults, her best-known work, *A Wrinkle in Time*, won the 1963 Newbery Medal.

A comma splice can be corrected by breaking the run-on into two separate sentences, adding a conjunction after the comma, or replacing the comma with a semicolon.

Read the following paragraph:

L'Engle submitted her manuscript for *A Wrinkle in Time* to many different publishers, twenty-six of them rejected it. The twenty-seventh agreed to publish it. L'Engle's work also includes plays and poetry, as well as her autobiography. *A Wrinkle in Time* is part of a series, other books in the series are *A Wind in the Door, A Swiftly Tilting Planet, Many Waters,* and *An Acceptable Time.*

4. In the above paragraph, underline each complete, correct sentence.

5. In the paragraph above, draw brackets around any run-on sentence(s).

6. If a run-on is a comma splice, circle the comma that incorrectly "splices" the sentences together.

Revising Sentences, Fragments, and Run-ons

7. Decide whether each word group below is a sentence (S), fragment (F), or run-on (R). Circle the corresponding letter. Rewrite the sentences with correct capitalization and punctuation. Revise the fragments and run-on sentences to make it a complete, correct sentence.

   a. meg murry's journey, a long and difficult one   S / F / R

   _____

   b. she has found her father, and they have escaped camazotz   S / F / R

   _____

   c. they were forced to leave behind charles wallace, he is her younger brother   S / F / R

   _____

   d. charles wallace is in the grip of the "black thing"   S / F / R

   _____

   e. now meg, on her way to camazotz to get him   S / F / R

   _____

   f. meg feels afraid, she persists in her mission   S / F / R

   _____

8. Rewrite the following paragraph, correcting fragments and run-ons.

   A *Wrinkle in Time* first published in 1962. It is the first book in Madeleine L'Engle's Time Quintet. Which is a series of five books that involve travel in time. The book includes ideas from quantum physics, one of those ideas is the tesseract. Supernatural beings use the tesseract to transport Meg Murry and other characters across the universe.

 **Check Your Understanding**

What questions can you ask yourself, when editing your work, to check for sentence fragments? How can you tell whether a fragment is used for effect?

What questions can you ask yourself to check for run-on sentences and comma splices in your work?

Add the questions to your Editor's Checklist.

Practice

With a partner, exchange drafts of your hero narrative and examine the writing specifically for correct use of complete sentences with correct punctuation. Put an exclamation point next to any sentence fragments or run-on sentences. Evaluate any fragments to determine whether they are unintentional or are used for effect. If they are unintentional, work with your partner to revise them. Also revise any run-ons or comma splices.

Learning Targets

- Identify and apply effective techniques and strategies for writing groups.
- Revise and edit a narrative draft through a collaborative writing group.

Preview

In this activity, you will participate in a writing group to provide feedback to your peers about their writing and revise your own work based on peer feedback.

Writing Group Roles

For groups to be effective, each member must participate to help achieve the goals of the group. The purpose of writing groups is to:

- Provide an open-minded place to read, respond to, and revise writing.
- Provide meaningful feedback to improve writing based on specific criteria.
- Create specific roles to solicit and manage sharing and responding.
- Focus on posing open-ended questions for the writer to consider.

Writing group members have roles and responsibilities.

Role	Guidelines	Discussion/Response Starters
The Reader: Reads the text silently, then aloud. Begins the conversation after reading.	The Reader's purpose is to share an understanding of the Writer's words. The Reader provides the writer with oral or written instructions on how to improve their writing. The Reader follows all listeners' guidelines as well.	Reader's and Listeners' compliments: • I liked the words you used, such as … • I like the way you described … • This piece made me feel … • This piece reminded me of … • I noticed your use of _____ from the Hero's Journey when you …
The Listeners: Take notes and prepare open-ended questions for the Writer or make constructive statements.	The Listeners begin with positive statements, using "I" statements to talk about the writing, not the Writer. The Listeners use the writer's checklist to produce thoughtful questions that will help strengthen the writing.	Reader's and Listeners' comments and suggestions: • I really enjoyed the part where … • What parts are you having trouble with? • What do you plan to do next? • I was confused when …
The Writer: Listens to the draft, takes notes, responds to questions, and asks questions for clarification.	As his or her work is being read aloud by another, the Writer can get an overall impression of the piece. The Writer follows oral or written instructions to improve the writing. The Writer asks questions to get feedback that will lead to effective revision.	Writer's questions: • What do you want to know more about? • Which part does not make sense? • Which section of the text does not work? • How can I improve this part?

1. Summarize the purpose and process of working in a successful writing group.

The Revision Process

Very few people are able to write a perfect first draft, so revising is a typical part of the writing process—even for famous writers. In an interview done for *The Paris Review* in 1956, the interviewer asked Ernest Hemingway about his writing.

> Interviewer: How much rewriting do you do?
> Hemingway: It depends. I rewrote the ending of *Farewell to Arms*, the last page of it, 39 times before I was satisfied.
> Interviewer: Was there some technical problem there? What was it that had stumped you?
> Hemingway: Getting the words right.
> (from Ernest Hemingway, "The Art of Fiction," *The Paris Review* Interview, 1956)

2. Writing groups can help you revise and get your words right. Throughout this unit, you have started a narrative about a hero. As you think about revising your draft, what are some guiding questions you might ask? You might use the Embedded Assessment 1 Scoring Guide to prompt your questions to focus on clarity, development, organization, style, word choice, and sentence variety.

Introducing the Strategy: Self-Editing, Peer-Editing

Editing your writing is a part of the writing process (self-editing). This strategy can be used with a partner (peer-editing) to examine a draft closely to identify areas that may need to be corrected for structure, ideas, language, grammar, punctuation, capitalization, or spelling. Peer editors need to provide clear oral or written instructions for how the writer can improve the writing.

3. In addition to asking questions, having a writer's checklist can help you revise. Next, you will work with members of your writing group to create, on separate paper, a writer's checklist for your Hero's Journey narrative. This checklist should reflect your group's input about the following:

- **Ideas:** Think of the purpose and development of the writing, the topic, and the details.
- **Structure:** Think of the type of writing and its purpose, as well as the organization and clarity of the writing. Revisit your hook and decide whether it is adequate or needs revision.
- **Use of language:** Think about style, clarity, figurative language, descriptive details, transitions, word choice, sentence variety, and so on.

4. After completing your writer's checklist, your writing group will read and discuss each member's draft of the Hero's Journey narrative. Group members should trade roles of Reader, Listener, and Writer as they proceed through each draft, following the information in the chart at the beginning of Activity 1.9.

Using Resources and References to Revise

How does a writer improve a text through revision? Deep revision takes time and effort. Skilled writers do the following:

- **Add** ideas and language to improve the development of ideas.
- **Delete** irrelevant, unclear, and repetitive ideas and language to improve pacing, clarity, and effect.
- **Rearrange** ideas to improve organization.
- **Substitute** ideas and language for effect such as improving sentence variety, tailoring style, or refining word choice to be more precise.

5. Have students number and label the sequence of events in their narratives to check how naturally and effectively the events unfold. Then have them summarize the sequences with partners to verify that they make sense.

6. Use the writer's checklist you created, the feedback from your peers, and the revision strategies above to guide your revision. Share one of your revisions with the class by explaining specifically what you revised and how it improved your writing.

Editing a Draft

7. New writers sometimes confuse revision with editing or proofreading. Both are extremely important in creating a polished piece of writing, but they are different and separate processes.

- Revision focuses on ideas, organization, and language and involves adding, deleting, rearranging, and substituting words, sentences, and entire paragraphs.
- Editing focuses on conventions of standard English. It involves close proofreading and consulting reference sources to correct errors in grammar and usage, capitalization, punctuation, and spelling.
- After drafting a text, students often either revise *or* edit rather than doing both. Skipping either step in the writing process greatly affects the quality of your final draft.

8. It is essential that writers take the time to edit drafts to correct errors in grammar and usage, capitalization, punctuation, and spelling. Return to your draft and self-edit and peer-edit to strengthen the grammar and language conventions in your draft. Be sure to create a new writer's checklist that contains specific areas of concern.

☑ Check Your Understanding

Use a combination of self-editing and peer-editing to strengthen the language and grammar in your draft, and correct errors in capitalization, punctuation, and spelling. Use online tools , such as spelling and grammar checkers and online dictionaries, to verify your writing when you are unsure.

⬆ Independent Reading Checkpoint

What accomplishments did the protagonist in your independent reading text achieve? What vivid language did the author use to describe these accomplishments? Explain why you think these accomplishments do or do not make this character a hero. Describe any personal connections that you have made to this text. Use complex and compound-complex sentences in your explanation, and include correctly punctuated dialogue from the excerpt.

Writing a Hero's Journey Narrative

 ASSIGNMENT

Think about all the heroes you have encountered in fiction and real life. What type of hero appeals to you? Write and create an illustrated narrative about an original hero. Use the Hero's Journey archetype to develop and structure your ideas. Orally present your narrative to your classmates.

Planning and Prewriting: Take time to make a plan for your narrative.	▪ What characteristics will your hero possess, and what setting will you choose? ▪ What are the essential elements of a narrative that you will need to include? ▪ What prewriting strategies will you use to plan the organization?
Drafting: Create a draft that includes the elements of an effective narrative.	▪ How will you introduce characters, context, and setting and establish a point of view? ▪ How will you use dialogue, details, and description to create an original, believable hero? ▪ How will you sequence events logically and naturally using steps of the Hero's Journey archetype? ▪ How will you provide a conclusion or resolution that follows from and reflects on the events of the narrative? ▪ How will you find or create illustrations to capture key imagery, emphasize ideas, or add interest?
Evaluating and Revising: Create opportunities to review and revise your work.	▪ When will you share your work with your writing group? ▪ What is your plan to incorporate suggestions and ideas for revisions into your draft? ▪ How can you improve connotative diction and imagery to create tone and mood? ▪ How can the Scoring Guide help you evaluate how well your draft meets the requirements of the assignment?
Checking and Editing: Confirm that your final draft is ready for publication.	▪ How will you proofread and edit your draft to demonstrate command of the conventions of standard English capitalization, punctuation, spelling, grammar, and usage? ▪ How will you create a title and assemble your illustrations in an appealing manner? ▪ How will you prepare a final draft for publication and presentation?

Reflection

After completing this Embedded Assessment, think about how you went about accomplishing this task and respond to the following:

• How did your understanding of the Hero's Journey archetype help you create an original narrative?

SCORING GUIDE

Scoring Criteria	Exemplary	Proficient	Emerging	Incomplete
Ideas	The narrative • creates a complex, original protagonist • establishes a clear point of view, setting, and conflict • uses precise and engaging details, dialogue, imagery, and description • includes a variety of enhancing visuals.	The narrative • creates a believable, original protagonist • establishes point of view, setting, and conflict • uses adequate details, dialogue, imagery, and description • includes sufficient visuals.	The narrative • creates an unoriginal or undeveloped protagonist • establishes a weak point of view, setting, or conflict • uses inadequate narrative techniques • includes insufficient, unrelated, or inappropriate visuals.	The narrative • lacks a protagonist • does not establish point of view, setting, or conflict • uses minimal narrative techniques • includes few or no visuals.
Structure	The narrative • engages and orients the reader with detailed exposition • sequences events in the plot effectively, including a variety of steps from the Hero's Journey archetype • uses a variety of transitional strategies effectively and purposefully • provides a thoughtful resolution.	The narrative • orients the reader with adequate exposition • sequences events in the plot logically, including some steps of the Hero's Journey archetype • uses transitional words, phrases, and clauses to link events and signal shifts • provides a logical resolution.	The narrative • provides weak or vague exposition • sequences events unevenly, including minimal or unclear steps of the Hero's Journey archetype • uses inconsistent, repetitive, or basic transitional words, phrases, and clauses • provides a weak or disconnected resolution.	The narrative • lacks exposition • has minimal plot with no apparent connection to the Hero's Journey archetype • uses few or no transitional strategies • lacks a resolution.
Use of Language	The narrative • is presented using effective volume, clarity, and eye contact • demonstrates command of the conventions of standard English capitalization, punctuation, spelling, grammar, and usage (including appropriate use of a variety of moods).	The narrative • is presented using appropriate volume, pronunciation, and eye contact • demonstrates adequate command of the conventions of standard English capitalization, punctuation, spelling, grammar, and usage (including appropriate use of moods).	The narrative • is presented with some attention to eye contact, volume, and pace of delivery • demonstrates partial or inconsistent command of the conventions of standard English capitalization, punctuation, spelling, grammar, and usage.	The narrative • is presented with little attention to eye contact, volume, and pacing • lacks command of the conventions of standard English capitalization, punctuation, spelling, grammar, and usage; frequent errors obscure meaning.

Unpacking Embedded Assessment 2

Learning Targets

- Reflect on previous learning and make connections to new learning.
- Identify and analyze the skills and knowledge necessary to be successful in completing Embedded Assessment 2.

Preview

In this activity, you will begin thinking about how to write a definition essay about heroism.

Making Connections

In the first part of this unit, you learned about the archetype of the Hero's Journey, and you wrote your own illustrated narrative depicting a protagonist who makes a heroic journey. In this half of the unit, you will continue thinking about heroism and what makes a hero; your work will culminate in an essay in which you create your definition of a hero.

Essential Questions

Reflect on your understanding of Essential Question 1: How has your understanding of the concept of a hero changed over the course of this unit? Then respond to Essential Question 2, which will be the focus of the rest of the unit: How does the Hero's Journey archetype appear in stories throughout time?

Developing Vocabulary

Re-sort the vocabulary from the first half of the unit, using the QHT strategy. Compare the new sort with your original QHT sort. In a concise statement, describe how your understanding has changed.

Use a dictionary to find the origin for each term. Group the words by their origins (Latin, Greek, French, Middle English, and so on). Then study the words in each category and describe anything you notice about each group. Compare your list with a partner's list.

Unpacking Embedded Assessment 2

Read the assignment for Embedded Assessment 2 closely to identify and analyze the components of the assignment.

 Think about people who deserve status as a hero from the past, from the present, from life, and from literature. What defines a hero? Write a multi-paragraph essay that develops your definition of heroism. Be sure to use strategies of definition (function, example, and negation) to guide your writing.

Using the assignment and the Scoring Guide, work with your class to analyze the prompt and create a graphic organizer to use as a visual reminder of the required concepts (what you need to know) and skills (what you need to do). Copy the graphic organizer in your Reader/Writer Notebook.

After each activity, use this graphic to guide reflection about what you have learned and what you still need to learn in order to be successful on the Embedded Assessment.

INDEPENDENT READING LINK
Reading Plan
Continue your exploration of *heroism* by choosing a fiction or nonfiction text about a historical or modern hero for your independent reading. Research the author of the text to find out why they might have chosen to write about this particular hero.

Learning Strategies

Note-taking
Graphic Organizer
Discussion Groups

VOCABULARY

LITERARY

Tone is a writer's or speaker's attitude toward a subject.
Diction is a writer's or speaker's choice of words.
Denotation is the direct meaning of a word or expression, as distinguished from the ideas or meanings associated with it or suggested by it.
Connotation is the implied associations, meanings, or emotions associated with a word.

ACADEMIC

Nuance refers to a subtle difference or distinction in meaning.

Learning Targets

- Differentiate between denotation and connotation.
- Analyze how connotation creates tone.

Preview

In this activity, you will think about how an author creates tone using diction.

Understanding Tone

In literature, being able to recognize the tone of a story or poem or essay is an important skill in understanding the author's purpose. An author who is trying to create a comedy skit needs to choose content and language that communicates humor rather than sadness. Writers purposefully select diction to create an appropriate tone.

1. What is the connection between tone and diction? Many words have a similar denotation, but one must learn to distinguish among the connotations of these words in order to accurately identify meaning and tone. Careful readers and writers understand nuances in word meanings. This means that they recognize that words have varying levels of meaning.

   Examples: *House*, *home*, *abode*, *estate*, *shack*, *mansion*, and *hut* all describe or denote a place to live, but each has a different connotation that determines meaning and tone.

2. Create examples like the one above illustrating ranges of words that have the same denotation but different connotations. Independently, write your examples below and then pair with another student to share your words.

My Notes

3. Use one of the examples you just created to discuss how connotation connects to tone.

Identifying Nuances in Diction

4. On the following page are some common tone words and their synonyms. Use a print or digital dictionary to determine or clarify each synonym's precise meaning. After taking notes on the denotation of each word, number the words to indicate the various levels of meaning, from least intense to most intense (1 = least intense). If your group feels that two words have the same connotation and level of meaning, give them the same ranking.

Angry: upset, enraged, irritated, sharp, vexed, livid, infuriated, incensed

Happy: mirthful, joyful, jovial, ecstatic, lighthearted, exultant, jubilant, giddy

Sad: poignant, despondent, sentimental, lugubrious, morose, woeful, mournful, desolate

Honest: sincere, candid, outspoken, forthright, frank, unbiased, blunt

Calm: placid, still, bored, composed, peaceful, tranquil, serene, soothing

Nervous: anxious, apprehensive, hesitant, fretful, agitated, jittery, afraid

Smart: wise, perceptive, quick-witted, clever, sagacious, intellectual, brainy, bright, sharp

5. Prepare to present your findings to the class. Use the outline below to prepare for your presentation.

Our group studied words that have the same denotation as ____________.

The most intense word is ____________, which means ____________.

One would feel ____________ if / when ____________ [specific situation].

The least intense word is ____________, which means ____________.

One would feel ____________ if / when ____________ [specific situation].

Our favorite word is ____________, which means ____________.

One would feel ____________ if / when ____________ [specific situation].

6. While other groups present, listen to comprehend, and take notes. You will be responsible for applying this vocabulary in future activities.

Check Your Understanding

Read the sentences and identify the tone using words from the list above. Explain how word choice changes the connotation of each sentence.

Jack skipped out of the house.

Jack stormed out of the house.

Learning Strategies

TP-CASTT
Diffusing
Paraphrasing
Summarizing
Close Reading
Marking the Text
Freewriting

My Notes

Learning Targets

- Analyze and compare text structures across genres.
- Make connections between elements in different genres.

Preview

In this activity, you will read a poem and an informational text on similar subjects and compare them.

Setting a Purpose for Reading

- As you read, underline and label evidence of a Hero's Journey so that you can compare it with and contrast it to other texts.
- Circle unknown words and phrases. Try to determine the meaning of the words by using context clues, word parts, or a dictionary.

About the Author

Nina Cassian (1924–2014) was a prominent writer in Romania until she was exiled for her poems satirizing the Romanian president's regime. She sought refuge in the United States and lived in New York City for many years. Cassian wrote more than 50 volumes of work, including poetry, fiction, and books for children. Cassian was also a journalist, film critic, and composer of classical music.

Poetry

A Man

by **Nina Cassian**

While fighting for his country, he lost an arm
And was suddenly afraid:
"From now on, I shall only be able to do things by halves.
I shall reap half a harvest.

5 I shall be able to play either the tune
or the accompaniment on the piano,
but never both parts together.
I shall be able to bang with only one fist
on doors, and worst of all

10 I shall only be able to half hold
my love close to me.
There will be things I cannot do at all,
applaud for example,
at shows where everyone applauds."

15 From that moment on, he set himself to do
everything with twice as much enthusiasm.
And where the arm had been torn away
a wing grew.

Making Observations

- What emotions do you feel while reading the poem?
- What lines from the poem seem to be the most powerful?

Returning to the Text

- Return to the text as you respond to the following questions. Use text evidence to support your responses.
- Write any additional questions you have about the poem in your Reader/Writer Notebook.

1. What kinds of things is the man afraid of not being able to do? What do these worries tell you about his character?

_____

_____

_____

_____

2. Is the last sentence of this poem meant to be understood literally or figuratively? How does the connotation of "wing" help create the mood of the poem?

_____

_____

_____

_____

Working from the Text

Introducing the Strategy: TP-CASTT

This reading strategy is used to analyze a poetic text by identifying and discussing each topic in the acronym: *Title, Paraphrase, Connotation, Attitude, Shift, Title* again, and *Theme*. The strategy is a guide designed to lead you in an analysis of a literary text. It is most effective if you begin at the top and work your way down the elements. However, you will find that as you study one element, you will naturally begin to explore others. For example, a study of *connotation* often leads to a discussion of *tone* and *shifts*. Revisiting the *title* often leads to a discussion of the *theme*, or author's message.

3. Use the TP-CASTT strategy to analyze the poem. Record your responses in the graphic organizer that follows. Read the poem several times, each time analyzing more deeply aspects of the TP-CASTT strategy and recording your responses.

4. After reading the poem several times, return to the TP-CASTT graphic organizer, and write a brief paragraph to summarize the poem and explain the author's message.

Strategy	Response/Analysis
Title: After reading the text, think about why the author chose the title.	**Analysis:**
Paraphrase: After diffusing the text, translate the most challenging lines of the poem into your own words (you may need to reread the text several times). Then briefly summarize the poem in such a way that the meaning is maintained.	**Poem Summary:**
Connotation: Mark the text by highlighting the diction (words and phrases) used for positive effect (color 1) and/or negative effect (color 2). Then study the diction to determine a pattern (e.g., mostly negative, begins negatively but ends positively) and record your analysis.	**Pattern: (+/−)**
Attitude (Tone): Determine how the speaker feels about the subject of the poem. (There might be more than one tone.) Highlight words that convey tone. Be sure to use precise tone words (e.g., mournful, not sad). Finally, summarize the tone.	**Tone Summary:**
Shift: Identify shifts, such as in the speaker, setting, subject, tone, or images. After marking the text with a star and numbering each, study and explain the shifts.	**Shifts:**
Title: Examine the title to determine the deeper meaning. Look beyond the literal, even if the title is simple (e.g. "Choices"). Record ideas.	**Deeper Meaning:**
Theme: Determine the author's message about life implied in the poem. After you identify a subject (e.g., friendship), write a statement about the subject that sounds like a piece of advice (e.g., For a friendship to survive, one must be selfless, not selfish). Record your theme statement(s).	**Theme Statement(s):**

My Notes

_____

_____

_____

_____

_____

_____

_____

_____

_____

_____

_____

_____

_____

_____

GRAMMAR & USAGE

Nonrestrictive Phrases & Clauses

A nonrestrictive phrase or clause is a group of words that gives extra information about a noun in the sentence. It is set off by commas to show that the information is not necessary to understand what the sentence is about.

In paragraph 2 of the article, the writer uses a nonrestrictive phrase to explain who Tristan Eugene Segers is: " ... Eugene Segers, a 2002 graduate of Lake Stevens High School, was driving ... " The phrase "a 2002 graduate of Lake Stevens High School" is extra information that is not necessary to the understanding of the sentence. Locate several more examples of nonrestrictive phrases in the article and share with a partner.

shrapnel: small fragments of a bomb after it explodes

Setting a Purpose for Reading

- As you read, underline and label evidence of a Hero's Journey so that you can compare it with and contrast it to other texts.
- Circle unknown words and phrases. Try to determine the meaning of the words by using context clues, word parts, or a dictionary.

About the Author

Inspired by the work of _Washington Post_ journalists during the Watergate era, Gale Fiege longed to be a newspaper reporter. She served as editor of the campus newspaper at Western Washington University in the late 1970s. Since then, she has been a reporter on a number of newspapers in Washington state, including the _Everett Daily Herald_. The skill Fiege thinks is most important to her job is the ability to listen well.

Article

Soldier home after losing his leg in Afghanistan

_by_ **Gale Fiege**

1   LAKE STEVENS—It started out as just another day in the Zabul Province of southern Afghanistan.

2   On Sept. 18, 2010, Army Pfc. Tristan Eugene Segers, a 2002 graduate of Lake Stevens High School, was driving his armored patrol vehicle when a homemade bomb exploded in the road underneath Segers' floorboard.

3   One of the vehicle's 800-pound tires was found a half-mile away.

4   Just below his knee, Segers' right leg was gone. He had **shrapnel** sticking out of his eyeballs, face and arms.

5   After nearly two years of surgeries and rehabilitation in Texas, Segers, a handsome 28-year-old, moved back to Snohomish County last week in time to celebrate Independence Day with his folks in the home where he grew up.

6   Segers is married now to his high school girlfriend, Lindsay Blanchard. They are expecting a baby boy in October. He plans to return to culinary arts school this fall and they are about to move into an apartment in the Bothell area.

7   Until his official Army retirement date on Aug. 21, he is Cpl. Segers, the owner of a Purple Heart.[1]

---

[1] The _Purple Heart_ is a medal given to U.S. military personnel who are injured in the line of duty

8   Segers wears shorts in the warm summer weather, not even pretending to hide his prosthetic leg. He has run a marathon. A specially designed gas pedal is on the left side of his slate-gray Toyota Tacoma truck.

9   Nothing is stopping him.

10   "Everybody's injury is different and everybody handles it in their own way. There is no way to measure it, whether it's physical or mental," Segers said. "I just kept telling the doctors that I didn't want my life to be different than it was before. Of course, the loss of a leg changed me. But it doesn't define me or the rest of my life."

11   Segers was enjoying a promising start to a career as a chef when the economic recession forced him to consider joining the Army. He figured he would serve in the family tradition set by his father and grandfather.

12   After **grueling** training in the hot Georgia sun, he landed a spot in the Army's 101st Airborne Pathfinder Division, an **elite** infantry unit, and was sent to Afghanistan in February 2010 to work on personnel recovery missions.

13   After the explosion, Segers was stabilized and flown to the Army hospital in Landstuhl, Germany.

14   "My eyes were completely bandaged and I was in a lot of pain. The stretchers were on bunks in the airplane, so when I woke up it felt like I was in a coffin," Segers said. "I was so glad to hear the voice of my buddy, Andrew Leonard, a guy from Boston who had been injured earlier."

15   Tristan Segers can't say enough good things about the surgeons, psychiatrists, physical therapists and other staff at the Army hospital, as well as the numerous charitable organizations such as the Fisher House Foundation that help wounded veterans.

16   "I was truly cared for," he said. "The rehabilitation was **rigorous** and I pushed it, building back my muscles and learning to use the prosthetic leg.

17   "But they never told me I was doing a good job for fear that I might get **complacent**. There were many guys there who had given up on life."

18   "Most of the time when people see my leg, they think I've been in a car accident or something. But sometimes an old veteran will stop me and thank me for my service," Segers said. "I didn't do anything special, but if the progress I have made motivates another wounded veteran to keep going, then that's great."

> **grueling:** physically demanding
> **elite:** made of the best and most able
> **rigorous:** full of difficulty
> **complacent:** satisfied

Making Observations
- What was most surprising about the article?
- What connections do you see between the article and the poem?

Returning to the Text
- Reread the article to answer these text-dependent questions.
- Write any additional questions you have about the article in your Reader/Writer Notebook.

5. What kind of person is Segers? Include details from the article that support your answer.

_____

_____

_____

_____

6. The author uses the word "folks" in paragraph 5 to mean "family." What effect does this word choice have?

_____

_____

_____

_____

7. Choose a statement made by Segers that expresses the central idea driving Segers's life now. What facts in the story support this idea?

_____

_____

_____

_____

8. Notice how the language shifts as it describes Segers's Army assignment. What is an "elite" infantry unit? What are "personnel recovery missions"?

_____

_____

_____

_____

Working from the Text
9. Return to the poem "A Man." What effect do the short line lengths have on the beginning of the poem? How does that shift in the last stanza?

10. Explain the author's purpose for writing the article about Segers. Then, analyze how the text structure contributes to the purpose.

11. How is the structure of the article different from the poem?

12. What message does each text reveal about the concept of heroism? Write a summary that supports your interpretation using evidence from both the poem and the article.

☑ Check Your Understanding

In your Reader/Writer Notebook, compare how the characters in the poem and the article exemplify the concept of a hero. How are these heroes similar and different? Include evidence from each text in your response.

Introducing the Strategy: Freewriting

The **freewriting** strategy allows writers to write freely without pressure to be correct or complete. A freewrite gives a writer the freedom to write in an informal style and get ideas on paper in preparation for a more complete and formal writing assignment. This strategy helps writers refine and clarify thoughts, spark new ideas, and/or generate content during drafting or revision.

13. Before you complete the writing prompt, use the freewriting strategy to prepare.

📝 Informational Writing Prompt

Write an essay about a challenge you have faced that includes examples of specific things you did to overcome adversity. Be sure to:

- Clearly explain the challenge you faced.
- Cite specific examples and experiences that helped you overcome your challenge.
- Summarize your outcome clearly.
- Use appositives to add additional information to sentences in your essay. Edit your work to make sure that you use commas correctly to set off nonrestrictive phrases and clauses.

Learning Strategies

Brainstorming
Manipulatives
Graphic Organizer
Prewriting

My Notes

Learning Targets

- Analyze characteristics and structural elements of informational texts.
- Synthesize information to create a deeper understanding of heroism.

Preview

In this activity, you will analyze a model definition essay and explain how it uses the definition strategies.

Preparing for Informational Writing

1. How are informational and narrative writing similar? How are they different? Consider both characteristics and structural elements such as theses, features, and organizational patterns in your analysis. List ideas below, and then create a graphic organizer on a separate paper to show your thinking.

Similarities	Differences

2. You are often asked to define vocabulary terms and to explain your understanding of what something means. Abstract concepts, such as heroism, can also be defined. Practice thinking about how to define an abstract concept by working in a small group or with a partner to develop a list of words that describe each of the concepts below.

- freedom
- responsibility
- sacrifice
- friendship

☑ Check Your Understanding

Working with the same partner or group, write a few sentences defining one of the abstract concepts you discussed.

Writing to Define

For Embedded Assessment 2, you will be writing a definition essay to share your personal understanding of the concept of heroism. To write this definition of heroism, you will need various strategies and knowledge to create an expanded definition of the concept. First, you can expand your collection of words that describe heroes and heroism.

3. **Defining heroes:** Generate a list of

   - **Adjectives** that could describe what a hero is:
     A hero is (adjective) brave,

   - **Nouns** that could define what a hero shows:
     A hero shows (noun) courage,

   - **Verbs** that could define what a hero does:
     A hero (verb) fights,

4. After sharing and consulting print and digital resources, such as a thesaurus, group synonyms by part of speech and sort them by their nuances (subtle differences in meanings). Record these terms in your Reader/Writer Notebook for future reference. Your teacher will provide you with oral instructions on how to create a Word Wall card with your terms and their parts of speech.

Defining a Concept

Part of defining any concept is finding ways to describe the concept to make it clear to others. The logical structure of an informational definition essay consists of an introduction, a body, and a conclusion. To clarify, develop, and organize ideas, body paragraphs often use three definition strategies: function, example, and negation.

- **Definition by function:** Paragraphs using the **function** strategy explain how the concept functions or operates in the real world.

- **Definition by example:** Paragraphs using the **example** strategy use specific examples of the concept from texts or life.

- **Definition by negation:** Paragraphs using the **negation** strategy explain what something is by describing what it is not. For example, an author may state, "Although tomatoes are often included in vegetable salads, a tomato is a fruit, not a vegetable." In this example, the negation is saying what a tomato is not, as well as what a tomato is.

5. Read the following passages of definition and decide whether they contain definition by function, example, and/or negation. Be able to explain why you categorized ideas as you did. First, highlight the topic being defined. Then, decide the type of definition being used.

   - "But just for the purposes of this discussion, let us say: one's family are those toward whom one feels loyalty and obligation, and/or from whom one derives identity, and/or to whom one gives identity, and/or with whom one shares habits, tastes, stories, customs, memories." (Marilynn Robinson, "Family." *The Death of Adam: Essays on Modern Thought*. Houghton Mifflin, 1998)

ACADEMIC VOCABULARY

Describing the function of something is telling how something is used. The verb to *function* means "to act as or to operate as."

Just as a negative answer would be a no, to negate is to deny or make ineffective. The noun negation means "showing what something is not in order to prove what it is."

My Notes

- "It's always seemed odd to me that *nonfiction* is defined, not by what it *is*, but by what it is *not*. It is *not* fiction. But then again, it is also *not* poetry, or technical writing or libretto. It's like defining classical music as *nonjazz*." (Philip Gerard, *Creative Nonfiction*. Story Press, 1996)

- "Love is patient and kind; love does not envy or boast; it is not arrogant or rude. It does not insist on its own way; it is not irritable or resentful; it does not rejoice at wrongdoing, but rejoices with the truth. Love bears all things, believes all things, hopes all things, endures all things. Love never ends." (*The Bible*, I Corinthians 13:4–8a)

Setting a Purpose for Reading

- As you read, highlight the author's definition of heroism and underline evidence that he gives to support his definition.
- Circle unknown words and phrases. Try to determine the meaning of the words by using context clues, word parts, or a dictionary.

About the Author

After serving in the Vietnam War, Oliver Stone became a movie director. He is best known for his controversial retellings of historical events. Stone's films have explored historical subjects, such as the Vietnam War and President Kennedy's assassination. Stone has won two Academy Awards for Best Director for the films *Platoon* and *Born on the Fourth of July*. He also won an Academy Award for Best Screenplay Writing for *Midnight Express*.

Article

Where I Find My Heroes

by **Oliver Stone**
from McCall's Magazine, November 1992

1   It's not true that there are no heroes anymore—but it is true that my own concept of heroism has changed radically over time. When I was young and I read the Random House biographies, my heroes were always people like George Washington and General Custer and Abraham Lincoln and Teddy Roosevelt. Men, generally, and doers. Women—with the exception of Clara Barton, Florence Nightingale, and Joan of Arc—got **short shrift**. Most history was oriented toward male heroes.

short shrift: little attention

2 But as I've gotten older, and since I've been to war, I've been forced to reexamine the nature of life and of heroism. What is true? Where are the myths?

3 The simple acts of heroism are often overlooked—that's very clear to me not only in war but in peace. I'm not **debunking** all of history: Crossing the Delaware was a magnificent action. But I am saying that I think the meaning of heroism has a lot to do with evolving into a higher human being. I came into contact with it when I worked with Ron Kovic, the **paraplegic** Vietnam vet, on *Born on the Fourth of July*. I was impressed by his life change, from a patriotic and strong-willed athlete to someone who had to deal with the total surrender of his body, who grew into a nonviolent and peaceful advocate of change in the Martin Luther King, Jr., and Gandhi tradition. So heroism is tied to an evolution of consciousness....

4 Since the war, I've had children, and I'm wrestling now with the everyday problems of trying to share my knowledge with them without overwhelming them. It's difficult to be a father, to be a mother, and I think that to be a kind and loving parent is an act of heroism. So there you go—heroes are everyday, common people. Most of what they do goes **unheralded**, unappreciated. And that, ironically, is heroism: not to be recognized.

5 Who is heroic? Scientists who spend years of their lives trying to find cures for diseases. The teenager who says no to crack. The inner-city kid who works at McDonald's instead of selling drugs. The kid who stands alone instead of joining a gang, which would give him an instant identity. The celebrity who remains modest and treats others with respect, or who uses his position to help society. The student who defers the immediate pleasure of making money and finishes college or high school. People who take risks despite fears. People in wheelchairs who don't give up. ...

6 We have a lot of **corruption** in our society. But we mustn't assume that everything is always basely motivated. We should allow for the heroic impulse—which is to be greater than oneself, to try to find another version of oneself, to grow. That's where virtue comes from. And we must allow our young generation to **strive** for virtue, instead of **ridiculing** it.

WORD CONNECTIONS

Etymology
The English word **advocate** was first used in the mid-1300s to refer to someone who argues a case in court. It was derived from the French word *avocar*, meaning "spokesman," which was itself derived from the Latin *advocatus*, meaning "one called to aid." The word *advocate* was first used as a verb in the 1640s.

debunking: proving false
paraplegic: someone who cannot move their legs
unheralded: overlooked
corruption: fraud
strive: to work hard for
ridiculing: making fun of

Working from the Text

6. Reread the essay, paying close attention to the author's definition of heroism, the strategies he uses to support this definition, and his final clarification of his definition. Work with a partner to analyze what each paragraph of the essay says and does by completing the graphic organizer. Then write a paragraph in your Reader/Writer Notebook analyzing how the structure of the essay contributes to the author's purpose of defining heroism.

Paragraph	What It Says	What It Does
1		
2		
3		
4		
5		
6		

7. The heroes mentioned by Oliver Stone are listed below. You will participate in an informal inquiry task to find information about one of these traditional heroes. First, follow along as your teacher models how to generate a list of questions about George Washington for informal inquiry. Then, choose one of the other heroes listed and create your own set of questions. Use the Internet, a classmate, and your teacher's guidance to help you locate information. Working in small groups, discuss what makes this person a hero.

- George Washington
- General Custer
- Abraham Lincoln
- Teddy Roosevelt
- Martin Luther King, Jr.

- Clara Barton
- Florence Nightingale
- Joan of Arc
- Ron Kovic
- Mohandas Gandhi

 INDEPENDENT READING LINK

Read and Discuss

Think about the historical or modern hero you are reading about independently. How is he/she an example of a heroic type? Would this person fit Oliver Stone's definition of a hero? Explain your answer. Present your ideas orally.

Beginning a Definition of Hero

8. After reading and thinking about definition strategies and heroes, use the graphic organizer that follows to begin organizing your definition of a hero according to the three different strategies for definition: function, example, and negation.

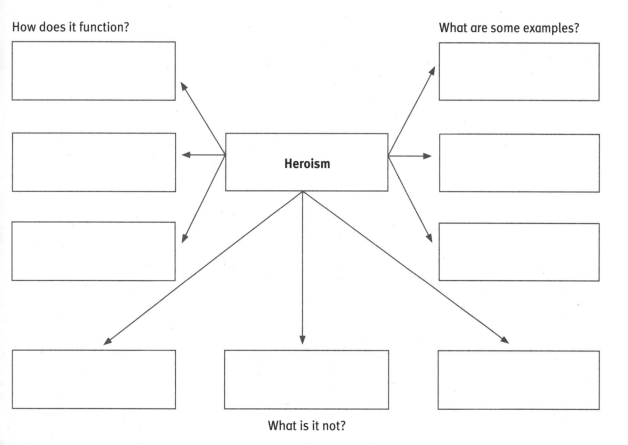

How does it function?

What are some examples?

Heroism

What is it not?

☑ Check Your Understanding

Quickwrite: Describe a person you know or have read about who is a "hero."

LANGUAGE & WRITER'S CRAFT: Embedded Quotations

Use quotation marks to show that you are using someone else's exact words. When you use the author's exact words in a sentence, it is called an embedded quotation. To introduce the quote, use a signal word or phrase from the box below, followed by a comma. Then use quotation marks to frame the quotation. Remember to capitalize the first word of the quotation.

Use this formula to ensure that you are punctuating quotations properly:

author's name + signal word + comma + quotation marks + author's words + quotation marks

Common Signal Words & Phrases	
according to	notes
argues	proposes
claims	says
concludes	states
explains	writes

In his article, Olive Stone says, "It is not true that there are no heroes anymore—but it is true that my own concept of heroism has changed radically over time."

Notice how there are quotation marks on both ends of the quotation so the reader knows where it starts and stops.

PRACTICE Add punctuation as needed to correct the embedded quotations.

1. According to Oliver Stone the simple acts of heroism are often overlooked.

2. In his article, Stone says to be a kind and loving parent is an act of heroism.

3. Svetlana Fedorov argues the American diet relies too heavily on processed foods.

📝 Informational Writing Prompt

Think about how to define a hero by how he or she functions or acts. Draft a paragraph that establishes the function of a hero. Cite examples from texts you have read throughout this unit. Remember that the function strategy explains how an idea or concept operates in the world. Be sure to:

- Begin with a topic sentence that states how a hero functions in the world.
- Provide supporting examples (paraphrased and directly quoted) from life and from the texts you have read and provide commentary to develop ideas.
- Punctuate embedded quotations correctly.
- Use transitions to create coherence.

Historical Heroes: Examples

Learning Targets

- Compare texts across genres to analyze how structure contributes to meaning.
- Use examples to develop an engaging written response.
- Integrate ideas from multiple texts to build knowledge and vocabulary about a theme.

Preview

In this activity, you will read a set of paired passages and work in expert groups to compare the features that appear in both genres.

Learning Strategies

TP-CASTT
Diffusing
Close Reading
Marking the Text
Paraphrasing
Summarizing
Rereading

Setting a Purpose for Reading

- As you read, underline sentences or phrases that develop the key concept.
- Circle unknown words and phrases. Try to determine the meaning of the words by using context clues, word parts, or a dictionary.

About the Author

Dr. Phineas D. Gurley (1816–1868) was the pastor of the New York Avenue Presbyterian Church (in Washington, DC), which Abraham Lincoln attended during his presidency. Gurley was also Chaplain of the United States Senate. Gurley preached this funeral sermon in the White House East Room on April 19, 1865, four days after Lincoln's assassination.

KNOWLEDGE QUEST

Knowledge Question:

What kinds of ideals motivate heroes to act?

In Activity 1.14, you will read two texts about a hero: Abraham Lincoln or Frederick Douglass. While you read, build knowledge about the theme relating to the ideals that motivate heroes, and think about your answer to the Knowledge Question.

Sermon

from White House Funeral Sermon for Abraham Lincoln

by **Dr. Phineas D. Gurley**

He is dead; but the God in whom he trusted lives, and He can guide and strengthen his successor, as He guided and strengthened him. He is dead; but the memory of his virtues, of his wise and patriotic counsels and labors, of his calm and steady faith in God lives, is precious, and will be a power for good
5 in the country quite down to the end of time. He is dead; but the cause he so **ardently** loved, so ably, patiently, faithfully represented and defended—not for himself only, not for us only, but for all people in all their coming generations, till time shall be no more—that cause survives his fall, and will survive it. The light of its brightening prospects flashes cheeringly to-day **athwart** the gloom
10 occasioned by his death, and the language of God's united **providences** is telling us that, though the friends of Liberty die, Liberty itself is **immortal**. There is no assassin strong enough and no weapon deadly enough to **quench**

ardently: passionately
athwart: across or against
providences: guardianship exercised by a deity
immortal: living forever
quench: to put an end to

its inextinguishable life, or arrest its onward march to the conquest and empire of the world. This is our confidence, and this is our consolation, as we
15 weep and mourn to-day. Though our beloved President is slain, our beloved country is saved. And so we sing of mercy as well as of judgment. Tears of gratitude mingle with those of sorrow. While there is darkness, there is also the dawning of a brighter, happier day upon our stricken and weary land. God be praised that our fallen Chief lived long enough to see the day dawn
20 and the daystar of joy and peace arise upon the nation. He saw it, and he was glad. Alas! alas! He only saw the *dawn*. When the *sun* has risen, full-orbed and glorious, and a happy reunited people are rejoicing in its light—alas! alas! it will shine upon his grave. But that grave will be a precious and a **consecrated** spot. The friends of Liberty and of the Union will **repair** to it in years and ages
25 to come, to pronounce the memory of its occupant blessed, and, gathering from his very ashes, and from the rehearsal of his deeds and virtues, fresh **incentives** to patriotism, they will there renew their vows of **fidelity** to their country and their God.

consecrated: dedicated to a sacred purpose
repair: to come together
incentives: rewards
fidelity: loyalty

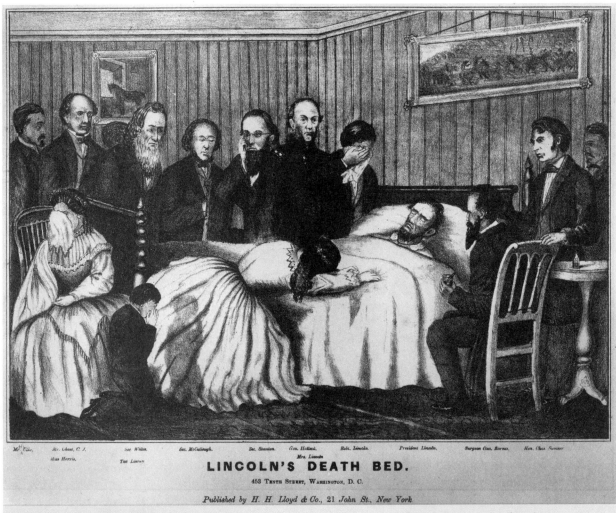

LINCOLN'S DEATH BED.
453 Tenth Street, Washington, D. C.
Published by H. H. Lloyd & Co., 21 John St., New York

Abraham Lincoln on his deathbed, surrounded by family members and members of his cabinet. April 15, 1865/ The Nation's Martyr.

VOCABULARY

Knowledge Quest

- What ideals seemed to motivate Lincoln?
- What additional knowledge about heroes, and Lincoln as a hero specifically, did you gain from reading this sermon?

LITERARY

An **allegory** is a literary technique of extending a metaphor through an entire poem or story so that objects, persons, and actions in the text are equated with meanings that lie outside the text.

About the Author

Walt Whitman (1819–1892) is now considered one of America's greatest poets, but his untraditional poetry was not well received during his lifetime. As a young man, he worked as a printer and a journalist while writing free-verse poetry. His collection of poems, *Leaves of Grass*, first came out in 1855, and he revised and added to it several times over the years. During the Civil War, he worked in Washington, caring for injured soldiers in hospitals. This poem is an example of an **allegory**.

My Notes

Poetry

O Captain! My Captain!

by **Walt Whitman**

O Captain! my Captain! our fearful trip is done;

The ship has weather'd every **rack**, the prize we sought is won;

The port is near, the bells I hear, the people all exulting,

While follow eyes the steady keel, the vessel grim and daring:

5   But O heart! heart! heart!

      O the bleeding drops of red,

        Where on the deck my Captain lies,

          Fallen cold and dead.

 KNOWLEDGE QUEST

Knowledge Question:
What kinds of ideals motivate heroes to act?

rack: windy storm

O Captain! my Captain! rise up and hear the bells;

10 Rise up—for you the flag is flung—for you the bugle trills;

For you bouquets and ribbon'd wreaths—for you the shores a-crowding,

For you they call, the swaying mass, their eager faces turning;

   Here Captain! dear father!

     This arm beneath your head;

15   It is some dream that on the deck,

      You've fallen cold and dead.

My Captain does not answer, his lips are pale and still;

My father does not feel my arm, he has no pulse nor will;

The ship is anchored safe and sound, its voyage closed and done;

20 From fearful trip the victor ship comes in with object won:

   Exult O shores, and ring O bells!

    But I with **mournful** tread,

     Walk the deck my Captain lies,

      Fallen cold and dead.

⊘ Knowledge Quest

- According to Whitman what motivated Lincoln as a hero?
- How does Whitman's knowledge of Lincoln compare with Gurley's knowledge of Lincoln?

mournful: sad

Returning to the Text

- Return to the texts as you respond to the following questions. Use text evidence to support your responses.
- Write any additional questions you have about the sermon and the poem in your Reader/Writer Notebook.

White House Funeral Sermon for Abraham Lincoln

1. What effect does the quote, "... though the friends of Liberty die, Liberty is immortal" have on the reader?

_____

_____

_____

_____

2. How do Dr. Gurley's contrasting statements about grief and hope create a structure that aptly describes that moment in history?

_____

_____

_____

_____

O Captain! My Captain!

3. What is the effect of the short lines that conclude each stanza in Whitman's poem? How do they contrast with the longer lines?

_____

_____

_____

_____

4. As an allegory representing the death of Abraham Lincoln, who does the Captain represent? What does the ship represent? What does the trip or voyage represent?

_____

_____

_____

_____

5. How does Whitman establish the same mood of sorrow and hope in his poem as Dr. Gurley does in his sermon? Explain by choosing a line that represents the mood.

_____

_____

_____

_____

My Notes

6. **KQ** Dr. Gurley capitalizes the word "liberty" in his sermon. Why might he have done that?

_____

_____

_____

_____

7. **KQ** Based on Dr. Gurley's sermon and Whitman's poem, what can you infer Lincoln was fighting for *most*?

_____

_____

_____

_____

Setting a Purpose for Reading

- As you read, underline the sentences that develop the main idea.
- Circle unknown words and phrases. Try to determine the meaning of the words by using context clues, word parts, or a dictionary.

About the Author

Robert Hayden (1913–1980) was born in Detroit, Michigan. He had a lifelong love of literature and became a teacher and writer. Through his work for the Federal Writers' Project in the 1930s, he studied African American history and folk life, both of which became inspirations for his works of poetry. Slavery and emancipation were recurring themes in his work.

Poetry

Frederick Douglass

by **Robert Hayden**

> When it is finally ours, this freedom, this liberty, this beautiful
> and terrible thing, needful to man as air,
> usable as earth; when it belongs at last to all,
> when it is truly instinct, brain matter, **diastole**, **systole**,
> 5 reflex action; when it is finally won; when it is more
> than the **gaudy** mumbo jumbo of politicians:
> this man, this Douglass, this former slave, this Negro
> beaten to his knees, **exiled**, visioning a world
> where none is lonely, none hunted, alien,

KNOWLEDGE QUEST

Knowledge Question:

What kinds of ideals motivate heroes to act?

diastole: the act of the heart filling with blood
systole: the act of the heart pumping blood
gaudy: showy in a tasteless way
exiled: forced to leave one's native land

10 this man, superb in love and logic, this man

      shall be remembered. Oh, not with statues' **rhetoric**,

      not with legends and poems and wreaths of bronze alone,

      but with the lives grown out of his life, the lives

      fleshing his dream of the beautiful, needful thing.

⬠ Knowledge Quest

- What knowledge about Frederick Douglass did you gain from reading the poem?
- According to Hayden, what motivated Douglass?

About the Author

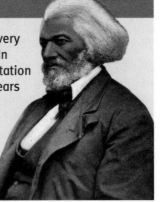

Frederick Douglass (1818?–1895) was born into slavery in Maryland. He learned to read as a house servant in Baltimore. In 1838, Douglass escaped from his plantation and settled in Massachusetts. After spending two years abroad, he published an antislavery newspaper and was an adviser to President Lincoln during the Civil War. He was later appointed to positions in the U.S. government never before achieved by an African American, including U.S. Marshal and Minister to Haiti.

Autobiography

from The Narrative of the Life of Fredrick Douglass, an American Slave

by **Frederick Douglass**

1 I felt assured that if I failed in this attempt, my case would be a hopeless one—it would seal my fate as a slave forever. I could not hope to get off with anything less than the severest punishment and being placed beyond the means of escape. It required no very vivid imagination to depict the most frightful scenes through which I should have to pass in case I failed. The wretchedness of slavery, and the blessedness of freedom, were perpetually before me. It was life and death with me. But I remained firm, and, according to my resolution, on the third day of September, 1838, I left my chains, and succeeded in reaching New York without the slightest interruption of any kind. How I did so—what means I adopted—what direction I travelled, and by what mode of conveyance—I must leave unexplained, for the reasons before mentioned.

My Notes

 KNOWLEDGE QUEST

Knowledge Question:

What kinds of ideals motivate heroes to act?

rhetoric: language or speech

My Notes

_____

_____

_____

_____

_____

_____

_____

_____

_____

_____

_____

_____

WORD CONNECTIONS

Roots & Affixes

In the word **sympathy**, the Greek root *path* means "feeling." Someone who *sympathizes* with a person facing a painful struggle is able to feel that person's sorrow. The root has the same meaning in words such as *apathy* ("lack of feeling") and *empathy* ("identifying with the feelings of others").

mariner: one who works on a ship

damp: lessen

ardor: strong devotion

fugitive: one who flees

brethren: people sharing in a similar situation

bonds: ties used to keep one in place

scathing: harshly critical

denunciations: formal accusations of wrongful activities

2   I have been frequently asked how I felt when I found myself in a free State. I have never been able to answer the question with any satisfaction to myself. It was a moment of the highest excitement I ever experienced. I suppose I felt as one may imagine the unarmed **mariner** to feel when he is rescued by a friendly man-of-war from the pursuit of a pirate. In writing to a dear friend, immediately after my arrival at New York, I said I felt like one who had escaped a den of hungry lions. This state of mind, however very soon subsided; and I was again seized with a feeling of great insecurity and loneliness. I was yet liable to be taken and subjected to all the tortures of slavery. This in itself was enough to **damp** the **ardor** of my enthusiasm. But the loneliness overcame me. There I was in the midst of thousands, and yet a perfect stranger; without home and without friends, in the midst of thousands of my own brethren—children of a common Father, and yet I dared not to unfold to any one of them my sad condition. I was afraid to speak to any one for fear of speaking to the wrong one, and thereby falling into the hands of money-loving kidnappers, whose business it was to lie in wait for the panting fugitive, as the ferocious beasts of the forest lie in wait for their prey. [I]n the midst of plenty, yet suffering the terrible gnawing of hunger—in the midst of houses, yet having no home—among fellow–men, yet feeling as if in the midst of wild beasts, whose greediness to swallow up the trembling and half-famished **fugitive** is only equalled by that with which the monsters of the deep swallow up the trembling and half-famished fish upon which they subsist—I say let him be placed in this most trying situation—the situation in which I was placed—then, and not till then, will he fully appreciate the hardships of, and know how to sympathize with, the toil-worn and whip-scarred fugitive slave.

...

3   In about four months after I went to New Bedford, there came a young man to me, and inquired if I did not wish to take the "Liberator." I told him I did; but just having made my escape from slavery, I remarked that I was unable to pay for it then. I, however, finally became a subscriber to it. The paper came, and I read it from week to week with such feelings as it would be quite idle for me to attempt to describe. The paper became my meat and my drink. My soul was set all on fire. Its sympathy for my **brethren** in **bonds**—its **scathing denunciations** of slaveholders—its faithful exposures of slavery—and its powerful attacks upon the upholders of the institution—sent a thrill of joy through my soul, such as I had never felt before!

4   I had not long been a reader of the "Liberator," before I got a pretty correct idea of the principles, measures and spirit of the anti-slavery reform. I did with a joyful heart, and never felt happier than when in an anti-slavery meeting. I seldom had much to say at the meetings, because what I wanted to say was said so much better by others. But, while attending an anti-slavery convention at Nantucket, on the 11th of August, 1841, I felt strongly moved to speak, and was at the same time much urged to do so by Mr. William C. Collin, a gentleman who had heard me speak in the colored people's meeting at New Bedford. It was a severe cross, and I took it up reluctantly. The truth was, I felt myself a slave, and the idea of speaking to white people weighed me

down. I spoke but a few moments, when I felt a degree of freedom, and said what I desired with considerable ease. From that time until now, I have been engaged in pleading the cause of my brethren—with what success, and with what devotion, I leave those acquainted with my labors to decide.

⌀ Knowledge Quest

- What motivated Frederick Douglass to become a hero?
- What heroic ideals does Douglass represent?

Returning to the Text

- Return to the texts as you respond to the following questions. Use text evidence to support your responses.
- Write any additional questions you have about the poem and autobiography excerpt in your Reader/Writer Notebook.

Frederick Douglass

8. In the first six lines, circle all the uses of the words "it" and "thing." What is "it"? How is it described?

_____

_____

_____

_____

9. Review the tribute to Douglass. What cause did he champion? What impact did he have on others?

_____

_____

_____

_____

The Narrative of the Life of Frederick Douglass, an American Slave

10. What images in paragraph 2 does Douglass use to describe his first feelings of freedom and his fear of capture?

_____

_____

_____

_____

11. What did the "Liberator" write about? Why did it send "a thrill of joy" through Douglass's soul?

_____

_____

_____

_____

12. What kind of mental, emotional, and physical courage did Douglass convey in this excerpt from his autobiography?

_____

_____

_____

_____

13. **KQ** In paragraph 2, how does Douglass's use of the word "fugitive" help you understand what motivated him to act? What part of a Hero's Journey is being a fugitive like?

_____

_____

_____

_____

14. **KQ** How does Lincoln's motivation to fight for freedom compare with Douglass's? What does this say about each man?

_____

_____

_____

_____

 INDEPENDENT READING LINK

Read and Recommend

You can continue to build your knowledge about heroes by reading other articles at ZINC Reading Labs. Search for keywords such as *heroes* or *activists*.

⊘ **Knowledge Quest**

Use your knowledge of Lincoln or Douglass to discuss with a small group your understanding of what motivates heroes to act. Be sure to:

- Provide evidence from the text that supports your thinking.
- Ask and answer questions that connect the ideas of group members.

Working from the Text

15. Study paragraph 3 from the excerpt of Frederick Douglass's autobiography. Underline the key elements of a paragraph: topic sentence; supporting details; and commentary. Analyze whether you think the paragraph succeeds as a well-developed paragraph or not. Tell why.

16. Use the following table to record details about your assigned hero's character expressed in each of the texts you just read. Then in your Reader/Writer Notebook, write about the structure of paragraph 2 in the excerpt from Frederick Douglass's autobiography.

Text 1: _____	Text 2: _____
Quality: Evidence:	Quality: Evidence:
Quality: Evidence:	Quality: Evidence:
Quality: Evidence:	Quality: Evidence:

☑ Check Your Understanding

Write a topic sentence that compares the two texts you read. How are they similar? How are they different?

 Gaining Perspectives

Think about how heroes such as Lincoln and Douglass fought for rights that are in the United States Constitution. What would they think about how voting rights have changed? With a group, role-play a conversation between Lincoln and Douglass. Assign roles for Lincoln, Douglass, and a person living today in the 21st century. What do you think they could teach you about using the power to vote to be a hero? When you are finished, summarize in your Reader/Writer Notebook the conversation that your group developed.

☑ Focus on the Sentence

Different types of sentences can be used for different purposes. Review these four sentence types.

A statement tells someone information. A question asks others for a response and ends with a question mark. An exclamation expresses emotion and typically ends with an exclamation point. A command tells another person to do something. A command may not have a subject, because it is understood that the subject is the person or thing being addressed. Read these sample sentences about heroism.

Statement: Everyday people can become heroes.

Question: Who is your hero?

Exclamation: The woman who saved me is a hero!

Command: Strive to be heroic.

Study the image below and its caption. Write four different sentences about Abraham Lincoln and Frederick Douglass.

Color Lithograph by William Edouard Scott depicts Frederick Douglass appealing to President Lincoln and his cabinet to enlist black soldiers in the Civil War, 1943

Statement: _____

Question: _____

Exclamation: _____

Command: _____

17. Review the elements of a well-developed explanatory body paragraph before responding to the Writing Prompt.

- **Topic Sentence:** Paragraphs begin with a sentence that includes a subject and an interpretation. The two main functions of a topic sentence are to make a point that supports the thesis of the essay and to indicate the central idea of the paragraph.

- **Support:** Specific and relevant facts, details, examples, and quotations are used to support the topic sentence and thesis and to develop ideas.

- **Commentary:** Commentary explains the significance of the supporting detail in relation to the thesis and further develops ideas. It also brings a sense of closure to the paragraph.

☑ Check Your Understanding

In your Reader/Writer Notebook, make a brainstorming web for Abraham Lincoln and a second one for Frederick Douglass. On each web, write 5–10 facts about the hero.

> **✍ Writing to Sources: Informational Text**
>
> Think about the four texts in this activity. Explain how Abraham Lincoln and Frederick Douglass were heroic. Draft a definition paragraph using the elements of a well-developed explanatory body paragraph. Be sure to:
>
> - Begin with a topic sentence that answers the prompt.
> - Provide supporting details and commentary to develop ideas.
> - Use domain-specific vocabulary and precise language for the purpose and audience.

Transitions and Quotations

Learning Strategies

Marking the Draft

Adding

Substituting

VOCABULARY

ACADEMIC

Coherence is the clear and orderly presentation of ideas in a paragraph or essay. Using transitional words or phrases both within and across paragraphs can help to create coherence in a multi-paragraph essay.

Learning Targets

- Examine and appropriately apply transitions and embedded quotations to create coherence in writing.

Preview

In this activity, you will learn how to use transitions and embed quotations in your writing.

Reviewing and Extending Transitions

You have learned that transitions connect ideas. Writers use transitional words and phrases to create coherence and to help readers move smoothly through the essay. In formal writing, transitions establish relationships between one thought and the next, both within and across body paragraphs.

Transitions are used for different purposes:

To offer evidence:	To introduce an interpretation:	To compare and contrast:
Most important,	Therefore,	Although _____,
For example,	For these reasons,	Even though _____,
For instance,	Consequently,	Instead,
According to _____,	Furthermore,	On the other hand,
To illustrate,	In addition,	On the contrary,
In this case,	Moreover,	Rather,
	Thus,	Yet,/But,/However,
		Still,
		Nevertheless,
		In contrast,
		Similarly,
		Likewise,
		In the same way,

To add information:	To clarify:	To conclude:
Additionally,	In other words,	As a result,
In addition,	For instance,	Therefore,
For example,	That is,	Thus,
For instance,	Put another way,	Finally,
Likewise,		
Finally,		
Equally important,		
Again,		

1. The following sample paragraph is based on a folklore story from China about a girl, Mulan, who chooses to go to war in place of her ill father. Mark the draft to indicate where transitions could be added to create coherence.

Mulan is courageous because she has the ability to disregard fear for a greater good. Mulan takes her father's place in the Chinese army because she knows that he is hurt. It is a crime punishable by death to impersonate a man and a soldier. Mulan has the strength and the nerve to stand up for her father and protect him. She gathers all of her courage and leaves before anyone can stop her, which is what courage is all about. Her pluck allows her to face the impossible and not think about the outcome, the fear or the danger, until she is far enough to be ready for it. The heroes that we look up to are everyday heroes, ordinary, average people who have conquered huge challenges by finding the strength and the courage within themselves to continue on. "A hero is an ordinary individual who finds the strength to persevere and endure in spite of overwhelming obstacles" (Christopher Reeve). Mulan is an ordinary young person who finds courage and strength to continue training and fighting in battles, even though she may be frightened. It is impossible to endure and overcome fearful obstacles when you have fear of them. Courage is what gives heroes the drive to move forward. The heroes that have the courage and the will to move on are the heroes that we all know and admire, the ones that we strive to be like.

Providing Support

Supporting details can be paraphrased or directly quoted, depending on the writer's purpose and intended effect. Examine the difference between a paraphrase and an embedded quotation.

Paraphrase: Early in the story, Mulan reveals that she knows she will hurt her family if she is true to herself (*Mulan*).

Embedded Quotation: Early in the story, Mulan reveals her fears when she sings, "Now I see, that if I were truly to be myself, I would break my family's heart" (*Mulan* 5).

Note that an embedded quotation shows a more detailed and precise knowledge of the text.

A direct quotation *should not*:	A direct quotation *should*:
contain a simple idea that a writer could easily paraphrase	contain a complex idea that is thought-provoking
repeat an idea that has already been said	add another layer of depth to the writing
stand alone	be smoothly embedded into the writing; begin with a transition and lead-in
be lengthy	be no more than three lines

Use the acronym TLQC to help you remember how to embed a quotation smoothly. The letters stand for Transition, Lead-in, Quote, Citation.

Element	Definition/Purpose	Example
Transition	Use as a bridge to link ideas and strengthen cohesion and fluency.	**Early in the story,** Mulan reveals her fears when she sings, "Now I see, that if I were truly to be myself, I would break my family's heart."
Lead-in	Use to set the context for the information in the quote (complex sentences work well).	Early in the story, **Mulan reveals her fears when she sings,** "Now I see, that if I were truly to be myself, I would break my family's heart."
Quote	Use ideas from a credible source to strengthen your ideas, illustrate a point, and/or support your controlling idea.	Early in the story, Mulan reveals her fears when she sings, **"Now I see, that if I were truly to be myself, I would break my family's heart."**
Citation	Include author's last name or the title of the work, if the author is unknown, and page number to give credit to the author and to make your writing credible to the reader.	Early in the story, Mulan reveals her fears when she sings, "Now I see, that if I were truly to be myself, I would break my family's heart" (***Mulan* 5**).

Note: If you are citing a different type of source, such as a website, provide the first piece of information listed in a source citation.

2. Return to the sample paragraph and revise the writer's ideas about *Mulan* by smoothly embedding Christopher Reeve's quote (already there, but not carefully embedded) and by adding the following quotation from the film:

Mulan: "It's going to take a miracle to get me into the army."

☑ Check Your Understanding

Return to the paragraph you wrote about Lincoln and Douglass as historical heroes. Mark your draft to indicate missing or ineffective transitions. Then, revise the organization by adding or substituting transitional words and phrases to create coherence both within and across paragraphs. Next, find a significant quote in two of the texts you have read and add those ideas into your paragraph by smoothly embedding the quotes and adding academic citations.

Reflection: What types of transitions did you add during your revision? Why? How do the direct quotations strengthen your ideas?

Learning Strategies

Quickwrite
Marking the Text
Drafting
Substituting

My Notes

Learning Targets

* Understand the negation strategy of definition.
* Develop an engaging idea using the negation strategy.

Preview

In this activity, you will read a definition essay about the concept of a "gentleman" and evaluate how the author used the negation strategy.

Review of the Negation Strategy

1. Review the negation definition strategy:

Paragraphs using the negation strategy explain what something is by showing what it *is not*. Pointing out what the subject *is not* can make what it *is* clearer to the reader. For example, here is an excerpt from a definition of a horse that uses the negation strategy:

> A horse, a zebra, and a mule, though alike in many ways, have significant differences. A horse, unlike a zebra, can be tamed and trained. And unlike a mule, which is a sterile beast of burden, a horse is a valued breeder of future generations of racing champions and hardworking ranch animals.

Setting a Purpose for Reading

* As you read, underline examples of the negation strategy.
* Circle unknown words and phrases. Try to determine the meaning of the words by using context clues, word parts, or a dictionary.

About the Author

John Henry Newman (1801–1890) was a scholar and clergyman who became an influential figure at Oxford College. Newman was a pioneer of the Oxford Movement, which sought to inject more Catholic teachings and traditions into the Protestant-leaning Church of England. Some of his works, including the seminal *Parochial and Plain Sermons*, helped influence the ideals of the Oxford Movement. In 1845, he converted to Roman Catholicism. Then in 2010, Pope Benedict XVI beatified Newman, meaning Newman was officially bestowed as someone in the church to be glorified and exalted.

Essay

A Definition of a Gentleman

by **John Henry Newman**

1   The true gentleman in like manner carefully avoids whatever may cause a jar or a jolt in the minds of those with whom he is cast;—all clashing of opinion, or collision of feeling, all restraint, or suspicion, or gloom, or resentment; his great concern being to make everyone at their ease and at home. (2) He has his eyes on all his company; he is tender towards the bashful, gentle towards the distant, and merciful towards the **absurd**; he can recollect to whom he is speaking; he guards against unseasonable allusions, or topics which may irritate; he is seldom prominent in conversation, and never **wearisome**. (3) He makes light of favours while he does them, and seems to be receiving when he is conferring. (4) He never speaks of himself except when compelled, never defends himself by a mere retort, he has no ears for **slander** or gossip, is scrupulous in imputing motives to those who interfere with him, and interprets everything for the best. (5) He is never mean or little in his disputes, never takes unfair advantage, never mistakes personalities or sharp sayings for arguments, or **insinuates** evil which he dare not say out. (6) From a long-sighted prudence, he observes the **maxim** of the ancient **sage**, that we should ever conduct ourselves towards our enemy as if he were one day to be our friend.

from *The Idea of a University*, by John Henry Newman, originally delivered as a series of lectures in 1852

absurd: ridiculous
wearisome: tiring
slander: spoken lies about someone
insinuates: implies
maxim: truthful adage
sage: wise person

INDEPENDENT READING LINK

Read and Connect

Your independent reading choice can be used as a source in your definition essay. Write about how the protagonist of your reading faced and overcame obstacles and challenges. Then discuss with a classmate why you think this text will be valuable in writing your definition essay. Be sure to provide clear reasons for your recommendation.

My Notes

Working from the Text

2. In your Reader/Writer Notebook, make a T-chart. Label one side "A Gentleman" and label the other side "NOT a Gentleman." Fill in the T-chart accordingly.

 Writing to Sources: Informational Text

Write about what heroism is not. Use the negation strategy to distinguish what heroism is from what it is not. Be sure to:

- Begin with a topic sentence that answers the prompt.
- Provide supporting details and commentary to develop ideas.
- Cite examples from the texts you have read.
- Use transitions to create coherence.

 Check Your Understanding

Exchange your draft with a partner. List your partner's ideas of what heroism is not. Check to see if his or her ideas make sense. Make notes where the draft can be improved. To prompt more ideas, list what heroism is, then list the opposite to tell what heroism is not.

Explanatory Writing Focus: Organization

Learning Targets

- Identify and evaluate the effectiveness of the structural elements of a definition essay.
- Draft a thesis and outline ideas for a definition essay.

Preview

In this activity, you will learn techniques to plan, draft, and revise your definition essay.

My Notes

Planning a Definition Essay

1. Review the Scoring Criteria for Embedded Assessment 2. What defines a proficient definition essay? List required skills and concepts for each category.

Ideas	
Organization	
Use of Language	

Introduction

The **introduction** to an essay has three main parts (listed in the order in which they should appear):

I. **The Hook:** If the opening lines are dull or confusing, the reader loses interest right away. Therefore, you must write an opening that grabs the reader's attention. Lure your readers into the piece with a hook—an anecdote, compelling question, quote, or intriguing statement (AQQS)—to grab them so firmly that they will want to read on.

- **Anecdote:** Begin with a brief anecdote (a story from real life) that relates to the point of your essay.
- **Question:** Ask a thought-provoking universal question relating to the concept of your thesis. You will answer this question in your essay. Don't ask simplistic questions such as "How would you feel if . . .?" or "What would you do if . . .?"

My Notes

- **Quote:** Find a quote to state an ordinary idea in an extraordinary or provocative way or state a provocative idea in an ordinary way. Either will grab the reader's interest. This quote can come from any source: someone you know, someone famous, or a song.
- **Intriguing statement:** Knock down a commonly held assumption or define a word in a new and startling way.

II. **The Bridge:** This writing represents the content between the hook and the thesis (the controlling idea of the essay). The purpose of the bridge is to make a clear and concise connection between these two parts. The bridge is also the place where a writer provides necessary background information to set the context for the ideas in the essay.

III. **The Thesis:** Your thesis is your response to the writing prompt, and it includes information about both the topic and your interpretation of it. The thesis is the single most important part of the essay in establishing focus and coherence; all parts of the essay should work to support this idea. Your thesis should be a clear and precise assertion. It should not be an announcement of your intent, nor should it include the first person (*I/my*).

A thesis should show a level of sophistication and complexity of thought. You may want to try to create a complex sentence as your thesis statement. Complex sentences contain a dependent clause that begins with a dependent marker, such as *because, before, since, while, although, if, until, when, after, as,* or *as if.*

Evaluating and Revising Introductions

2. Read the following introductions. For each one, identify, label, and evaluate the three parts of the introduction: hook, bridge, and thesis.

Sample 1

Aristotle said, "The beauty of the soul shines out when a man bears with composure one heavy mischance after another, not because he does not feel them, but because he is a man of high and heroic temper." When people go through calamity with poise, it is not because they don't feel anything; it is because they are of a heroic nature. Heroism is being brave and helping other people before yourself, but it does not always have a happy ending.

Sample 2

"A hero is no braver than an ordinary person, but is braver five minutes longer." When heroes keep on going and keep battling a challenge or problem, it makes them that much more heroic. Anyone could just give up, but heroes keep going. Instead of stressing over satisfying everyone, heroes know that their best is good enough and focus on doing the right thing. Heroism is putting others before yourself and directly facing challenges, but not always saving or satisfying everyone.

3. Now reread each introductory paragraph, evaluate its effectiveness, and mark it for revision. Use these questions to aid your evaluation:

- Is the hook engaging?
- If the hook is a quote, is it integrated smoothly?
- Is there a bridge that effectively links the hook to the thesis?
- Is the thesis a clear and precise interpretation of the topic?
- Is the use of language formal or informal?
- Is the language effective? Where can it be made clearer, or where can ideas be stated more smoothly?

☑ Check Your Understanding

Revise one of the two sample paragraphs on the previous page based on your evaluation and discussion of how it could benefit by additional content, reworking sentences, and using more precise or formal diction.

Revising Thesis Statements

Examine the following model thesis statement, and then see how the statement has been revised to have a complex sentence structure with a beginning dependent clause.

- **Model thesis statement:** Heroism involves selflessness and dedication to a challenge. It means helping others without desire for recognition or stardom.
- **Revised model: Because** heroism involves selflessness, it requires dedication to a challenge and helping others without desire for recognition or stardom.

4. What is the value of combining the two sentences in this way? How does it improve the clarity of ideas in the thesis statement?

5. Now follow the model to revise the remaining thesis statements on the next page. Create a complex sentence structure by using a dependent marker to create a dependent clause at the beginning of the sentence. Revise other elements as needed for smooth expression while still keeping the same ideas.

My Notes

- **Thesis statement:** Heroism means taking action when you are needed, showing dedication to your quest, and not giving up even when the odds are against you.

  Revised thesis statement:

- **Thesis statement:** Heroism means putting others before oneself and directly facing challenges, but not always saving or satisfying everyone.

  Revised thesis statement:

- **Thesis statement:** Heroism is being brave and helping other people before yourself, but it does not always guarantee a happy ending.

  Revised thesis statement:

Writing a Concluding Paragraph

The concluding paragraph in an essay is the last thing your reader takes from your essay. Try to make the reader think in a new way, feel emotional, or feel enlightened. Choose the ending carefully. Avoid clichés or something stale, such as "The end," "That is all I have to say," or "That's my definition of heroism." Make your readers feel that they have arrived somewhere by sharing with them what you have learned, discovered, or realized.

The following are some possible ways to conclude your essay.

- Be genuine. Explain why this topic is important to you and/or important in life.
- If you used a quote as your hook, refer back to it. If you didn't use a quote, use one to guide your conclusion.
- You may finish by reviewing the paper's main point, but with new insight.
- Direct the readers into the future. How does an understanding of this topic relate to future thought or action? What will or should happen in the months or years ahead?

WORD CONNECTIONS

Etymology

The word cliché means "something that is overused." It derives from the French word *clicher*, meaning "to click," which resembled a sound made when using printing plates. One method of creating printing plates was called *stereotype*, and this method could produce the same image repetitively. The word *stereotype* is now used as a synonym of *cliché*.

Evaluating and Revising Conclusions

6. As you read examples of a conclusion, identify which technique the writer used and how effective the conclusion is.

Sample 1

The best heroes out there are those that put others before themselves. How do we know when someone is a hero? When they face challenges with pure determination, but don't save or satisfy everyone in the end. It blows us away every time a hero can fix sticky situations, but it is more important to know that a hero is doing what they're doing for the protection of everyone else. Making mistakes is what makes everything else that they do even more spectacular.

Sample 2

Heroes often look like the normal people we see walking down the street and they might be the plainest form of normal there is. Behind that normal appearance there have been struggle and challenge that have turned into wisdom. Heroes have to not only overcome challenges, but have done it with dignity. Heroes have grown from their experiences and now put a different value on life itself. Heroes are absolutely essential to life, for without heroes we would have no one to admire or set our goals to their standards.

☑ Check Your Understanding

Revise one of the two paragraphs above based on your evaluation and discussion of how it could benefit by additional content, reworking sentences, and using more precise or formal diction.

Writing Body Paragraphs

Body paragraphs are the meat of your essay. Outlined by the thesis, they include the reasons, plus the details and examples, that provide the support for your thesis. Part of the strength of your support is synthesizing, or pulling together, facts, examples, and details from your experiences and from texts and resources you have read or studied. As you write body paragraphs, be sure to include the following:

- A topic sentence that introduces the focus of the paragraph
- A concluding sentence that follows from the information and explanations presented
- Facts, details, and examples relevant and sufficient to make your point
- Commentary that explains why these details and examples are significant
- Paraphrases and embedded quotations conveying important details and examples
- Transitions to show your understanding of the content by showing the connections among ideas

WORD CONNECTIONS

Cognates
The English word **synthesizing** has the same meaning as its Spanish cognate *sintetizar*.

My Notes

Evaluating and Revising Body Paragraphs

7. Read the following body paragraph and evaluate its effectiveness. Look at the transitions, facts, details, examples, and commentary, as well as the skill with which paraphrases and embedded quotations are handled.

> Heroism is trying your hardest, no matter the obstacles, to go beyond the needs of yourself to help others. A son writes about how his mother, Ana, has an obstacle, but does all that she can to fight it, and does not complain. He says that she fights cancer with a smile and "hasn't let it slow her down, either" (Gandara). This shows that even though she could complain and give up fighting the disease, she tries her hardest, which inspires her loved ones. In addition, in the movie *Mulan*, the main character wants to help her father by enlisting in the army, which is impossible according to Chinese law because she is a girl. Instead of giving up on this, Mulan decides to pretend to be a man and goes to extremes to keep up her charade. This is heroic because her father, being the only male in his family, had to enlist in the army, yet he was too sick to fight and would have undoubtedly died in the conflict. Facing illness or danger with courage for the sake of another is inspiring and heroic.

☑ Check Your Understanding

Return to the texts you have read and studied in this unit. Begin to think about which ones you can use to help support your definition of heroism. Make a list of the texts, the heroes, and the events you may be able to use in your essay. Begin to categorize them as you think of each definition strategy: function, example, and negation.

Publishing for Your Intended Audience

8. Once you have written, revised, and edited your definition essay, you will need to publish it. Think about your intended audience. Is it your teacher? Classmates? Parents? School newspaper readers? Should the final product be hand-written, typed, or online? What should you include, if anything, in the header or footer? Follow the Embedded Assessment checklist and the instructions from your teacher to publish the final product in a way that is suitable for your audience.

Drafting the Embedded Assessment

Think about people who deserve status as a hero from the past, from the present, from life, and from literature. What defines a hero? Draft an insightful thesis statement using a complex sentence structure. Then outline ideas for your essay. Remember to return to your work in Activity 1.13 on defining a hero.

Hero Definition Essay Outline

I. **INTRODUCTION**

Hook: (What would make an effective hook?)

Bridge: (background information and connections)

Thesis: (state your original definition)

II. **BODY PARAGRAPH 1** (Function/Example/Negation)

Topic Sentence: (connect to thesis)

Supporting Detail: (list source)

Paraphrase, quotations, examples with commentary

Supporting Detail: (list source)

III. **BODY PARAGRAPH 2** (Function/Example/Negation)

Topic Sentence: (connect to thesis)

Supporting Detail: (list source)

Paraphrase, quotations, examples with commentary

Supporting Detail: (list source)

IV. **BODY PARAGRAPH 3** (Function/Example/Negation)

Topic Sentence: (connect to thesis)

Supporting Detail: (list source)

Paraphrase, quotations, examples with commentary

Supporting Detail: (list source)

V. **CONCLUSION**

(What would make an effective conclusion?)

 Independent Reading Checkpoint

Look back at the article about Tristan Segers in Activity 1.12. Compare how his life and the life of the hero in your independent reading text fit into the hero's archetype that you have learned about in this unit.

Writing a Definition Essay

 ASSIGNMENT

Think about people who deserve status as heroes—from the past, from the present, from life, and from literature. What defines a hero? Write a multi-paragraph essay that develops your definition of heroism. Be sure to use strategies of definition (function, example, and negation) to guide your writing.

Planning and Prewriting: Take time to make a plan for your essay.	■ Which activities and texts have you collected that will help you refine and expand your definition of a hero? ■ What prewriting strategies (such as freewriting, outlining, or using graphic organizers) could help you brainstorm ideas and organize your examples?
Drafting: Write a multi-paragraph essay that effectively organizes your ideas.	■ How will you provide a hook, a bridge, and a thesis in the introduction? ■ How will you use the strategies of definition (function, example, negation) in your support paragraphs? ■ How will your conclusion demonstrate the significance of heroism and encourage readers to accept your definition?
Evaluating and Revising: Create opportunities to review and revise your work.	■ During the process of writing, when can you pause to share with and respond to others? ■ What is your plan to include suggestions and revision ideas in your draft? ■ How can the Scoring Guide help you evaluate how well your draft meets the requirements of the assignment?
Checking and Editing for Publication: Confirm that your final draft is ready for publication.	■ How will you proofread and edit your draft to demonstrate command of the conventions of standard English capitalization, punctuation, spelling, grammar, and usage? ■ How will you create a title and assemble your illustrations in an appealing manner? ■ How will you publish your final draft in a way that is appropriate for the audience?

Reflection

After completing this Embedded Assessment, think about how you went about accomplishing this task and respond to the following:

- Explain how the activities in this unit helped prepare you for success in the Embedded Assessment.
- Which activities were especially helpful, and why?

SCORING GUIDE

Scoring Criteria	Exemplary	Proficient	Emerging	Incomplete
Ideas	The essay • uses all three strategies of definition effectively to define a hero • maintains a precise and original thesis • integrates relevant supporting details and evidence (quotes and paraphrases) with citations and commentary.	The essay • uses strategies of definition (function, example, negation) to define a hero • maintains a clear thesis • includes adequate supporting details and evidence (quotes and paraphrases) with citations and commentary.	The essay • uses insufficient strategies of definition to define a hero • has an unclear or unfocused thesis • includes inadequate supporting details and evidence; may have inconsistent citations and/or weak commentary.	The essay • does not define a hero using strategies of definition • has no discernible thesis • lacks supporting details, citations, and/or commentary.
Structure	The essay • introduces the central idea with an engaging hook, bridge, and thesis • organizes ideas into focused support paragraphs that progress smoothly • creates coherence with the purposeful use of a variety of transitions and topic sentences • provides an insightful conclusion.	The essay • introduces the topic with a hook, bridge, and thesis • organizes ideas into support paragraphs that progress logically • creates coherence with the use of transitions and topic sentences • provides a conclusion that follows from the ideas presented.	The essay • includes an ineffective or partial introduction • has unrelated, undeveloped, or insufficient support paragraphs • uses transitions and topic sentences ineffectively or inconsistently • provides a weak, illogical, or repetitive conclusion.	The essay • lacks an introduction • has minimal, absent, or flawed support paragraphs • uses few or no transitions and topic sentences • lacks a conclusion.
Use of Language	The essay • uses consistent diction and style appropriate for an academic audience • demonstrates command of the conventions of standard English capitalization, punctuation, spelling, grammar, and usage (including complex sentences).	The essay • uses diction and style that is generally appropriate for an academic audience • demonstrates adequate command of the conventions of standard English capitalization, punctuation, spelling, grammar, and usage (including complex sentences).	The essay • uses diction or a style that is basic or inappropriate to an academic audience • demonstrates partial or inconsistent command of the conventions of standard English capitalization, punctuation, spelling, grammar, and usage.	The essay • uses flawed diction • lacks command of the conventions of standard English capitalization, punctuation, spelling, grammar, and usage; frequent errors obscure meaning.

VISUAL PROMPT
The perfect society may mean different things to different people. How does this image represent one vision of an ideal society? Is this similar or different from what you envision a perfect society to be?

THE CHALLENGE OF UTOPIA

The year was 2081, and everyone was finally equal. They weren't only equal before God and the law. They were equal every which way. Nobody was smarter than anybody else. Nobody was better looking than anybody else. Nobody was stronger or quicker than anybody else.

—from "Harrison Bergeron" by Kurt Vonnegut

UNIT 2

The Challenge of Utopia

GOALS

- To analyze a novel for thematic development
- To recognize and analyze literary elements in a novel
- To analyze characteristics of argumentative and informational texts by evaluating ideas, structure, and language
- To develop informative/ explanatory texts using the compare/contrast organizational structure
- To develop effective arguments using logical reasoning, relevant evidence, and persuasive appeals for effect

VOCABULARY

ACADEMIC
perspective
Socratic
seminar
argument
illustration
analogy
anecdote
debate
controversial
research

LITERARY
science fiction
protagonist
antagonist
flashback
foreshadowing

CONTENTS

ACTIVITY	CONTENTS	

Texts not included in these materials.

My Independent Reading List

Learning Strategies

Think-Pair-Share
QHT
Close Reading
Marking the Text
Paraphrasing
Graphic Organizer

Learning Targets

- Preview the big ideas and vocabulary for the unit.
- Identify and analyze the skills and knowledge necessary to be successful in completing Embedded Assessment 1.

Preview

In this activity, you will begin exploring the concepts of utopia and dystopia and unpack the first Embedded Assessment for the unit.

Making Connections

We probably all agree that we would like to live in an ideal society where everyone is free and happy, but what does that actually mean, and why do definitions of the ideal society differ so greatly? In this unit, you will read, write, and engage in various types of collaborative discussions to explore these universal questions. Then you will move from discussion and explanation into debate and effective argumentation as you research and develop a claim about a contemporary issue.

Essential Questions

The following Essential Questions will be the focus of the unit study. Respond to both questions in your Reader/Writer Notebook.

1. To what extent can a perfect or ideal society exist?
2. What makes an argument effective?

Developing Vocabulary

Create a QHT chart in your Reader/Writer Notebook and sort the Vocabulary Terms on the Contents page. Use print or online resources to move all of the words into the "T" column by the end of the unit. Keep in mind that there is more to knowing a new word than just learning the definition. Truly knowing a word also involves an understanding of its pronunciation, origin, and part of speech.

INDEPENDENT READING LINK

Reading Plan

During this half of the unit, you will read a science fiction novel together as a class. The protagonist in this novel is a hero fighting against a challenge in society. Think about a challenge in your own society that interests you. Research news articles, narrative nonfiction texts, or contemporary short stories that discuss that challenge and what people are trying to do to fix it. Note the texts you will select to read independently in your "My Independent Reading List" space on the Contents page.

Unpacking Embedded Assessment 1

Read the assignment for Embedded Assessment 1: Writing an Informational Essay.

 Think about how writers organize and develop ideas in informational writing. Use an informational structure to communicate your understanding of the concept of dystopia and/or the concept of the Hero's Journey. Select one of these prompts:

- Write an essay that compares and contrasts life in a dystopian society with modern-day society.
- Write an essay that explains how the protagonist (hero) changes as a result of conflict with his dystopian society (Road of Trials). Explain how this change connects to the novel's theme (the Crossing or Return Threshold).

Work with your class to paraphrase the expectations and create a graphic organizer to use as a visual reminder of the required concepts and skills.

Informational Writing: Compare/Contrast

Learning Targets

- Evaluate the use of the organizational pattern of compare/contrast to present a thesis in an informational text.
- Write a paragraph that uses the compare/contrast organizational pattern to present a key idea.

Preview

In this activity, you will read and analyze a text that compares and contrasts utopian and dystopian novels. You will then think about the characteristics of each genre, the relationship between the two genres, and how modern-day novels connect to utopian and dystopian stories from the past.

Learning Strategies

Graphic Organizer
QHT
Close Reading
Marking the Text
Rereading
Brainstorming
Drafting

My Notes

Review of Informational Writing

You have had many experiences writing informational text. Every time you explain something or define a concept or idea, you are writing an informational text. One form of informational writing is **compare/contrast**. This method of organization is an important model of explanation to master and can be used in many different writing situations.

1. Brainstorm ideas for topics for different school subjects that would require you to write a compare/contrast essay.

2. Writers use planning and prewriting to decide how to organize their ideas. The table that follows shows two methods of organizing a compare/contrast essay, using "ancient *vs.* modern civilizations" as a topic.

Subject-by-Subject Organization	Feature-by-Feature Organization
Discuss all the features of one subject. Then discuss all the features of the other.	Select a feature common to both subjects, and then discuss each subject in light of that feature. Then go on to the next feature.

Subject A: Ancient Civilization
    Government
    Education
    Social Norms
Subject B: Modern Civilization
    Government
    Education
    Social Norms
	Government
	    Subject A: Ancient Civilization
	    Subject B: Modern Civilization
	Education
	    Subject A: Ancient Civilization
	    Subject B: Modern Civilization
	Social Norms
	    Subject A: Ancient Civilization
	    Subject B: Modern Civilization

3. Why would a writer select one organizational structure over the other?

My Notes

Setting a Purpose for Reading

- While you read, use two different colored pens to underline details that describe the similarities and differences between utopian and dystopian societies.
- Circle unknown words and phrases. Try to determine the meanings of the words by using context clues, word parts, or a dictionary.

About the Author

Benjamin Obler is a modern-day instructor and novelist. Originally from Minneapolis, Minnesota, Obler teaches writing at Gotham Writer's Workshop in New York City. He received an MFA in Creative Writing from the University of Glasgow, Scotland. He's been on BBC Radio and was interviewed at Strand bookstore for a documentary film about coffee. His first novel, *Javascotia*, was published in 2009.

Essay

In a Dreadfully Perfect World

by **Benjamin Obler**

1 When Katniss Everdeen draws back her bow to unleash the arrow that will help free her outcast friends in *The Hunger Games* (2013), few moviegoers were likely thinking of Thomas More's[1] novel of 500 years earlier. Nevertheless, if it weren't for More's *Utopia* (1516), perhaps a whole genre of novels would not exist today. Utopian novels, portraying imagined, idealized societies began with More, and out of them grew dystopian novels in which, typically, societies grow more corrupt, diabolical, and inhumane. Though the two genres are vastly different, and in some ways completely opposite, utopian and dystopian fiction are interrelated and rely upon each other.

2 More's novel is set on an island called Utopia, where everyone is employed and work days are only six hours long. People are not burdened by property ownership or the drive to earn money. In fact, they are free to take from the supply stores whatever food they need. Because the laws are so simple,

---

[1] Thomas More, or "Sir Thomas More," as he is sometimes called, was knighted by King Henry in the 1520s. More is also referred to as Saint Thomas More because of his involvement in the Catholic Church.

WORD CONNECTIONS

Roots and Affixes

The word utopia comes from the Greek *ou*, meaning "no" or "not," and *topos*, meaning "place." But its meaning is closer to *eutopia*, made from the English prefix *eu*, meaning "good," and *topos*. Which of the two words, *eutopia* or *utopia*, would better describe a place with a pink sky? A world with no war or poverty? A dystopia is a community or society, usually fictional, that is in some important way undesirable or frightening. The word dystopia comes from the Latin prefix *dys-*, meaning "bad" or "abnormal," and the Greek word *topos*.

there's no need for lawyers. All Utopians agree that war is barbaric, so wars never happen. Just about every aspect of life is perfect, and all woes and pains have vanished.

3   More's work is the earliest of its kind, and since then all stories that **depict** any **idealized** outcome have been described as *utopian*. Utopian texts are essentially hopeful, imagining positive outcomes and the disappearance of those traits of real life that bring suffering—inequality, poverty, injustice, bigotry. In utopian stories, peacefulness and reason prevail over chaos and greed. Conversely, dystopian texts depict the worst possible outcomes of societal strife, often involving the aftermath of social change that went wrong and led to **oppression** or chaos.

4   Utopian works were popular for a long time before dystopian novels became more common. Writers across three centuries turned to the imagined place to project their hopes. In More's time, the novel was a relatively new way to talk about ideas of civic life and analyze customs and rules. With the utopian novel, writers could awaken the public imagination to what harmony might be possible.

5   In 1619, Johann Valentin Adreae published *Christianopolis*, which tells of a distant island city where the citizens use no money and own no property. Economic equality rules, and all material goods needed for life are provided by the state. Tommaso Campanella produced a similar novel, *City of the Sun*, in 1623, featuring a peaceful place where property is communal and money is not needed. Campanella improved on More's six-hour workday, making the workday on his island of Taprobane only four hours long. Abolishment of slavery, good education for all, and rule by bright, capable people—life on the island was utopian in every way.

6   Remote settings such as islands are a popular feature of the utopian genre. Francis Bacon's *The New Atlantis* (1624) features an island, as did utopian works by several other writers. Other utopian worlds were found near the north pole, or through underground caves. It seemed that for writers to envision a harmonious society, it had to be completely unconnected from any system in place in any western nation at the time.

7   In contrast, dystopian works typically depict settings that are distantly removed from us not by geography, but by time. The typical dystopian society springs up from the foundations of our own society sometime in the future. For example, Lois Lowry's *The Giver* is set in a futuristic time, when many problems have been solved. Likewise, in Ray Bradbury's *Fahrenheit 451*, the setting is an unnamed American city of the future. Dystopias are projections of today's society in more advanced stages. For example, imbalances of power grow more imbalanced, limited rights become greatly restricted, and partial oppression becomes totalitarian rule. Writers of dystopian works want these connections to the current time and place to be clearly understood. The purpose of many

12   VTOPIAE INSVLAE TABVLA.

Plan of the island of Utopia. Illustration from Thomas More's novel, depicting an idealized society living on an imaginary island.

depict: represent
idealized: better than something actually is
oppression: unjust rule or treatment

My Notes

dystopian stories is to illustrate the potential for terror and catastrophe that lurks in our existing systems. To set a dystopian novel in some imaginary island would defeat the purpose of delivering such chilling possibilities to readers.

8 In the 18th century, utopian novels began to **proliferate**, and the societies depicted in them grew more extreme. By 1755, Étienne-Gabriel Morelly, in his novel *Code de la Nature* (Nature's Code), advocates for the abolition of property, trade, politics, marriage, privilege, and law. Everything that stands in the way of individual liberty is **eradicated**.

9 Subsets of the utopian genre emerged, such as the feminist utopia. The first was *The Blazing World* (1666) by Margaret Cavendish. In it, a shipwrecked young woman reaches a foreign land via the North Pole. She is crowned empress and uses her power to keep the kingdom free from war, religious division, and unfair sexual discrimination. Elizabeth Burgoyne Corbette's *New Amazonia* is another example. Her setting is Ireland in the year 2472. Because they are corrupt, men are barred from political office. Everyone is vegetarian.

10 The appeal of the perfect world had a powerful hold on some writers. Theodor Hertzka, a political economist, wrote *Freiland* (*Freeland*) (1890) about an imaginary utopian colony in Africa. Then he tried (unsuccessfully) to create a real village, Freeland, in Africa.

11 A key difference between utopias and dystopias is their relationship to the real world. Hertzka tried to establish a real-world replica of his fictional colony. But no writer would ever try to create a real-world replica of their fictional dystopia. Utopias are written in earnest, as admirable models, whereas dystopias are devised to serve as warnings of what we should never let our world become.

12 The utopian craze peaked with Edward Bellamy's *Looking Backward: 2000–1887*. First published in 1888, it was the third largest best-seller of its time. In the novel, the protagonist Julien West wakes in the year 2000. The United States is now a socialist utopia. People work shorter hours and retire at age 45. Production and distribution of goods is smooth and efficient thanks to a regimented labor force. Selling 400,000 copies by 1897, Bellamy's novel set the market ablaze for such utopian works. Between 1860 and 1887, no fewer than 11 such works of fiction were published in the United States by various authors.

13 By comparison, a list of popular dystopian novels published between 2000 and 2015 contains at least 75 titles.

14 Utopias and dystopias are siblings, and one of their similarities is foresight. In casting their imaginations forward, many writers of both utopian and dystopian novels have described technologies that were impossible for the time. For example, Bellamy's character is taken to a store that cuts out middlemen, much like a modern-day Costco or Sam's Club. The concept of credit cards is introduced, and Bellamy also predicts both sermons and music being available in the home through cable "telephone," much like the internet during its early, wired days.

WORD CONNECTIONS

Roots and Affixes

When it comes to opposition, the words beneficent and malevolent describe a person or an action's intent. Generally, words with the prefix *bene-* (good, well) have positive connotations, and words that begin with *male-* (bad, wrong) have negative connotations.

proliferate: multiply quickly
eradicated: wiped out completely

15 But utopias are in the eyes of the beholder—a matter of interpretation. For example, in Bellamy's book, one judge presides over all court cases, appointing two colleagues to represent the prosecution and defense. This is meant to seem simple and elegant—incorruptible. But from another point of view a single judge enforcing all law amounts to dictatorship, and the appointment of colleagues smells of corruption, creating ample opportunity for self-serving deals. To some total equality is the ideal, but to others the measures taken to achieve that equality would be repression. Utopias such as the one depicted in Corbette's *New Amazonia* would not be a utopia to everyone.

16 This highlights a similarity between utopias and dystopias. In any real society or form of government, there are **beneficent** people and **malevolent** people. Some people respect order, obey the law, are kind and peaceful. Others break laws, serve themselves, lie, and manipulate the system to their advantage. What utopian and dystopian works have in common is that they both unbalance reality, making everything starkly black and white, taking away one aspect and leaving the other. In this way, utopian and dystopian novels are very much alike. They both exaggerate things for dramatic effect, capture our imaginations, and make us feel the stark power of what might be.

Making Observations
- What details in the essay stand out to you?
- What similarities between utopias and dystopias surprise you?

A typical element in dystopian works is oppression. In *The Hunger Games*, characters deal with oppression and totalitarianism from a powerful government system. In turn, citizens, such as Katniss Everdeen (played by actress Jennifer Lawrence), must fight to survive.

beneficent: good-intentioned
malevolent: evil-intentioned

Evaluating Details to Determine Key Ideas

4. Examining details in a text can help readers understand the key ideas the author wants to convey. Look back at your color-coded underlining of the similarities and differences between utopian and dystopian societies. Use those details you underlined to create a Venn diagram in your Reader/Writer Notebook. Evaluate the details you organized into the Venn diagram to determine the key ideas in this text.

Analyzing the Photograph

5. How do the details in the photograph help you better understand an element of the text? Make a statement about the details. Then connect them to the text.

Returning to the Text

- Return to the text as you respond to the following questions. Use text evidence to support your responses.
- Write any additional questions you have about the essay in your Reader/Writer Notebook.

6. Find the sentence from paragraph 1 that best illustrates the relationship between utopian and dystopian genres. Explain why this is the author's thesis statement.

_____

_____

_____

_____

7. Which words does the author use to describe utopian and dystopian novels? Why does the author use these words?

_____

_____

_____

_____

8. Why is the footnote in paragraph 1 placed after that particular sentence?

_____

_____

_____

_____

9. When it comes to setting, why might an author of a utopian novel choose a mountaintop or the bottom of the ocean? Why might this be a difficult setting in which to place a dystopian society, and where would be better?

_____

_____

_____

_____

10. Reread paragraph 9, in which the author gives two examples of feminist utopias. Based on the examples, how would you define a feminist utopia?

_____

_____

_____

_____

11. Who or what is a _beholder_? Why does the author say that "utopias are in the eyes of the beholder," and how does he connect this expression to the rest of the text?

_____

_____

_____

_____

12. What is the relationship between reality and a utopia or dystopia? How might a utopian or dystopian novel help readers understand more about real life?

_____

_____

_____

_____

13. According to the essay, how has the popularity of utopian and dystopian stories changed over time?

_____

_____

_____

_____

Working from the Text

14. Examine how the text "In a Dreadfully Perfect World" is organized. As you analyze the organization, write the focus of each paragraph in the My Notes section. Underline transitional words and phrases that help you follow the changes in focus. Arrange the results of your paragraph-by-paragraph examination in the graphic organizer that follows.

Structure of "In a Dreadfully Perfect World"	
Paragraphs:	**Focus of that text:**
1 through 3	
4 through 6	
7	
8 through 10	
11 through 14	
15	
16	

15. Explain the author's purpose and thesis. How does the text structure contribute to the author's purpose and the development of the thesis? Provide textual evidence to support your analysis.

Creating Coherence

In Unit 1, you learned that *coherence* in writing is the clear and orderly presentation of ideas in a paragraph or essay. One way a writer creates coherence is to use transitional words, phrases, and sentences to link ideas within and between paragraphs. The following chart lists some transitional words and phrases that create coherence in compare/contrast essays.

Transitions That Compare		Transitions That Contrast	
likewise	as well as	although	nevertheless
similarly	the same as	instead	still
in the same way	both	even though	however
in comparison	like	on the other hand	yet/but
in like manner	also	on the contrary	rather
by the same token	compared to	in contrast	conversely

16. Sort the transitions using the QHT strategy. Then practice using some of the transitions on a subject that you know about, such as *short stories versus poetry*. Write a few sentences in your Reader/Writer Notebook.

☑ Check Your Understanding

To prepare for your Writing to Sources activity, return to the Venn diagram you made in your Reader/Writer Notebook in step 4 in which you compared and contrasted the concepts of utopia and dystopia. Think of ways utopian and dystopian works are alike and different. Write a sentence about a way they are alike. Then write a sentence about a way they are different. In each sentence, try to link ideas by using a transitional word or phrase.

LANGUAGE & WRITER'S CRAFT: Verb Moods

Verbs have moods, just like tenses. A verb's mood can change the tone of a sentence in different ways. There are five major verb moods:

Indicative: Makes a declaration. *Example:* A dystopian novel gives readers a warning about the future.

Imperative: Expresses a command. *Example:* Read this essay about Thomas More.

Interrogative: Asks a question. *Example:* What did you learn about Thomas More?

Conditional: Indicates a **conditional** state. *Example:* If a novel is set in the future, then it's a dystopian story.

Subjunctive: Expresses a **hypothetical** situation. *Example:* I wish I could live on a faraway island.

The conditional and subjunctive moods are similar, but they express different things. In general, the conditional mood expresses situations that are *almost certain* to come true, while the subjunctive mood expresses situations that *are unlikely* and more imaginary or speculative.

Consider this sentence from the passage:

Example: *If an author includes malevolent aspects in a novel, then the text is about a dystopian society.*

PRACTICE What verb mood is this sentence expressing? First tell what verb mood is expressed, and then rewrite the sentence using one of the other 5 verb moods described above.

Writing to Sources: Informational Text

After reading "In a Dreadfully Perfect World," write a short paragraph comparing and contrasting utopian and dystopian societies, settings, and characteristics. Be sure to:

- Begin with a topic sentence that clearly states the comparison/contrast you plan to explore.
- Explain at least one difference and one similarity between the two subjects.
- Organize ideas logically (subject-by-subject or feature-by-feature). Refer to the chart at the beginning of this activity to review these organizational structures.
- Create coherence by using transitional words and phrases.
- Support your explanations and ideas with evidence from the text.

Utopian Ideals and Dystopian Reality

Learning Strategies

Close Reading
Rereading
Diffusing
Paraphrasing
Marking the Text
Shared Reading
Think Aloud

Learning Targets

- Closely read a story and explain how its setting influences the values and beliefs of its characters.
- Make connections between a character's beliefs and values and the events of a story.
- Integrate ideas from multiple texts to build knowledge and vocabulary about utopian and dystopian societies.

Preview

In this activity, you will read a story and expand your understanding of the concepts of utopia and dystopia.

My Notes

The Concept of Utopia

As you read in the previous activity, a utopia is an ideal or perfect community or society. It is a real or imagined place considered to be ideal or perfect (politically, socially, economically, technologically, ecologically, religiously, etc.). People in a utopia lead civilized lives filled with peace, fulfillment, and happiness.

The Western idea of utopia originates in the ancient world, where legends of an earthly paradise (e.g., Eden in the Old Testament, the mythical Golden Age of Greek mythology), combined with the human desire to create, or re-create, an ideal society, helped form the utopian idea.

When Sir Thomas More wrote the book *Utopia* in 1516, he described a perfect political and social system on an imaginary island named Utopia. Since then, the term *utopia* has entered the English language, meaning any place, state, or situation of ideal perfection.

Both the desire for Eden-like perfection and an attempt to start over in "unspoiled" America led religious and nonreligious groups and societies to set up communities in the United States. These experimental utopian communities were committed to such ideals as simplicity, sincerity, and brotherly love.

Once the idea of a utopia was created, its opposite, the idea of a dystopia, was also created. Such societies appear in many works of fiction, particularly in stories set in a speculative future.

Setting a Purpose for Reading

- As you read, label text that hints at whether the story's setting is utopian or dystopian. Make notes where you are confused about the setting.
- Circle unknown words and phrases. Try to determine the meaning of the words by using context clues, word parts, or a dictionary.

KNOWLEDGE QUEST

Knowledge Question:

Why do utopias often become dystopias?

In Activity 2.3, you will read one text and view two illustrations depicting a utopia and a dystopia. While you read and build knowledge about the topic, think about your answer to the Knowledge Question.

unceasing: nonstop
vigilance: observation

About the Author

Kurt Vonnegut (1922–2007) was one of the most influential American writers of the 20th century. His hallmark blend of dark satire, humor, and science fiction defines works such as *Cat's Cradle* (1963), *Slaughterhouse-Five* (1969), and *Breakfast of Champions* (1973). As an outspoken humanist, or someone who thinks humans have value and should solve problems rationally, he served as honorary president of the American Humanist Association.

Short Story

Harrison Bergeron

by **Kurt Vonnegut**

1   THE YEAR WAS 2081, and everybody was finally equal. They weren't only equal before God and the law. They were equal every which way. Nobody was smarter than anybody else. Nobody was better looking than anybody else. Nobody was stronger or quicker than anybody else. All this equality was due to the 211th, 212th, and 213th Amendments to the Constitution, and to the **unceasing vigilance** of agents of the United States Handicapper General.

2   Some things about living still weren't quite right, though. April for instance, still drove people crazy by not being springtime. And it was in that clammy month that the H-G men took George and Hazel Bergeron's fourteen-year-old son, Harrison, away.

3   It was tragic, all right, but George and Hazel couldn't think about it very hard. Hazel had a perfectly average intelligence, which meant she couldn't think about anything except in short bursts. And George, while his intelligence was way above normal, had a little mental handicap radio in his ear. He was required by law to wear it at all times. It was tuned to a government transmitter. Every twenty seconds or so, the transmitter would send out some sharp noise to keep people like George from taking unfair advantage of their brains.

4   George and Hazel were watching television. There were tears on Hazel's cheeks, but she'd forgotten for the moment what they were about. On the television screen were ballerinas.

5   A buzzer sounded in George's head. His thoughts fled in panic, like bandits from a burglar alarm.

6   "That was a real pretty dance, that dance they just did," said Hazel.

7   "Huh," said George.

8   "That dance—it was nice," said Hazel.

9   "Yup," said George. He tried to think a little about the ballerinas. They weren't really very good—no better than anybody else would have been, anyway. They were burdened with sash weights and bags of birdshot, and their faces were masked, so that no one, seeing a free and graceful gesture or a pretty face, would feel like something the cat drug in. George was toying with the vague notion that maybe dancers shouldn't be handicapped. But he didn't get very far with it before another noise in his ear radio scattered his thoughts.

10   George winced. So did two out of the eight ballerinas.

11   Hazel saw him wince. Having no mental handicap herself, she had to ask George what the latest sound had been.

12   "Sounded like somebody hitting a milk bottle with a ball peen hammer," said George.

13   "I'd think it would be real interesting, hearing all the different sounds," said Hazel a little envious. "All the things they think up."

14   "Um," said George.

15   "Only, if I was Handicapper General, you know what I would do?" said Hazel. Hazel, as a matter of fact, bore a strong resemblance to the Handicapper General, a woman named Diana Moon Glampers. "If I was Diana Moon Glampers," said Hazel, "I'd have chimes on Sunday—just chimes. Kind of in honor of religion."

16   "I could think, if it was just chimes," said George.

17   "Well—maybe make 'em real loud," said Hazel. "I think I'd make a good Handicapper General."

18   "Good as anybody else," said George.

19   "Who knows better than I do what normal is?" said Hazel.

20   "Right," said George. He began to think glimmeringly about his abnormal son who was now in jail, about Harrison, but a twenty-one-gun salute in his head stopped that.

21   "Boy!" said Hazel, "that was a **doozy**, wasn't it?"

22   It was such a doozy that George was white and trembling, and tears stood on the rims of his red eyes. Two of the eight ballerinas had collapsed to the studio floor, and were holding their temples.

23   "All of a sudden you look so tired," said Hazel. "Why don't you stretch out on the sofa, so's you can rest your handicap bag on the pillows, honeybunch." She was referring to the forty-seven pounds of birdshot in a canvas bag, which was padlocked around George's neck. "Go on and rest the bag for a little while," she said. "I don't care if you're not equal to me for a while."

24   George weighed the bag with his hands. "I don't mind it," he said. "I don't notice it any more. It's just a part of me."

doozy: something that is unusually good, bad, severe, etc.

My Notes

25 "You been so tired lately—kind of wore out," said Hazel. "If there was just some way we could make a little hole in the bottom of the bag, and just take out a few of them lead balls. Just a few."

26 "Two years in prison and two thousand dollars fine for every ball I took out," said George. "I don't call that a bargain."

27 "If you could just take a few out when you came home from work," said Hazel. "I mean—you don't compete with anybody around here. You just sit around."

28 "If I tried to get away with it," said George, "then other people'd get away with it—and pretty soon we'd be right back to the dark ages again, with everybody competing against everybody else. You wouldn't like that, would you?"

29 "I'd hate it," said Hazel.

30 "There you are," said George. "The minute people start cheating on laws, what do you think happens to *society*?"

31 If Hazel hadn't been able to come up with an answer to this question, George couldn't have supplied one. A siren was going off in his head.

32 "Reckon it'd fall all apart," said Hazel.

33 "What would?" said George blankly.

34 "Society," said Hazel uncertainly. "Wasn't that what you just said?

35 "Who knows?" said George.

36 The television program was suddenly interrupted for a news bulletin. It wasn't clear at first as to what the bulletin was about, since the announcer, like all announcers, had a serious speech **impediment**. For about half a minute, and in a state of high excitement, the announcer tried to say, "Ladies and Gentlemen."

37 But he finally gave up, handed the bulletin to a ballerina to read.

38 "Oh, that's all right—" Hazel said of the announcer, "he tried. That's the big thing. He tried to do the best he could with what God gave him. He should get a nice raise for trying so hard."

39 "Ladies and Gentlemen," said the ballerina, reading the bulletin. She must have been extraordinarily beautiful, because the mask she wore was hideous. And it was easy to see that she was the strongest and most graceful of all the dancers, for her handicap bags were as big as those worn by two-hundred pound men.

40 And she had to apologize at once for her voice, which was a very unfair voice for a woman to use. Her voice was a warm, luminous, timeless melody. "Excuse me—" she said, and she began again, making her voice absolutely uncompetitive.

impediment: disorder

41 "Harrison Bergeron, age fourteen," she said in a grackle squawk, "has just escaped from jail, where he was held on suspicion of plotting to overthrow the government. He is a genius and an athlete, is under-handicapped, and should be regarded as extremely dangerous."

42 A police photograph of Harrison Bergeron was flashed on the screen—upside down, then sideways, upside down again, then right side up. The picture showed the full length of Harrison Bergeron against a background calibrated in feet and inches. He was exactly seven feet tall.

43 The rest of Harrison's appearance was Halloween and hardware. Nobody had ever borne heavier handicaps. He had outgrown hindrances faster than the H-G men could think them up. Instead of a little ear radio for a mental handicap, he wore a tremendous pair of earphones, and spectacles with thick wavy lenses. The spectacles were intended to make him not only half blind, but to give him whanging headaches besides.

44 Scrap metal was hung all over him. Ordinarily, there was a certain symmetry, a military neatness to the handicaps issued to strong people, but Harrison looked like a walking junkyard. In the race of life, Harrison carried three hundred pounds.

45 And to offset his good looks, the H-G men required that he wear at all times a red rubber ball for a nose, keep his eyebrows shaved off, and cover his even white teeth with black caps at snaggle-tooth random. "If you see this boy," said the ballerina, "do not—I repeat, do not—try to reason with him."

46 There was the shriek of a door being torn from its hinges.

47 Screams and barking cries of consternation came from the television set. The photograph of Harrison Bergeron on the screen jumped again and again, as though dancing to the tune of an earthquake.

48 George Bergeron correctly identified the earthquake, and well he might have—for many was the time his own home had danced to the same crashing tune. "My God—" said George, "that must be Harrison!"

49 The realization was blasted from his mind instantly by the sound of an automobile collision in his head.

50 When George could open his eyes again, the photograph of Harrison was gone. A living, breathing Harrison filled the screen.

51 Clanking, clownish, and huge, Harrison stood—in the center of the studio. The knob of the uprooted studio door was still in his hand. Ballerinas, technicians, musicians, and announcers cowered on their knees before him, expecting to die.

52 "I am the Emperor!" cried Harrison. "Do you hear? I am the Emperor! Everybody must do what I say at once!" He stamped his foot and the studio shook.

GRAMMAR & USAGE

Conventions

An **ellipsis** is a row of three dots (...) that indicates something has been omitted from within a quoted passage, usually because it doesn't apply to the point the writer is trying to convey. Look at paragraph 42 from the story. If you only want to quote the part of the paragraph that describes Harrison, you could use ellipses to indicate the portion you removed, like so:

A police photograph of Harrison Bergeron was flashed on the screen ... The picture showed the full length of Harrison against a background calibrated in feet and inches. He was exactly seven feet tall.

When you use an ellipsis, be sure that your revised quote doesn't change the intent of the original meaning. If your quoted text uses more ellipses than words, consider paraphrasing it rather than using a direct quotation.

As you prepare to write your analysis, look for instances where you can use ellipses to clarify your text.

grackle: a small bird known for its unpleasant call

hindrances: artificial limitations

symmetry: balance; arrangement

consternation: alarm; bewilderment

Parallel Structure

Parallel structure (or parallelism) is the use of a repeated word pattern. It is used to show the reader that two or more things are of equal importance. For example, look at this sentence.

I love my cat because she is warm, she is furry, and she is affectionate.

This sentence uses parallel structure to explain the writer's feelings for the cat. The words used to describe the cat (warm, furry, affectionate) are arranged in a parallel structure so they equally emphasize each quality for the reader.

Look for instances in paragraphs 51 and 53 where Vonnegut uses parallel structure. What words does he use to create this parallel structure? What punctuation does he use? What effects does Vonnegut's use of this structure create?

gamboled: frolicked; played

53 "Even as I stand here," he bellowed, "crippled, hobbled, sickened—I am a greater ruler than any man who ever lived! Now watch me become what I can become!"

54 Harrison tore the straps of his handicap harness like wet tissue paper, tore straps guaranteed to support five thousand pounds.

55 Harrison's scrap-iron handicaps crashed to the floor.

56 Harrison thrust his thumbs under the bar of the padlock that secured his head harness. The bar snapped like celery. Harrison smashed his headphones and spectacles against the wall.

57 He flung away his rubber-ball nose, revealed a man that would have awed Thor, the god of thunder.

58 "I shall now select my Empress!" he said, looking down on the cowering people. "Let the first woman who dares rise to her feet claim her mate and her throne!"

59 A moment passed, and then a ballerina arose, swaying like a willow.

60 Harrison plucked the mental handicap from her ear, snapped off her physical handicaps with marvelous delicacy. And last of all he removed her mask.

61 She was blindingly beautiful.

62 "Now—" said Harrison, taking her hand, "shall we show the people the meaning of the word dance? Music!" he commanded.

63 The musicians scrambled back into their chairs, and Harrison stripped them of their handicaps, too. "Play your best," he told them, "and I'll make you barons and dukes and earls."

64 The music began. It was normal at first—cheap, silly, false. But Harrison snatched two musicians from their chairs, waved them like batons as he sang the music as he wanted it played. He slammed them back into their chairs.

65 The music began again and was much improved.

66 Harrison and his Empress merely listened to the music for a while—listened gravely, as though synchronizing their heartbeats with it.

67 They shifted their weights to their toes.

68 Harrison placed his big hands on the girl's tiny waist, letting her sense the weightlessness that would soon be hers.

69 And then, in an explosion of joy and grace, into the air they sprang!

70 Not only were the laws of the land abandoned, but the law of gravity and the laws of motion as well.

71 They reeled, whirled, swiveled, flounced, capered, **gamboled**, and spun.

72 They leaped like deer on the moon.

73   The studio ceiling was thirty feet high, but each leap brought the dancers nearer to it.

74   It became their obvious intention to kiss the ceiling. They kissed it.

75   And then, neutralizing gravity with love and pure will, they remained suspended in air inches below the ceiling, and they kissed each other for a long, long time.

76   It was then that Diana Moon Glampers, the Handicapper General, came into the studio with a double-barreled ten-gauge shotgun. She fired twice, and the Emperor and the Empress were dead before they hit the floor.

77   Diana Moon Glampers loaded the gun again. She aimed it at the musicians and told them they had ten seconds to get their handicaps back on.

78   It was then that the Bergerons' television tube burned out.

79   Hazel turned to comment about the blackout to George. But George had gone out into the kitchen for a can of beer.

80   George came back in with the beer, paused while a handicap signal shook him up. And then he sat down again. "You been crying," he said to Hazel.

81   "Yup," she said.

82   "What about?" he said.

83   "I forget," she said. "Something real sad on television."

84   "What was it?" he said.

85   "It's all kind of mixed up in my mind," said Hazel.

86   "Forget sad things," said George.

87   "I always do," said Hazel.

88   "That's my girl," said George. He winced. There was the sound of a riveting gun in his head.

89   "Gee—I could tell that one was a doozy," said Hazel.

90   "You can say that again," said George.

91   "Gee—" said Hazel, "I could tell that one was a doozy."

Ⓚ Knowledge Quest

- Which details about the characters stood out to you?
- What events seem strange to you?

☑ Focus on the Sentence

Before analyzing the story more closely, use what you have observed so far to complete the following sentences.

Harrison Bergeron is an exceptional fourteen-year-old boy because _____

_____

Harrison Bergeron is an exceptional fourteen-year-old boy, but _____

_____

Harrison Bergeron is an exceptional fourteen-year-old boy, so _____

_____

Returning to the Text

- Return to the text as you respond to the following questions. Use text evidence to support your responses.
- Write any additional questions you have about the short story in your Reader/Writer Notebook.

1. What is George's "little mental handicap radio," and what is its purpose?

_____

_____

_____

_____

2. Why is the punishment for removing weight from the "handicap bag" so harsh? Find textual evidence to support your answer.

_____

_____

_____

_____

3. According to this society, what makes George, his son, and the ballerinas so dangerous? Cite textual evidence to support your inference.

_____

_____

_____

_____

4. **KQ** In paragraph 30, why might the author have italicized the word *society* in the sentence "The minute people start cheating on laws, what do you think happens to *society*?"

_____

_____

_____

_____

5. What does Harrison's rebellion against the government's handicapping tell you about his character and values? Support your response with evidence from the text.

_____

_____

_____

_____

6. Examine the author's choice of verbs to describe the actions of Harrison and the ballerina in motion. What is the intended effect?

_____

_____

_____

_____

7. Explain how George's handicap prevents him and Hazel from reacting appropriately to their son's death. Cite evidence from the text to support your response.

_____

_____

_____

_____

8. How is the story's theme reflected in the conversation between Hazel and George that concludes the story?

_____

_____

_____

_____

My Notes

9. What has been done to make the society in the story utopian? Have those steps been successful, or is the society dystopian? Explain by comparing the story's setting to the definitions of *utopian* and *dystopian*.

10. **KQ** Which ideals in "In a Dreadfully Perfect World" are most like the ideals of the society in "Harrison Bergeron"? How does this story offer one example of the negative effects of that ideal?

Setting a Purpose for Viewing

- Highlight words or phrases in the caption that surprise or interest you.
- Use the My Notes section to briefly summarize each illustration.

KNOWLEDGE QUEST

Knowledge Question:

Why do utopias often become dystopias?

Illustrations of utopias often depict pollution-free natural environments. Here the utopia is isolated like a floating island.

Illustrations of dystopias often depict polluted futuristic cities. The dystopia here appears as protected as a fortress.

Knowledge Quest

- How does each illustration make you feel?
- What details and colors in each illustration make you feel a certain way?

Returning to the Images

- Return to the illustrations as you respond to the following questions. Use evidence to support your responses.
- Write any additional questions you have about the images in your Reader/Writer Notebook.

11. **KQ** The words *utopia* and *dystopia* have the same Greek root, *topos*, meaning "place." How would you describe each of these places? How do these pictures make it easy to compare a utopia and a dystopia?

12. Compare the colors the artists used in each illustration. Why do you think the artists chose those colors?

13. Which environment looks more inviting? What evidence supports your thinking?

14. Read the captions. What figurative language can you find? What is important about the words *like* and as in the captions?

15. **KQ** How are an isolated island and a protected fortress alike? What inferences can you draw from these two illustrations to help you answer the question, "Why do utopias often become dystopias?"

INDEPENDENT READING LINK

You can continue to build your knowledge about this theme by reading related fiction at ZINC Reading Labs.

Select the **fiction** filter and type keywords such as *utopia, dystopia,* or *alternate future* in the **Search all ZINC articles** field.

 ZINC

 Knowledge Quest

Use your knowledge about "Harrison Bergeron" and the images to discuss with a partner how your understanding of why utopias often become dystopias has changed. Be sure to:

- Explain your answer to your partner, be specific and use as many details as possible.
- When your partner explains his or her answer, ask for clarification by posing follow-up questions as needed.
- After the discussion, write down the ideas you talked about.

Working from the Text

16. Return to the text and take notes on the setting and the rules of the society. Underline any sentences that give you this information.

17. Use your annotations about the setting and the rules of the society to complete the following chart. Practice embedding quotations in your responses.

Analyzing the Setting	Interpretation	Response with Embedded Quotation
What "ideal" is the society based upon?		
What rules exist to create and maintain this ideal?		
How was this utopian ideal transformed into a dystopian reality?		
What new problems were created?		

18. Choose a character and explain how the setting of the story influences their values and beliefs. Embed quotations in your response.

☑ Check Your Understanding

Throughout the story, George shows signs that he knows there is something wrong with the handicapping system. Find two direct quotes that support this statement.

✍ Writing to Sources: Informational Text

Write a short paragraph explaining how "Harrison Bergeron" conveys the conflict between the needs or ideals of society and the realities of individuals. Be sure to:

- Begin with a topic sentence that describes the setting and explains how it influences the values and beliefs of characters.
- Provide examples from the text and use at least one direct quotation to support your ideas.
- Write sentences using the words *utopia* and *dystopia* in ways that demonstrate their meanings.

GRAMMAR & USAGE

Conventions

Brackets ([ ]) are most often used to clarify the meaning of quoted material. If it isn't clear what your quoted material is about, consider using brackets to clarify it.

For example, if you quote line 21 without providing any context, the reader won't know what "that" refers to. You can add context by using brackets.

"Boy!" said Hazel, "that [the noise] was a doozy, wasn' t it?"

As you prepare to write your analysis, look for instances where you can use brackets to clarify your text.

Language Checkpoint:
Using Subject-Verb Agreement

Learning Targets
- Understand how to use verbs that agree with their subjects.
- Revise writing to check for subject-verb agreement.

Preview
In this activity, you will examine, identify, and demonstrate subject-verb agreement.

Subject-Verb Agreement

Complete sentences always have a subject and a verb. In other words, someone or something—the subject—*is* or *does* something. The word that expresses what the subject is or does is called the verb. Making the verb match the subject is called **subject-verb agreement**.

1. Read the following sentences about "Harrison Bergeron" by Kurt Vonnegut. Underline the subjects and circle the verbs.
   a. A buzzer sounds in George's head.
   b. A news bulletin interrupts the television program.
   c. Screams come from the television set.

2. What do you notice about the subjects and verbs in the sentences above? With a partner, look at the subjects and verbs and make an observation about what makes them agree.

   _____

   _____

3. Read the following excerpt from a student's analysis of "Harrison Bergeron." Find the subjects and verbs in each sentence and write them in the chart that follows. Then decide whether each subject is singular or plural.

   In Kurt Vonnegut's story, the main character is not allowed to think. Because his intelligence is far above average, as soon as he begins to have a thought, a buzzer sounds in his head. The sounds of bells, sirens, and other awful noises chase away his thoughts. As a result, his intelligence remains at the level of average people. The conflict begins when George sees his missing son on television. Although his memories quickly escape him, they linger and haunt him nonetheless.

Subjects and Verbs	Singular (S) or Plural (P)
character is	S

4. With your partner, look at the subjects and verbs you added to the chart. Then read the observation you wrote earlier about what makes subjects and verbs agree and decide whether to add anything to your observation.

Subject-Verb Agreement in Long Sentences

Writers have to pay careful attention to subject-verb agreement, especially in longer sentences where the subject and the verb are not next to each other.

5. Read the following sentences from a student's analysis of "Harrison Bergeron." Identify the subjects and verbs by underlining the subject and circling the verb. Then decide whether the subjects and verbs agree or not.

   a. The United States Handicapper General, resembling Hazel Bergeron, applies handicaps to people with positive attributes.

   b. A rubber ball on his perfectly formed nose hides Harrison Bergeron's attractiveness.

   c. The newscaster, a man with a serious speech impediment, was unable to deliver his announcement.

6. Work with a partner to come up with a way to check for subject-verb agreement in long sentences.

Editing

Read the following paragraph from a student's essay about "Harrison Bergeron." Work with a partner to check whether subjects and verbs agree. Mark the text to show how you would correct any mistakes you notice. Remember that sentences may contain more than one subject and verb.

[1] Hazel, who is considered to have too many emotions, are of average intelligence. [2] However, the United States Handicapper General, the person who regulates each citizen's emotions, appearance, intelligence, and skill, always ensure that Hazel's emotions stay in check. [3] She forget her emotions almost instantly. [4] At the same time, Hazel, despite the government's best efforts, seem unable to escape her emotions. [5] Even though she cannot remember why she is upset, she find herself crying frequently. [6] The image of her son on television, for instance, bring her to tears.

☑ Check Your Understanding

Imagine that you are editing a classmate's writing and you notice this sentence:

Intelligence, strength, and good looks, qualities that Harrison Bergeron possesses, is just what the government is trying to control.

In your own words, write an explanation so that your classmate understands how to correct the sentence. Then add an item to your Editor's Checklist to help you remember how to check your writing for subject-verb agreement.

_____

_____

Practice

Return to the summary you wrote in Activity 2.3, and check it for subject-verb agreement. Trade your work with a partner. Be sure to:

- Underline subjects and circle verbs in the summary.
- Check that subjects and verbs agree.

Previewing the Novel

Learning Strategies

Visualizing
Levels of Questions
Inferring
Graphic Organizer
Note-taking
Discussion Groups

WORD CONNECTIONS

Etymology

Fantasy comes from the Old French word *fantasie* ("fantasy"), the Latin word *phantasia* ("imagination"), and the Ancient Greek word *phantasia*, meaning "apparition." The literary genre of fantasy is imaginative fiction crafted in a setting other than the real world. It involves creatures and events that are improbable or impossible in the world as we know it.

VOCABULARY

LITERARY

Science fiction is a genre in which the imaginary elements of the story could be scientifically possible. The **protagonist** of a fictional work is its hero or central character; the term is the opposite of **antagonist**, a character who actively opposes the main character.

Learning Targets

- Collaboratively analyze the opening chapters of a fictional text, citing text evidence to support your analysis.
- Examine the relationship between character and setting in a fictional text.

Preview

In this activity, you will analyze and explain utopian and dystopian themes within a fictional text.

Genre Study: Science Fiction

You will read a novel that questions whether a utopian society is possible. Such novels generally fit into the genre of **science fiction** because they are set in the future or in an alternate reality. There is generally a pronounced scientific or technological aspect to the story's setting.

1. Read the following text to gather more information about science fiction (from readwritethink.org). As you read, highlight the characteristics of science fiction.

> Science fiction is a genre of fiction in which the stories often tell about science and technology of the future. It is important to note that science fiction has a relationship with the principles of science—these stories involve partially true/partially fictitious laws or theories of science. It should not be completely unbelievable with magic and dragons because it would then venture into the genre of fantasy. The plot creates situations different from those of both the present day and the known past. Science fiction texts also include a human element, explaining what effect new discoveries, happenings, and scientific developments will have on us in the future. Science fiction texts are often set in the future, in space, on a different world, or in a different universe or dimension. Early pioneers of the genre of science fiction are H. G. Wells (*The War of the Worlds*) and Jules Verne (*20,000 Leagues Under the Sea*). Some well-known 20th-century science fiction texts include *1984* by George Orwell and *Brave New World* by Aldous Huxley.

Making Inferences

Preview the novel you will be reading as a class. Remember that to *infer* is to make an educated guess.

2. The cover art of a novel usually displays aspects of the novel's content. Study the cover of the class novel. Based on what it shows and what you know about the science fiction genre, what can you infer about the story?

- Setting:

  _____

- Characters (**protagonist** and **antagonist**):

  _____

- Plot:

  _____

• Theme: _____

_____

Preparing to Read

3. Use the graphic organizer to note evidence that reveals important information about the protagonist and setting. Then make inferences based on the evidence.

Literary Element	Evidence (page #)	Inferences
Protagonist _____ (name)		
Setting (description of the society/the way of life)		

4. In your Reader/Writer Notebook, begin a personal vocabulary list. Make inferences and use digital and print resources, context clues, and your knowledge of word roots to identify, record, and define at least five new words. Apply these same strategies to new words in later readings.

Levels of Questions

Remember that questioning a text on multiple levels can help you explore its meaning more fully. Read the definitions and write an example of each type of question, based on texts you have read in this unit. Before, during, and after reading sections of the class novel, you should routinely pose Level 1 and 2 questions. Record these questions as they come to you in your Reader/Writer Notebook.

• A **Level 1** question is **literal** (the answer can be found in the text).

• A **Level 2** question is **interpretive** (the answer can be inferred based on textual evidence).

• A **Level 3** question is **universal** (the answer is about a concept or idea beyond the text).

My Notes

5. Select and record an interesting quotation—relating to the protagonist and setting—that you think is important to understanding the conflict or theme. Then analyze the idea and form two thoughtful questions for discussion. Record your ideas in the graphic organizer.

Quotation (page #)
Analysis
Questions Level 1:
Level 2:

INDEPENDENT READING LINK

Read and Respond

What challenges are faced by the protagonist of your independent text? How do these challenges illustrate the conventions of dystopian literature? Is the challenge the protagonist faces similar to that of the class novel? If so, how? Write a summary of what you have read so far, citing information from sources outside the text, in your Reader/Writer Notebook.

☑ Check Your Understanding

Using the questions you have created for the novel you are reading, participate in a brief discussion about the society the novel presents and the protagonist's role in it. How does society influence the values and beliefs of the protagonist?

Contemplating Conflicting Perspectives

Learning Strategies

Shared Reading
Close Reading
Rereading
Questioning the Text
Note-taking
Discussion Groups

Learning Targets

- Identify conflicting perspectives within the novel and explain how themes are developed through interactions between characters.
- Identify and analyze the importance of specific vocabulary to the story.

Preview

In this activity, you will identify conflicting perspectives among the characters.

ACADEMIC

VOCABULARY

Perspective is a point of view or a specific attitude toward something. Your *perspective* is how you look at or interpret situations or events. Differences in perspective can sometimes cause conflict.

Perspectives

1. Other than the protagonist, who are the most important characters so far in the story? What do you know about each of these characters? Make a list of these characters and provide a brief description of each.

2. Which of these characters usually agree with one another? Which of these characters tend to disagree?

3. Conflict among people or between people and society is a result of conflicting **perspectives.** Support this idea by identifying a topic that has created the most important conflict so far in the story and contrast two different perspectives about the topic.

Topic:	
Character 1:	**Character 2:**
Perspective:	**Perspective:**
Textual Evidence (#):	**Textual Evidence (#):**

4. Write questions for discussion based on the information you provided in the chart.

   • **Level 1 (literal, factual):**

   • **Level 2 (interpretive):**

5. Which characters are questioning society? Analyze how the theme is developed through the interaction between these characters.

6. Continue to expand your personal vocabulary list in your Reader/Writer Notebook. Use digital and print resources, context clues, and your knowledge of word roots to identify, record, and define at least five new words.

7. In addition to creating differences in characters' perspectives, authors create differences between the perspectives of the characters and that of the reader. Support this idea by identifying a topic and comparing and contrasting a character's perspective with your own perspective. This time, include the main reason for each perspective and provide evidence from the text for each reason.

Topic:	
Character's Perspective:	**My Perspective:**
Main Reason:	**Main Reason:**
Textual Evidence (page #)	**Textual Evidence (page #)**

☑ Check Your Understanding

Write a summary of the plot of the novel so far. Tell how the characters' conflicting perspectives influence the events.

LANGUAGE & WRITER'S CRAFT: Subject-Verb Agreement and Prepositions

Recall what you learned earlier in this unit about subject-verb agreement:

- Complete sentences always have a **subject** and a **verb**.
- The **subject** is whatever the sentence is about.
- The **verb** is the word that tells what the subject *is* or *does*.
- Making the verb match the subject is called **subject-verb agreement**.

PRACTICE Circle the choices that create sentences with correct subject-verb agreement.

The colors is/are beautiful.

The prettiest color/colors is blue.

The antique dealer was/were asked for an appraisal.

The police is/are investigating several local burglaries.

Subject-verb agreement can be a little confusing when a preposition or prepositional phrase is part of a sentence, as shown in these incorrect examples:

- The dogs at the dog track runs faster than the average pet.
- A vase of wildflowers make a lovely centerpiece.

Both sentences are incorrect because the person who wrote them chose a verb that agrees with the **object** of the **preposition** instead of the **subject** of the **sentence**. Here is how those two sentences should be written:

- The **dogs** at the dog track **run** faster than the average pet.
- A **vase** of wildflowers **makes** a lovely centerpiece.

PRACTICE: Review the following sentences for subject-verb agreement. Copy them into your Reader/Writer Notebook, and edit the sentences that have errors.

A dealer in rare books were asked to look at the collection.

Many secrets in the universe has yet to be discovered.

Shouts from the crowd are frightening the baby.

Writing to Sources: Informational Text

Identify the perspectives of two characters and explain how those perspectives highlight a conflict in the story. Explain how the conflict between characters develops a theme in the novel. Be sure to:

- Create a topic sentence that compares or contrasts the perspectives.
- Provide examples from the text and at least one direct quotation.
- Write at least one sentence that includes a prepositional phrase while maintaining correct subject-verb agreement.

Questioning Society

Learning Strategies

Shared Reading
Marking the Text
Questioning the Text
Socratic Seminar
Fishbowl

WORD CONNECTIONS

Etymology
Censorship comes from the Latin word *censor*. A censor in Rome was responsible for counting citizens and for supervising and regulating their morals. The suffix *-ship* makes the word a noun.

My Notes

Learning Targets

- Make connections between specific rules and laws in a fictional society and those of present society, referencing the text and notations from additional research and reading materials.
- Participate collaboratively on this topic in a Socratic Seminar.

Preview

In this activity, you will read a short article about banned books and make connections to the novel you are reading.

Setting a Purpose for Reading

- As you read this article, underline words and phrases that relate to big concepts that you have been thinking about in this unit. Prepare to summarize and discuss these concepts.

- Circle unknown words and phrases. Try to determine the meaning of the words by using context clues, word parts, or a dictionary.

- Jot down any questions that you may have while you read in the My Notes area.

Article

Banned Books Week:
Celebrating the Freedom to Read

from **the American Library Association**

1   Banned Books Week (BBW) is an annual event celebrating the freedom to read and the importance of the First Amendment. Held during the last week of September, Banned Books Week highlights the benefits of free and open access to information while drawing attention to the harms of censorship by spotlighting actual or attempted bannings of books across the United States.

2   Intellectual freedom—the freedom to access information and express ideas, even if the information and ideas might be considered unorthodox or unpopular—provides the foundation for Banned Books Week. BBW stresses the importance of ensuring the availability of unorthodox or unpopular viewpoints for all who wish to read and access them.

3   The books featured during Banned Books Week have been targets of attempted bannings.

Fortunately, while some books were banned or restricted, in a majority of cases the books were not banned, all thanks to the efforts of librarians, teachers, booksellers, and members of the community to retain the books in the library collections. Imagine how many more books might be challenged—and possibly banned or restricted—if librarians, teachers, and booksellers across the country did not use Banned Books Week each year to teach the importance of our First Amendment rights and the power of literature, and to draw attention to the danger that exists when restraints are imposed on the availability of information in a free society.

Working from the Text

1. Review details in the article and determine the key idea. Which details directly support the key idea behind Banned Book Week? Explain the author's purpose for writing the article.

2. **Quickwrite:** Explain why access to books is important to our society. What societal value does access to information symbolize? You may reference the text in your response.

Novel Study

A story's setting is not simply the time and place in which it occurs. It is also the social environment in which characters live, act, and make choices. Social surroundings influence the values and beliefs of their inhabitants. Readers who are sensitive to this aspect of setting are better able to understand the behavior of the characters. That understanding makes the theme of a literary piece easier to detect.

3. Give an example of how the setting of "Harrison Bergeron" connects to the title character and the story's theme. How does that story's setting compare with that of your novel?

GRAMMAR & USAGE

Capitalization of Proper Nouns

Look at the first three words of the first paragraph of the article. You know that a noun is a word that names a person, place, thing, or idea. A **proper noun** is one that names a *particular* person, place, thing, or idea. For example, "Banned Book Week" names a week set aside for a particular purpose (unlike phrases such as "last week," "this week," or "next week," which are common terms with no special significance). Note that when a phrase is used instead of a single word to designate a particular person, place, thing, or idea, every word in that phrase begins with a capital letter.

The acronym "BBW" is also in all caps; this is standard practice for an acronym, a particular kind of abbreviation made up of the first letter of each word in a phrase. An acronym is treated as a word on its own.

Proper nouns are capitalized wherever they appear in a sentence. As you read the text, look for other capitalized proper nouns. Analyze why they are proper nouns (they denote a particular month or a particular item on a famous list of items). As you examine them, think of similar examples of each.

4. How does the setting of "Harrison Bergeron" connect to the plot? Which events in the story are influenced by the setting?

5. How are books viewed in the society of your novel's protagonist? How does that society's view of books compare with that of the society in which you live?

6. What sort of books do you think might be banned in Harrison Bergeron's society? Explain.

7. Think about the society in the novel you are reading. Which rules and/or laws do you completely disagree with?

8. Take notes in the following chart to prepare for a collaborative discussion.

State the rule or law (paraphrase or directly quote)	Analyze: Underlying Value	Evaluate: State why you disagree with the rule or law, and then form a thoughtful Level 3 question to spark a meaningful conversation with your peers.
1. page(s): ___		Response: Level 3 Question:
2. page(s): ___		Response: Level 3 Question:
3. page(s): ___		Response: Level 3 Question:

9. Continue to expand your personal vocabulary list in your Reader/Writer Notebook. Use digital and print resources, context, and knowledge of word roots to identify, record, and define at least five new words.

☑ Check Your Understanding

What do you think our country would be like if the government could ban books? State your thesis and give three examples to back it up. Record your answer in your Reader/Writer Notebook.

Introducing the Strategy: Socratic Seminar

A Socratic Seminar is a type of collaborative discussion designed to explore a complex question, topic, or text. Participants engage in meaningful dialogue by summarizing what is said, asking one another questions, making comments, and using textual evidence to support responses. The goal is for participants to arrive at a deeper understanding of a concept or idea by the end of the discussion. A Socratic Seminar is not a debate.

10. You will next participate in a Socratic Seminar. During the seminar, follow these rules for collegial discussions:

- Challenge yourself to build on others' ideas by summarizing those ideas orally before asking questions in response to them. To do this effectively, you will have to listen closely to comprehend and evaluate.

- Make clear transitions between your ideas to maintain coherence throughout the discussion.

- Work to achieve a balance between speaking and listening within a group. Make sure everyone has a chance to speak. Allow quiet time during the discussion so that people have a chance to formulate a thoughtful response.

- Have you heard the expression: "Be a frog, not a hog or a log"? What do you think that means? Set two specific and attainable goals for the discussion:

    Speaking Goal:

    Listening Goal:

ACADEMIC

The word **Socratic** is an adjective formed from the name of the philosopher Socrates, who was famous for using the question-and-answer method in his search for truth and wisdom.

A **seminar** is a term used to describe a small group of students engaged in intensive study.

VOCABULARY

My Notes

Oral Discussion sentence starters:

- I agree with your idea relating to ... , but it is also important to consider ...
- I disagree with your idea about ... , and I would like to point out ...
- You made a point about the concept of ... How are you defining that?
- On page ___, (a specific character) says ... I agree/disagree with this because ...
- On page ___, (a specific character) says ... This is important because ...
- On page ____, we learn ... , so would you please explain your last point about ... ?
- Add your own:

Introducing the Strategy: Fishbowl

Fishbowl is a speaking and listening strategy that divides a large group into an inner and an outer circle. Students in the inner circle model appropriate discussion techniques as they discuss ideas, while students in the outer circle listen to comprehend ideas and evaluate the discussion process. During a discussion, students have the opportunity to experience both circles.

11. Engage in the Socratic Seminar.

- When you are in the *inner* circle, you will need your work relating to rules and laws, a pen or pencil, and the novel.
- When you are in the *outer* circle, you will need a pen or pencil and the note-taking sheet that follows.

12. **Quickwrite:** Reflect on the ideas you discussed during the Socratic Seminar. Then, in the genre of your choice, write to the protagonist of the novel you are reading, explaining your thoughts on his or her society's laws and rules. Before you begin writing, you should consider your topic, purpose, and audience. What genre would be most appropriate? Use a strategy such as creating a t-chart, brainstorming the pros and cons of the genre you are considering, or discussing your ideas with a shoulder partner.

Socratic Seminar Notes
Topic: Rules and Laws in a Utopian/Dystopian Society

Listening to Comprehend

- **Interesting points:**
    1. _____:

    2. _____:

    3. _____:

- **My thoughts:**
    1.

    2.

    3.

Listening to Evaluate

- **Speaking:**
    Strength:

    Challenge:

- **Listening:**
    Strength:

    Challenge:

Reflection

- I <u>did/did not</u> meet my speaking and listening goals.
  Explanation:

- I am most proud of:

- Next time I will:

A Shift in Perspective: Beginning the Adventure

Learning Strategies

Summarizing
Close Reading
Marking the Text
Skimming/Scanning
Rereading
Drafting

VOCABULARY

LITERARY

A **flashback** is an interruption in the sequence of events to relate events that occurred in the past.

Foreshadowing is the use of clues to hint at events that will occur later in the plot.

My Notes

Learning Targets

- Identify how the Departure stage of the Hero's Journey archetype provides a framework for understanding the actions of the protagonist.
- Analyze how an author uses nonlinear plot development.
- Organize coherent writing by using transitions.

Preview

In this activity, you will analyze the protagonist's journey.

Plot Development

When a writer presents the events of a story the way events happen in real life—in time order—it is called linear plot development. Sometimes, though, a writer needs to tell about an event from the past or hint about an event in the future. To share an event that happened at a point in time before the time of the story, a writer uses **flashback**. To hint at a future event, a writer uses **foreshadowing**. The use of such techniques is called nonlinear plot development.

1. Conduct a close read of the assigned passage. How does the author let you know that what you are about to read is a flashback? Make notes in the graphic organizer that follows.

Flashbacks in the Novel	
Signal	**Notes**

2. Reread the passage, but this time identify examples of foreshadowing, and use them to make inferences. Write your evidence and inferences in the following graphic organizer.

Evidence of foreshadowing in the novel	Inference about what is being foreshadowed

3. Both flashback and foreshadowing affect the plot and conflict of the story. With your group, discuss how these techniques help the reader think about the conflict. Compare the plot of the novel to a story that only uses linear plot development.

The Departure

4. What can you infer about the protagonist in this story? Make an inference based on relevant *descriptions* (e.g., appearance, thoughts, feelings), *actions*, and/or *dialogue*. Support your inference with evidence from the text. Follow this format:

Topic Sentence: State an important character trait.

- **Supporting Detail/Evidence:** Provide a transition, lead-in, and specific example that demonstrates the trait.
- **Commentary/Analysis:** Explain how the evidence supports the trait.
- **Commentary/Analysis:** Explain why this character trait is important to the story.

5. In Unit 1, you studied the Hero's Journey archetype. What do you remember about the departure? In the left column, provide a brief summary of the initial steps and their importance.

Stage 1: The Departure

Stage and Definition	Connection to the Story
Step 1: The Call to Adventure	
Step 2: Refusal of the Call	
Step 3: The Beginning of the Adventure	

WORD CONNECTIONS

Roots and Affixes

Sequential is the adjective form of the word *sequence*, which comes from the Latin root *sequi*, meaning "to follow."

Chronological order means "time order," reflecting the origin of the word in *chronos*, a Greek word meaning "time."

6. The protagonist is considered the hero of the story. Readers most often identify with his or her perspective. While you read, use sticky notes to mark text that could reflect the protagonist's Departure. On each note, comment on the connection to the archetype.

7. Continue to expand your personal vocabulary list in your Reader/Writer Notebook. Use digital and print resources, context, and knowledge of word roots to identify, record, and define at least five new words.

8. There are a few things you should remember as you skim/scan the first half of the story and revisit your sticky notes on the Departure.

   • Remember that the Hero's Journey is organized sequentially, in chronological order (although some steps may occur at the same time or not at all). This means that once you connect a step to the story, the next step in the journey must reflect an event that occurs later in the story.

   • Because this task is based on interpretation, there is more than one correct answer. To convince an audience of your interpretation, you must be able to provide a convincing explanation.

   • Go back to The Departure chart, and add connections to the story. Use this information in your response to the prompt that follows.

☑ Focus on the Sentence

In preparation for writing, create an outline of the protagonist's departure in your novel by completing each sentence that follows.

First, the protagonist _____

_____

Then _____

_____

As a result, _____

_____

Next, the protagonist _____

_____

Finally, _____

_____

✍ Writing to Sources: Informational Text

Explain the beginning of the protagonist's journey using the first three steps of the Hero's Journey archetype to guide your explanation. Be sure to:

• Establish a clear controlling idea.

• Develop ideas with relevant and convincing evidence from the text (include at least one direct quotation) and analysis.

• Use appropriate and varied transitions to create coherence and clarify the relationships among ideas (i.e., steps in the Hero's Journey).

Navigating the Road of Trials

Learning Strategies

Close Reading
Rereading
Graphic Organizer
Shared Reading
Marking the Text
Note-taking
Discussion Group

Learning Targets

- Analyze how a character's dialogue influences the events of a narrative.
- Demonstrate how the Initiation stage of the Hero's Journey archetype provides a framework for the protagonist in the class novel.

Preview

In this activity, you will continue to analyze the journey taken by the novel's protagonist.

The Initiation

1. Review the Initiation stage of the Hero's Journey. What do you remember about:

   Step 4. The Road of Trials

   Step 5. The Experience with Unconditional Love

2. In the previous activity, you interpreted the protagonist's Departure. Now begin your interpretation of the next two steps in the protagonist's journey: the Road of Trials and the Experience with Unconditional Love.

   - List three significant trials (conflicts)—in chronological order—that occur *after* the event you identified as Step 3 of the Hero's Journey.
   - If possible, connect the experience with unconditional love to the trial.
   - Analyze how the *trial* and the *experience with unconditional love* affect the protagonist.

My Notes

Trial (focus on conflicts with other characters and society)	Experience with Unconditional Love	Effect (actions; words; thoughts/feelings)
1.		
2.		
3.		

3. Who is the antagonist in the story? How would you describe this character? What does he or she value or believe? What motivates this person and how does this influence events in the novel?

4. Prepare for a small group discussion by continuing to focus on the *trials* and *unconditional love* experienced by the protagonist. Use sticky notes for the following:

   • Mark conflicts reflected in dialogue spoken by other characters and analyze how the dialogue affects the protagonist's perspective on his society, encouraging him to reject their way of life.

   • Mark evidence of *unconditional love* reflected in dialogue spoken by other characters and analyze how the dialogue affects the protagonist's perspective on his society, encouraging him to reject their way of life.

5. Continue to expand your personal vocabulary list in your Reader/Writer Notebook. Use digital and print resources, context, and knowledge of word roots to identify, record, and define at least five new words.

6. Using the notes you have prepared about important dialogue, engage in a small group discussion based on the following prompt.

   Discussion Prompt: Analyze how specific lines of dialogue provoke the protagonist to make the decision to reject his dystopian society.

☑ Check Your Understanding

Quickwrite: Think back over the group discussion about dialogue and conflict that you participated in for question 6. Prepare a brief written summary of the points your group made.

✍ Writing to Sources: Informational Text

In a paragraph, explain how the trials (conflicts) experienced by the main character in your novel and the evidence of unconditional love are representative of the Hero's Journey archetype. Explain how these events develop the theme of the novel. Be sure to:

• Include a topic sentence.
• Use evidence from the novel.
• Show an understanding of the steps of the journey archetype.
• Check your writing for correct subject-verb agreement.

The End of the Journey

Learning Strategies

Discussion Groups
Shared Reading
Close Reading
Note-taking
Drafting

Learning Targets

- Contrast the hero and another character in the novel and consider how their differences convey the author's message in the text.
- Explore the final stage of the Hero's Journey archetype and its portrayal in the novel.
- Analyze the theme of the class novel.

Preview

- In this activity, you will write a reflection of how your protagonist has changed over the course of the novel, citing evidence from the text as support.

My Notes

Characterization Using Appositives

1. Remember that an appositive is a noun or a pronoun that identifies or explains another noun or pronoun. Look at the following examples using the characters from "Harrison Bergeron."
   - Harrison Bergeron, an exceptional individual, was handicapped by society.
   - George, Harrison's father, is forced to wear a little mental handicap radio.
   - Hazel, a person of average intelligence, is not handicapped.

2. Write two sentences, each using an appositive, to describe the protagonist of the novel.

☑ Focus on the Sentence

Try using an appositive to add more information to one of the sentences you wrote about the protagonist, and rewrite it in the space that follows.

Character Transformation

3. Think about the protagonist's Departure into the Hero's Journey (Stage 1) and his *Road of Trials*. How has the character changed as a result of these trials or conflicts? Use the following sentence frame to explain the change. Be sure to provide evidence to support your interpretation.

   In the beginning, the protagonist was _____, but after

   _____, he becomes _____.

4. What do you remember about the *boon* in Stage 2, the Initiation of the Hero's Journey?

   Step 6: The Ultimate Boon:

My Notes

_____
_____
_____
_____
_____
_____
_____
_____
_____

INDEPENDENT READING LINK

Read and Connect

Find information on a person who has experienced a challenge similar to the protagonist in the class novel. What has this person's journey been? How is it similar and different to that of your protagonist? Does this person embody the concept of a "hero?" Why or why not? Write your response in your Reader/Writer Notebook.

LANGUAGE & WRITER'S CRAFT: Active *vs.* Passive Voice

Some sentences have three main parts, a subject, a verb, and an object. In sentences with an object, the verb has a voice. The "voice" shows whether or not the subject performs the action identified by the verb. In a sentence with an *active* voice, the subject performs the action stated by the verb. In a sentence with a *passive* voice, the subject is acted upon by the verb.

In the **active voice**, the *subject* is doing the main action of the sentence:

A news bulletin **interrupted** **the television program**.

The subject, a news bulletin, performs the action of the verb, *to interrupt*. The television program is the object of the verb *interrupted*.

In the **passive voice**, the action is happening to the subject:

The television program **was interrupted for** **a news bulletin**.

The focus of the sentence has shifted to the television program rather than a news bulletin. Notice that the subject and object in the passive sentence changed places. Also notice that the verb *to be* is used.

When you revise your work, look for the subject, verb, and the object in each sentence. Where are they placed? Is the object of the verb's action where the subject should be? Revising your work to the active voice makes your language clearer and more direct.

Example: Look at these passive sentences based on "Harrison Bergeron":

Harrison was taken by H-G men.

A police photograph of Harrison Bergeron was flashed on the screen.

PRACTICE: Rewrite the sentences above in the active voice.

_____

---

5. How do conflicts with society (including characters who believe in the society's way of life) transform the character into a hero? What are the hero's behaviors and motivations that influence these events and the resolution to the conflicts? As you read, take notes in the chart that follows.

Conflict with Society	Heroic Traits Revealed through Conflict	Connection to Theme

6. Continue to expand your personal vocabulary list in your Reader/Writer Notebook. Use digital and print resources, context, and knowledge of word roots to identify, record, and define at least five new words.

7. Interpret the hero's *boon*: What did the hero achieve through this journey?

8. Which characteristics helped the hero to achieve the *boon* or influence the resolution to the conflict? Explain.

Writing Introductory Paragraphs

9. Read and analyze the following samples of introductory paragraphs. Which one would be used to write an essay structured as compare/contrast? Which would introduce an essay based on a different informational organizational structure?

Sample 1

People say that kids are a lot like their parents, but in Kurt Vonnegut's short story "Harrison Bergeron," this is definitely not the case. Harrison Bergeron, the protagonist, and Hazel Bergeron, Harrison's mother, have close to nothing in common. Hazel is completely average and therefore content, while her son is completely superior and therefore rebellious.

Sample 2

A hero must be willing to take risks and have the courage to go against the norm to help others. "Harrison Bergeron" by Kurt Vonnegut is a story of how society holds back its most talented members in search of the supposed ideal of equality. Harrison Bergeron, the protagonist, is a would-be hero who is struck down before he has the opportunity to begin, much less complete, his hero's journey.

☑ Check Your Understanding

In small groups, discuss the trials experienced by the main character in your novel. With your classmates, discuss whether these trials are examples of the Hero's Journey archetype. Use evidence from the novel to support your discussion.

✏ Writing to Sources: Informational Text

Analyze the two prompts that follow. Notice that each prompt requires a different organizational structure. Choose one of the prompts and write a response.

Writing Prompt 1: Think about the protagonist's characteristics, what he achieved, and how he changed by the end of the story. Contrast the protagonist with another character from his society. Be sure to:

- Introduce the topic clearly, establishing a clear controlling idea.
- Provide examples from the text (including at least one direct quotation) and analysis to support your ideas.
- Sequence ideas logically using the appropriate compare/contrast structure.
- Choose the appropriate verb mood for the ideas you want to express.
- Write in active voice unless the passive voice is specifically needed.

Writing Prompt 2: Think about the final stage in the Hero's Journey: the Crossing or Return Threshold. What does the hero learn about life (theme) as a result of the events that take place? Be sure to:

- Introduce the topic clearly, establishing a clear controlling idea.
- Provide examples from the text (including at least one direct quotation) and analysis to support your ideas.
- Sequence ideas logically to explain how the protagonist's transformation connects to what he learns.
- Choose the appropriate verb mood for the ideas you want to express.
- Write in active voice unless the passive voice is specifically needed.

🔒 Independent Reading Checkpoint

As a culminating project for your independent reading, you will share your research about a challenge in society with the class. Complete a RAFT (Role, Audience, Format, Topic) to plan a first draft. Choose a format, or genre that is appropriate for your audience, topic, and purpose. Then, discuss your ideas with a partner. After you have finalized your ideas, create your first draft.

Writing an Informational Essay

 ASSIGNMENT

Think about how writers organize and develop ideas in informational writing. Use an informational organizational structure to communicate your understanding of the concept of dystopia or the concept of the Hero's Journey. Select one of the prompts that follow.

- Write an essay that compares and contrasts life in the dystopian society of the novel you read with our modern-day society.
- Write an essay that explains how the protagonist (hero) changes as a result of conflict with his dystopian society (Road of Trials) and how this change connects to the novel's theme (the Crossing or Return Threshold).

Planning and Prewriting: Take time to plan your essay.	■ Which prompt do you feel better prepared to respond to with examples from literature and real life? ■ What prewriting strategies (such as freewriting or graphic organizers) could help you brainstorm ideas and organize your examples?
Drafting: Write a multi-paragraph essay that effectively organizes your ideas.	■ How will you introduce the topic clearly and establish a controlling idea (thesis)? ■ How will you develop the topic with well-chosen examples and thoughtful analysis (commentary)? ■ How will you logically sequence the ideas using an appropriate structure and transitions? ■ How will your conclusion support your ideas?
Evaluating and Revising the Draft: Create opportunities to review and revise your work.	■ During the process of writing, when can you pause to share and respond with others in order to elicit suggestions and ideas for revision? ■ How can the Scoring Guide help you evaluate how well your draft meets the requirements of the assignment?
Checking and Editing for Publication: Confirm your final draft is ready for publication.	■ How will you proofread and edit your draft to demonstrate command of the conventions of standard English capitalization, punctuation, spelling, grammar, and usage? ■ How did you use TLQC (transition/lead-in/quote/citation) to properly embed quotations? ■ How did you ensure use of the appropriate voice and mood in your writing?

Reflection

After completing this Embedded Assessment, think about how you went about accomplishing this task and respond to the following:

- How has your understanding of utopia and dystopia developed through the reading in this unit?

SCORING GUIDE

Scoring Criteria	Exemplary	Proficient	Emerging	Incomplete
Ideas	The essay • maintains a focused thesis in response to one of the prompts • develops ideas thoroughly with relevant supporting details, facts, and evidence • provides insightful commentary and deep analysis.	The essay • responds to one of the prompts with a clear thesis • develops ideas adequately with supporting details, facts, and evidence • provides sufficient commentary to demonstrate understanding.	The essay • has an unclear or unrelated thesis • develops ideas unevenly or with inadequate supporting details, facts, or evidence • provides insufficient commentary to demonstrate understanding.	The essay • has no obvious thesis • provides minimal supporting details, facts, or evidence • lacks commentary.
Structure	The essay • has an engaging introduction • uses an effective organizational structure for a multi-paragraph essay • uses a variety of transitional strategies to create cohesion and unity among ideas • provides an insightful conclusion.	The essay • has a complete introduction • uses an appropriate organizational structure for a multi-paragraph essay • uses transitional strategies to link or compare and contrast ideas • provides a conclusion that supports the thesis.	The essay • has a weak or partial introduction • uses an inconsistent organizational structure for a multi-paragraph essay • uses transitional strategies ineffectively or inconsistently • provides a weak or unrelated conclusion.	The essay • lacks an introduction • has little or no obvious organizational structure • uses few or no transitional strategies • provides no conclusion.
Use of Language	The essay • conveys a consistent academic voice by using a variety of literary terms and precise language • embeds quotations effectively • demonstrates command of the conventions of standard English capitalization, punctuation, spelling, grammar, and usage (including a variety of syntax).	The essay • conveys an academic voice by using some literary terms and precise language • embeds quotations correctly • demonstrates adequate command of the conventions of standard English capitalization, punctuation, spelling, grammar, and usage (including a variety of syntax).	The essay • uses insufficient language and vocabulary to convey an academic voice • embeds quotations incorrectly or unevenly • demonstrates partial or inconsistent command of the conventions of standard English capitalization, punctuation, spelling, grammar, and usage.	The essay • uses limited or vague language • lacks quotations • lacks command of the conventions of standard English capitalization, punctuation, spelling, grammar, and usage; frequent errors obscure meaning.

Unpacking Embedded Assessment 2

Learning Targets

- Review vocabulary, using a dictionary to improve understanding of difficult terms.
- Review the assessment and scoring guide and paraphrase the expectations.

Preview

In this activity, you will begin to explore the skills and knowledge necessary to write an effective argumentative essay.

Making Connections

It can be said that writers of fiction, especially dystopian novels, are trying to make a point or criticize some aspect of society. In this part of the unit, you will think about how you can have an impact by creating a well-reasoned argument about a social issue important to you.

Essential Questions

Reflect on your understanding of Essential Question 1: To what extent can a perfect or ideal society exist? Then respond to Essential Question 2, which will be the focus of the rest of the unit: What makes an argument effective?

Developing Vocabulary

Re-sort the Academic and Literary Vocabulary using the QHT strategy. Use a dictionary to look up any words still in the Q column. Review their definitions. Choose one word from the list and write a concise statement about how your understanding of this term has improved.

Unpacking Embedded Assessment 2

Closely read the Embedded Assessment 2 assignment.

Write an argumentative essay in which you convince an audience to support your claim about a debatable idea. Use your research and experience or observations to support your argument.

Now consult the Scoring Guide and work with your class to paraphrase the expectations. Create a graphic organizer to use as a visual reminder of the required concepts and skills.

After each activity, use this graphic organizer to guide reflection about what you have learned and what you still need to learn in order to be successful in completing the Embedded Assessment.

My Notes

INDEPENDENT READING LINK

Reading Plan

While creating an argumentative essay, you will have the opportunity to read texts on your own. Choose argumentative texts, including speeches and essays, to inspire your writing. Use the Resources section of your book, your Reading Lists and Logs, and your teacher to help you select appropriate texts. As a class, brainstorm and share recommendations. Record your choices on the My Independent Reading List.

Understanding Elements of Argumentation

Learning Strategies

Marking the Text
Graphic Organizer

VOCABULARY

ACADEMIC

An **argument** is a logical appeal, supported by reasons and evidence, to persuade an audience to take an action or agree with a point of view.

Learning Targets

- Explore the genre of argumentative writing.
- Understand the parts of an argumentative essay.

Preview

In this activity, you will read and analyze part of an eighth-grader's written argument.

Looking Ahead to Argumentative Writing

Based on your current understanding, how are informational and argumentative writing similar? How are they different?

Similarities:

Differences:

Main Parts of an Argument

People convince skeptical people to change their opinions every day. You observe this in politics and in school—even at home. Do certain people simply have a way with words, or is there a strategy to help you become more persuasive? To begin building your powers of persuasion, study the four main components in an argumentative essay.

Parts of an Argument	Explanation	Helpful Questions
Claims	• offer solutions to problems • try to convince a reader to change his thoughts or actions related to a problem • based on reasons	What do you think about this problem?
Reasoning	• logical grounds that show that your claim is important • link between the claim and evidence	Why do you believe this?
Evidence	• data or facts that support your claim	How do you know your idea is right?
Counterclaims	• an alternate point of view that challenges your claim	What other solutions to the problem are possible?

Setting a Purpose for Reading

- As you read, annotate the text using four colors of highlighters to identify claims, evidence, reasoning, and counterclaims.
- Jot down questions you have about the essay in the My Notes section.
- Circle unknown words and phrases. Try to determine the meaning of the words by using context clues, word parts, or a dictionary.

Essay

Private Eyes

by **Brooke Chorlton (an eighth-grader from Washington State)**

1 "Private eyes, they're watching you, they see your every move," sang the band Hall and Oates in their 80s hit "Private Eyes." A popular song three decades ago is quite relevant to life today. We do not live very private lives, mainly due to the Internet, whose sole purpose is to help people share everything. But there are still boundaries to what we have to share. Employers should not require access to the Facebook pages of potential or current employees because Facebook is intended to be private, is not intended to be work-related, and employers do not need this medium to make a good hiring decision.

2 It is true that the Internet is not private, and it is also true that Facebook was not created to keep secrets; it is meant for people to share their life with the selected people they choose as their "friends." However, Facebook still has boundaries or some limits, so that members can choose what to share. As a fourteen-year-old girl I know for a fact, because I have seen it, that when you are setting up your Facebook account, you are able to choose the level of security on your page. Some choose to have no security; if someone on Facebook were to search them, they would be able to see all of their friends, photos, and posts. And, according to *Seattle Times* journalists Manuel Valdes and Shannon McFarland, "It has become common for managers to review publically available Facebook Profiles." The key words are "publically available." The owners of these profiles have chosen to have no boundaries, so it is not as big a deal if an employer were to look at a page like this. But others choose to not let the rest of the world in; if you search them, all that would come up would be their name and profile picture. That is all: just a name and a picture. Only the few selected to be that person's friends are allowed into their online world, while the strangers and stalkers are left out in the cold. It is not likely that you would walk up to a stranger and share what you did that weekend. Orin Kerr, a George Washington University law professor and former federal **prosecutor**, states that requiring someone's password to their profile is, "**akin** to requiring [their] house keys." If we expect privacy in our real world life, shouldn't we be able to have privacy in our online life as well?

prosecutor: a person who institutes legal proceedings against someone
akin: similar

Working from the Text

1. As you reread the essay, use four different colored highlighters to identify the parts of the writer's argument. Mark the writer's claim with the first color, reasons with the second color, evidence with the third color, and counterclaim with the fourth color. Then turn to a partner and take turns explaining each element of the argument.

2. Based on your highlighted information and your rereading, what is the writer's purpose? Why does the writer end the essay with a question?

3. Who is the writer's audience? Use textual evidence to support your answer.

4. Discuss whether or not the writer's claim is believable. Which reasons and evidence are the most compelling? Was the counterclaim more believable than the claim? Explain your answer.

Beginning to Construct an Argument

5. Think of a technology-related topic that has two sides that can be argued. Decide which side of the issue you want to argue. Brainstorm possible topics and claims.

   Topics:

   _____

   _____

   _____

   _____

   Claims:

   _____

   _____

   _____

   _____

   _____

   _____

   _____

Refining Your Claim

☐ Choose one of the claims from your brainstorm that is most appealing to you. Then confirm that you agree with your claim by asking yourself, "What do I believe about this issue or problem?"

☐ Ask yourself, "Why do I believe this?" Explain your reasoning. If you struggle to come up with a reason, revisit your claim and be sure this is the position you want to take.

☐ When you have at least three solid reasons, ask yourself, "How do I know this idea is right?"

☐ Consider possible counterclaims. Ask yourself, "What other solutions are possible?" Think about these alternatives and how someone else might defend them.

☐ If your claim is strongly supported, you are ready for peer-editing. If not, revise your claim and repeat the above steps.

Peer-Editing

Switch papers with your designated partner. As you read your partner's claim and supporting information, consider the following questions and share your answers:

- Does the claim take a strong and clear position?
- Do the reasons support the claim?
- Which reasons are strong? Which reasons need more development?

Consider the advice from your peer to help you revise your claim and reasoning.

 Gaining Perspectives

Since the invention of the Internet, the way people interact with each other has changed. As you just read in the essay "Private Eyes," it is more difficult to keep your life private, even if you have the proper security settings. With a partner, discuss how social media can cause problems at school and in your community. Then think about what other things beside social media can cause conflicts between you and your classmates. Record your ideas in a two-column chart with these headings: "Problems Caused by Social Media" and "Problems Caused by Other Things." Then use the chart to summarize your discussion in your Reader/ Writer Notebook. As a final step, work with your partner to come up with a solution for one of the problems in your chart. Present your idea orally to another pair of students in your class.

☑ Check Your Understanding

Now that you have revised your claims, share them orally in small groups or with the whole class. As you present your ideas, be sure to make eye contact and maintain adequate volume and clear pronunciation so that you communicate your ideas effectively.

Learning Targets

- Plan both sides of a debate using rhetorical appeals.
- Use anecdote, illustration, or analogy to support a claim.

Preview

In this activity, you will learn about rhetorical appeals and how they can strengthen an argumentative essay.

VOCABULARY

ACADEMIC

Illustration explains how your solution or point of view will result in something good for the audience.

An **analogy** is a comparison between two things, typically for the purpose of explanation or clarification.

An **anecdote** is a short narrative of an interesting, amusing, or biographical incident.

A **debate** is an informal or formal discussion in which opposing arguments are put forward. A debate usually focuses on a debatable or controversial issue.

📖 INDEPENDENT READING LINK

Read and Discuss

Choose one essay or speech from your Independent Reading List that contains a compelling claim or argument. What makes the claim or argument effective? Share your ideas with a partner. Compare your examples, compiling a list of similarities, including strategies they both use to build a strong argument. As a class, build a detailed list of ways an author creates a compelling claim. Document your response in your Reader/Writer Notebook.

Rhetorical Appeals

1. Rhetorical appeals are an important part of creating a convincing and persuasive argument. Read the definitions that follow to understand how writers or speakers use each type of appeal. Included are some examples of rhetorical devices that fall under each category of rhetorical appeals.

Appeal	Meaning
Logos	• an appeal to reason; providing logical reasoning and evidence in the form of description, narration, and/or exposition • **illustration** (example or story that helps explain or justify a point) • **analogy** (uses a more familiar concept to help explain an unfamiliar one)
Pathos	• an appeal to emotions; using descriptive, connotative, and figurative language for effect; providing an emotional **anecdote**; or developing tone
Ethos	• an appeal based on trust or character; demonstrating that you understand the audience's point of view; making the audience believe that you are knowledgeable and trustworthy; showing that you have researched your topic by supporting reasons with appropriate, logical evidence and reasoning

2. Create a visual of each type of appeal to help you remember its definition.

Introducing the Strategy: Debate

The purpose of a **debate** is to provide an opportunity to collect and orally present evidence supporting the affirmative and negative arguments of a proposition or issue. During a debate, participants follow a specific order of events and often have a time limit for making their points. Participants need to advocate their position using rhetorical appeals, like the ones listed above, while employing eye contact, speaking rate, volume, enunciation, a variety of natural gestures, and conventions of language to communicate their ideas effectively. Listen to your teacher as he or she explains each of these elements of good oral communication.

Preparing to Debate

A debate provides an opportunity to practice creating a reasoned argument and to identify and use appeals when trying to convince others of your point of view. You will engage in a debate on a topic from the article that follows.

3. Read and respond to the following news article, first by circling any words you don't know that you think are important, and next by deciding whether you are for or against the legislation.

Article

Representative Urges Action on the Media

In order to combat what he calls the dangerous increases in teens' harmful media habits, Representative Mark Jenkins has recently introduced legislation that would make it a crime for anyone under the age of 18 to engage with more than two hours of media a day on the weekdays and three hours a day on the weekends. The bill defines "media" as television, radio, commercial magazines, non-school related Internet and any blogs or podcasts with advertising. Penalties for violation can range from forfeiture of driver's licenses and media counseling to fines for parents or removal of media tools (TVs, computers, phones, etc.). Monitoring systems will be set up in each Congressional district through the offices of Homeland Security and the National Security Agency. Rep. Jenkins could not be reached for comment because he was appearing on television.

4. Read the debate prompt (always posed as an interrogative sentence).

   Debate: Should the government restrict media usage for anyone under the age of 18 to two hours a day on weekdays and three hours a day on weekends?

5. Use the following tables to plan arguments for both sides of the issue. Consider valid reasons for and against the debate topic, find evidence in support of the arguments, and brainstorm various rhetorical appeals to help persuade the audience. Try to use at least one anecdote, illustration, and analogy. During the debate, you will use these notes to argue your side of the issue.

YES, the government should restrict media usage because:		
Reason 1:	Evidence:	Appeals:
Reason 2:	Evidence:	Appeals:

NO, the government should not restrict media usage because:		
Reason 1:	Evidence:	Appeals:
Reason 2:	Evidence:	Appeals:

Engaging in a Debate

6. When it is your turn to speak, engage in the debate and be sure to reflect on and adjust your statements as your classmates present their arguments. Be able to argue either claim. Keep in mind the elements of argument and the different types of appeals. Be sure to use appropriate eye contact, speaking rate, volume, enunciation, a variety of natural gestures, conventions of language, and a clear voice when speaking in a debate. Use the following sentence starters as support during the debate:

   - I agree with your point about ... , but it is also important to consider ...
   - I disagree with your point about ... , and I would I like to counter with the idea that ...
   - You made a good point about ... , but have you considered ...
   - Your point about ... is an appeal to emotions, and so it is not a logical reason/explanation. Evidence shows ...

7. When it is your turn to listen, evaluate others' arguments for their use of rhetorical appeals. Record notes in the following chart as you identify examples of effective and ineffective appeals and the rhetorical devices used. Then provide a brief explanation for each example.

Use of Rhetorical Appeals	Explain and Evaluate

8. After the debate, reflect on the ideas you shared and the ideas you heard from your classmates. How would you adjust your initial response to the debate prompt now that you have heard new evidence?

☑ Check Your Understanding

Prepare for discussion by answering these questions in your Reader/Writer Notebook: What types of rhetorical appeals provided the most effective support for the topic during the debate? What, if any, appeals were convincing enough to make you change your mind about the issue? Explain your answers.

9. Review your claims from the previous lesson and identify whether or not you used any *logos*, *pathos*, or *ethos* appeals to support your claims. If you did, label them; if you did not, add at least one of these appeals to your argument. As a class, share your findings. Discuss how *logos*, *pathos*, and *ethos* can strengthen your claims.

Learning Strategies

Marking the Text
Close Reading
Rereading

Learning Targets

- Identify and analyze parts of arguments, including counterarguments.
- Determine the intended audience in two texts.
- Integrate ideas from multiple texts to build knowledge and vocabulary about self-driving cars.

Preview

In this activity, you will read and analyze two texts that take different sides on an issue.

Setting a Purpose for Reading

- As you read, annotate the text using four colors of highlighters to identify claims, evidence, reasoning, and counterclaims.
- Circle unknown words and phrases. Try to determine the meaning of the words by using context clues, word parts, or a dictionary.

About the Author

Edward Humes is a Pulitzer Prize-winning journalist and author of over a dozen books. As a reporter, Humes pursued complex stories that other writers ignored or overlooked. This led him to a career writing nonfiction books and introducing his readers to the surprising aspects of ordinary places such as juvenile court and landfills.

Essay

The Promise of a Post-Driver Life

In this third in a series of opinion essays by thought leaders, a Pulitzer Prize–winning author forecasts the future of transportation

by **Edward Humes**

1   What would surprise you most about your morning commute if you woke up to find yourself beamed 80 years into the future? Self-driving cars would be a good guess—but no. **Autonomous** transport will be **ubiquitous** by the 2040s, if not sooner. Shared fleets of driverless, personal transit will be unremarkable by 2096. The future shock in 80 years will be the end of everything we hate most about car society today: parking, traffic jams, and motor death itself.

2   A leading killer of Americans under the age of 35—vehicle crashes—will have become less common in 2096 than death by a lightning strike.

> **INDEPENDENT READING LINK**
>
> **Knowledge Question:**
> How are humans the biggest flaw behind self-driving cars?
>
> Across Activities 2.13, 2.15, and 2.16, you will read an essay, an editorial, and two articles about self-driving cars. While you read and build knowledge about the topic, think about your answer to the Knowledge Question.

> **autonomous:** without the help of humans
> **ubiquitous:** everywhere at once

My Notes

3 The long fight by Consumer Reports and others against unsafe cars has been invaluable, but only the rise of truly autonomous cars will finally address the most deadly and enduring design flaw in our vehicles: the human behind the wheel. And that shift, seemingly radical today but utterly commonsense tomorrow, can transform for the better our cities, our economy, our environment, and our way of life.

4 If we play our cards right.

5 It's easy to forget that, 80 years ago, cars lacked even the most basic safety measures. It took many decades before cars had seat belts, laminated safety glass, airbags, crumple zones, and child safety seats that actually work.

6 While safety technology has made many crashes more survivable and prevented some others, it can't truly overcome bad driving. And make no mistake: Bad driving is the primary cause of fatal car crashes, most of which are the result of driving too drunk, too fast, or too distracted.

7 The phrase "car crash" is a pointed choice here. The everyday term "car accident" is a lie we tell ourselves as almost all crashes result from avoidable acts of negligence, recklessness, foolishness, or law breaking. In the 1920s, these were rightly called "motor killings." Today's **euphemism** of "accidents" allows us to pretend that the toll of bad driving is the unavoidable cost of modern mobility. And so we **avert** our gaze from the carnage on U.S. roads: an estimated 38,300 deaths and 4.4 million serious injuries in 2015 alone …

8 The encouraging news is that recent trends in auto safety aren't just about shielding us during crashes—which is critical and saves lives—but about endeavoring to prevent disaster in the first place. This evolution began with antilock brakes and electronic stability control in the '80s and '90s, and continues today with collision-avoidance systems that can commandeer the brakes when sensors perceive a crash is **imminent**.

9 The way forward is clear: We need a **concerted** effort to add more layers of carefully tested and validated autonomy to cars, ultimately pushing human drivers out of the loop.

10 Cruise-control tech already in most cars—a **primitive** form of autonomy—could be repurposed to prevent drivers from exceeding posted speed limits. (Not to mention that speed limits are too high to begin with. We allow cars to do 40 mph where pedestrians are present, knowing this may kill almost half the people struck at this speed. At 20 mph, pedestrian fatalities fall to 7 percent.)

11 Blood alcohol touch sensors currently in the prototype stage could end drunken driving for good by shutting off the car and automatically summoning a ride-share.

euphemism: the substitution of a mild word for a harsh one
avert: to turn away
imminent: about to happen
concerted: planned together by agreement
primitive: first or earliest

My Notes

12 And smartphones—a leading factor in distracted driving—can be forced by an even smarter car into voice-command-only status. Countless lives and many millions in medical and insurance costs could be saved with these simple advances …

13 Here's what 2096 could look like if the promise is nurtured into reality, along with a few other key advances that will transform transportation.

Cities Will Be Remade

14 Because driverless cars can move bumper to bumper safely in much skinnier lanes with no traffic jams, new urban cores can devote 40 to 60 percent of space previously used for street and parking **infrastructure** to public and open space. And because these will be shared electric fleets rather than individually owned gas burners, air quality will improve while fossil-fuel dependence wanes.

Mass Transit Will Be Transformed

15 Bus-sized robot coaches can also platoon bumper to bumper—forming de facto trains—then peel off for various stops to suit passengers. Country, suburb, and city can be seamlessly linked. Driving alone in a car for a long distance will be viewed as a shockingly wasteful historical absurdity.

People Will Become Healthier

16 Repurposed streets and shared fleets will de-emphasize car culture, and encourage walking and biking for short trips. This could result in a triumph over obesity and heart disease as Americans embrace exercise as a natural part of everyday life.

The Movement of Goods Will Be Revolutionized

17 Advanced 3D printing will make a great deal of shipping and global trade **obsolete** as manufacturing will become a local activity. Consumers will buy a product design online, then it will be "printed" at the neighborhood 3D shop for pickup. Meanwhile, giant solar airships and airliner-sized drones will move other cargo across the globe.

Going to Work May Become a Perk

18 Augmented reality, digital commuting, and virtual meetings will make daily commuting an option, not a requirement. But face-to-face brainstorming, camaraderie with peers, and the need for human connection will keep many of us commuting. And why not? In a world with personal rapid transit, walkable and bikeable streets, and no traffic jams, there'll be nothing to dread about rush hour.

⊘ Knowledge Quest

- What details in the article surprised you?
- What additional questions do you have about self-driving cars?

infrastructure: basic framework of a system
obsolete: no longer used

Returning to the Text

- Return to the text as you respond to the following questions. Use text evidence to support your responses.
- Write any additional questions you have about the essay in your Reader/Writer Notebook.

1. Which text features were the most effective in helping you understand the article?

_____

_____

_____

_____

2. Why does the author begin the essay with a rhetorical question? Explain its purpose.

_____

_____

_____

_____

3. Reread paragraph 3. Explain the metaphor of a "design flaw." What does it mean, and why does he say it?

_____

_____

_____

_____

4. In paragraph 7, the author states that calling a car crash an "accident" is a euphemism. What point is he making? How does this statement set a tone for his argument?

_____

_____

_____

_____

5. What is the purpose of the bold headings in the last five paragraphs of the article?

_____

_____

_____

_____

6. Which of the author's appeals made the greatest impact on you? Explain how it supported the author's claim.

_____

_____

_____

_____

7. KQ In paragraph 11, what can you infer about the meaning of the word *prototype* based on its context?

_____

_____

8. KQ How does the author's use of the metaphor "design flaw" point to a larger irony about self-driving cars?

_____

_____

Working from the Text

9. Now that you have read and analyzed the essay, complete the chart that follows. Restate the author's claim in your own words. Then add three pieces of evidence or appeals and the specific rhetorical devices used from the text. Compare your chart with a partner's and then work together to create a counterclaim. Think about what someone would say if she or he believed autonomous cars were dangerous or unrealistic. Be sure to consider your audience as you build your counterclaim. Take turns with your partner debating these claims.

Claim		
Evidence or Appeal 1	**Evidence or Appeal 2**	**Evidence or Appeal 3**

My Notes

- As you read, annotate the text using four colors of highlighters to identify claims, evidence, reasoning, and counterclaims.
- Circle unknown words and phrases. Try to determine the meaning of the words by using context clues, word parts, or a dictionary.

About the Author

The Times Editorial Board is comprised of 10 members from different backgrounds who speak for the *Los Angeles Times*. They produce editorials, articles that express the newspaper's viewpoint on various issues. Every week they meet as a team, sharing ideas, debating their virtues, dissecting flaws, and finalizing the topics they will pursue. A group consensus determines the editorials they produce.

Editorial

It's Time to Tap the Brakes on Self-Driving Cars

by **The Times Editorial Board**

1 Carmakers and tech companies are in a race to put autonomous vehicles on the road, and it's time for **regulators** to tap the brakes.

2 This month the National Highway Traffic Safety Administration revealed that it is investigating two crashes involving Tesla vehicles allegedly operating on autopilot. Tesla's autopilot feature is a semi-autonomous system that uses cameras, radar and sensors to steer the car, change lanes, adjust speed and even find a parking space and parallel park. It's not supposed to turn a Tesla sedan into a self-driving car, but there's **ample** evidence on YouTube of people driving with their hands off the steering wheel, playing games and even climbing into the back seat while their car is hurtling down a freeway.

3 In May, a driver died in Florida when his Tesla Model S sedan on autopilot slammed into a tractor-trailer that had turned across the road in front of him ... Tesla said that neither the autopilot nor the driver noticed the white side of the tractor trailer against a brightly lighted sky, and so the brake was not applied. The second accident happened when a Tesla sport utility vehicle hit a guardrail on the Pennsylvania Turnpike, crossed traffic and rolled over. The driver told state police that he was in autopilot mode; the cause is still under investigation.

4 Although Tesla has been far more aggressive than its rivals in making cutting-edge driverless technology readily available to its customers, other automakers aren't far behind in rolling out advanced "driver assist" systems. Yet there are still no rules governing the use of this sort of technology—

 KNOWLEDGE QUEST

Knowledge Question:

How are humans the biggest flaw behind self-driving cars?

---

regulators: people who control requirements

ample: more than enough

whether partially autonomous, like autopilot, or fully self-driving, like Google's steering-wheel-less prototype. And at this point, there are no standardized tests the cars are required to pass before regular folks take them on the road. Who gets to decide when an autonomous car is ready for the public? Current policies let the car's manufacturer make that call, restrained only by the fear of liability.

5   Regulators must intervene. The technology is already being deployed, and it's time to set standards for when an autonomous-driving feature has been tested enough and is considered safe enough for widespread use. Public roads shouldn't be uncontrolled laboratories for vehicle safety experiments.

6   But this is no easy job. There is immense pressure from driverless-car supporters and safety advocates to get more autonomous technology on the road as soon as possible because, at the end of the day, self-driving cars will probably be much safer than cars driven by erratic, distracted humans. (More than 90% of crashes are caused by human error.) Transportation safety regulators, as well as manufacturers, have to figure out how to do more real-world, independently verified stress-testing to hone the technology without people dying in the process. If that means slowing the rush to roll out driverless cars, that's OK.

7   This month, NHTSA is supposed to release guidelines to manufacturers for the safe operation of fully autonomous vehicles. The agency has said rigorous testing and ample data on performance are necessary, but the agency's guidelines are expected to be suggestions, not mandates, because NHTSA needs the flexibility to respond to a rapidly evolving industry. Until the federal government sets testing and performance standards for driverless technology, states will be left to come up with their own policies on when and how to allow autonomous vehicles, potentially resulting in a patchwork of laws that confuses consumers and confounds carmakers.

8   California lawmakers directed the state in 2012 to develop rules to allow the testing and eventual use of driverless cars, but because of the issue's complexity and the shortage of precedents, the state is already a year and a half behind schedule. Draft regulations issued late last year sounded logical at the time—because autonomous vehicles are still so new, the state would require licensed drivers to stay behind the wheel, ready to take over if the system failed. The problem, as the fatal Tesla autopilot crash demonstrates, is that drivers are not a reliable backup. They learn to trust the car, perhaps too quickly and too much; they let their guard down and may not be prepared to act in a split second to prevent a crash. California ought to reconsider whether requiring a driver behind the wheel makes an autonomous vehicle safe enough for the public roadways.

My Notes

_____

intervene: come between people who disagree

immense: huge

hone: improve or perfect

mandates: orders

precedents: decisions that serve as an example or standard liability; a legal responsibility

- What groups of people are mentioned in the article?
- What events and details in the article stood out to you?

Returning to the Text

- Return to the text as you respond to the following questions. Use text evidence to support your responses.
- Write any additional questions you have about the editorial in your Reader/Writer Notebook.

10. In the first paragraph, how does the author use figurative language to make a claim?

_____

_____

_____

11. Explain one way that the author supports the claim.

_____

_____

_____

_____

12. In paragraph 5, the author states, "Public roads shouldn't be uncontrolled laboratories for vehicle safety experiments." What kind of appeal is the author using? Explain your answer.

_____

_____

_____

_____

13. **KQ** How does the word *regulators* in paragraph 5 help you to understand the importance of their job?

_____

_____

_____

_____

14. Explain the counterclaim stated in paragraph 6 and how it is addressed.

_____

_____

_____

_____

15. Compare both texts on autonomous vehicles. What details might both authors agree on? Explain your answer.

_____

_____

_____

_____

16. KQ Based on the last two texts you've read, what is the main reason why it takes self-driving safety regulators so much time to craft sufficient regulations?

_____

_____

_____

_____

Working from the Text

17. Now that you have read and analyzed the editorial, complete the chart that follows. Restate the author's claim in your own words. Then add three pieces of evidence or appeals and the specific rhetorical devices used from the text.

Claim		
Evidence or Appeal 1	**Evidence or Appeal 2**	Evidence or Appeal 3

Gaining Perspectives

You have just read about the leading cause of death in people under the age of 35 is vehicle crashes. With a partner, discuss what types of behaviors in drivers and their passengers would lead to an accident that are not mentioned in the article. Then think of solutions other than driverless cars that might lower the number of crashes. Record ideas in a 2-column chart. When you are finished, write about your conclusions in your Reader/Writer Notebook.

Write a Review

18. Time to put your evaluative skills to the test. In the same way that people write book or movie reviews, you will write a review of an argument. Choose one of the arguments on self-driving cars. Then analyze each of the elements listed in the chart that follows. After you complete your chart, evaluate the argument by explaining which elements were effective and which were not. When you write your review, be sure to include an evaluation of the way the author handles audience, claims, counterclaims, and appeals. Then share and discuss your review with a peer.

Audience

Who is the intended audience? How do you know?

Claims and Counterclaims

What is the main argument? What opposing argument does the author include?

Appeals

Which types of appeals and rhetorical devices are used? Provide examples.

WORD CONNECTIONS

Multiple Meaning Word

When you hear the word sound, you probably think of noise, but *sound* has many meanings. It can mean free from error, showing good judgment, or being logically valid, such as in "sound advice" or a "sound argument." A "sound heart" is one free from defects, and a "sound sleep" describes sleep that was deep and undisturbed.

What Is Sound Reasoning?

Sound reasoning stems from a valid argument whose conclusion follows from its premises. A **premise** is a statement upon which an argument is based or from which a conclusion is drawn. In other words, a premise is an assumption that something is true.

For example, consider this argument:
Premise: A implies B;
Premise: B implies C;
Conclusion: Therefore, A implies C.

Although we do not know what statements A, B, and C represent, we are still able to judge the argument as valid. We call an argument "sound" if the argument is valid *and* all the statements, including the conclusion, are true.

This structure of **two premises** and **one conclusion** forms the basic argumentative structure. Aristotle held that any logical argument could be reduced to two premises and a conclusion.

Premises: If Socrates is a man, and all men are mortal,

Conclusion: then Socrates is mortal.

A logical fallacy is an error in reasoning that makes an argument invalid or unsound. A logical fallacy can be used in an argument by accident or for the purpose of misleading the audience. Common fallacies include:

- claiming too much
- oversimplifying a complex issue
- supporting an argument with abstract generalizations
- false assumptions
- bandwagon appeals
- circular reasoning
- incorrect premises

Example: *We need to pass a law that stupid people cannot get a driver's license*. This statement incorrectly equates driving skills with intelligence.

Avoid logical fallacies by being sure you present relevant evidence and logical and sound reasoning—the cornerstones of effective argumentation.

19. Examine this statement. Is it valid and sound? Explain why or why not.

    Premises: If texting is distracting, and distracted driving can result in an accident,

    Conclusion: then texting can result in an accident.

20. Using your understanding of sound reasoning, go back to each of the two texts on self-driving vehicles. Study the arguments of each author, paying close attention to the premises. Note and explain the purpose of any logical fallacies or faulty reasoning. Has your confidence in the authors changed? Why or why not?

📝 Writing to Sources: Argument

Now that you have evaluated both arguments for sound or faulty reasoning including logical fallacies, select one of them to challenge. After selecting an argument, choose one quote from the text to support your challenge. Use the TLQC format you learned in Unit 1 (Activity 1.15) to state the importance of the evidence. Be sure to:

- Use the TLQC format for introducing quoted material.
- Write in the active voice.
- Use quotation marks around direct quotes.
- Use ellipses when necessary to show that words have been left out.

Take turns presenting. Then discuss how sound or faulty reasoning and the use of logical fallacies impacts your opinion of the author as well as your attitude toward his or her claims.

Learning Targets

- Identify the components of a debatable claim.
- Use valid reasons and evidence to support a debatable claim.

Preview

In this activity, you will write and support a debatable claim.

VOCABULARY

ACADEMIC
A controversial topic is a topic that can be debated. A controversy occurs when there are two sides that disagree with each other.

Debatable and Non-Debatable Claims

You have already brainstormed topics and possible claims. It may seem obvious, but it is important to be sure your topic and claim are debatable.

- If a claim is **debatable**, it is controversial; that is, two logical people might disagree based on evidence and reasoning used to support the claim. Example: *Self-driving cars present a danger on roadways.*

- If a claim is **non-debatable**, it is a fact; therefore, it cannot be argued. Example: *Self-driving cars are already on the road in many locations.* This could be an informational topic, but is not suitable for argument.

1. Summarize the difference between a debatable and a non-debatable claim while maintaining the meaning of the concepts.

2. Write one debatable and one non-debatable claim relating to each topic that follows.

   Topic: the amount of time teens spend using technology

   - Debatable:

   - Non-debatable:

   Topic: the age at which someone should have a social media account

   - Debatable:

   - Non-debatable:

INDEPENDENT READING LINK

Read and Discuss

Think about the topic of your nonfiction independent reading book. Write a debatable claim based on the information from the book. Share your claim with a partner and have them confirm that your claim is debatable. Provide evidence to support your claim and confirm with your partner that your evidence supports your claim. Then share your responses orally with the class.

Forming and Supporting a Debatable Claim

3. Use the following steps to form and support a debatable claim for the topic you chose in Activity 2.11.

Step 1: Write a debatable claim for each side of an issue relating to the topic.

Topic: _____

Side 1	**Side 2**
Claim:	Claim:

Step 2: Highlight the claim you will support.

Step 3: Freewrite: Answer the following questions in your Reader/Writer Notebook. How can you support the claim you chose? How much logical reasoning can you use? Will you depend on pathos? How can you support your claim with evidence and sound reasoning?

Step 4: Identify and analyze your **audience**. Who would support the other side? Be specific! Consider the kind of information, language, and overall approach that will appeal to your audience. Ask yourself the following questions:

- What does the audience know about this topic (through personal experience, research, etc.)?
- What does the audience value related to this topic?
- How might the audience disagree with me? What objections will the audience want me to address or answer?
- How can I best use *logos* to appeal to and convince this audience?
- How will I use language to show that I am worth listening to on this subject?

Step 5: Now that you better understand your audience, plan to address at least two counterclaims by identifying potential weaknesses of your argument within opposing reasons, facts, or testimony. Use this format:

My audience might argue_____, so I will counter by arguing or pointing out that _____.

☑ Check Your Understanding

Quickwrite: Why is it necessary to identify your audience as precisely and accurately as possible before you draft your argument? What might go wrong if you do not have a strong sense of who the audience is?

Learning Strategies

Skimming/Scanning
Close Reading
Marking the Text
Note-taking

VOCABULARY

ACADEMIC

Research (*v.*) means locating information from a variety of sources.

Research (*n.*) is the information found from investigated sources.

My Notes

Learning Targets

- Create a model research plan before reading.
- Write a list of research questions and update them after reading.
- Evaluate sources for reliability, credibility, and bias.
- Integrate ideas from multiple texts to build knowledge and vocabulary about self-driving cars.

Preview

In this activity, you will go through the process of creating a model research plan.

Developing a Research Plan

1. Once you have chosen your topic, created a claim, and considered possible counterclaims, you are ready to conduct a more extensive process of gathering information to support your own ideas. This process is called a **research** plan and without making one, you could waste hours on information that proves to be of little value. A strong research plan includes five components. Brainstorm the steps in the research process and discuss with classmates. Put the steps in order and share.

Writing Research Questions

2. An effective research question is open-ended, directly related to a claim, and purposeful, meaning that the answer will be used to support the argument. Use your topic to generate a central research question. Then break your main question into a subset of related questions.

Main research question:

Sub-questions:

Locating and Evaluating Sources

Many people rely on the Internet for their research, because it is often more convenient and efficient than searching through paper books. To find relevant information on the Internet, use effective search terms to begin your research. Try to choose terms that narrow your results. For example, searching on the term "cars" will return broad information, whereas searching "self-driving cars" will return results more closely in line with that topic.

The Internet contains a lot of useful information, but it also has a great deal of information that is unreliable, biased, or lacking in credibility. You must carefully examine websites to avoid trusting sites that contain unreliable information from unknown sources. Faulty information and unreliable sources can undermine the validity of your argument.

3. You can evaluate both print and Internet sources using six separate criteria, including authority, accuracy, credibility, reliability, timeliness, and purpose/audience. Use a dictionary or work with your classmates and teacher to define each term in the graphic organizer that follows. Then review questions that you can ask yourself when evaluating sources based on each criterion.

Source Criteria	Definition	Questions to Consider
1. Authority		Who is the audience? What organization is behind this information? What are the qualifications of the author or organization to write about this topic?
2. Accuracy		Determine if the content of the source is fact, opinion, or propaganda. If you think the source is offering facts, are the sources clearly indicated? Is any information omitted from the source?
3. Credibility		Is the information trustworthy? Does it show any biases for or against the topic, including the omission of relevant details? Is the source using faulty reasoning such as bandwagon appeals, repetition, or loaded language?
4. Reliability		Can you verify the information presented? Are there other sources that contradict or confirm the source? Is information omitted?
5. Timeliness		How old is the source? Some sources become dated when new research is available, but other sources of information can remain quite sound.
6. Purpose/ Audience		What is the purpose of this information? To whom is it directed?

4. Your teacher will provide you with an outside source. Read the text closely. Then use the criteria listed above to evaluate the text to determine reliability, credibility, and bias.

Primary and Secondary Sources

When choosing credible and reliable sources, you will find **primary** and **secondary sources**. Primary sources are original documents; they are often used in historical research. For example, if you are researching the era of the Holocaust, you might use the primary resource of *The Diary of a Young Girl*, by Anne Frank. You might find an excerpt from the diary in a secondary source written about the Holocaust or on the Internet.

5. As you conduct your research, consider if the sources you find are primary or secondary sources? How do you know?

Preparing for Research

6. As a class, you will practice finding evidence from a variety of outside sources to strengthen and support an argument. First, form two or three research questions about the class topic of self-driving cars:

7. Which types of sources are best for the information you seek? List at least three and explain your choices.

8. What search terms will you use to narrow your search for sources with relevant information on the topic and claim?

Researching and Reading Academic Texts

Much research information is taken from academic texts, which can be challenging to read. An effective strategy for reading these texts is to pay attention to their **text features**.

There are five broad categories of graphical and print features found in academic texts:

• **Text organization** identifies text divisions (e.g., chapters, sections, introductions, summaries, and author information).

• **Headings** help readers understand the information (e.g., titles, labels, and subheadings).

• **Graphics** show information visually to add or clarify information (e.g., diagrams, charts and tables, graphs, maps, photographs, illustrations, paintings, time lines, and captions).

• **Format and font size** signal to the reader that certain words are important (e.g., boldface, italics, or a change in font).

• **Layout** includes aids such as insets, bullets, and numbers that point readers to important information.

9. Scan the article "The Very Human Problem Blocking the Path to Self-Driving Cars." Pay attention to the text features, and use them to help you better understand the article. Then think about the information you expect to find in this article. In what ways do you think it might be useful in answering your research questions?

Setting a Purpose for Reading

- As you read, annotate the text using four colors of highlighters to identify claims, evidence, reasoning, and counterclaims.
- Circle unknown words and phrases. Try to determine the meaning of the words by using context clues, word parts, or a dictionary.
- Read the article with your research questions in mind. As you read, write any new or refined questions in the My Notes section.

About the Author

Alex Davies is a Senior Associate Editor for WIRED, where he writes mainly about self-driving cars. He oversaw the launch of WIRED's transportation section and continues to manage, edit, and write for it. He has written for WIRED, CNN, Business Insider, and more. According to Business Insider, he says that his greatest driving feat is piloting a 1998 Ford Escort through the Rocky Mountains in the dead of winter.

Article

The Very Human Problem Blocking the Path to Self-Driving Cars

by **Alex Davies**

1   It was a game of Dots that pushed Erik Coelingh to rethink his entire approach to self-driving cars. Coelingh, Volvo's head of safety and driver assist technologies, was in a **simulator**, iPad in hand, swiping this way and that as the "car" drove itself, when he heard an alert telling him to take the wheel. He found the timing less than **opportune**.

2   "They gave the message when I was close to getting a high score," he says. Jolted away from the absorbing task, he had no idea of what was happening on the "road," or how to handle it. "I just realized," he says, "it's not so easy to put the game away."

3   The experience helped confirm a thesis Coelingh and Volvo had been testing: A car with any level of autonomy that relies upon a human to save the day in an emergency poses almost insurmountable engineering, design, and safety challenges, simply because humans are for the most part horrible

My Notes

🧭 KNOWLEDGE QUEST

Knowledge Question:
How are humans the biggest flaw behind self-driving cars?

---

simulator: machine that creates a likeness or model of something

opportune: favorable or well-timed

backups. They are inattentive, easily distracted, and slow to respond. "That problem's just too difficult," Coelingh says.

4   And so Volvo, and a growing number of automakers, are taking you out of the equation entirely. Instead of developing autonomous vehicles that do their thing under most circumstances but rely upon you take the wheel in an emergency—something regulators call Level 3 autonomous capability—they're going straight to full autonomy where you're simply along for the ride.

5   Google figured this out around 2012, when it decided that full autonomy—no steering wheel, no pedals, no human backup—was the best way forward. Almost everyone else has embraced this way of thinking, abandoning the step-by-step approach and promising to begin launching fully robotic cars within a few years. The shift came as automakers recognized the difficulty of the "handoff"—getting the person behind the wheel to take control at a moment's notice.

6   Automakers also saw only **incremental** improvements in safety, convenience, and value by advancing from Level 2 autonomy—cars that can keep their lane and handle rush-hour gridlock—to more sophisticated systems that still require human intervention. Going straight to levels 4 and 5 and offering a fully autonomous vehicle creates new markets, and new opportunities to challenge the likes of Uber and Google.

The Handoff Conundrum

7   It should be noted that these designations, defined by SAE International, are squidgy, and don't directly correlate to specific vehicles automakers are developing. For the sake of this discussion, Level 3 autonomy defines cars capable of basic decision-making like when to change lanes or pass other vehicles. The human at the wheel can check out entirely to, say, play an iPad game, but must be ready to take control if something goes amiss—a sensor fails, for example, or the car's map doesn't quite match the terrain.

8   Level 3 seems like a natural evolution of the tech you find in Tesla's Autopilot, which demands **vigilance** even if not everybody obeys. More work for the robot, less for the human. But it's a **Herculean** challenge for engineers and designers. "Having a human there to resume control is very difficult," says Bryan Reimer, an MIT researcher who studies driving behavior. Once relieved of the burden of constantly paying attention, people are quick to lose focus, and getting them back on task is difficult. Imagine you're watching the final moments of *The Shining* when someone suddenly turns on the light and tosses you a Rubik's cube. How quickly could you register what's happening, let alone attempt to solve the puzzle? Now you see the challenge of the handoff.

My Notes

9   To make Level 3 work, the car must verify its human hasn't, say, dozed off. This involves installing cameras and sensors to monitor things like head position and gaze direction. It means providing visual, aural, and haptic alerts to get the person's attention. And it requires making absolutely sure the autonomous technology is robust and sophisticated enough to handle any situation for the 5 to 10 seconds needed for the human to realize what's happening and take control.

10   Simply put, solving this problem is almost as difficult as figuring out how to make cars drive themselves. That's why Google—whose autonomous effort is now called Waymo—almost immediately abandoned any thought of building anything but a fully autonomous car. It started with a system that could handle highway driving with human oversight. Google's engineers soon realized those humans were **lulled** into paying zero attention, and that they were all but useless in such circumstances. So they started pursuing full autonomy ...

11   Beyond being difficult to achieve, Level 3 autonomy is difficult to justify. If every car on the road featured Level 2 capabilities, fatal automobile collisions would drop by 80 percent, according to Delphi, one of the world's largest automotive industry suppliers. Level 3 doesn't advance the ball much further, so why bother? Full autonomy, on the other hand, brings safety improvements while also bringing mobility to people who cannot drive, automating deliveries, and creating other opportunities.

🖉 Knowledge Quest

- How do you feel about self-driving cars after reading the article? Are you optimistic or doubtful?
- What questions will you ask yourself as you reread the article?

☑ Focus on the Sentence

Before analyzing the article more closely, take a moment to summarize the ideas of the experts cited in the article. Write a sentence with each of the appositives that follow. Use your own words to summarize each expert's ideas while maintaining the meaning of their words.

Volvo's head of safety and driver assist technologies

_____

_____

an MIT researcher who studies driving behavior

_____

_____

lulled: given a false sense of security

Returning to the Text

- Return to the text as you respond to the following questions. Use text evidence to support your responses.
- Write any additional questions you have about the article in your Reader/Writer Notebook.

10. What is the problem referred to in the title of the article?

_____

_____

_____

_____

11. Why does the author open the article with an anecdote about a self-driving simulator?

_____

_____

_____

_____

12. Reread paragraphs 4–7. What is the main premise of the article?

_____

_____

_____

_____

13. In paragraph 7, what does the word *amiss* mean? Use context clues to explain your definition.

_____

_____

_____

_____

14. Reread paragraph 8. How does the author use an analogy to help the reader understand the difficulty of switching from autopilot back to human-controlled driving?

_____

_____

_____

_____

15. What evidence does the author include to support the idea that fully autonomous vehicles are the best next step in vehicle technology? Why might he have chosen this example?

_____

_____

_____

_____

16. How does the author address counterclaims in the last two paragraphs?

_____

_____

_____

_____

17. KQ The author uses the words *autonomous* and *autonomy* throughout the article to describe the vehicles of the future. What utopian ideals based on human desires do these words suggest?

_____

_____

_____

_____

18. KQ Over the past three articles you've read about self-driving cars, which human flaw do you think is the most compelling one? Why?

_____

_____

_____

_____

Working from the Text

19. Divide into groups of 2–3 and discuss whether or not the author of this article is a credible source. Review your chart to evaluate the authenticity of this article. Think about the evidence he presents, the way he uses information from primary sources to support his claims, and the way he addresses counterclaims.

20. Now return to the class research plan and research question and sub-questions. Based on the information in the article and your teacher's guidance, revise the questions. Complete the chart to help you organize your ideas. Then review the chart and ask yourself: what additional questions come to mind, and what previous questions need to be updated? Make any revisions to the research plan as needed. Do you need to look for other types of resources? Then discuss these changes with your group.

Research Questions	Information from Article	Additional/Revised Questions

☑ Check Your Understanding

Now that your teacher has guided you through the research process with your class research questions, use these skills for your own research topic. Write a main research question and sub-questions for the topic you have selected. Then find three reliable sources you could consult to find information that answers your research questions.

21. Now it is your turn to identify and gather relevant information from a variety of sources to support the claim you have chosen. After identifying sources, read them closely and take notes on how ideas from one source connect to, refute, or build on ideas from the other sources. Synthesize this information in your Reader/Writer Notebook.

✍ Explain How an Author Builds an Argument

One of the arguments the author makes in "The Very Human Problem Blocking the Path to Self-Driving Cars" is that only fully autonomous car technology is worth pursuing. Write a paragraph analyzing the author's argument in support of this position. Be sure to:

- Provide a clear thesis statement.
- Paraphrase the author's argument.
- List specific details that support the author's premise.
- Include your own commentary on whether the author was successful.

Gathering and Citing Evidence

Learning Strategies

Graphic Organizer
Summarizing
Paraphrasing
Note-taking
Marking the Text
Questioning the Text

Learning Targets

- Understand how to paraphrase source material.
- Cite sources and use source materials ethically.
- Integrate ideas from multiple texts to build knowledge and vocabulary about the topic of self-driving cars.

Preview

In this activity, you will learn how to rephrase an author's words and give credit to sources.

Conducting Research

You have started to conduct research on a topic and claim of your choice, create research questions, use effective search terms, and find appropriate sources from which you can take information to use as evidence. Now, you will learn how to give credit to your sources in your writing.

Citing Sources and Creating a Bibliography

Drawing on and adding to other people's ideas is at the heart of research. But researchers must be careful to use others' ideas ethically and to avoid plagiarism. This is why citing sources and creating a thorough and accurate bibliography is such an important part of any research project. In addition to giving credit in your essay, you should also provide a Works Cited page or an Annotated Bibliography to document your research sources. A Works Cited page uses a standard format to list every source you use. An Annotated Bibliography includes the citation of the source plus a summary or commentary.

Citation Formats

Works Cited Entry:

Davies, Alex. "The Very Human Problem Blocking the Path to Self-Driving Cars." *Wired*. 1 January 2017, wired.com, Accessed 15 July 2017.

In-text Citation:

Human beings have been described as "symbol-using animals" (Burke 3).

1. To practice note-taking and generating a bibliography entry, complete the following research card using information from "The Very Human Problem Blocking the Path to Self-Driving Cars."

   Source Citation:

   How can this source help you to support your argument?

   What makes this source credible?

My Notes

INDEPENDENT READING LINK

Read and Connect

As you read your independent text, connect something the author says to the following: another text you have read, something in society it reminds you of, and something you have experienced. Paraphrase what the author says by rewriting it in your own words. Then explain your connections.

My Notes

Setting a Purpose for Reading

- As you read, annotate the text using four colors of highlighters to identify claims, evidence, reasoning, and counterclaims.
- Circle unknown words and phrases. Try to determine the meaning of the words by using context clues, word parts, or a dictionary.

About the Author

Laurel Hamers is a staff writer for *Science News*, where she writes extensively about developments in scientific technology. Although she grew up wanting to be a scientist, her career path changed when she realized that she prefers sharing other people's discoveries to making her own. She earned a bachelor's degree in biology from Williams College and studied science journalism at the UC Santa Cruz Science Communication Program.

Article

Five Challenges for Self-Driving Cars

Experts weigh in on the roadblocks and research efforts
by **Laurel Hamers**

1   Self-driving cars promise to transform roadways. There'd be fewer traffic accidents and jams, say **proponents**, and greater mobility for people who can't operate a vehicle. The cars could fundamentally change the way we think about getting around.

2   The technology is already rolling onto American streets: Uber has introduced self-driving cabs in Pittsburgh and is experimenting with self-driving trucks for long-haul commercial deliveries. Google's prototype vehicles are also roaming the roads. (In all these cases, though, human supervisors are along for the ride.) Automakers like Subaru, Toyota, and Tesla are also including features such as automatic braking and guided steering on new cars.

3   "I don't think the 'self-driving car train' can be stopped," says Sebastian Thrun, who established and previously led Google's self-driving car project.

4   But don't sell your minivan just yet. Thrun estimates 15 years at least before self-driving cars outnumber conventional cars; others say longer. Technical and scientific experts have weighed in on what big roadblocks remain, and how research can overcome them.

⊘ KNOWLEDGE QUEST

Knowledge Question:
How are humans the biggest flaw behind self-driving cars?

proponents: supporters

Sensing the Surroundings

5   To a computer, a highway on a clear day looks completely different than it does in fog or at dusk. Self-driving cars have to detect road features in all conditions, regardless of weather or lighting. "I've seen promising results for rain, but snow is a hard one," says John Leonard, a roboticist at MIT.

6   Sensors need to be reliable, compact and reasonably priced—and paired with detailed maps so a vehicle can make sense of what it sees.

7   Leonard is working with Toyota to help cars respond safely in variable environments, while others are using data from cars' onboard cameras to create up-to-date maps. "Modern **algorithms** run on data," he says. "It's their fuel."

Unexpected Encounters

8   Self-driving cars struggle to interpret unusual situations, like a traffic officer waving vehicles through a red light. Simple rule-based programming won't always work because it's impossible to code for every scenario in advance, says Missy Cummings, who directs a Duke University robotics lab.

9   Body language and other contextual clues help people navigate these situations, but it's challenging for a computer to tell if, for example, a kid is about to dart into the road. The car "has to be able to abstract; that's what artificial intelligence is all about," Cummings says.

10   In a new approach, her team is investigating whether displays on the car can instead alert pedestrians to what the car is going to do. But results suggest walkers ignore the newfangled displays in favor of more old-fashioned cues — say, eyeballing the speed of the car.

> **algorithms:** sets of rules to solve problems

My Notes

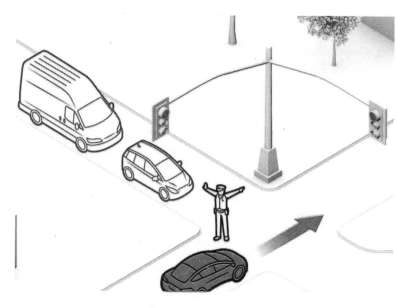

Human-Robot Interaction

11 Even with fully autonomous vehicles on the horizon, most self-driving cars will be semiautonomous for at least the foreseeable future. But figuring out who has what responsibilities at what time can be tricky. How does the car notify a passenger who has been reading or taking a nap that it's time to take over a task, and how does the car confirm that the passenger is ready to act?

12 "In a sense, you are still concentrating on some of the driving, but you are not really driving," says Chris Janssen, a cognitive scientist at Utrecht University in the Netherlands.

13 His lab is studying how people direct their attention in these scenarios. One effort uses EEG machines to look at how people's brains respond to an alert sound when the people are driving versus riding as a passive passenger (as they would in a self-driving car). Janssen is also interested in the best time to deliver instructions and how explicit the instructions should be.

Ethical Dilemmas

14 In exploring the ethical questions of self-driving cars, Iyad Rahwan, an MIT cognitive scientist, has confirmed that people are selfish: "People buying these cars, they want cars that prioritize the passenger," says Rahwan—but they want other people's cars to protect pedestrians instead (*SN Online: 6/23/16*).

15 In an online exercise called the Moral Machine, players choose whom to save in different scenarios. Does it matter if the pedestrian is an elderly woman? What if she is jaywalking? Society will need to decide what rules and regulations should govern self-driving cars. For the technology to catch on, decisions will have to incorporate moral judgments while still **enticing** consumers to embrace automation.

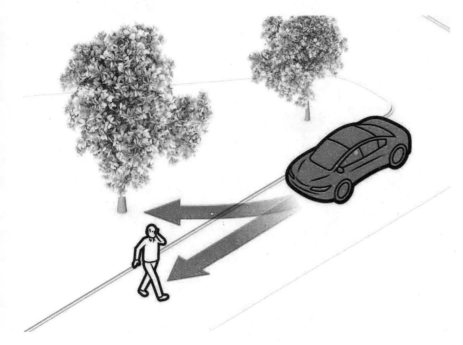

enticing: leading someone on by inspiring hope or desire

Cybersecurity

16   In 2015, hackers brought a Jeep to a halt on a St. Louis highway by wirelessly accessing its braking and steering via the onboard entertainment system. The demonstration proved that even conventional vehicles have **vulnerabilities** that, if **exploited**, could lead to accidents.

17   Self-driving cars, which would get updates and maps through the cloud, would be at even greater risk. "The more computing **permeates** into everyday objects, the harder it is going to be to keep track of the vulnerabilities," says Sean Smith, a computer scientist at Dartmouth College.

18   And while terrorists might want to crash cars, Smith can imagine other **nefarious** acts: For instance, hackers could disable someone's car and hold it for ransom until receiving a digital payment.

vulnerabilities: areas that are open to attack

exploited: misused or taken advantage of

permeates: passes into every part of

nefarious: wicked

References

B. Bower. Moral dilemma could put brakes on driverless cars. Science News Online. June 23, 2016.

J. F. Bonnefon, A. Shariff, and I. Rahwan. The social dilemma of autonomous vehicles. *Science*. Vol. 352, June 24, 2016, p. 1573. doi: 10.1126/science.aaf2654.

B. Bower. Morality play. *Science News*. Vol. 176, September 12, 2009, 16

U.S. Department of Transportation and National Highway Traffic Safety Administration. Federal Automated Vehicles Policy: Accelerating the Next Revolution in Roadway Safety. September 2016.

Ⓧ Knowledge Quest
- What is one new detail you learned about the challenges of self-driving cars?
- Which ideas from the article seem most important to you?

Returning to the Text
- Return to the text as you respond to the following questions. Use text evidence to support your responses.
- Write any additional questions you have about the article in your Reader/Writer Notebook.

2. Reread paragraphs 1-4 and analyze the thesis that is presented. What evidence is provided by the author to support her thesis throughout the article?

_____

_____

_____

_____

3. In paragraph 3, why does Thrun refer to the self-driving car technology as a train?

_____

_____

_____

_____

4. Who is the intended audience? Explain your answer with evidence from the text.

_____

_____

_____

_____

5. **KQ** The author used *cybersecurity* as a heading for paragraphs 16-18. What do the words *vulnerabilities*, *accidents*, *risk*, *crash*, *nefarious*, and *ransom* in these paragraphs tell you about cybersecurity? Why did the author use the heading "Cybersecurity" when writing about human flaws?

_____

_____

_____

_____

6. **KQ** What is the main reason in all four texts in Activities 2.13, 2.15, and 2.16 that self-driving cars fail?

_____

_____

7. What impact could hackers have on self-driving cars?

_____

_____

8. Explain the author's purpose in writing the article. How does the author's use of print and graphic features achieve her purpose?

_____

_____

_____

_____

INDEPENDENT READING LINK

You can continue to build your knowledge about this topic by reading other articles at ZINC Reading Labs. Search for keywords such as *self-driving cars*.

ZINC

⊘ Knowledge Quest

Use your knowledge of the four texts to consider how humans are the biggest flaw behind self-driving cars. Write an explanatory essay that responds to the question: How are humans the biggest flaw behind self-driving cars? Be sure to:

• Include a clear statement about each authors' ideas.
• Explain how the details in each text support and elaborate the author's central idea.
• Cite and quote evidence from the texts to support your ideas.

☑ Focus on the Sentence

Use information from the article to complete the following sentences.

If a self-driving car encounters snow or fog, _____

_____

Since self-driving cars get data through the cloud, _____

_____

Until society decides what rules should govern self-driving cars, _____

_____

_____

Working from the Text

9. Use two index cards to create a source card and an information card. On the source card, create a citation for this article.

10. On the other card, create an information card that you could use to support an argument essay. On the front of the card, write an important quote from the article. On the back of the card, paraphrase the quote by putting it in your own words. Finally, add your commentary on why this information is important. Keep in mind that paraphrasing another writer's ideas and adding your own original commentary can help you avoid plagiarism by using your own words and ideas to explain or expand on the subject.

Writing to Sources: Argument

Imagine that you have been called to court to testify either for or against the author's claim in "The Very Human Problem Blocking the Path to Self-Driving Cars." Prepare your statement to the court by stating the author's claim as well as why you support or challenge it. Incorporate evidence from the other articles you have read, particularly "Five Challenges for Self-Driving Cars," giving credit to the authors for any ideas you use. Be sure to:

- State your claim.
- Incorporate evidence by paraphrasing and/or quoting.
- Show your reasoning with commentary.
- Properly cite your source(s).

Organizing and Revising Your Argument

Learning Strategies

Writer's Checklist
Discussion Groups
Oral Reading
Sharing and Responding
Self-Editing/Peer-Editing

Learning Targets

- Synthesize information from multiple sources to refine arguments and develop a supported argument.
- Edit drafts for organization and development as well as sentence-level errors.

Preview

In this activity, you will refine your argument and finalize your research plan by creating an outline.

My Notes

Monitor Progress by Creating and Following a Plan

You have gone through a model of the research process and conducted research on your own topic for the argumentative essay you will write for the Embedded Assessment.

Now you will focus on completing your research and finding evidence for your argument. You will also work on organizing and communicating your argument.

1. First, look at the chart that follows. Where are you in the process of researching for your essay? Check off the steps you have already completed, but remember that you can go back to revise your claim or find additional support for your argument, if necessary. In the third column, add planning notes for completing each step of the process.

Research Plan for My Argumentative Essay

Check Progress	Step of Research Process	Notes
	Identify the issue or problem; establish a claim.	
	Form a set of questions that can be answered through research.	
	Locate and evaluate sources. Gather evidence for claims and counterclaims.	
	Interpret and synthesize evidence from multiple sources.	
	Communicate findings.	

2. Study your research questions and sub-questions, noting which ones you have located additional information about or already answered. Then complete the chart to refine your research questions, determine where more information is needed, synthesize information from your findings so far, and refine your argument.

What I Know Now	What I Still Need to Learn	Where I Can Look

Original Research Question: _____

Refined Research Question: _____

Research Questions:

Works Consulted Source + Citation	Notes/Examples/Quotes/Connections
Sample citation for a website: Davies, Alex. "The Very Human Problem Blocking the Path to Self-Driving Cars." *Wired*. 1 January 2017, wired.com, Accessed 15 July 2017.	

Peer Huddle

3. Divide into groups of 3–4 students. Take turns presenting the results of your research. As your peers present, note anything that is unclear or needs more information. Share your feedback.

Argumentative Essay Outline

4. A clear organizational structure is essential to a successful essay. Fill in the blank spaces in the following outline with your claim and the reasons and evidence you will use to support it.

I. **Introduction**

  A. Attention-getting hook

  B. Background information/definition of terms

  C. Claim (Thesis):

II. **Body paragraphs**

  A. Reason 1:   C. Reason 3:

    Evidence: Evidence:

  B. Reason 2:   D. Counterclaim:

    Evidence: Evidence:

                                Rebuttal:

III. **Conclusion follows from and supports the argument**

  A. Restate claim

  B. Connect back to hook

  C. State specific call to action

Sharing and Responding in Writing Groups

5. Prepare for discussion by doing the following:

- Revisit your outline and think about its organization.
- Think about your research notes and decide where the information fits in your argument.
- At the top of your draft, make a list of vocabulary and transitions you might use while discussing your ideas.
- Determine whether you should adjust your claim to reflect the new information.
- Create three copies of the graphic organizer in Step 7 on which you will take notes for your peers.
- Review the rules for collegial discussions and decision-making from Activity 2.6.

6. Gather the materials you will need for the discussion group: the draft outline of your argument, your research cards, and a pen or pencil.

7. Create a town hall meeting with your group members. First, elect a leader who will run the meeting. Then, take turns presenting your outlines. As each person presents, complete this chart to note any areas where you can help your peers write stronger outlines. Finally, discuss strategies you can use to strengthen your outlines based on this information.

Area of Focus	Strengths	Areas for improvement

8. Work with a peer to use the Writer's Checklist to help each other as you write. Check each other's writing after each stage: Ideas/Development; Organization; and Use of Language. Start with a focus on big issues such as organization, ideas, and style. Then focus on sentence-level issues, such as using commas properly, correct spelling, sentence variety, and subject-verb agreement. Make sure you have properly cited sources and used either direct quotations or paraphrasing to avoid plagiarism.

Writer's Checklist

Use this checklist to guide the sharing and responding to your partner.

IDEAS/DEVELOPMENT

☐ The writer has a clear claim (thesis).
☐ The writer supports his or her claim with logical reasoning and relevant evidence from accurate, credible sources.
☐ The writer effectively uses appeals to *logos* and *pathos*.
☐ The writer addresses counterclaims effectively.

ORGANIZATION

☐ The writer clearly introduces the claim at the beginning of the argument.
☐ The writer organizes reasons and evidence logically.
☐ The writer effectively uses transitional words, phrases, and clauses to create cohesion and clarify the relationships among ideas.
☐ The writer provides a concluding statement or section that follows from and supports the argument presented.

USE OF LANGUAGE

☐ The writer effectively and correctly embeds quotations and paraphrases clearly to strengthen evidence and create convincing reasoning while avoiding plagiarism.
☐ The writer includes all required elements of citations and correctly punctuates them.
☐ The writer uses a formal style, including proper references of sources to express ideas and add interest.
☐ The writer uses precise and clear language in the argument rather than vague or imprecise vocabulary.
☐ The writer uses a variety of sentence types.

LANGUAGE & WRITER'S CRAFT: Correct Capitalization

All strong research papers contain paraphrases and quotations from a variety of sources. Remember that the first word in a direct quotation should be capitalized. However, indirect quotations do not need to be capitalized. Similarly, if you use a piece of a sentence, you do not need to capitalize it unless it is capitalized in the original text. See the chart for examples.

Quotation or Paraphrase	Explanation of Capitalization
According to the author, "Body language and other contextual clues help people navigate these situations, but it's challenging for a computer to tell if, for example, a kid is about to dart into the road."	Because the sentence is taken word for word from the text, set it off with a comma, insert quotation marks, and capitalize the first letter of the sentence that is quoted.
According to the author, computers have difficulty making determinations based on body language and context alone.	Because this is an *indirect quote*, no additional capitalization is needed.
According to the author, although people are able to use body language clues, "... it's challenging for a computer to tell if, for example, a kid is about to dart into the road."	This quotation does not include the beginning of the sentence. Therefore, capitalization is not required.

PRACTICE Review the draft of your essay, highlighting any quotations or paraphrases. Check each example to ensure that you have capitalized correctly.

☑ Check Your Understanding

Create a flowchart that shows the order in which the five steps of a research project should be completed. Clearly label each step.

📦 Independent Reading Checkpoint

You have read a variety of sources relating to your topic. Which information supports your claim? Which information counters your claim? How can you use this information to strengthen your argument? Prepare your answers in the form of a brief oral presentation.

Writing an Argumentative Essay

 ASSIGNMENT

Write an argumentative essay in which you convince an audience to support your claim about a debatable idea. Use your research and experience or observations to support your argument.

Planning and Prewriting: Take time to make a plan for generating ideas and research questions.	■ What prewriting strategies (such as outlining or webbing) can you use to select and explore a controversial idea? ■ How will you draft a claim that states your position? ■ What questions will guide your research? ■ How will you make sure you have written work that is appropriate for your audience?
Researching: Gather information from a variety of credible sources.	■ What types of sources are best for the information you seek? ■ What criteria will you use to evaluate sources? ■ How will you take notes to gather, interpret, and synthesize information and evidence? ■ How will you create a bibliography or Works Cited page? ■ How will you present the results of your research?
Drafting: Convince your audience to support your claim.	■ How will you select the best reasons and evidence from your research to support your claim? ■ How will you use persuasive appeals (logos, ethos, pathos) in your essay? ■ How will you introduce and respond to counterclaims? ■ How will you organize your essay logically with an introduction, transitions, and concluding statement?
Evaluating and Revising the Draft: Create opportunities to review and revise your work.	■ During the process of writing, when can you use the Writer's Checklist to revise your argumentative essay? ■ How can the Scoring Guide help you evaluate how well your draft meets the requirements of the assignment?
Checking and Editing for Publication: Confirm that your final draft is ready for publication.	■ How will you proofread and edit your draft to demonstrate command of the conventions of standard English capitalization, punctuation, spelling, grammar, usage, and formal style? ■ How did you use TLQC (transition/lead-in/quote/citation) to properly embed quotations?

Reflection

After completing this Embedded Assessment, think about how you went about accomplishing this task and respond to the following:

• How can you use discussion and/or debate in the future to explore a topic?

SCORING GUIDE

Scoring Criteria	Exemplary	Proficient	Emerging	Incomplete
Ideas	The essay • supports a claim with compelling, relevant reasoning and evidence • provides extensive evidence of the research process • addresses counterclaim(s) effectively • uses a variety of persuasive appeals.	The essay • supports a claim with sufficient reasoning and evidence • provides evidence of the research process • addresses counterclaim(s) • uses some persuasive appeals (*logos, ethos, pathos*).	The essay • has an unclear or unfocused claim and/or inadequate support • provides insufficient evidence of the research process • addresses counterclaims ineffectively • uses inadequate persuasive appeals.	The essay • has no claim or claim lacks support • provides little or no evidence of research • does not reference a counterclaim • fails to use persuasive appeals.
Structure	The essay • has an introduction that engages the reader and defines the claim's context • follows a logical organizational structure • uses a variety of effective transitional strategies • contains an insightful conclusion.	The essay • has an introduction that includes a hook and background • follows an adequate organizational structure • uses transitional strategies to link ideas • has a conclusion that supports and follows from the argument.	The essay • has a weak introduction • uses an ineffective or inconsistent organizational strategy • uses basic or insufficient transitional strategies • has an illogical or unrelated conclusion.	The essay • lacks an introduction • has little or no obvious organizational structure • uses few or no transitional strategies • lacks a conclusion.
Use of Language	The essay • uses precise diction and language effectively to convey tone and persuade an audience • demonstrates command of the conventions of standard English capitalization, punctuation, spelling, grammar, and usage • includes an accurate, detailed annotated bibliography.	The essay • uses diction and language to convey tone and persuade an audience • demonstrates adequate command of the conventions of standard English capitalization, punctuation, spelling, grammar, and usage • includes a generally correct and complete annotated bibliography.	The essay • uses basic or weak diction and language • demonstrates partial command of the conventions of standard English capitalization, punctuation, spelling, grammar, and usage; for the most part, errors do not impede meaning • includes an incorrect or insufficiently annotated bibliography.	The essay • uses confusing or vague diction and language • lacks command of the conventions of standard English capitalization, punctuation, spelling, grammar, and usage • does not include an annotated bibliography.

VISUAL PROMPT
How can public art like this help people remember the Holocaust and also look toward the future? How do you think the arts can help change the world?

THE CHALLENGE TO MAKE A DIFFERENCE

I remember: It happened yesterday, or eternities ago. A young Jewish boy discovered the Kingdom of Night. I remember his bewilderment, I remember his anguish. It all happened so fast. The ghetto. The deportation. The sealed cattle car. The fiery altar upon which the history of our people and the future of mankind were meant to be sacrificed. I remember he asked his father: Can this be true? This is the twentieth century, not the Middle Ages. Who would allow such crimes to be committed? How could the world remain silent?

–from Elie Wiesel's Nobel Peace Prize Acceptance Speech

GOALS

- To compare thematic development in multiple literary texts in different genres
- To work collaboratively to plan and perform oral presentations
- To organize a draft with a purposeful structure, including an introduction, transitions, and a conclusion
- To research and summarize information from a variety of sources about an issue of national or global significance
- To advocate a position using rhetorical appeals while employing effective presentation techniques

VOCABULARY

ACADEMIC
communication
résumé
euphemism
slogan

LITERARY
drama
found poem

CONTENTS

ACTIVITY	CONTENTS	

*Texts not included in these materials.

My Independent Reading List

Learning Strategies

Think-Pair-Share
QHT
Close Reading
Marking the Text
Paraphrasing
Graphic Organizer

Learning Targets

- Discuss the big ideas and vocabulary for the unit.
- Paraphrase the skills and knowledge necessary to be successful in completing the Embedded Assessment.

Preview

In this activity, you will preview some of the unit's content and begin thinking about a panel discussion that you will present with a group.

Making Connections

In the first part of this unit, you will read texts about the Holocaust that show both the tragedy of historical events and the ways in which people reacted to those events. This study will help prepare you to research current issues from around the world and choose one for which to create a persuasive multimedia campaign.

Essential Questions

The following Essential Questions will be the focus of the unit study. Respond to both questions.

1. Why is it important to learn about the Holocaust?

2. How can one person make a difference?

INDEPENDENT READING LINK

Reading Plan

In this unit, you will be reading selections related to events surrounding World War II and the genocide of a people based on their religion. You may want to read a novel or nonfiction narrative from the additional titles mentioned in this unit. Book lists are available in the back of this book, and you can use book discussions and recommendations from classmates to help you choose. Use your Reader/ Writer Notebook to create an independent reading plan and to take notes on any questions, comments, or reactions you might have to your reading. Refer to these notes as you participate in discussions with classmates throughout the unit. Add the titles that you choose to read during the unit to the My Independent Reading List on the Contents page.

Developing Vocabulary

Use a QHT chart to sort the terms on the Contents page. Remember, one academic goal is to move all words to the "T" column by the end of the unit. Learning a new word means more than learning just its meaning. When you look up the vocabulary terms in this unit, pay attention to the different kinds of information the dictionary provides, including the word's pronunciation, syllables, origin, and part of speech. Record what you learn about each term in your Reader/Writer Notebook.

Unpacking Embedded Assessment 1

Read the assignment for Embedded Assessment 1:

Present a panel discussion that includes an oral reading of a significant passage from the texts read by your group. Your discussion should explain how the theme or central idea of "finding hope in times of despair" is developed in each text.

After you closely read the Embedded Assessment 1 assignment and use the Scoring Guide to further analyze the requirements, work with your class to paraphrase the expectations. Create a graphic organizer to use as a visual reminder of the required concepts and skills.

Preparing for Literature Circles

Learning Targets
- Identify and practice skills for active listening and effective speaking.
- Participate in a group discussion about quotations related to the unit theme.

Preview
In this activity, you will think about ways to be a good listener and speaker, and you will practice the skills in a group discussion.

Learning Strategies
Note-taking
Graphic Organizer
Previewing
Predicting
Summarizing
Discussion Groups

ACADEMIC
Communication is a process of exchanging information between individuals. It can include both verbal (words) and nonverbal (expressions, gestures) language. Effective communication is the result of both the speaker and the listener making an effort.

Preparing for Listening and Speaking

1. As a student, you have probably spent years observing teachers and other students who demonstrate both effective and ineffective speaking and listening skills. To help you identify good speaking and listening skills, create two T-charts in your Reader/Writer Notebook, one for Listening and one for Speaking. Brainstorm effective and ineffective listening and speaking habits and practices. Add to your chart during the class discussion.

2. Read the following information to learn more about effective **communication** in collaborative groups. All members of a group need to communicate effectively to help the group work smoothly to achieve its goals. Group members should allow opportunities for everyone to participate. To help ensure a successful group experience, follow these guidelines.

As a Speaker:
- Come prepared to the discussion, having read or researched the material being studied.
- Organize your thoughts before speaking.
- Ask questions to clarify and to connect to others' ideas.
- Respond to others' questions and comments with relevant evidence, observations, anecdotes, analogies, illustrations, and ideas.
- Use an appropriate level of formality for classroom discussions, as well as appropriate eye contact, a variety of natural gestures, clear speaking rate, adequate volume, and clear pronunciation.

As a Listener:
- Listen to comprehend, analyze, and evaluate others' ideas.
- Avoid barriers to listening such as daydreaming, fidgeting, or having side conversations.
- Listen actively by taking notes, summarizing, asking questions, and making comments.

Collaborative Discussions

3. Following are quotations about the topic of hope and despair. With your group, take turns reading each quotation aloud and sharing an interpretation of its meaning. When other group members share their interpretations, listen actively to understand them, and ask questions to clarify your understanding. As you discuss each quotation, comment on what the quotation actually says, as well as any meanings that might be inferred from it. Practice using the appropriate register, vocabulary, tone, and voice in your responses, comments, and questions to the group.

My Notes

Quotation	Interpretation
"When I despair, I remember that all through history the way of truth and love has always won. There have been tyrants and murderers and for a time they seem invincible, but in the end, they always fall—think of it, always." —Mahatma Gandhi	
"The road that is built in hope is more pleasant to the traveler than the road built in despair, even though they both lead to the same destination." —Marion Zimmer Bradley	
"The difference between hope and despair is a different way of telling stories from the same facts." —Alain de Botton	
"My theory has always been, that if we are to dream, the flatteries of hope are as cheap, and pleasanter, than the gloom of despair." —Thomas Jefferson	
"There is no despair so absolute as that which comes with the first moments of our first great sorrow, when we have not yet known what it is to have suffered and be healed, to have despaired and have recovered hope." —George Eliot	

4. Reflect on your group's discussion of the quotes. Identify challenges and set specific goals for improving your speaking, listening, and reading skills.

	Challenges	Goals
Speaking		
Listening		
Reading		

Forming Literature Circles

5. For this activity, you will be reading and discussing the texts included in the Literature Circle Text Collection. In your discussion group, choose a different Holocaust text for each group member to preview.

6. Form a new group with other students who are previewing the same Holocaust text. Use the following graphic organizer to preview the text.

Title:	Author:
Genre:	Length:

Predictions based on title and images:

Summary of the information provided in the description or review:

Information about the author or poet:

Personal response after reading a passage:

This text sounds ...

This text reminds me of ...

Someone who would like this text ...

7. Go back to your original discussion group and take turns presenting your previews. Use the graphic organizer that follows to take notes on each text as you hear it described. If needed, continue on a new page in your Reader/Writer Notebook.

WORD CONNECTIONS

Etymology

The word holocaust comes from the Greek words *holos*, meaning "whole" or "entire," and *caustos*, meaning "burn." During World War II, the mass killing of European Jews, Roma, Slavs, and people with physical or mental disabilities during Hitler's regime was referred to as a *holocaust*. It wasn't until 1957, however, that it became a proper name, *Holocaust*.

My Notes

Text Preview Note-Taking Graphic Organizer

Title	An Interesting Point Made About the Text	My Thoughts/Comments/Questions

Composing Letters

8. Work with a partner to discuss the following model letter. Note the different sections of the letter, such as the date, greeting, body, and closing. Then discuss the purpose of the letter.

October 17, 2020

Dear Principal Clark,

I am writing on behalf of a group of students who would like to begin a poetry group here at Edison Junior High. The school supports other groups that reflect a variety of interests, but the school has no group for students who love to read and write literary poems.

A poetry group would allow us to meet on school grounds to discuss and share poetry. It would allow us to build our interest in literature and our skills as writers. It would allow us to offer each other peer reviews and other advice on our writing.

You might think that a poetry group appeals to only a small population of students, but don't let that stop you from approving the group. We would be just as pleased with a writers group that includes all genres, including short stories, plays, and nonfiction.

Please see the attached sheet for the signatures of the seven students who are already interested in joining the group.

Sincerely,

Jay Garcia, 8th grade

---

9. Now work independently to write a letter to your teacher that explains your opinion about your three choices from the Text Preview. Use the format of a letter that follows. Be sure to explain why you made your choices. Your teacher will use the information in your letter while creating the Literature Circle groups. Be aware that some, but not necessarily all of your choices will be on your group's reading list.

[Class]

[Date]

Dear [teacher],

[explain first choice]

[explain second choice]

[explain third choice]

Sincerely,

[name]

---

10. Collaborate with your assigned Literature Circle group to create a plan for reading your Holocaust texts using a chart like the one that follows. Be sure to set clear goals for reading, as well as deadlines for meeting those goals.

Reading Schedule

Text 1: _____

Text 2: _____

Text 3: _____

Date Assigned	Date Due	Reading Selection	Role	Number of Journal Entries

11. Before each Literature Circle meeting, collaborate on an agenda that includes clear goals and deadlines for the meeting. While conducting your meeting, set time limits for speakers, take notes when group members are speaking , and vote on any key issues that arise.

Understanding Literature Circle Discussions

Learning Strategies

Diffusing
Literature Circles
Questioning the Text
Summarizing
Note-taking
Discussion Groups

My Notes

Learning Targets

- Analyze Literature Circle role descriptions and demonstrate an understanding of one role by creating a résumé of the skills needed to perform it.
- Read a narrative with the purpose of learning more about the Holocaust.
- Practice Literature Circle roles by participating in a collaborative discussion.

Preview

In this activity, you will learn about the roles in a Literature Circle, describe one role in depth, and practice your role in a discussion about a Holocaust narrative.

Understanding Literature Circle Roles

Read the following information about Literature Circle roles. For each role, think about the skills required and consider your personal strengths.

Discussion Leader

Your job is to develop a list of questions you think your group should discuss about the reading selection. Use your knowledge of Levels of Questions to create thought-provoking, interpretive (Level 2), and universal (Level 3) questions that connect to understanding the content and themes of the text. Try to create questions that encourage your group to consider many ideas. Help your group to explore these important ideas and share their reactions. You are in charge of facilitating the day's discussion.

Diction Detective

Your job is to carefully examine the diction (word choice) in the reading selection. Search for words, phrases, and lines or passages that are especially descriptive, powerful, funny, thought-provoking, surprising, or even confusing. List the words or phrases and explain why you selected them. Then analyze the intended effect, asking and answering questions such as the following: What is the author trying to say? How does the diction help the author achieve his or her purpose? What tone do the words indicate?

Bridge Builder

Your job is to build bridges between the events of the text and other people, places, or events in school, the community, or your own life. Look for connections between the text, yourself, other texts, and the world. Also, when reading a narrative, make connections between what has happened before and what might happen as the narrative continues. Look for the character's internal and external conflicts and the ways that these conflicts influence his or her actions. When reading poetry, make connections between the beginning and ending of the poem. Is there a shift in the narrator's attitude or perspective about the subject of the poem?

Reporter

Your job is to identify and report on the key points of the reading assignment. When reading a narrative, make a list or write a summary that describes how the setting, plot, point of view, and characters are developed in the reading selection. Consider character interactions, major events that occur, and shifts in the setting or mood that seem significant. When reading poetry, consider the context of the poem. What does the reader know about the poet? What are the circumstances surrounding the text? Who is the target audience? Share your report at the beginning of the group meeting to help your group focus on the key ideas presented in the reading. Like that of a newspaper reporter, your report must be concise yet thorough.

Artist

Your job is to create an illustration to clarify information, communicate an important idea (e.g., about setting, character, conflict, or theme), and/or to add interest to the discussion. It can be a sketch, cartoon, diagram, flowchart, or a piece that uses visual techniques for effect. Show your illustration to the group without any explanation. Ask each group member to respond, either by making a comment or asking a question. After everyone has responded, explain your picture and answer any questions that have not been answered.

Assigning Literature Circle Roles

1. Create a résumé using the following template to apply for a role.

> **Name:**
>
> **Role (Job Description):** Choose one of the roles and summarize the requirements.
>
> **Skills:** Describe the skills you have that will help you perform this role (e.g., reading, artistic skills, etc.).
>
> **Experience:** Describe similar experiences you have had and how they will help you in this role.
>
> **Activities:** Describe any classwork or extracurricular activities that have prepared you for the role.

2. Use your résumés to distribute role assignments in your group. Record these assignments on your reading schedule.

3. Create a table tent for your role by folding an index card or construction paper. On the side facing your group, write the role title and a symbolic image. On the side facing you, write a description of your role and bullet points listing the requirements. Be specific so that the next person who has this role will understand what to do.

ACADEMIC
A résumé is a brief written account of personal, educational, and professional qualifications and experience, prepared by an applicant for a job.

VOCABULARY

My Notes

Practicing Literature Circle Roles

4. Before you begin reading, think about these questions: How old do you think someone should be when they first learn about the Holocaust? Why would someone write a children's book about such a disturbing subject?

5. Create a double-entry journal in your Reader/Writer Notebook, keeping your Literature Circle role in mind. For example, the discussion leader may want to record passages that inspire questions, while the artist might record interesting imagery.

6. After you read, use the notes from your double-entry journal to prepare for your role. When everyone in the group is ready, practice conducting a Literature Circle meeting. Before you begin your discussion, collaborate on an agenda that establishes your goals, deadlines, and time limits for speakers. As you listen, take notes on and summarize interesting ideas presented by group members, and form questions and comments in response. As you respond to others, use an appropriate register, vocabulary, tone, and voice. If any key issues come up, vote in a democratic fashion.

Discussion Note-Taking Graphic Organizer

An Interesting Point Made by a Member of My Group	My Thoughts/Comments/Questions

7. Reflect on your discussion. Review your responses in the graphic organizer.

   • What contributed most to your understanding or appreciation of the text?

   • What did you learn about the Holocaust through the narrative and discussion?

LANGUAGE & WRITER'S CRAFT: Combining Sentences

Combining sentences adds variety and interest to your speaking and writing. It also helps ideas move smoothly from one to the next.

One way to combine sentences is by using conjunctions. There are two kinds of conjunctions, and each is used to create a specific type of sentence.

Coordinating Conjunctions

> *for, and, nor, but, or, yet, so*

Use a coordinating conjunction when combining two complete sentences to create a compound sentence. Always use a comma when creating a compound sentence.

> Authorities took people from their homes. Family members were separated from one another.

> Authorities took people from their homes, and family members were separated from one another.

Remembering the word *FANBOYS* can help you remember the seven coordinating conjunctions.

Subordinating Conjunctions

> Single word examples: *after, although, as, because, before, if, since, unless, until, when, while*

> Multiple word examples: as *if, as soon as, as though, even though, no matter how, so that*

Use a subordinating conjunction to make one of the sentences dependent on the other. When combining two complete sentences in which one has been made dependent on the other, the result is a complex sentence.

> The Christians in Holland are also living in fear. Their sons are being sent to Germany.

> The Christians in Holland are also living in fear because their sons are being sent to Germany.

As you can see, *because their sons are being sent to Germany* is not a full sentence. It is dependent on the first sentence and is subordinate to it.

Always use a comma when you place the dependent clause before the independent clause when combining sentences.

Because their sons are being sent to Germany, the Christians in Holland are also living in fear.

PRACTICE Combine these two sentences. First make a compound sentence, and then make a complex sentence.

> I wanted to come back to warn you. No one is listening to me.

☑ Focus on the Sentence

Write two short sentences about facts you learned in your reading or discussion about the Holocaust. Then combine the ideas from the two sentences into one longer sentence.

Sentence 1: _____

Sentence 2: _____

Combined Sentence: _____

Learning Targets

- Read and analyze an excerpt from a memoir and a poem.
- Compare thematic development in two literary texts in different genres.
- Participate collaboratively in a discussion to analyze and compare themes of literary texts.
- Integrate ideas from multiple texts to build knowledge and vocabulary about the theme of standing up for others.

Preview

In this lesson, you will read an excerpt from a memoir and a poem about the Holocaust. Then you will compare the themes of the literary works in a collaborative discussion.

My Notes

Foreshadowing

As you learned in Unit 2, writers often use techniques such as foreshadowing and flashbacks to add interest to their narratives. Instead of using a linear plot in which each event happens in chronological order, they develop a plot that moves backward and forward in time. The excerpt that you are about to read is an example of foreshadowing. When you read the About the Author on Elie Wiesel, think about how knowing this information about his life helps you identify and analyze the foreshadowing in the excerpt.

Setting a Purpose for Reading

- As you read, underline any examples you find in which people are being separated from each other.
- Circle unknown words and phrases. Try to determine the meaning of the words by using context clues, word parts, or a dictionary.

About the Author

Elie Wiesel (1928–2016) was a teenager in 1944 when he and his whole family were taken from their home to the Auschwitz concentration camp and later to Buchenwald. Wiesel wrote his internationally acclaimed memoir *Night* about his experiences in the camps. In addition to writing many other books, Wiesel became an activist who spoke out about injustices in many countries around the world. He was awarded the Nobel Peace Prize in 1986.

Memoir

from Night

by **Elie Wiesel**

1 AND THEN, one day all foreign Jews were expelled from Sighet[1]. And Moishe the Beadle[2] was a foreigner.

2 Crammed into cattle cars by the Hungarian police, they cried silently. Standing on the station platform, we too were crying. The train disappeared over the horizon; all that was left was thick, dirty smoke.

3 Behind me, someone said, sighing, "What do you expect? That's war …"

4 The deportees were quickly forgotten. A few days after they left, it was rumored that they were in Galicia[3], working, and even that they were content with their fate.

5 Days went by. Then weeks and months. Life was normal again. A calm, reassuring wind blew through our homes. The shopkeepers were doing good business, the students lived among their books, and the children played in the streets.

6 One day, as I was about to enter the **synagogue**, I saw Moishe the Beadle sitting on a bench near the entrance.

7 He told me what had happened to him and his companions. The train with the deportees had crossed the Hungarian border and, once in Polish territory, had been taken over by the Gestapo[4]. The train had stopped. The Jews were ordered to get off and onto waiting trucks. The trucks headed toward a forest. There everybody was ordered to get out. They were forced to dig huge trenches. When they had finished their work, the men from the Gestapo began theirs. Without passion or haste, they shot their prisoners, who were forced to approach the trench one by one and offer their necks. Infants were tossed in the air and used as targets for the machine guns. This took place in the Galician forest, near Kolomay. How had he, Moishe the Beadle, been able to escape? By a miracle. He was wounded in the leg and left for dead …

8 Day after day, night after night, he went from one Jewish house to the next, telling his story and that of Malka, the young girl who lay dying for three days, and that of Tobie, the tailor who begged to die before his sons were killed.

9 Moishe was not the same. The joy in his eyes was gone. He no longer sang. He no longer mentioned either God or Kabbalah[5]. He spoke only of what he

---

[1] **Sighet:** a town in Romania
[2] **Beadle:** a minor church official; a caretaker of a synagogue
[3] **Galicia:** a former province of Austria, now in parts of Poland and Ukraine
[4] **Gestapo:** the secret police in Nazi Germany
[5] **Kabbalah:** a Jewish religious tradition that strives to explain how the universe works

---

KNOWLEDGE QUEST

Knowledge Question:
Why should people stand up for each other?

In Activity 3.4, you will read a memoir and a poem on the theme of separating people so they don't stand up for each other. While you read and build knowledge about the Holocaust and how the Nazis separated people, think about your answer to the Knowledge Question.

GRAMMAR & USAGE

Participle Verb Forms

The participle forms of verbs can be used as adjectives. There are two participial forms: present (ending in *-ing*) and past (usually ending in *-d*). Note the use of these participles as adjectives in the text: **"reassuring wind"**(paragraph 5) and **"waiting** trucks" (paragraph 7).

A participle may occur in a participial phrase, which includes the participle plus any complements and modifiers. The whole phrase serves as an adjective. For example: **"Crammed into cattle cars by the Hungarian police,** they…" (paragraph 2).

As you read the memoir, look for more examples of participles and participial phrases.

---

synagogue: a building that houses Jewish religious services

Today this historical train car stands as a memorial at the site of the Auschwitz II–Birkenau concentration camp.

My Notes

had seen. But people not only refused to believe his tales, they refused to listen. Some even insinuated that he only wanted their pity, that he was imagining things. Others flatly said that he had gone mad.

10 As for Moishe, he wept and pleaded:

11 "Jews, listen to me! That's all I ask of you. No money. No pity. Just listen to me!" he kept shouting in the synagogue, between the prayer at dusk and the evening prayer.

12 Even I did not believe him. I often sat with him, after services, and listening to his tales, trying to understand his grief. But all I felt was pity.

13 "They think I'm mad," he whispered, and tears, like drops of wax, flowed from his eyes.

14 Once, I asked him the question: "Why do you want people to believe you so much? In your place I would not care whether they believed me or not …"

15 He closed his eyes, as if to escape time.

16 "You don't understand," he said in despair. "You cannot understand. I was saved miraculously. I succeeded in coming back. Where did I get my strength? I wanted to return to Sighet to describe to you my death so you might ready yourselves while there is still time. Life? I no longer care to live. I am alone. But I wanted to come back to warn you. Only no one is listening to me. …"

17 This was toward the end of 1942.

18 Thereafter life seemed normal once again. London radio, which we listened to every evening, announced encouraging news: the daily bombings of Germany and Stalingrad, the preparation of the Second Front. And so we, the Jews of Sighet, waited for better days that surely were soon to come.

Knowledge Quest
- Which part of the memoir stands out to you? Why?
- What details do you notice about the narrator, Elie Wiesel?

☑ Focus on the Sentence

Answer the following questions to expand on the sentence provided.

They refused to believe Moishe's stories.

Who? _____

When? _____

Why? _____

Use your responses to write an expanded sentence:

_____

_____

_____

_____

Returning to the Text

- Return to the text as you respond to the following questions. Use text evidence to support your responses.
- Write any additional questions you have about the memoir in your Reader/Writer Notebook.

1. What does the use of the pronouns *they* and *we* in paragraph 2 suggest about the narrator's point of view? How does this point of view reflect the theme of the excerpt?

_____

_____

_____

_____

2. When the foreign Jews are deported from Sighet, one person says, "'What do you expect? That's war ...'" (paragraph 3). How does the wartime setting affect the characters' beliefs and emotions? What evidence can you find of how the setting affects the characters' actions?

_____

_____

_____

_____

3. Identify the word *insinuated* in paragraph 9. Work with a partner to identify context clues in the passage that reveal the word's meaning. Then write a dictionary entry for *insinuated* that includes its meaning, syllables, and part of speech. Then use a print or online dictionary to confirm the details of your entry, revising as necessary.

_____

_____

_____

_____

4. What is Moishe the Beadle's motivation for returning to Sighet? What is the effect of his return?

_____

_____

_____

_____

5. Reread the About the Author at the beginning of this activity. How does its information help to reveal that this excerpt is an example of foreshadowing?

_____

_____

_____

_____

6. KQ The footnote for the word *Gestapo* in paragraph 7 is defined as "the secret police in Germany." What does this tell you about what the Nazis didn't want others to know?

_____

_____

_____

_____

7. KQ What did you learn about standing up for others who are being treated badly from Wiesel's memoir? How was this conveyed by his use of foreshadowing?

_____

_____

_____

_____

Setting a Purpose for Reading

- As you read, underline the groups that the Nazis separated people into. Also circle any of the group names that are unfamiliar.
- Circle unknown words and phrases. Try to determine the meaning of the words by using context clues, word parts, or a dictionary.

About the Author

Martin Niemöller (1892–1984) was a German Protestant pastor. During World War II, he opposed Hitler's religious policies and was sent to concentration camps. He survived and, after the war, joined the World Peace Movement. This poem is his response to the question "How could it happen?"

  INDEPENDENT READING LINK

Read and Respond

As you read independently, look for examples of flashback and foreshadowing. Write down two or three examples, along with a brief description of how each illustrates the literary device.

Poetry

First They Came for the Communists

by **Martin Niemöller**

KNOWLEDGE QUEST

Knowledge Question:
Why should people stand up for each other?

> When the Nazis came for the communists,
> I remained silent;
> I was not a communist.
>
> When they locked up the social democrats,
> 5 I remained silent;
> I was not a social democrat.
>
> When they came for the trade unionists,
> I did not speak out;
> I was not a trade unionist.
>
> 10 When they came for the Jews,
> I did not speak out;
> I was not a Jew.
>
> When they came for me,
> there was no one left to speak out.

WORD CONNECTIONS

Roots and Affixes

The Latin root *commun* in **communist** means "common." There are a few distinctions in the definition of *common*. In this case it refers to something that is shared or owned together by several people or groups. In communism, land and factories are owned by the community.

To explore this root further, determine the meaning of *communal*, which also includes the root *commun*, and use the word in a sentence.

Knowledge Quest

- What are your first thoughts about the poem?
- What emotion do you feel after reading the poem's final lines?

Returning to the Text

- Return to the text as you respond to the following questions. Use text evidence to support your responses.
- Write any additional questions you have about the poem in your Reader/Writer Notebook.

8. How does each stanza contribute to a developing sense of doom? Which words does the poet use to build the mood in the poem?

_____

_____

_____

_____

9. Describe the poet's use of punctuation. What is the effect of using punctuation in this way?

_____

_____

_____

_____

10. Why do you think the poet ends the poem with a two-line stanza rather than a three-line stanza like the others? How does this change in the stanza's length reflect his message?

_____

_____

_____

_____

11. KQ What connotations does the word *communist* have in the poem? How are the connotations different from the denotation of the word?

_____

_____

_____

_____

12. **KQ** What is the poet's reason for not "speaking out"? How is this reason similar to Wiesel's "Night"? How is this reason deceiving?

_____

_____

_____

_____

 Knowledge Quest

Use your knowledge of the three texts about the Holocaust to discuss with a partner the role that bystanders played in the Holocaust. Why should people stand up for each other? Be sure to:

• Explain your answer to your partner, be specific and use details.
• When your partner explains his or her answer, ask for clarification by posing follow-up questions as needed.
• After the discussion, write down the ideas you talked about.

 INDEPENDENT READING LINK

You can continue to build your knowledge about the Holocaust and the importance of being an upstander by reading informational texts at ZINC Reading Labs. Search for keywords such as *Holocaust, activists,* or *bullying.*

 ZINC

 Gaining Perspectives

You've been reading texts about how the Nazis singled out Jews, along with other groups they deemed undesirable or dangerous, for arrest, detainment, and later extermination. You have also been learning about standing up for others. Imagine seeing someone at school being bullied by classmates. Making sure that you remain safe, what steps could you and your friends take? Whom could you ask for help? How could you get their help quickly to prevent physical or emotional harm to the one being bullied? Discuss the risks and benefits with a small group of peers. Use the Round Table Discussion graphic organizer to record everyone's ideas for a thoughtful decision-making process that you and your friends could follow as upstanders. When you have finalized your plan, record it in your Reader/Writer Notebook.

Working from the Text

13. Work collaboratively while participating in a Literature Circle discussion about the two texts you read in this activity. Use the descriptions of each Literature Circle role in Activity 3.3 to guide your group's thinking and analysis before completing the following compare-contrast chart.

14. Now that you participated in a Literature Circle discussion, use your ideas from the discussion to compare and contrast both texts. Consider each text's structure, language, and theme. Then record your ideas in the following Compare-Contrast graphic organizer.

	Excerpt from *Night*	"First They Came for the Communists"
Structure: *How are the ideas presented? How are events or ideas organized? What is the genre of the text?*		
Language: *How do the words make you feel? Why might the author have chosen one word over another?*		
Theme: *How are the events described in* Night *similar to those described in the poem? What lesson has each narrator learned from experiencing these events?*		

☑ **Focus on the Sentence**

Use details from the graphic organizer to complete the following sentences.

Although the texts are structured differently, _____

_____

While the excerpt from Night contains descriptive language, _____

_____

Even though the texts are different genres, _____

_____

Analyzing an Allegory

Learning Targets

- Use sensory and other descriptive details to create mental images of a story as it is read aloud.
- Identify and analyze connections among the themes of Holocaust texts in multiple genres.
- Work collaboratively to plan and perform a dramatic interpretation of an assigned passage.

Preview

In this lesson, you will think about how a children's story connects to the themes of other texts about the Holocaust, and you will work in a group to present a dramatic interpretation of a passage.

Setting a Purpose for Reading

- As you listen to the story, make a list in your Reader/Writer Notebook of any unfamiliar words and write down any questions that you have.
- Make notes of any connections that you notice among the three texts about the Holocaust that you have studied so far.

About the Author

Eve Bunting (1928–) was born in Ireland and grew up in a household with parents who loved to read. In 1958, she moved to California with her husband and three young children. After taking a writing class, Bunting started to get her children's stories and books published. Several of her books have received awards. Even though picture books are her favorite genre, she often writes about serious and difficult topics. As a result, her books are enjoyed by young readers and adults alike.

Making Observations

- What happens in the story?
- What do the characters and events remind you of?

My Notes

Returning to the Text

- Listen to your teacher read the story again, and use details from the story to complete the following chart.
- Write any additional questions you have about the story in your Reader/Writer Notebook.

How do the other animals respond to the demand of the Terrible Things?	How do the other animals respond after the Terrible Things have taken the animals?
When the Terrible Things come for "every creature with feathers on its back"	
Frogs, squirrels, porcupines, rabbits, fish:	Porcupine, squirrels:
	Little Rabbit:
	Big Rabbit:
When the Terrible Things come for "every bushy-tailed creature"	
Frogs, porcupines, fish, rabbits:	Little Rabbit:
	Big Rabbit:

How do the other animals respond to the demand of the Terrible Things?	How do the other animals respond after the Terrible Things have taken the animals?
When the Terrible Things come for "every creature that swims"	
Rabbits, porcupines:	Little Rabbit:
	Big Rabbit:
When the Terrible Things come for "every creature that sprouts quills"	
Rabbits:	Little Rabbit:
	Big Rabbit:
When the Terrible Things come for "any creature that is white"	
	Little Rabbit:

1. How are the Little Rabbit, Wiesel, and the speaker in the poem "First They Came for the Communists" similar? How are their actions and desires similar?

_____

_____

_____

_____

Working from the Text

2. Why would authors choose to use an allegory to tell a story?

3. After listening and taking notes, meet with your Literature Circle groups and, using your notes and insights, discuss how this text connects to the previous two texts you have read. Discuss the three different genres presented and why they are effective and appropriate for the topic, audience, and purpose.

☑ Check Your Understanding

Reflect on your Literature Circle discussion. What connections can you make among the texts that you have read so far in this unit?

Planning a Dramatic Performance

4. Work collaboratively to plan and perform a dramatic interpretation of your assigned passage. Mark the text for pauses, emphasis, volume, and tone to convey important ideas and to add interest.

5. Rehearse your interpretation, and then present to the other group that shares your passage. Use an appropriate register, vocabulary, tone, and voice.

6. Reflect on your group's dramatic interpretation. What did your group do well? What will you do differently next time?

✍ Writing to Sources: Informational Text

Write a paragraph explaining how the theme of this story is similar to the theme of Wiesel's excerpt and Niemöller's poem. Be sure to:

- Begin with a topic sentence that responds to the prompt and states a theme.
- Provide textual evidence from the texts and commentary for support.
- Use precise diction to inform or explain.

Dangerous Diction

Learning Targets

- Use print and digital resources to explain the meaning, word origin, and other aspects of Holocaust-related vocabulary.
- Participate collaboratively in a discussion about the Holocaust using newly acquired vocabulary.

Preview

In this lesson, you will think carefully about the language associated with the Holocaust and use Holocaust-related vocabulary in a group discussion.

Learning Strategies

Graphic Organizer
Discussion Groups

ACADEMIC

Euphemisms are offensive expressions that are substituted for ideas that are considered too harsh or blunt. A common example of a euphemism is saying that something fell off the back of a truck when it was actually stolen.

Understanding Euphemism

The Nazis deliberately used euphemisms to disguise the true nature of their crimes. Euphemisms replace disturbing words using diction with more positive connotations.

1. Work with a small group to analyze how the Nazis manipulated language to disguise the horror of their policies. Research the term *euphemism* and how they were used in Nazi Germany. If doing an online search, use effective search terms to find the true meanings of the terms in this graphic organizer.

Euphemism	Denotation (Literal Definition)	Meaning in Context of the Holocaust	Analyze the Difference in Connotation
relocation			
disinfecting or delousing centers			
camp			
The Final Solution			

2. To discuss the Holocaust, you will need to be familiar with Holocaust-related vocabulary. In your Literature Circle groups, use print or digital resources to research and explain each of the terms listed on the following. Record as much information as possible about each term, including its meaning, pronunciation, syllables, and part of speech. Also, investigate each term's origin if possible, explaining any Greek or Latin roots or other word parts. Then synthesize the information to write a thorough explanation of each term.

Holocaust Vocabulary	Definition/Explanation
antisemitism	
concentration camp	
death camp	
genocide	
gestapo	
Holocaust	
Nazi	
persecution	
propaganda	
SS (Schutzstaffel)	
Star of David	

WORD CONNECTIONS

Etymology

Euphemism contains the Greek prefix *eu-*, meaning "well" or "pleasing," and the Greek root *pheme*, which has the meaning of "speak." A person who uses a euphemism speaks with pleasing words.

People in ancient Greece were superstitious about using certain words in religious ceremonies. Euphemisms were used instead to be more pleasing.

3. In your Literature Circle groups, hold a discussion that connects the above terms to the Holocaust texts you have already studied. The Discussion Leader in your group should note each "hit," or each time a group member appropriately uses one of the terms in a response. At the end of the discussion, add up the hits to see how well your group did at using newly acquired vocabulary in discussion.

☑ Check Your Understanding

Use your growing knowledge of the Holocaust to write five sentences on the topic, with each of your sentences using one of the vocabulary words in the chart. Write two statements, one question, one command, and one exclamation.

Exploring the Museum

Learning Strategies

Oral Reading
Note-taking
Discussion Groups
Graphic Organizer
Summarizing

Learning Targets

- Summarize information gathered from a Holocaust website and contribute events to a historical time line.
- Work within a group to choose talking points and plan a collaborative presentation to present them.
- Organize a draft with a purposeful structure, including an introduction, transitions, and a conclusion.

Preview

In this lesson, you will gather information about the Holocaust from a website and work with a group to turn that information into a presentation.

My Notes

Researching the Holocaust

1. Setting (time and place) is important in any story, but why is it especially important in a Holocaust narrative?

2. The United States Holocaust Memorial Museum in Washington, D.C., has a large collection of primary and secondary sources about the events and people of the Holocaust. Work collaboratively to research and take notes on your assigned topics by exploring the museum's website, starting with the page "The Holocaust: A Learning Site for Students." Record the sources you use and differentiate whether they are primary or secondary resources.

3. Each of the topics on the Learning Site links to a different web page. Visit the website to explore your topics. Take notes on a graphic organizer like the one that follows in order to prepare your talking points for a presentation on the Holocaust. Your talking points should contain interesting information that leads to an exploration of the theme, or central idea.

   Step 4 has a list of topics about the Holocaust. Your teacher will assign each group a topic (column) and individual subjects within that topic to research. As you research, neatly copy your key dates and events onto individual index cards to add to the collaborative time line after your presentation.

My Group's Topic:

Topic 1:	Topic 2:
Notes for Talking Points:	Notes for Talking Points:
Summaries and Dates of Key Events:	Summaries and Dates of Key Events:

4. Mark the chart to indicate your assignment by circling the title of your group's topic (column) and highlighting or placing a check mark by the topics you are responsible for.

Nazi Rule	Jews in Prewar Germany	The "Final Solution"	Nazi Camp System	Rescue and Resistance
• Hitler Comes to Power • The Nazi Terror Begins • SS Police State • Nazi Propaganda and Censorship • Nazi Racism • World War II in Europe • The Murder of the Handicapped • German Rule in Occupied Europe	• Jewish Life in Europe Before the Holocaust • Antisemitism • The Boycott of Jewish Businesses • The Nuremberg Race Laws • The "Night of Broken Glass" • The Evian Conference • Voyage of the *St. Louis* • Locating the Victims	• Ghettos in Poland • Life in the Ghettos • Mobile Killing Squads • The Wannsee Conference and the "Final Solution" • At the Killing Centers • Deportations • Auschwitz	• Prisoners of the Camps • "Enemies of the State" • Forced Labor • Death Marches • Liberation • The Survivors • The Nuremberg Trials	• Rescue in Denmark • Jewish Partisans • The Warsaw Ghetto Uprising • Killing Center Revolts • The War Refugee Board • Resistance Inside Germany

Source: Copyright © United States Holocaust Memorial Museum, Washington, D.C.

5. Gather with your group and present the results of your research. Work together to plan a collaborative presentation based on your group's most interesting or important talking points. Decide which point(s) each person will discuss, how long each person will speak, who will present the introduction and conclusion, and which types of delivery will be most effective. Also, plan how to transition effectively between talking points. Once everyone has an assignment, take time to prepare individual talking points. Then return to the group and rehearse putting the presentation together. Take notes in the following outline to organize your presentation.

Organization of Presentation	Assignment
Introduction: Begin with a dramatic interpretation of a startling fact, statistic, or anecdote from the site and preview what is to follow in the presentation.	Dramatic Interpretation: Preview:
Transition: **Talking Point 1:** Topic:	
Transition: **Talking Point 2:** Topic:	
Transition: **Talking Point 3:** Topic:	
Transition: **Talking Point 4:** Topic:	
Conclusion: Summarize a thoughtful question or thematic connection.	Brief Summary: Question or Connection:

6. As you rehearse your presentation, use this chart to evaluate yourself and the rest of your group.

Element of Expressive Oral Reading/Speaking	Proficient	Emerging
Enunciation: Pronunciation of words	Enunciation is clear, correct, and effective throughout the reading and enhances the listener's understanding.	Mumbling, incorrect or indistinct pronunciation hinders the listener's understanding.
Pitch: Vocal highs and lows	Variety in vocal highs and lows enhances the listener's understanding of the passage.	Mostly monotone
Volume: Variety in volume	Variety in volume enhances the listener's understanding of the passage.	Too quiet
Tempo: Appropriate pacing (fast or slow)	Appropriate pacing enhances the listener's understanding of the passage.	Too fast or too slow
Phrasing: Pausing at appropriate points and adding emphasis to some words	Pauses and emphasis enhance the listener's understanding of the passage.	No pauses or emphasized words

7. Deliver your presentation and add the information from your index cards to the collaborative time line.

8. As you view the other presentations, take notes in this chart, drawing a line under each new presentation.

Presentation Topic and Speaker Names	Facts and Information About the Topic	My Opinion and Evaluation of the Talking Points	Questions I Still Have

9. Use the notes and outline from your presentation to draft an informational essay.

10. Reflect on your group's collaborative presentation:

   • What did your group do well?

   • What will you do differently next time?

☑ **Check Your Understanding**

In your Reader/Writer Notebook, draw three conclusions about the Holocaust. Then make a list of any additional questions you have about the presentations or timeline.

Presenting Voices

ACTIVITY
3.8

Learning Targets

- Choose a specific Holocaust victim and gather relevant biographical information about him or her through research.
- Identify active and passive voice, and use each voice correctly to achieve an appropriate effect.
- Plan, write, and revise a draft that tells the story of a person's life.

Preview

In this lesson, you will research the life of a specific Holocaust victim and use the information to draft a narrative telling their life story.

Researching the Holocaust

1. During the Holocaust, many people fit into one of the following categories based on either their circumstances or decisions that they made. Try to think of individual examples of each from your reading, research, and/or prior knowledge. Which group do you think was the largest? Which was the smallest?

Victims:

Perpetrators:

Rescuers:

Bystanders:

☑ Focus on the Sentence

Write three questions about this image.

Artifacts featured at the Holocaust Museum in Washington, D.C., are primary sources that help to tell the story of the Holocaust.

Question 1. _____

Question 2. _____

Question 3. _____

Learning Strategies

Note-taking
Graphic Organizer
Drafting
Adding
Substituting
Oral Reading

WORD CONNECTIONS

Roots and Affixes
Perpetrator contains the Latin root *petrare*, which means "to bring about." It derives from *pater*, which means "father," as seen in *paternity* and *patriarch*. Adding the suffix *-or*, which means "one that performs a specific action," makes *perpetrator* refer to the person who brings about, or commits, a certain action. It is commonly associated with doing something wrong or illegal.

 INDEPENDENT READING LINK

Read and Respond
In the narrative you are reading independently, find a few instances where the author uses the active voice and a few uses of the passive voice. Rewrite each sentence in the other voice.

2. Choose an ID card from the Holocaust Museum website. Take notes on each section of your card, using the chart to organize information. As you learn about your chosen person, try to see the world through his or her eyes. Then in preparation for the Narrative Writing Prompt, present the results of your research to your group.

Name: **Date of Birth:** **Place of Birth:**
Biographical Background:
Experiences from 1933 to 1939:
War Years:
Future and Fate:

LANGUAGE & WRITER'S CRAFT: ACTIVE AND PASSIVE VOICE

When writing or speaking, it is usually better to use active voice instead of passive voice. However, skilled writers and speakers use voice for effect, and sometimes the passive voice works better. Study these examples. How is the effect different in each sentence?

Passive: Relocation camps were used to destroy whole villages.

Active: The Nazis used the camps to empty whole villages of their citizens.

Notice that the passive voice sentence does not mention the people who were doing the destroying. It has a softer effect. The active voice sentence is more engaging and powerful. Depending on what tone the writer wants to create, either sentence could be effective.

PRACTICE Find some examples of active and passive voice in your reading or writing. Write several examples in your Reader/Writer Notebook and try changing them to the opposite voice to see which has more impact.

Narrative Writing Prompt

Using the information you learned in your research about a Holocaust victim, draft a story about the victim's experiences. Be sure to:

- Use narrative techniques (dialogue, pacing, description, and reflection) to develop events and characters.
- Establish a context and use first-person point of view (I).
- Sequence events logically and naturally using your notes as a guide.
- Use active and passive voice effectively.

3. Revise your writing to show your understanding of voice and mood by adding or substituting for effect. Also revisit the organizational outline introduced in Activity 3.7 Step 5. Then check your work to be sure you have included transitions to convey sequence and signal shifts and to connect the relationships among experiences and events. Reflect on your editing: How does using voice and mood for effect strengthen your writing?

My Notes

Presenting the Narrative

4. Revisit the evaluation criteria introduced in Activity 3.7 Step 6 before you prepare for your oral reading. Remember to enunciate clearly by pronouncing words correctly, to vary your pitch as to not be monotone, to vary your volume, to pace yourself, and to pause at appropriate points for emphasis.

5. Prepare and present an oral reading of your revised narrative to a small group of your peers. Use the chart in Activity 3.7 Step 6 to provide feedback about each speaker's strengths and weaknesses.

Check Your Understanding

How did the process of researching a person from the Holocaust and trying to see the world from that person's perspective add to your understanding of the Holocaust? What evidence supported your understanding of the Holocaust experience? Discuss with a partner.

Learning Strategies

Predicting
Graphic Organizer
Drafting
Oral Reading
Discussion Groups

My Notes

Learning Targets

- Analyze film clips from a movie about the Holocaust and note details about setting, characters, plot, and mood.
- Explain how screenwriters use such literary elements as setting, character, plot, and mood to develop a theme.
- Write an informational text on the Holocaust and present an effective oral reading of the written draft.

Preview

In this lesson, you will watch film clips from a movie about the Holocaust and think about how its theme is developed through literary elements. Then you will write an informational essay and present it.

About the Film

Life Is Beautiful is a fictional story about a family in Italy that is sent to a concentration camp. The father and son are Jewish, but the mother is not. The father tries to protect his son from the ugly realities of the Holocaust by making it seem as if they are playing a game whose prize is a real tank. *Life Is Beautiful* was released in the United States in 1997 and received wide acclaim and numerous awards, including three Academy Awards. The Academy Award for Best Actor went to Roberto Benigni, who cowrote, directed, and starred in the film.

Finding Hope in Times of Despair

1. Return to Activity 3.2 and reread the quotes. Notice that each speaker uses the opposites of hope and despair to say something about life. How do you think this conflict between opposites might be portrayed in film?

2. Based on the information in the About the Film, predict conflicts that the father might encounter as he tries to convince his son that the concentration camp is just a game.

3. Work in groups of four to take notes on setting, character, plot, and mood in each film clip. Share notes and trade jobs after each clip to complete the following graphic organizer.

	Setting	Character(s)	Plot	Mood
Clip 1				
Clip 2				
Clip 3				
Clip 4				

☑ Check Your Understanding

Was the mood of the film appropriate for the topic of the film? Why or why not? Discuss your opinions in a small group using the following discussion prompts.

Discussion Prompts:

A. What is your reaction to a film about the Holocaust that has so much comedy in it?

B. What aspects of the Holocaust, as portrayed in the film, are similar to or different from what you learned in your research?

C. How and when did the mood change during the film clips, and what settings, characters, or events caused those shifts? Consider the following image of the scene in your discussion.

Roberto Benigni in the film *Life Is Beautiful*, which he cowrote, directed, and starred in.

✍ Writing to Sources: Informational Text

One of the themes of *Life Is Beautiful* is the ability to find the good in a very difficult situation. Write a draft of an informational essay that describes some of the ways Holocaust victims found hope in the dark reality of their lives. Make sure you use at least two examples from the movie and/or the texts in your writing. Be sure to:

• Begin with a meaningful topic sentence that responds to the prompt.

• Provide two or more examples from the movie and/or texts.

• Combine simple sentences, when possible, to create more complex sentences, and use transitions to connect ideas.

• Provide a conclusion that summarizes your response.

Prepare and present an oral reading of your written draft. Use the chart in Activity 3.7 to guide your preparation. Present your response to another pair of students. Provide feedback about ideas and oral reading.

Dramatic Tone Shifts

Learning Targets

- Understand and identify the features of the drama genre.
- Analyze how dialogue and other features of drama are used in a play to develop character and plot, convey tone, and reveal theme.

Preview

In this lesson, you will read an excerpt from a play and think about how its features work together to tell a story and share a message.

Genre Study: Drama

Just like a short story or novel, a play tells a story through literary elements like characters, setting, and plot. However, unlike prose fiction, drama presents these elements through a special structure. These structural differences allow the drama to be performed onstage with actors. Take a look at the following chart.

Element of Drama	Definition	Example
Cast of Characters	A list of the characters that appear in a play, usually presented at the beginning	**Families living in the hidden attic:** Mr. Frank and Mrs. Frank: Anne and Margot Frank's parents
Stage Directions	Directions to the actors about how to act out each part of the play, usually presented in italic type	*(Night. Everyone is asleep. Suddenly, Mrs. Frank sits up in bed.)*
Dialogue	The words that the characters speak to each other, which move along the action of the play	**Mrs. Frank:** *(In a whisper.)* Otto. Listen. The rat!
Acts	The main sections of a play	Act 1
Scenes	Smaller sections of a play that happen within an act	Act 2, Scene 2

Learning Strategies

Skimming/Scanning
Marking the Text
Close Reading
Oral Reading
Discussion Groups
Drafting

VOCABULARY

LITERARY

Drama is a genre of literature that is intended to be performed before an audience. A drama is driven by characters' words and actions. The setting of a drama can be established through props and costumes.

My Notes

My Notes

Setting a Purpose for Reading

- As you read, look for elements of drama in the text. Label elements "C" for cast of characters, "SD" for stage directions, and "D" for dialogue.
- Circle unknown words and phrases. Try to determine the meaning of the words by using context clues, word parts, or a dictionary.
- Record questions you have about the play or the genre.

About the Authors

Frances Goodrich (1891–1984) and Albert Hackett (1900–1995) were both writers and actors; they married in 1931. Together they wrote numerous plays and film screenplays. In 1955 they adapted Anne Frank's *The Diary of a Young Girl* for the stage, where it received several Tony Award nominations, including a win for best play. The play also was awarded the Pulitzer Prize for Drama in 1956.

Drama

from The Diary of Anne Frank

by Frances Goodrich and Albert Hackett

Families living in the hidden attic:

Mr. Frank and Mrs. Frank: Anne and Margot Frank's parents

Margot and Anne: sisters, 18 and 13 years old

Mr. van Daan and Mrs. van Daan: Mr. van Daan worked with Otto Frank
5 in Amsterdam

Peter van Daan: their son

Mr. Dussel: older; dentist who also lives in the attic

Others:

Miep Gies: close friend of the Frank family

10 Eisenhower: the voice of the American general

Scene: Anne, Mr. Dussel, Mr. van Daan, Mr. Frank, Mrs. van Daan, Mrs. Frank, Margot, Peter, Miep, Eisenhower

(Night. Everyone is asleep. Suddenly, Mrs. Frank sits up in bed.)

MRS. FRANK: *(In a whisper.)* Otto. Listen. The rat!

15 MR. FRANK: *Edith, please. Go back to sleep. (He turns over. Mrs. Frank gets up, quietly creeps to the main room, stands still. There is a tiny crunching sound. In the darkness, a figure is faintly illuminated, crouching over, gnawing on something.*

INDEPENDENT READING LINK

Read and Connect

Find an instance in the narrative you are reading independently where the tone shifts dramatically. How is it similar to or different from the tone shift in the play? What language is used to indicate a shift?

Mrs. Frank moves closer, turns on the light. Trembling, Mr. van Daan jumps
20 *to his feet. He is clutching a piece of bread.)*

MRS. FRANK: *My God, I don't believe it! The bread! He's stealing the bread!*
(Pointing at Mr. van Daan.) Otto, look!

MR. VAN DAAN: *No, no. Quiet.*

MR. FRANK: *(As everyone comes into the main room in their nightclothes.)*
25 *Hermann, for God's sake!*

MRS. VAN DAAN: *(Opening her eyes sleepily.) What is it? What's going on?*

MRS. FRANK: It's your husband. Stealing our bread!

MRS. VAN DAAN: It can't be. Putti, what are you doing?

MR. VAN DAAN: Nothing.

30 MR. DUSSEL: It wasn't a rat. It was him.

MR. VAN DAAN: Never before! Never before!

MRS. FRANK: I don't believe you. If he steals once, he'll steal again. Every
day I watch the children get thinner. And he comes in the middle of the
night and steals food that should go to them!

35 MR. VAN DAAN: *(His head in his hands.)* Oh my God. My God.

MR. FRANK: Edith. Please.

MARGOT: Mama, it was only one piece of bread.

MR. VAN DAAN: *(Putting the bread on the table. In a panic.)* Here. *(Mrs.*
Frank swats the bread away.)

40 MR. FRANK: Edith, he couldn't help himself! It could happen to any one
of us.

MRS. FRANK: *(Quiet.)* I want him to go.

MRS. VAN DAAN: Go? Go where?

MRS. FRANK: Anywhere.

45 MRS. VAN DAAN: You don't mean what you're saying.

MR. DUSSEL: I understand you, Mrs. Frank. But it really would be
impossible for them—

MRS. FRANK: They have to! I can't take it with them here.

MR. FRANK: Edith, you know how upset you've been these past—

50 MRS. FRANK: That has nothing to do with it.

MR. FRANK: We're all living under terrible strain. *(Looking at Mr. van*
Daan.) It won't happen again.

MR. VAN DAAN: Never. I promise.

MRS. FRANK: I want them to leave.

55 MRS. VAN DAAN: You'd put us out on the street?

MRS. FRANK: There are other hiding places. Miep will find something.
Don't worry about the money. I'll find you the money.

GRAMMAR & USAGE

Pronoun Antecedents

An **antecedent** is a word or
group of words that a pronoun
refers to. Mrs. Frank says,
"They have to! I can't take it
with them here." To whom is
she referring? The preceding
part of the play indicates that
Mrs. Frank is referring to the
van Daans. This statement
would be confusing if readers
did not know the antecedent
(in this example, the van
Daans).

As you read, notice pronouns
and make sure you know their
antecedents. Being clear about
antecedents can often improve
your comprehension of a text.

The Diary of Anne Frank was staged as a play for the first time by Leon de Winter at the renowned Hamburg Ernst Deutsch Theater in Germany on August 27, 2015, starring Kristin Suckow as Anne.

My Notes

MRS. VAN DAAN: Mr. Frank, you told my husband you'd never forget what he did for you when you first
60 came to Amsterdam.

MRS. FRANK: If my husband had any obligation to you, it's paid for.

MR. FRANK: Edith, I've never seen you like this, for God's sake.

65 ANNE: You can't throw Peter out! He hasn't done anything.

MRS. FRANK: Peter can stay.

PETER: I wouldn't feel right without Father.

ANNE: Mother, please. They'll be killed on the street.

70 MARGOT: Anne's right. You can't send them away.

MRS. FRANK: They can stay till Miep finds them a place. But we're switching rooms. I don't want him near the food.

MR. DUSSEL: Let's divide it up right now.

MARGOT: (*As he gets a sack of potatoes.*) We're not going to divide up
75 some rotten potatoes.

MR. DUSSEL: (*Dividing the potatoes into piles.*) Mrs. Frank, Mr. Frank, Margot, Anne, Peter, Mrs. van Daan, Mr. van Daan, myself … Mrs. Frank, Mr. Frank …

MARGOT: (*Overlapping.*) Mr. Dussel, please. Don't! No more. No more,
80 Mr. Dussel! I beg you. I can't bear it. (*Mr. Dussel continues counting nonstop. In tears.*) Stop! I can't take it …

MRS. FRANK: All this … all that's happening …

MR. FRANK: Enough! Margot. Mr. Dussel. Everyone—back to your rooms. Come, Edith. Mr. Dussel, I think the potatoes can wait. (*Mr. Dussel
85 goes on counting. Tearing the sack from Mr. Dussel, the potatoes spilling.*) Just let them wait! (*He holds out his hand for Mrs. Frank. They all go back to their rooms. Peter and Mrs. van Daan pick up the scattered potatoes. Not looking at each other, Mr. and Mrs. van Daan move to their separate beds. The buzzer rings frantically, breaking the silence.*) Miep? At this hour?
90 (*Miep runs up the stairs, as everyone comes back into the main room.*)

MIEP: (*Out of breath.*) Everyone … everyone … the most wonderful, incredible news!

MR. FRANK: What is it?

MIEP: (*Tears streaming down her cheeks.*) The invasion. The invasion has
95 begun! (*They stare at her, unable to grasp what she is telling them.*) Did you hear me? Did you hear what I said? The invasion! It's happening—right now! (*As Mrs. Frank begins to cry.*) I rushed to tell you before the workmen got here. You can feel it in the streets—the excitement! This is it. They've landed on the coast of Normandy.

100 PETER: The British?

MIEP: British, Americans … everyone! More than four thousand ships! Look—I brought a map. *(Quickly she unrolls a map of Normandy on the table.)*

105 MR. FRANK: *(Weeping, embracing his daughters.)* For over a year we've hoped for this moment.

MIEP: *(Pointing.)* Cherbourg. The first city. They're fighting for it right now.

MR. DUSSEL: How many days will it take them from Normandy to the Netherlands?

MR. FRANK: *(Taking Mrs. Frank in his arms.)* Edith, what did I tell you?

110 MR. DUSSEL: *(Placing the potatoes on the map to hold it down ashe checks the cities.)* Cherbourg. Caen. Pont L'Eveque. Paris. And then … Amsterdam! *(Mr. van Daan breaks into a **convulsive** sob.)*

MRS. VAN DAAN: Putti.

MR. FRANK: Hermann, didn't you hear what Miep said? We'll be free
115 … soon. *(Mr. Dussel turns on the radio. Amidst much static, Eisenhower's voice is heard from his broadcast of June 6, 1944.)*

EISENHOWER: *(Voice-over.)* People of Western Europe, a landing was made this morning on the coast of France by troops of the Allied Expeditionary Force. This landing is part of the concerted United Nations
120 plan for the liberation of Europe …

MR. FRANK: *(Wiping tears from his eyes.)* Listen. That's General Eisenhower. *(Anne pulls Margot down to her room.)*

EISENHOWER: *(Voice-over, fading away.)* … made in conjunction with our great Russian allies. I have this message for all of you. Although the
125 initial assault may not have been made in your own country, the hour of your liberation is approaching. All patriots …

ANNE: *(Hugging Margot.)* Margot, can you believe it? The invasion! Home. That means we could be going home.

MARGOT: I don't even know what home would be like anymore. I can't
130 imagine it—we've been away for so long.

ANNE: Oh, I can! I can imagine every little detail. And just to be outside again. The sky, Margot! Just to walk along the canal!

MARGOT: *(As they sit down on Anne's bed.)* I'm afraid to let myself think about it. To have a real meal—*(They laugh together.)* It doesn't seem
125 possible! Will anything taste the same? Look the same? *(Growing more and more serious.)* I don't know if anything will ever feel normal again. How can we go back … really?

Making Observations

- What do the stage directions tell you that the dialogue alone does not?
- What happens in this excerpt of the play?

GRAMMAR & USAGE

Punctuation
Punctuation helps to clarify meaning in sentences. Notice the varied punctuation in the drama.

Ellipses (…) are used to show pauses or to show that words are omitted, or left out.

A **colon** (:) is used in a script to follow the name of the speaker. It can also be used to introduce a list or a statement.

An **exclamation point** (!) is used to show excitement.

A **dash** (—) is used to set off or emphasize content.

Parentheses () indicate an aside or additional information.

Look for examples of these types of punctuation as you reread the play excerpt.

WORD CONNECTIONS

Word Relationships
Concerted and **conjunction** are similar in meaning. *Concerted* describes the combined efforts of people or groups that work together to achieve a goal. Think of a concert where musicians and singers perform together to make music. You could also say these musicians are working in *conjunction with each other,* meaning they are working together at the same time to put on a great show.

convulsive: marked by violent shaking

Returning to the Text

- Return to the text as you respond to the following questions. Use text evidence to support your responses.
- Write any additional questions you have about the play in your Reader/Writer Notebook.

1. Quote dialogue that expresses Mrs. Frank's anger. Why is she so angry when the scene begins?

   _____

   _____

   _____

   _____

2. Identify an example of stage directions that are essential to understanding the action in the scene. How would the play be different if the stage directions were not included? How do they help to develop the dramatic action in the scene?

   _____

   _____

   _____

   _____

3. After Mrs. Frank catches Mr. van Daan sneaking bread, the stage directions say, "*Mrs. Frank swats the bread away.*" What does this action suggest about what motivates her? What other example of her behavior fits this pattern?

   _____

   _____

   _____

   _____

4. Analyze this line of dialogue from the play:
   MR. FRANK: Enough! Margot. Mr. Dussel. Everyone—back to your rooms.
   How does Mr. Frank's statement affect the **action** of the play? What happens next as a result?

   _____

   _____

   What aspects of Mr. Frank's **character** does his statement reveal?

   _____

   _____

   What **resolution** in the plot does Mr. Frank's statement cause?

   _____

   _____

Working from the Text

5. In literature, tone refers to the narrator's attitude toward the characters, events, and other elements of the story. Sometimes, the tone will be consistent throughout a passage, but other times the tone can change, often in response to a character's action or an event in the story. In your group, discuss how and when the tone shifts in the play.

6. Use the following chart to analyze how the dialogue and stage directions help reveal the tone and move the plot forward. In the Context column, explain where the line of dialogue fits in the scene. In the Tone column, write a word or two to identify the tone of the play where the line is. In the final column, explain what effect the line of dialogue has on moving forward the plot.

Line from Play	Context	Tone	Effect on Plot
MR. VAN DAAN: (*His head in his hands.*) Oh my God. My God.			
ANNE: Mother, please. They'll be killed on the street.			
MIEP: (*Out of breath.*) Everyone ... everyone ... the most wonderful, incredible news!			
MR. FRANK: (*Wiping tears from his eyes.*) Listen. That's General Eisenhower.			

7. Decide on your roles for an oral reading of the scene with your group. Then prepare for the oral reading by skimming/scanning the scene independently, marking and annotating your own character's lines:

   • Mark connotative diction and label the tone you intend to use in speaking lines of dialogue.

   • Mark words of the dialogue that you will emphasize with a shift in volume or pitch.

   • Place slash marks in places where you will pause for effect.

8. Review your marked-up lines with a partner. Follow and give advice about how to improve the readings. Then conduct an oral reading, using your marks and annotations as a guide.

☑ Check Your Understanding

What is the mood of the play? Find evidence in the text to support your answer. Discuss with a partner or in a small group.

✍ Writing to Sources: Informational Text

Think about the characters in the scene from *The Diary of Anne Frank*. How does their dialogue reveal the characters and the conflicts of the story? How does it increase the reader's understanding of an aspect of the Holocaust experience? Draft a response that explains how specific dialogue is used to develop character(s) or plot and to reveal theme. Be sure to:

- Begin with a topic sentence that responds to the prompt.
- Provide textual evidence and commentary for support.
- Use transitional words and phrases to clarify how your ideas are related.
- Include a conclusion that summarizes your major points and supports your opening statement.

LANGUAGE & WRITER'S CRAFT: Pronoun–Antecedent Agreement

A **pronoun** is a word that takes the place of a noun or another pronoun. The word or group of words that a pronoun replaces is called its **antecedent**. A pronoun must agree with its antecedent in number, gender, and person. Understanding antecedents can improve both your reading and writing skills. In these examples, the pronoun is in bold type, and the antecedent is underlined.

Anne and **her** family were excited by Miep's news.

The Allied troops had landed, and **they** would fight **their** way to the Netherlands.

As a reader, boost your comprehension by knowing what or whom is being referred to. As a writer, use clear pronoun–antecedent agreement to help the reader understand your meaning and message.

PRACTICE Identify the pronouns and their antecedents in the following sentences. If you find an error in agreement, rewrite the sentence with correct pronoun–antecedent agreement.

1. Mrs. Frank wanted Mr. van Daan and their whole family to leave the annex.

2. But then, Anne defended Peter because she considered him to be his friend. her friend

3. After the news of the invasion, Anne and her sister Margot dreamed of returning to their home. correct

Look for examples of incorrect pronoun–antecedent agreement when you edit your informational essay. Revise each trouble spot to clarify what the pronoun is referring to.

Learning Targets

- Recognize how punctuation marks are used to indicate pauses and breaks within sentences, including in dialogue.
- Correctly punctuate dialogue when crafting a brief dramatic scene.

Preview

In this lesson, you will learn how to use punctuation marks in sentences and dialogue, and you will practice the skill by writing a short dramatic scene of your own.

Recognizing Punctuation Marks Within Sentences

Punctuation marks make texts easier to read and understand. They can show a writer's tone as well as organize thoughts. You already use many different punctuation marks in your formal writing.

1. Write a brief explanation of how each of these punctuation marks is used.

   period (.):

   question mark (?):

   exclamation point (!):

   comma (,):

   ellipsis (...):

   dash (—): A dash sometimes represents a sudden interruption in someone's thought or speech.

2. Read the following lines of dialogue taken from *The Diary of Anne Frank* (Activity 3.10). After each line, describe what the purpose or function of each punctuation mark is.

   MR. FRANK: Edith, you know how upset you've been these past—

   MRS. FRANK: That has nothing to do with it.

   dash (—): The dash indicates that Mr. Frank's dialogue is suddenly interrupted by Mrs. Frank's dialogue.

   MIEP: British, Americans ... everyone! More than four thousand ships! Look—I brought a map.

   ellipsis (...):

   dash (—):

Punctuating Pauses

A long sentence without *internal punctuation*—that is, punctuation that appears inside the sentence—runs the risk of being confusing to readers. Internal punctuation marks can clarify ideas in a sentence. They can also be used to create pauses that make dialogue sound more realistic.

Quick Guide to Internal Punctuation		
Comma (,)	indicates a brief pause in a sentence	Well, I didn't think about it that way.
Ellipsis (...)	indicates thought or speech that trails off or pauses	I wonder if ... I don't know if it'll work, but ... sure, let's try it.
Dash (—)	indicates a sudden break or interruption in thought or speech	If you push the start button first— hey, are you paying attention to my instructions?

3. Work with a partner to revise each of these sentences, using the punctuation mark indicated after the sentence.

   a. And then she opened up my book / Hey! / Did you just see that?

     Dash (—):

   b. The rocket wasn't tested / so I wonder if it will even succeed.

     Comma (,):

   c. There's a way this plan can work / If we put our heads together / Yeah, we'll have some ideas.

     Ellipsis (...):

4. Rewrite the following lines of dialogue to include appropriate internal punctuation, based on context.

   a. I'm just not sure. It's not coming to me. Maybe if I sleep on that idea for tonight.

   b. The way the performers are staging the action is incredible. Whoa! Did you see that?

   c. Joe may not appreciate that option so I will reconsider our plans for tonight.

Editing

Sometimes writers do not choose the most appropriate punctuation in their first drafts. Read the following student paragraph, and decide how to edit each numbered sentence.

The Diary of Anne Frank is a drama written by Frances Goodrich and Albert Hackett. [1] <u>Together the two</u> writers adapted Anne Frank's book for the stage. [2] One of the greatest accomplishments of their work is how natural the <u>dialogue sounds it feels</u> like you're right there in the room with the characters! For example, Mrs. Frank says, "If he steals once, he'll steal again ... And he comes in the middle of the night and steals food that should go to them!" [3] The tone and punctuation really make the emotion of the scene <u>very clear so it becomes much</u> more believable. [4] In real life, people interrupt each other all the <u>time so</u> characters in a play should do the same to make the scenes realistic.

☑ Check Your Understanding

What question(s) can you ask yourself whenever you write in order to ensure you are using internal punctuation correctly? Add the question(s) to your Editor's Checklist.

Practice

Reread the excerpt from *The Diary of Anne Frank* from Activity 3.10, and notice how the playwrights' use special punctuation to make the characters' dialogue believable. Then craft a small scene from your own imagination. Be sure to:

- Include dialogue for at least three characters in your scene.
- Use ellipses, dashes, or commas to indicate pauses, sudden interruptions, or dialogue that trails off.
- Ask a partner to review your work for correct use of punctuation.

A Tale of Survival and Hope

Learning Strategies

Marking the Text
Note-taking
Graphic Organizer
Outlining
Summarizing
Rehearsal

Learning Targets

- Analyze literary elements in an excerpt of historical fiction about the Holocaust.
- Understand how setting affects other story elements, such as character, plot, and theme.
- Collaborate to plan a panel discussion about the thematic focus of a passage.

Preview

In this lesson, you will read an excerpt from a historical novel based on a true story about Yanek Gruener, a Jewish boy in 1930s Poland who is taken prisoner by the Nazis. You will also collaborate in a panel about theme.

Making Adjustments While Reading

While reading complex texts, readers sometimes need to pause and make adjustments when their understanding breaks down. When you don't understand something you are reading, try the following adjustments:

- Reread the word, phrase, or sentence that you do not understand. Reread out loud to see if hearing the sentence helps you understand it.
- Use your background knowledge to make sense of what you are reading.
- Ask questions about the text. Jot down questions in the My Notes section, and return to them later to see if you know the answer after reading more of the text.
- Use annotations, like metacognitive markers, to note parts of the text where you have questions or comments.

Setting a Purpose for Reading

- As you read, underline the words that describe characters and highlight text that relates to the setting.
- Circle unknown words and phrases. Try to determine the meaning of the words by using context clues, word parts, or a dictionary.

About the Author

Alan Gratz (b. 1972) is an American author of young adult fiction. Gratz has published over a dozen novels, including *Prisoner B-3087* and *Code of Honor*. His work has received many awards, including a YALSA award for Best Fiction for Young Readers for *Prisoner B-3087*. His novel *Refugee* spent over 6 months on the *New York Times* bestseller list. Gratz has traveled across the world to teach writing, including to Japan and Indonesia, and is now settled in Asheville, North Carolina with his wife and children.

My Notes

_____
_____
_____
_____
_____
_____
_____
_____
_____
_____
_____
_____
_____
_____
_____
_____
_____
_____
_____

WORD CONNECTIONS

Multiple Meaning Words

The word **chamber** has several meanings, both as a noun and a verb. As a noun, it can refer to a private bedroom, or a more formal room like a courtroom, or a meeting hall where business is conducted. It can also refer to an enclosed space, such as the chambers of a human heart. As a verb, it can refer to the act of placing something in a chamber or housing something.

Novel

from # Prisoner B-3087

by **Alan Gratz**

1   After the shower nothing seemed to matter as much to me. I knew it was a game to the Nazis—kill us, don't kill us, to them it didn't really matter—but even so, I was glad I had made it through.

2   I had been ready to die. But when water came out of those showers, not gas, it was like I was born again. I had survived, and I would keep surviving.

3   I was alive.

4   The Nazis lined us up, still naked and shivering. First they shaved our heads. With our hair gone, we all looked alike—young and old. Next they marched us to a different room, where soldiers waited at tables with what looked like big oversized pencils with wires attached to them. As we worked our way toward them, person after person, I could hear screams of pain ahead of us. I had no idea what they were doing to us, but they weren't killing us. That was all that mattered, I told myself. I could handle pain.

5   By the time I got to the head of the line, I understood what was happening. We were being tattooed. I watched as the man ahead of me had letters and numbers carved into his skin in black ink with an electric needle. When it was my turn, the Nazi with the tattoo pencil grabbed my arm and started to write. The pain was awful as he dragged the vibrating needle over my skin, but I knew better than to cry out or beg him to stop. Besides, nothing could be worse than what had already happened to me. I had been in a gas chamber. I had looked up into the showerhead and waited for death to come, and it had passed me by. I was alive. A tattoo was nothing to me. Not in that moment.

6   B-3087.

7   That's what the Nazis carved into my skin, B for Birkenau, 3087 for my prisoner number. That was the mark they put on me, a mark I would have for as long as I lived. B-3087. That was who I was to them. Not Yanek Gruener, son of Oskar and Mina. Not Yanek Gruener of 20 Krakusa Street, Podgórze, Kraków. Not Yanek Gruener who loved books and science and American movies.

8   I was Prisoner B-3087.

9   But I was alive.

10   After the room where we were tattooed, we were taken to another room with a huge pile of old, used prisoner uniforms, and told to find something that fit. The soldiers made us run, beating us with clubs if we took too long to find

new pants and a shirt, so we took whatever we could as fast as we could. I ended up with pants that were too short and a shirt that was too big, but I was lucky to get a pair of wooden shoes that fit. That was important. Shoes were everything in the camps. I moved fast and wasn't beaten. I could play the game as well as anybody. I had made it this far, hadn't I? I was alive.

11 When we were showered and tattooed and dressed again, we were taken to our new barracks. They were worse than any barracks I'd seen yet. The ground at Birkenau was like a swamp, wet and thick with mud, and there were no floors in the barracks. There was no heat or electric light either. The bunks weren't beds but shelves, stacked three tall on top of one another, and they stuffed us in again as they had on the trains. There were no mattresses, no pillows, no blankets. Just old, wet straw, when there was anything at all. There were so many of us we could only all lie one direction or we couldn't lie down at all. It didn't matter. I was alive. I couldn't help thinking it over and over again.

12 I felt something at my feet, deep inside the shelf, and I reached down to get it. It was a scrap of colorful cloth, a bandanna or a handkerchief, probably left there by one of the gypsies who'd slept in these bunks before us. I tucked the scrap up under my head, hoping to use it as a bit of pillow against my ear, but there was something hard inside it. I unknotted the cloth and found an object hidden within: a little wooden horse. It was a simple children's toy, a rough carving that just hinted at four legs and a head, but it was smooth and dark like it had been played with. Some gypsy boy or a girl had loved this horse. Had somehow kept it with them always, right up until the very end. Had they known they were going to die? Had they left their little horse behind so it wouldn't die with them? So some part of them might survive and be remembered?

13 "We have a boy who is thirteen today," a man on my shelf said. I raised my head, as did one or two others. "Who will stand with him?"

14 No one stirred.

15 "Are there not ten men here who will make a **minyan** with us?"

16 "Be quiet," someone told him. "Go to sleep."

17 "How can you care about such things in a place like this?" someone else asked.

18 "It is even more important here and now," the man said.

19 Someone scoffed. "Tomorrow he will be dead. We all will. None of it matters anymore."

20 I was tired, and starving, and my arm burned from the tattoo. But suddenly I thought standing in a minyan for somebody's **bar mitzvah** was the most important thing in the world. Worth losing sleep over. Worth being punished or killed.

minyan: group of at least 10 Jews of-age needed for public worship

bar mitzvah: Jewish religious ceremony held when a boy turns thirteen, and is recognized as an adult member of the faith

21 "I'll do it," I said. The men around me were quiet for a minute after I spoke, and then someone else said yes. And another. And another. When there were ten of us, we climbed down onto the muddy floor, and the man who had first spoken began to pray. More men came down then, more than ten, until we filled the whole ground. The boy looked so young, but I knew I could be only one or two years older than he was. With a start, I realized I had probably missed my own birthday. I was fifteen now, maybe even sixteen. It was winter, but I had no idea what month it was, let alone what day. I had been in concentration camps for more than two years. I looked at the boy and remembered my own hasty bar mitzvah in Kraków. I had been so young then, a lifetime ago.

22 The ceremony was fast so we wouldn't be caught. When it was over, the men all whispered "Mazel tov" and climbed back onto their shelves. I went up to the boy and pressed the wooden horse into his hands, the only present I could give him. The boy looked at me with big, round eyes. Had I ever been so young? "We are alive," I told him. "We are alive, and that is all that matters. We cannot let them tear us from the pages of the world."

Making Observations

- What are some details you notice about the setting of the story?
- What characters do you meet in the story?

Returning to the Text

- Return to the text as you respond to the following questions. Use evidence from the text to support your responses.
- Write any additional questions you have about the excerpt in your Reader/Writer Notebook.

1. Examine the description in the first three paragraphs. What can you infer about why the narrator's shower made him feel like he was "born again"?

_____

_____

_____

_____

2. What can you infer about the setting of the narrative? Provide details that helped you form your inferences.

_____

_____

_____

_____

3. Reread the conversation that takes place over paragraphs 13 through 20. How does the setting affect the characters' feelings about the boy's birthday?

_____

_____

_____

_____

4. Reread paragraph 21. What does the narrator's willingness to stand with the boy reveal about his character?

_____

_____

_____

_____

5. Reread paragraph 22. How do the narrator's comments reveal the excerpt's theme?

_____

_____

_____

_____

Working from the Text

6. Both the narrator and the boy in the story had a thirteenth birthday. In the Jewish tradition, when a boy turns thirteen, he is given a bar mitzvah, a ritual to mark a boy's coming of age. How were the two boy's birthdays different? Working with a partner, use a Venn diagram like the one that follows to compare and contrast the two characters' thirteenth birthdays.

7. How does the boy's thirteenth birthday become a symbol of hope for the characters?

_____

_____

_____

_____

8. Fill in the following graphic organizer with information from the passage. Use your notes to prepare talking points that will guide a meaningful discussion of the text. Be sure to:

- Discuss how interactions between characters, events (plot), or place (setting) contribute to the development of a theme.
- Include details from the text, commentary (analysis), and questions to spark discussion.

Character 1:	Character 2:	Setting:

Summary of the Plot

Beginning:	Middle:	End:

Theme:

9. Work collaboratively to prepare the content of your panel discussion. Use the outline to plan your presentation. Draft an introduction and conclusion, and select and arrange talking points. Assign a speaker to each part of the presentation, and set a time limit for each. Have speakers practice using eye contact, gestures, and appropriate speaking rate and volume. When other groups present their panel discussions, listen actively to understand their points and share questions and comments, if possible.

Organization of Presentation	Assignment
Introduction: Begin with a dramatic interpretation of an important section of the narrative, and preview what is to follow in the presentation.	**Dramatic Interpretation:** **Preview:**
Transition: **Talking Point 1:** Topic:	
Transition: **Talking Point 2:** Topic:	
Conclusion: Summarize the main points of your discussion. Connect the story to the theme of "finding hope in times of despair."	**Brief Summary:** **Connection to Theme:**

10. Review the criteria from the Embedded Assessment Scoring Guide to prepare the delivery of your panel discussion.

11. After rehearsing your panel discussion, present it to another group. Use the Scoring Guide to provide specific feedback and suggestions for improvement. Focus on the quality of speakers' interpretation and evidence.

☑ Check Your Understanding

Quickwrite: How do you think the narrator will continue to affect the other boy's life in the story? Use text details to make predictions in your Reader/Writer Notebook.

✍ Writing to Sources: Informational Text

Write a short, objective summary of the excerpt from *Prisoner B-3087*, including its theme and how the characters, setting, and plot relate to the theme. Be sure to:

- Include a topic sentence that states the theme.
- Include details and quotes from the text in the summary.
- Explain how characters, setting, and plot relate to the theme.

Creating a Memorable Opening

Learning Strategies

Questioning the Text
Close Reading
Rereading
Discussion Groups

Learning Targets

- Read an excerpt from a diary and choose impactful language to use in a found poem.
- Work collaboratively to analyze the content and structure of a found poem.
- Present an oral reading of a found poem and listen actively to a partner's presentation, asking questions and making comments as appropriate.

Preview

In this lesson, you will read an excerpt from Anne Frank's diary and create a found poem from its words. You will then present an oral reading of your own found poem to a partner.

My Notes

Setting a Purpose for Reading

- As you read, circle examples of impactful language to use in a found poem.
- Circle unknown words and phrases. Try to determine the meaning of the words by using context clues, word parts, or a dictionary.

About the Author

Anne Frank (1929–1945) is one of the Holocaust's most famous victims. The Frank family fled Germany for Amsterdam, but eventually the Nazis also occupied the Netherlands. The family spent two years in hiding, during which Anne wrote of her thoughts and feelings to her imaginary friend, Kitty. The German authorities found the family's hiding place and sent them to concentration camps, where Anne perished at age 15. Her diary was found years later, and it continues to be read today as a moving narrative from the Holocaust.

My Notes

Diary

from

The Diary of a Young Girl

Wednesday, 13 January, 1943

by **Anne Frank**

Dearest Kitty,

1   This morning I was constantly interrupted, and as a result I haven't been able to finish a single thing I've begun.

2   We have a new pastime, namely, filling packages with powdered gravy. The gravy is one of Gies & Co.'s products. Mr. Kugler hasn't been able to find anyone else to fill the packages, and besides, it's cheaper if we do the job. It's the kind of work they do in prisons. It's incredibly boring and makes us dizzy and giggly.

3   Terrible things are happening outside. At any time of night and day, poor helpless people are being dragged out of their homes. They're allowed to take only a knapsack and a little cash with them, and even then, they're robbed of these possessions on the way. Families are torn apart; men, women and children are separated. Children come home from school to find that their parents have disappeared. Women return from shopping to find their houses sealed, their families gone. The Christians in Holland are also living in fear because their sons are being sent to Germany. Everyone is scared. Every night hundreds of planes pass over Holland on their way to German cities, to sow their bombs on German soil. Every hour hundreds, or maybe even thousands, of people are being killed in Russia and Africa. No one can keep out of the conflict, the entire world is at war, and even though the Allies are doing better, the end is nowhere in sight.

4   As for us, we're quite fortunate. Luckier than millions of people. It's quiet and safe here, and we're using our money to buy food. We're so selfish that we talk about "after the war" and look forward to new clothes and shoes, when actually we should be saving every penny to help others when the war is over, to salvage whatever we can.

5   The children in this neighborhood run around in thin shirts and wooden shoes. They have no coats, no socks, no caps and no one to help them. Gnawing on a carrot to still their hunger pangs, they walk from their cold houses through cold streets to an even colder classroom. Things have gotten so bad in Holland that hordes of children stop passersby in the streets to beg for a piece of bread.

6   I could spend hours telling you about the suffering the war has brought, but I'd only make myself more dejected. All we can do is wait, as calmly as possible, for it to end. Jews and Christians alike are waiting, the whole world is waiting, and many are waiting for death.

Yours,

Anne

Making Observations
- What questions do you have about the first few paragraphs?
- What emotions do you feel after reading the diary so far?

Returning to the Text
- Return to the text as you respond to the following questions. Use text evidence to support your responses.
- Write any additional questions you have about the diary entry in your Reader/Writer Notebook.

1. Why does Anne feel that she is fortunate? Cite evidence from the text to support your answer.

_____

_____

_____

_____

2. Analyze Anne Frank's language in the excerpt. What mood does the language create? Why? Include examples from the text in your response.

_____

_____

_____

_____

3. Based on the mood Frank portrays in this passage, what is the meaning of the word *dejected* in paragraph 6? Include examples of context clues that helped you uncover the meaning.

_____

_____

_____

_____

Working from the Text
4. In a previous activity, you read a play based on Anne Frank's diary. Identify the point of view used in each text. What could you learn from her diary that you could not learn from the play?

LITERARY

A found poem is verse that is created from a prose text by using the original words, phrases, images, and/or sentences but manipulating them and reformatting them into poetic lines.

5. The opening three paragraphs of the diary entry have been transformed into a model of a **found poem**. With a partner, conduct an oral reading using choral reading for effect.

"Wednesday, 13 January, 1943"

Everyone is afraid:

It is terrible outside.
Day and night
more of those poor miserable people
are being dragged off.

Families are torn apart.
Children coming home from school
find that their parents
have disappeared.

Women
return from shopping to find
their homes shut up and
their families gone.

The Dutch people,
their sons are being sent
to Germany.
Everyone is afraid …

6. The author of the found poem selected particular lines from the text and then transformed them into poetry. How does this transformation change the power of the language?

INDEPENDENT READING LINK

Read and Respond

Choose a passage from the Holocaust narrative you are reading independently to transform into a found poem. Perform an oral reading of your poem at the final Literature Circle meeting.

7. How does the structure of the lines in the found poem transform the text from prose to poetry? Which lines stand out? Why?

8. How would a dramatic interpretation of this found poem successfully open a panel discussion about the Holocaust?

9. Reread the diary entry again, highlighting words, phrases, and images you think are important. Then create your own found poem using the words and images you find compelling.

☑ Check Your Understanding

Plan a dramatic interpretation (i.e., oral reading) of the found poem you created. Present your oral reading to a partner and listen and provide feedback to your partner's oral reading.

⬚ Independent Reading Checkpoint

Respond to the first Reflection question in Embedded Assessment 1 as it relates to your independent reading narrative: How was the theme or central idea of "finding hope in times of despair" developed in the narrative you read independently?

Presenting Voices of the Holocaust

 ASSIGNMENT

Present a panel discussion that includes an oral reading of a significant passage from the texts read by your group. Your discussion should explain how the theme or central idea of "finding hope in times of despair" is developed in each text.

Planning: Discuss your ideas with your group to prepare a focus for your panel discussion.	■ How was the theme or central idea of "finding hope in times of despair" developed in your Holocaust texts? ■ If you read a narrative, how did supporting details such as character, point of view, plot, and setting contribute to the theme? If you read a poem, how did the language and structure contribute to the theme? ■ How will you find a significant passage for your oral reading that will help communicate the idea of "finding hope in times of despair"? ■ How will you assign talking points to each group member to include an introduction, at least two supporting details, and a conclusion?
Drafting: Write a draft of your talking point(s) that includes details from the text, commentary (analysis), and discussion questions.	■ How will the introductory talking point present a hook, summary of the text, and thematic statement? ■ How will the supporting talking points explain how literary elements contributed to theme? ■ How will the concluding talking point restate the theme, summarize the main points of the discussion, and elicit textual connections (text to self, text, or world) from the entire group?
Rehearsing: Rehearse and revise your panel discussion to improve the final presentation.	■ How will you prepare notes to provide constructive feedback and build on ideas and questions presented by other group members? ■ How will your group create smooth transitions between speakers? ■ How will you include your oral reading as you introduce and develop your explanation? ■ How will you use appropriate register, vocabulary, tone, and voice in order to establish and maintain a formal style? ■ How will you use eye contact, volume, and pronunciation to express your ideas clearly?

Reflection

After completing this Embedded Assessment, think about how you went about accomplishing this task, and respond to the following:

- How was the theme or central idea of "finding hope in times of despair" developed in the different Holocaust texts that you heard about in the panel discussions?
- What did you learn from studying and discussing texts about the Holocaust that you can apply to your own life?

SCORING GUIDE

Scoring Criteria	Exemplary	Proficient	Emerging	Incomplete
Ideas	The discussion • includes an effective oral reading of a significant text passage • presents a variety of significant ideas to explain how literary elements contribute to the development of a theme • provides relevant elaboration to develop the topic, including textual evidence, details, commentary, and questions.	The discussion • includes an oral reading of a text passage • presents adequate ideas to explain how literary elements contribute to the development of a theme • provides sufficient elaboration to develop the topic, including textual evidence, details, commentary, and questions.	The discussion • includes an ineffective passage or reading of a passage • presents unfocused or undeveloped ideas to explain how literary elements contribute to the development of a theme • provides insufficient or weak details to develop the topic.	The discussion • does not include an oral reading of a passage • does not explain how literary elements contribute to the development of a theme • provides minimal or irrelevant details.
Structure	The discussion • demonstrates strong evidence of effective collaboration and preparation • follows a logical and smooth organizational structure • uses transitional strategies effectively and purposefully.	The discussion • demonstrates sufficient evidence of collaboration and preparation • follows an adequate organizational structure • uses transitional strategies to create cohesion and clarify relationships.	The discussion • demonstrates insufficient evidence of collaboration and preparation • follows an uneven or ineffective organizational structure • uses transitional strategies inconsistently.	The discussion • demonstrates little or no collaboration and/or preparation • lacks any obvious organizational structure • does not use transitional strategies.
Use of Language	The speaker • communicates effectively with group members and the audience • uses consistently precise diction and academic language • demonstrates deep command of the conventions of standard English grammar, usage, and language (including active/passive voice).	The speaker • communicates appropriately with group members and the audience • uses sufficiently precise diction and academic language • demonstrates adequate command of the conventions of standard English grammar, usage, and language (including active/passive voice).	The speaker • communicates inappropriately or inconsistently with group members and/or the audience • uses insufficiently precise diction and academic language • demonstrates partial command of the conventions of standard English grammar, usage, and language.	The speaker • does not communicate well with the group or audience • uses flawed, confusing, or basic diction and language • has frequent errors in standard English grammar, usage, and language.

Literature Circle Text Collection

TEXT	CONTENTS	

About the Author

Lois Lowry (1937–) was born in Hawaii and grew up in New York, Pennsylvania, and Tokyo. She has written over forty books for young people and has received numerous awards for her writing, including two Newbery Medals for her books *Number the Stars* and *The Giver*. Lois Lowry was inspired to write *Number the Stars* after listening to stories told by her friend Annelise, who grew up in Denmark during World War II. Though Denmark surrendered to Germany, organized resistance groups and ordinary citizens helped almost all Jewish people in the country (over seven thousand people) escape to safety in Sweden.

Novel

from Number the Stars

by **Lois Lowry**

1   "Now," Peter said, looking at his watch, "I will lead the first group. You, and you, and you." He gestured to the old man and to the young people with their baby.

2   "Inge," he said. Annemarie realized that it was the first time that she had heard Peter Neilsen call her mother by her first name; before it had always been "Mrs. Johansen"; or in the old days, during the merriment and excitement of his engagement to Lise, it had been, occasionally, "Mama." Now it was Inge. It was as if he had moved beyond his own youth and had taken his place in the world of adults. Her mother nodded and waited for his instructions.

3   "You wait twenty minutes, and then bring the Rosens. Don't come sooner. We must be separate on the path so there is less chance of being seen."

4   Mrs. Johansen nodded again.

5   "Come directly back to the house after you have seen the Rosens safely to Henrik. Stay in the shadows and on the back path—you know that, of course."

6   "By the time you get the Rosens to the boat," Peter went on, "I will be gone. As soon as I deliver my group, I must move on. There is other work to be done tonight."

7   He turned to Annemarie. "So I will say goodbye to you now."

8   Annemarie went to him and gave him a hug. "But we will see you again soon?" she asked.

9   "I hope so," Peter said. "Very soon. Don't grow much more, or you will be taller than I am, little Longlegs!"

10   Annemarie smiled, but Peter's comment was no longer the lighthearted fun of the past. It was only a brief grasp at something that had gone.

11   Peter kissed Mama wordlessly. Then he wished the Rosens Godspeed, and he led the others through the door.

12   Mama, Annemarie, and the Rosens sat in silence. There was a slight commotion outside the door and Mama went quickly to look out. In a moment she was back.

13   "It's all right," she said, in response to their looks. "The old man stumbled a bit. But Peter helped him up. He didn't seem to be hurt. Maybe just his pride," she added, smiling a bit.

14   It was an odd word: pride. Annemarie looked at the Rosens, sitting there, wearing the misshapen, ill-fitting clothing, holding ragged blankets folded in their arms, their faces drawn and tired. She remembered the earlier, happier times: Mrs. Rosen, her hair neatly combed and covered, lighting the Sabbath candles, saying the ancient prayer. And Mr. Rosen, sitting in the big chair in their living room, studying his thick books, correcting papers, adjusting his glasses, looking up now and then to complain good-naturedly about the lack of decent light. She remembered Ellen in the school play, moving confidently across the stage, her gestures sure, her voice clear.

15   All of those things, those sources of pride—the candlesticks, the books, the daydreams of theater—they had all been left behind in Copenhagen. They had nothing with them now; there was only the clothing of unknown people for warmth, the food from Henrik's farm for survival, and the dark path ahead, through the woods, to freedom.

16   Annemarie realized, though she had not really been told, that Uncle Henrik was going to take them, in his boat, across the sea to Sweden. She knew how frightened Mrs. Rosen was of the sea: its width, its depth, its cold. She knew how frightened Ellen was of the soldiers, with their guns and boots, who were certainly looking for them. And she knew how frightened they all must be of the future.

17   But their shoulders were as straight as they had been in the past: in the classroom, on the stage, at the Sabbath table. So there were other sources, too, of pride, and they had not left everything behind.

About the Author

Irene Gut Opdyke (1918–2003) was born in Kozienice, Poland. While working for Nazi officers, she risked her life to save the lives of twelve Jews. When asked about her experiences later, she said, "You have to think with your heart and not with your head." She has been honored by many organizations and has received the Israel Medal of Honor and the Commander's Cross, the Polish Medal of Honor.

Memoir

from # In My Hands: Memories of a Holocaust Rescuer

by **Irene Gut Opdyke with Jennifer Armstrong**

The Villa

1 The instant I was able to get away after breakfast, I walked to the villa as quickly as I could—quickly enough to put a stitch in my side and to break a sweat in the heat. I unlocked the door and burst inside, dreading the sound of painters bumping ladders against the furniture. But it was silent. I was in time—assuming that my friends were indeed waiting in the basement. The smell of cabbage and potatoes lingered in the air.

2 Almost fearing what I might find, I opened the basement door and clattered down the stairs, my shoes making a racket on the wooden steps. "Hoo-ee! It's Irene!" I called out.

3 The first room was empty. Trying not to worry, I opened the door to the furnace room, praying to find my six friends—and Henry Weinbaum. The door creaked as it swung open into the gloom, and I called out again.

4 "It's Irene!"

5 There was an almost audible sigh of relief. One by one, figures emerged from the shadows: Ida, Lazar, Clara, Thomas, Fanka, Moses Steiner, and a young, handsome fellow I took to be Henry Weinbaum. I shook hands with them all silently, suddenly overcome with emotion. They were all there; they were safe and alive. And then, to my surprise, I found three strangers, who greeted me with an odd mixture of sheepishness and defiance.

6 "I'm Joseph Weiss," the eldest of the three said. "And this is Marian Wilner and Alex Rosen. Henry told us."

7 For a moment I was at a loss. I had ten lives in my hands now! But there wasn't time for lengthy introductions. The soldiers from the plant were due any minute to start painting.

8 "Hurry, everyone," I said. "You'll have time to stay in the attic until the house is painted. I'll check on you as often as I can. I don't need to tell you not to make any noise at all."

9 This was met with grim nods all around. Then we made our way upstairs. The attic was musty; dust swirled in a shaft of light from the high window, and the air smelled of mouse droppings. "Shoes off," I said. "Don't walk around unless you absolutely must."

10 I locked them in just as trucks ground to a halt out on the street.

11 I kicked the basement door shut on my way to let in the soldiers, and then unlocked the front door.

12 "This way," I said, stepping aside to usher them in with their painting equipment and drop cloths. When I glanced outside, I saw the major climbing out of a car.

13 "Guten Tag, Irene," he called cheerily.

14 I bobbed my head. "Herr Major."

15 "This is splendid," he said, rubbing his hands together as he came inside. "I'll move in in a week or so, when all the painting and repairs are finished, but in the meantime, I'd like you to move in right away, so that you can oversee things. Don't worry about your duties at the hotel— if you can serve dinner, Schulz can manage without you the rest of the time."

16 As he spoke, Major Rügemer strolled back and forth across the hallway, glancing into the rooms and nodding his approval. His footsteps echoed off the walls, and he muttered, "Ja, ja, ausgezeichnet," under his breath. Then, when another truckload of soldiers arrived, he went outside to meet them and show them around the garden: There were renovations to be made on the grounds, as well. I stood at the dining room window, watching him point out the gazebo and indicate which shrubs and trees should be removed and where new ones should be planted. Behind me, I could hear the painters beginning to shove furniture across the floors, exchanging jokes and commenting on the weather and the sour cabbagey smell left behind by the previous tenants. I heard one of them say " ... the major's girlfriend."

17 I gritted my teeth and prepared to spend the day keeping the soldiers away from the attic.

18 For the next few days, while the soldiers swarmed around the villa—painting, repairing, replanting—I contrived to smuggle food upstairs to the attic. I took fruit and cheese, cold tea, bread and nuts. I also took up two buckets to use for toilets. The attic was stuffy from the heat of summer, but we were reluctant to open the one window high on the wall. The fugitives had accustomed themselves to much more discomfort than this. They were willing to sit in the stifling heat, not speaking, just waiting. At night, when the workmen were gone and I had returned from the hotel, I was able to give my friends some minutes of liberty. They used the bathroom, stretched their legs, and bathed their sweating faces with cool water. But we did not turn on any lights, and we were still as silent as ghosts.

19 It wasn't long before the servants' quarters had been completely refurbished; I had seen to that. Telling the workmen that the major had ordered the work to be done from bottom to top, I directed them to start with the basement. Then, when it was finished, I waited until dark and triumphantly escorted my friends to their new quarters, fresh with the smell of sawdust and new paint instead of old cooking.

20 It was the start of a new way of life for all of us. Several of the men, being handy and intelligent, were able to rig up a warning system. A button was installed in the floor of the foyer,

under a faded rug. From it, a wire led to a light in the basement, which would flicker on and off when I stepped on the button. I kept the front door locked at all times, and when I went to see who might be knocking, I had ample opportunity to signal to the people in the basement. One flash would warn them to stand by for more news. Two flashes meant to be very careful, and constant flashing meant danger—hide immediately. We had also found the villa's rumored hiding place: A tunnel led from behind the furnace to a bunker underneath the gazebo. If there was serious danger, everyone could instantly scramble into the hole and wait for me to give them the all clear. The cellar was kept clear of any signs of occupation. Once the men had killed all of the rats living in the bunker under the gazebo, it could accommodate all ten people without too much discomfort.

21 There was food in plenty; Schulz kept the major's kitchen stocked with enough to feed a platoon, and once again, I could not help wondering if he had an inkling of what I was doing. I was also able to go to the Warenhaus whenever I needed to, for cigarettes, vodka, sugar, extra household goods, anything the major might conceivably need for entertaining in his new villa. Of course, the soldiers who ran the Warenhaus had no way of knowing that half of what I got there went directly into the basement, and I was certainly not going to tell them!

22 The basement was cool even in the intense summer heat; there was a bathroom, and newspapers, which I brought down after the major was finished with them. All in all, the residents of the basement enjoyed quite a luxurious hiding place.

23 And yet it almost fell apart when the major moved in at last.

24 "The basement is finished, isn't it?" he asked me when he arrived.

25 All the hairs on my arms prickled with alarm. "Do you have some plans for it, Major?" I asked, keeping my voice from showing my fear.

26 He unbuttoned the top button of his tunic. "I'm sure it will do very well for my orderly."

27 I felt the blood drain from my face, and Major Rügemer looked at me in surprise. "What is it?"

28 I did not have to fake the tears that sprang to my eyes. "Please don't move him in here," I pleaded. My mind raced with explanations. "I never told you this, but at the beginning of the war, I was captured by Russian soldiers and—and I was—" My throat closed up.

29 The major frowned at me. "You were what?"

30 They attacked me, sir." I saw his face flush, and I hurried on, more confident. "I cannot bear to have a young man living here. It brings back terrible memories for me. Please take pity on me."

31 Major Rügemer dragged his handkerchief from his pocket and blew his nose hard, shaking his head in anger. "War brings out the worst, the very worst in some people! Funny," he went on, "I always wondered why you didn't have a boyfriend, a pretty girl like you. I've never seen you flirt with the officers the way some other girls might do."

32 "I can do all of the work myself, Herr Major," I pressed. "You will not feel any lack."

33 He put his hand on my shoulder. "Of course, Irene. I wouldn't dream of making you unhappy."

34 I smiled up at him. Sometimes it made me cringe inside, to get what I wanted by playing up my femininity. Yet I knew it was the one power I had, and I would have been a fool not to use it. For my pretty face, for the affection he felt for me, the major would let me have my way.

35   We quickly fell into a routine. Once he had moved in, Major Rügemer left for the factory every morning at eight-thirty. I rose at seven-thirty to start his breakfast, which he ate in the dining room. Often, he asked me to sit and have a cup of coffee to keep him company, and we would chat about nothing—about the nest of blackbirds in the gazebo, or the way the middle C on the parlor piano stuck, or what kind of pickles went best with pork. Sometimes, if he was planning to entertain, we would discuss a menu for cocktails or dinner or after-dinner drinks. He stirred his coffee all the time in an absent way, and the spoon would clink-clink-clink against the cup as we talked.

36   Once he left the house, I locked the front door and left the key in the lock; this would make it impossible for the major to unlock the door from the outside and come in unexpectedly. This was the time when my friends in the basement could begin their day, taking showers, brewing coffee, listening to BBC war news on the radio while I cleaned the house. They read the paper and compared the official reports from Berlin with what they heard on the BBC. I returned to the factory every evening to serve dinner, but I always went home before the major.

37   And when he did return at night and rang the doorbell (I told him I kept the door locked out of nervousness), I opened the door and let him into a house that gave no hint that there were people living in the basement. It almost made me laugh, sometimes, to think of the absurdity and irony of it. Under any circumstances, it would have been hilarious, because this was the stuff of farce: upstairs, a deaf and snuffling codger, oblivious to the goings-on at his very feet, and below, the hunted stowaways, dining richly off the major's larder. They were like mice in a cheese shop guarded by a sleeping cat. Under the circumstances, however, I never did get all the way to laughter; a grim smile from time to time was all. This was, after all, a capital crime.

Irene Gut Opdyke with a photograph of seven of the twelve Jewish people she saved by hiding them in the cellar of a German major's house where she worked as a housekeeper as a Polish Catholic teenager during WWII.

About the Texts

I Never Saw Another Butterfly is an anthology of drawings and poetry written by children in the Terezin concentration camp in Czechoslovakia. Many scholars and artists were sent to Terezin, and although the camp had terrible living conditions, there was a rich culture of music, poetry, and art. Tens of thousands of children spent time at Terezin, and over 90 percent of them did not survive. The art and poetry left behind by the children was saved when the camp was liberated in 1945 and after ten years was finally put on exhibition for the world to see. Their poetry and art convey their experiences and their emotions to readers today.

Poetry

The Butterfly

by **Pavel Friedmann**

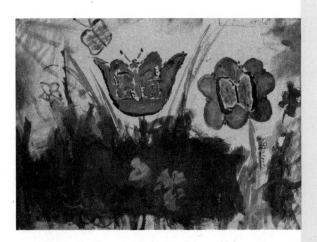

   The last, the very last,

   So richly, brightly, dazzlingly yellow.

   Perhaps if the sun's tears would sing
      against a white stone. ...

5 Such, such a yellow

   Is carried lightly 'way up high.

   It went away I'm sure because it wished to
      kiss the world good-bye.

   For seven weeks I've lived in here,

10 Penned up inside this ghetto.

   But I have found what I love here.

   The dandelions call to me

   And the white chestnut branches in the court.

   Only I never saw another butterfly.

15 That butterfly was the last one.

   Butterflies don't live in here,
      in the ghetto.

Poetry

On a Sunny Evening

by **Anonymous**

On a purple, sun-shot evening

Under wide-flowering chestnut trees

Upon the threshold full of dust

Yesterday, today, the days are all like these.

5 Trees flower forth in beauty,

Lovely, too, their very wood all gnarled and old

That I am half afraid to peer

Into their crowns of green and gold.

The sun has made a veil of gold

10 So lovely that my body aches.

Above, the heavens shriek with blue

Convinced I've smiled by some mistake.

The world's abloom and seems to smile.

I want to fly but where, how high?

15 If in barbed wire, things can bloom

Why couldn't I? I will not die!

About the Author

Jane Yolen (1939–) is an American author who publishes fantasy, science fiction, and children's books. Yolen has written over 300 books, including the *The Devil's Arithmetic*, an historical fiction novel about the Holocaust. In 1999 the book was made into a television film starring Kirsten Dunst. Yolen has won several awards for her writing, including the National Jewish Book Award, and was nominated for a Nebula award for *The Devil's Arithmetic*. She spends her time between Massachusetts and Scotland, where she spends four months of the year writing.

Novel

from The Devil's Arithmetic

by **Jane Yolen**

1   They sat on the benches naked and cold for a long time while the barber worked on each in turn. Hannah glanced around cautiously. With their hair gone, they all looked like little old men. She wondered what she looked like herself, resisting the urge to put her hand up to her head again. She would not think about it. Thinking was dangerous. In this place she would not think, only do.

2   After a while, time seemed to lose its reality. Only the *snick-snack* of the scissors and the occasional cry of the barber's victims marked the minutes. There was a dreamlike feeling in the room as if, Hannah thought, anything might happen next.

3   The woman in the blue dress entered the far door and stood for a long moment examining them all with a sour face. Hannah happened to be facing the door when she entered and, without meaning to, locked eyes with her. It was the woman who looked away first, calling out, "Schnell! into the next room. You must have clothes." She turned abruptly, signaling with her hand. For the first time Hannah noticed that she had only three fingers on her right hand.

4   *I wonder how she lost those fingers*, Hannah thought. *Was she born that way?* Then remembered she was not going to think. She rose with the others and shuffled out of the room after them.

5   For the first time, Hannah allowed herself to feel hungry. But when she began to wonder about when they might be fed, the still, small voice reminded her, *Don't think, do*. She reached out and found the hand of one of the children. Silently she squeezed the child's hand for comfort.

6   The room they were herded into was a small, low-ceilinged place with a single window high up under the eaves. It reminded Hannah of an attic somewhere, she couldn't remember where. An unadorned light bulb dangled down over several long wooden tables piled high with rags.

7   *"Shmattes!"* whispered a woman behind Hannah in a hoarse voice.

8   *"Choose!"* bellowed the three-fingered woman in blue.

9   *"Schnell!"*

10   Hannah took her turn at one of the tables and started to paw through the clothes. They were ragged and worn and smelled peculiar, with a lingering, dank odor, part old sweat and part something else Hannah did not even want to guess at. She hesitated.

11   "Choose, Jews. You cannot be fancy now."

12   *Don't think. Do.* Hannah put her hand onto the pile and came up with a dark gray dress with a dirty white collar and cuffs. There was a ragged rip along the hem and deep perspiration stains under the arms. Looking around, she saw that the other women were already slipping into whatever they had chosen. She raised the gray dress over her head and pulled it down. The material was silky and a bit stiff where it was stained. Buttoning the three buttons in front, she remembered suddenly how she had thought the dark blue dress Gitl had given her ugly, how she'd called it a rag. Even that small return of memory was a comfort. She'd called the dress a rag; she hadn't known anything about wearing rags then. Her arms strained the sleeves of the gray dress.

13   "Help the children," someone near her whispered.

14   It sounded like Gitl.

15   Hannah glanced down at the naked child by her side. Was it Tzipporah? The poor little thing had her thumb in her mouth. Her eyelids were a bruised bluish color and she swayed where she stood. Hannah rummaged quickly through the pile of clothes and found a blouse and jumper that looked as if they might fit. The child made no move to help, and Hannah had to dress her as if she were a doll, pushing her arms into the sleeves of the blouse as gently as she could.

16   They were herded directly into another room and made to line up single file. Another shaven-headed prisoner, with an odd-looking metal instrument, sat at a wooden table. There were guards at the door.

17   Hannah could hear a mumble of voices by the table, but she couldn't begin to guess what they were discussing. Holding Tzipporah's hand, she moved in the slow, shuffling barefooted rhythm of the line; wait, walk, wait, walk.

18   Closer to the table, she saw that the man was using the instrument to write something on each woman's arm. Strangely, no one protested or drew their arm away.

19   Another memory, hazier than the one about the dress, flooded back to her. *"This. . ."* She heard a familiar man's voice crying out. *"I'll give them this!"* She couldn't think who it was or what he was giving to whom. When she turned to see who was speaking, everyone behind her was silent, staring at the floor.

20   "Next!"

21 The man meant Hannah. She walked up to the table and sat down on a chair by the side of the table.

22 "Tell me your name," the man said. "I will give you a number in exchange."

23 That seemed simple enough, but she couldn't think of a name. There was none that came to her. From behind, Gitl whispered hoarsely, "Chaya. Chaya Abramowicz."

24 She said it aloud. "Chaya." It felt—and it did not feel—like hers.

25 The man looked at her and his eyes were the saddest she'd ever seen, a muddy brown, like river sludge. His mouth was puckered and old. It dropped open as easily as a slot in a machine, and a sound—not quite a cry—came out.

26 "I knew it would come," he whispered. "Some day. The *malach ha-mavis*."

27 "What? What?" Hannah asked.

28 That is my daughter's dress you are wearing. Chaya Abramowicz. My Chaya. I brought it as a present for her in Lublin."

29 "Chaya," Hannah said.

30 "The same name, too. God is good. Your name means life." His voice broke.

31 "Life," Hannah repeated.

32 He nodded, then shook his head, the one following the other like a single movement. "You are Chaya no longer, child. Now you are J197241. Remember it."

33 "I can't remember anything," Hannah said, puzzled.

34 "This you must remember, for if you forget it, *life* is gone indeed." The tattooing pen burned her flesh, leaving a trail of blue numbers in her arm above the wrist. J197241. She didn't cry. She wouldn't. It was something more she just remembered: her promise to Gitl.

35 When the man finished the number, he reached out and touched the collar of her dress, smoothing it down gently. "Live," he whispered. "For my Chaya. For all of our Chayas. Live. And remember."

36 There was a loud clearing of a throat and Hannah looked up into the guard's unsmiling face. "Next!" he said.

37 Little Tzipporah was next, and Hannah held the child on her lap, covering her eyes with ice-cold hands and crooning a song into her ears. It was a wedding song, the only song she could come up with, something about a madness forced upon them. The words didn't matter, only the melody, only the soothing rhythm. The child, Tzipporah, J197242, lay silent in her arms.

About the Interviewee

Thomas Buergenthal (1934–), former judge of the International Court of Justice and international human rights advocate, grew up in Czechoslovakia and is a survivor of the Auschwitz concentration camp. He was interviewed by Joan Ringelheim and Neenah Ellis as a part of the United States Holocaust Memorial Museum's "Life After the Holocaust" project, which documents oral histories from Holocaust survivors. In Buergenthal's memoir, *A Lucky Child: A Memoir of Surviving Auschwitz as a Young Boy*, he shares his journey from the Auschwitz and Sachsenhausen concentration camps to liberation.

Interview

from # Life After the Holocaust

Stories of Holocaust Survivors After the War

Interview Transcript with Thomas Buergenthal by **Joan Ringelheim and Neenah Ellis**

1 **NARRATOR:** The Netherlands—February 27, 2001.

2 **THOMAS:** We are at the International Court of Justice in The Hague in my office at the court. Ahm, on a very sort of *(laughs)* dark, dreary day …

3 **NARRATOR:** Judge Thomas Buergenthal is well known as a leading advocate of international human rights law, and for his pioneering work in international law. In March of 2000, he was elected the American judge for the principal judicial organ of the United Nations—the International Court of Justice.

4 **THOMAS:** It's a court where you deal only with disputes between states. So, for an international lawyer like me, this is a dream court and a dream come true. It's like being on the Supreme Court of the United States. This is the court that determines what is and what is not international law. Not that we're that important but in terms of those of us who believe in international law and practice international law, this is the Mecca to which you look. I should tell you that the notice to me that I was going to be the nominee of the United States for the Court came to me while I … had just done a visit to Auschwitz, my second visit, and I was in Cracow, had just come back from it, in the evening, in the hotel, when I received the call from the legal advisor. So, it was very special.

Oswiecim, Poland – July 23, 2011: Warning sign at Auschwitz concentration camp. It was the biggest Nazi concentration camp in Europe during World War II.

5 **NARRATOR:** Buergenthal's first visit to Auschwitz after the war was with his wife, Peggy. He returned again, close to the 55th anniversary of the day when, as a 10-year-old, he left the camp on a forced march. It was one of the infamous "death marches" that the retreating Nazis forced on most concentration camp prisoners, rather than leaving them to be liberated by the advancing Allied forces.

6 **THOMAS:** It was easier when my wife and I went, because it was summer and it was easier to take. When we were there on the 20th of January 19 ... of 2000, it was just as it was, as I remembered it in terms of the cold. The road was all ice. And all I could think about was, "How did I ever survive this?" Because I was dressed in the heaviest jacket with sweaters, with hat—and I was freezing! And I was there as a child with a little blanket and thin prison uniform and—and I made it. It's ... hard to believe.

[Thunder is heard, then sounds of war.]

7 **NARRATOR:** Those prisoners from the Auschwitz men's camp who survived the death march ended up in the concentration camp Sachsenhausen, near Berlin, Germany. In March, Thomas entered the infirmary, where two of his frostbitten toes were amputated. In April, when the battle over Berlin had already begun, Sachsenhausen was evacuated, and Thomas was left behind with the other prisoners who couldn't walk.

8 **THOMAS:** The next morning I got up, and it was very, very quiet except for the shooting coming closer. I crawled out, went out and looked up and saw in the entrance of the camp, over

the entrance on the inside—they always had a machine gun mounted with SS guards sitting on, and there was nobody there, the machine gun was empty. I came back and told people. Of course, nobody believed me (*laughing*) that this was happening. And then we just waited. And the shooting came closer. Then we began hearing small arms fire and suddenly sort of, I think it was in the early afternoon ... the camp had a big bell in the middle of this field, and a Russian soldier was ringing—was driven in with a jeep and was ringing the bell saying, "You're free." You know when I see pictures of people who were liberated by American troops, by British troops, they were liberated. We were sort of ... there were none of these scenes as far as I remember. The Russians just told us, "You can go." I mean, we felt a great sense of relief, because we expected to be shot. But I didn't have any sense of the tremendous joy that other people must have experienced. I was alone in many ways. I think if my parents had been there it would have been different.

9   **NARRATOR:** Thomas had been separated from his parents for several months. He was taken in by members of a Polish Army unit under Russian command. The soldiers assumed that he was a Christian Polish child. And Thomas had experienced enough discrimination to know that it was not safe to tell them that he was Jewish and from Czechoslovakia. The Polish he had learned in the ghetto of Kielce and in Auschwitz proved good enough for his new comrades.

10   **THOMAS:** They made me a small uniform. And I had shoes. They even gave me a small revolver—not a revolver—automatic pistol. I had—they had found a circus horse some place, a pony, and—because much of the army was still horse-drawn. They had—supplies of the Russian and Polish army was still brought in by horse-drawn carts. There was a lot of horses. And I had my horse, and I could keep up with the soldiers. And I had a wonderful time. (*Laughs.*) The strange thing is that the sort of—the absurdity of it, the comic aspect of it never occurred to me as a child. And, you know, at the same time I—all of this I thought was going to lead to my being reunited with my parents. And I never even thought that this wasn't going to happen. This was all part of a process. And in the meantime I could eat, and I no longer had to be afraid, and I had fun.

11   **NARRATOR:** The soldiers fed him bacon and bread. For the 10-year-old, none of it seemed out of the ordinary.

12   **THOMAS:** And I think it has a lot to do with having, being a child and taking a lot of these things for granted. This is life, and this is what happened. One day you don't have anything to eat, and the next day there's suddenly food. What I remember though is that I for years afterwards would always think that you should always eat before you did anything of importance because you never knew when you were going to eat again.

13   **NARRATOR:** Only one of the Polish soldiers, a Jew himself, found out that Thomas was Jewish. Eventually, he made arrangements for the boy to be taken to a Jewish orphanage. In 1946, his mother tracked him down, and Thomas was smuggled to Germany to be reunited with her. They settled in Goettingen, his mother's hometown. And suddenly, life took on different shades of normalcy. Going to school, catching up ...

14   **THOMAS:** With my mother we discussed—there was a lot of reminiscing about the camp and you know, "Where was this and that. What happened? ... " The truth of the matter is that we often laughed about things in retrospect, about things that happened that were funny, about

this or that that happened. So ahm, the human spirit—you couldn't take all of this, if it were only reminiscences about all of the terrible things. I saw the fact that I survived as a victory, that we had won over them. They wanted to kill us and we made it; we didn't give them the joy of killing us. So there was a tremendous sense of satisfaction, that of survival, unlike what one reads now that people supposedly feel bad that they survived and others didn't. We never had that feeling. Neither did my mother. Because my mother survived. I mean, we felt very bad that, for example, my father didn't survive. He died just shortly before the end of the war. But we never felt that—guilty about the fact of surviving. On the contrary.

[*German reporter heard in background*, "Goering ist gefragt worden, ob er hören kann."]

15 **NARRATOR:** In 1946, at the war crime trials in Nuremberg, 19 out of 22 German war criminals were convicted. Twelve were sentenced to death.

[*1946 sentence is read* " ... The International Military Tribunal sentences you to death by hanging ... "]

16 **THOMAS:** The first, almost first English words that I remember was "by hanging." I remember listening to the radio when they—when they announced the sentences. And we were, we were listening to that and with sort of, with joy ... And sitting on the balcony on a Sunday and seeing the German families taking a walk and my father hadn't come back. And at that point, you know, the desire of sort of seeing—when I first came back I would love to mount a machine gun on that balcony and shoot all of them. But then you realize that, you know these are people you don't know whether they killed your father. Most of them probably didn't. And you make friends. And you find for example, we lived in the house with somebody, who ah, a Catholic family that had actually helped the Jews in town, and had been in danger themselves. And so you—the sort of abstract hatred becomes transformed into the fact that they're human beings regardless of whether they're Germans or not Germans. And not every German was guilty.

17 **NARRATOR:** The only Jewish student in class, he never experienced antisemitism, yet never felt quite comfortable either. In 1951, Thomas left for America.

18 **NARRATOR:** Thomas ... was busy getting on with his life, college on a full scholarship— New York University Law School—Harvard Law School. Citizenship in 1957—marriage two years later. He never returned to live in Germany, but he remained in close contact with his mother until her death in 1991. At home, Thomas focused on his three sons who were born in the early '60s. At work, he was drawn to international law—a discipline of little interest to most American law students and lawyers at the time. He was also interested in human rights law, a relatively new discipline.

19 **THOMAS:** I don't know, I've often been asked, well, is it my experience that drove me to it. I'm never quite sure. Ah, but what I think is true is this: that I felt from my concentration camp experience where we always looked to the U.S. and to England to save us really, that in a situation where one was in trouble from a human rights point of view, one couldn't rely on the domestic scene, on the domestic environment, and you had to look—you had to have some international mechanisms that could protect you. Really the Universal Declaration of Human Rights had been adopted in '48, but nothing much was happening. And then in the early '50s the European Convention on Human Rights came into being, and I was fascinated ... wanted to see how did this work, really. Is there a chance that this might prevent what I went through?

20 **NARRATOR:** In addition to teaching and writing landmark books and articles on human rights law, Buergenthal has been a key member of several international bodies, including the United Nations Human Rights Committee, the Truth Commission for El Salvador, and the Claims Resolution Tribunal for Dormant Accounts in Switzerland.

21 **THOMAS:** What is impressive about it is not my career. I mean that—those things are often happenstance than anything else. But what is significant about it ... this is an example of the fact that one can overcome certain ... not I personally, but that we can overcome some of these murderous things that have happened and still be able to work for a better world! That to me has always been the sort of significant aspect of my activities. I spoke once in Germany, I think in connection when I got the honorary degree. And I said, "It's so wonderful when you think that when you go down the Rhine and when you remember that the Rhine was reinforced on both sides between France and Germany with cannons and today you don't even need a passport!" There's tremendous things that have happened that should give us a sense of optimism. Yet, you know, the cynics keep saying, nothing is changing. Lots of terrible things happening. But a lot of good things have been happening, and that—that should inspire people to want to do things.

About the Author

Abraham Sutzkever (1913–2010) was a poet who was known for his works about the Holocaust. He was born in Belarus and survived the Vilna ghetto, where his young son was killed by Nazis. Sutzkever and his wife joined a Jewish resistance group and later moved to Israel. Sutzkever mainly wrote in Yiddish. He was awarded the Israel Prize in 1985. In this poem, Sutzkever pays tribute to Yanova Bartoszewicz, a Polish woman who hid him during a period of mass killings.

Poetry

1980

by **Abraham Sutzkever**

And when I go up as a pilgrim in winter, to recover
the place I was born, and the twin to self I am in my mind,
then I'll go in black snow as a pilgrim to find
the grave of my saviour, Yanova.

She'll hear what I whisper, under my breath:
Thank you. You saved my tears from the flame.
Thank you. Children and grandchildren you rescued
   from death.
I planted a sapling (it doesn't suffice) in your name.

Time in its gyre spins back down the flue
faster than nightmares of nooses can ride,
quicker than nails. And you, my saviour, in your cellar you'll
   hide
me, ascending in dreams as a pilgrim to you.

You'll come from the yard in your slippers, crunching the
   snow
so I'll know. Again I'm there in the cellar, degraded and low,
You're bringing me milk and bread sliced thick at the edge.
You're making the sign of the cross. I'm making my pencil its
   pledge.

Learning Strategies

QHT
Close Reading
Paraphrasing
Graphic Organizer

My Notes

Learning Targets

- Reflect on and make connections between the lessons of the Holocaust and "taking action."
- Analyze the skills and knowledge needed to complete Embedded Assessment 2 successfully.

Preview

In this activity, you will preview Embedded Assessment 2 as a class.

Making Connections

During your study of narratives of the Holocaust, you were asked to think about the concept of "finding hope in times of despair." This idea is developed further in the last half of the unit by building on the idea of people taking action to create positive change in their communities and the world.

Essential Questions

Reflect on your understanding of the relationship between the first Essential Question *(Why is it important to learn about the Holocaust?)* and the second Essential Question *(How can one person make a difference?)*.

Developing Vocabulary

Dividing words into their individual syllables helps with pronunciation, decoding word parts, and spelling. Return to the Academic Vocabulary and Literary Terms at the beginning of the unit, and use a print or digital resource to determine the syllable breakdown of each word. You might notice that some words have different syllable breakdowns for spelling and pronunciation. Using the QHT strategy, re-sort the words based on your new learning.

1. Compare this sort with your original sort. How has your understanding changed?

2. Select a word from the chart (or a Holocaust-related term), and write a concise statement about your learning. How has your understanding of this word changed over the course of this unit?

Unpacking Embedded Assessment 2

Closely read the Embedded Assessment 2 assignment and the Scoring Guide.

 Develop a multimedia presentation that informs your peers about an issue of national or global significance and convinces them to take action. Work collaboratively to conduct and synthesize research into an engaging campaign that challenges your audience to make a difference.

Work with your class to paraphrase the expectations and create a graphic organizer to use as a visual reminder of the required concepts (what you need to know) and skills (what you need to do).

After each activity, use this graphic organizer to guide reflection about what you have learned and what you still need to learn in order to be successful in the Embedded Assessment.

INDEPENDENT READING LINK

Reading Plan

To support your learning in the second half of the unit, select a fiction or nonfiction narrative about someone who made a difference in the world or who tried to confront social injustice.

Making a Difference

Learning Targets

- Identify the purpose of PSAs (public service announcements) by analyzing their formats and imagery.
- Evaluate the effectiveness of imagery and language in PSAs.

Preview

In this activity, you will apply your understanding of the elements of multimedia by finding or creating a PSA for a cause you care about.

My Notes

Multimedia

1. How would you define *multimedia*? Use your understanding of word parts to determine the meanings of each part: *multi* and *media*. What is the connection between the words *medium* and *media*?

2. Work with a partner to brainstorm the different media for delivering information, including how you will communicate about the research you will be conducting in this unit, to an audience.

Media for Delivering Information

3. Discuss how you will choose which media to use when presenting your campaign at the end of this unit. What factors should you take into consideration?

ACADEMIC

A **slogan** is a memorable phrase or motto used to identify or promote a product or group. Slogans often rhyme and are short enough for people to remember easily.

Analyzing the Characteristics of Multimedia

Multimedia incorporates more than one kind of communication and includes text, images, audio, color, lighting, camera techniques, sound, and videos.

4. How effective are visuals in making a point about a significant issue? How do they compare with other media channels: speeches, articles, videos, radio announcements, and so on?

5. Look at the following two images. Each is intended as a "call to action" as part of a public service campaign to make a difference. Examine each of the visuals and determine its purpose. Note also that each image has text, including a **slogan**. How does a slogan help promote a goal?

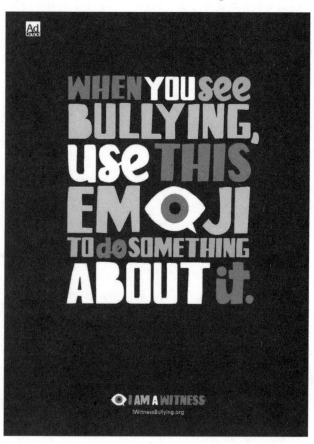

6. Evaluate the effectiveness of the imagery and the slogan for the PSAs above. Each image is associated with a website. What can you tell about the sponsors of the visuals by their web addresses?

7. As you explore each website, take notes about its images, slogans, audio, video, and additional media formats. Analyze the purpose of the presented information and describe how the purpose is helped by the graphic features. In your groups, discuss and evaluate the purpose of the information. Is it presented for social, commercial, public safety, or political purposes?

8. Choose a recorder to capture the insights and conclusions of your group discussion.

Website	Description	Purpose	Evaluation

9. **Quickwrite:** What kind of music would you combine with these campaigns to make them memorable? How might you use music to enhance your multimedia presentation?

LANGUAGE & WRITER'S CRAFT: Reviewing Participial Phrases

The **participle** forms of verbs can be used as adjectives. There are two participial forms: present (ending in *-ing*) and past (usually ending in *-d* or *-ed*).

> **rising** world concerns

> widely **used** media

A participle may be part of a participial phrase, which includes the participle plus any complements and modifiers. The whole phrase serves as an adjective. In the following example, the participial phrase appears in bold text; the participle itself is *located*.

Located 275 miles north of San Francisco, Arcata is ...

PRACTICE In the following space, write one sentence using a participle and one sentence using a participial phrase.

☑ Check Your Understanding

Find or create a paper advertisement for a cause you care about. Include a simple illustration and slogan. In small groups, evaluate the advertisements.

📝 Writing Prompt: Informational Text

Explain a cause that you believe in to your classmates. Use the RAFT strategy to plan a first draft including selecting an appropriate genre. Some genres to consider are campaign posters, speeches, public service announcements, or digital text such as websites, podcasts, or commercials. Be sure to:

- Include an opening statement that introduces your cause and why you support it.
- Choose an appropriate genre for the topic, audience, and purpose.
- Incorporate elements that are characteristic of the genre.

Never Forget, Never Again

Learning Strategies

SOAPSTone
Close Reading
Discussion Groups
Drafting
Rehearsal
Oral Reading

Learning Targets

- Analyze the parts of an argument.
- Write and present a short argumentative speech about a controversial issue.

Preview

In this activity, you will study the structure of an argumentative speech to help you create your own.

Setting a Purpose for Reading

- As you read the speech, underline words and phrases that produce strong emotions.
- Circle unknown words and phrases. Try to determine the meaning of the words by using context clues, word parts, or a dictionary.

Speech

from # The Nobel Acceptance
Speech Delivered by Elie Wiesel
in Oslo on December 10, 1986

My Notes

1   I am moved, deeply moved by your words, Chairman Aarvik. And it is with a profound sense of **humility** that I accept the honor—the highest there is—that you have chosen to bestow upon me. I know your choice **transcends** my person.

2   Do I have the right to represent the multitudes who have perished? Do I have the right to accept this great honor on their behalf? I do not. No one may speak for the dead, no one may interpret their **mutilated** dreams and visions. And yet, I sense their presence. I always do—and at this moment more than ever. The presence of my parents, that of my little sister. The presence of my teachers, my friends, my companions …

3   This honor belongs to all the survivors and their children and, through us, to the Jewish people with whose destiny I have always identified.

4   I remember: It happened yesterday, or eternities ago. A young Jewish boy discovered the Kingdom of Night. I remember his bewilderment, I remember his **anguish**. It all happened so fast. The ghetto. The **deportation**. The sealed cattle car. The fiery altar upon which the history of our people and the future of mankind were meant to be sacrificed.

5   I remember he asked his father: "Can this be true? This is the twentieth century, not the Middle Ages. Who would allow such crimes to be committed? How could the world remain silent?"

humility: modesty
transcends: goes beyond the limits of
mutilated: damaged beyond repair
anguish: agonizing pain
deportation: removal to another country

1986 Nobel Peace Prize winner and writer Elie Wiesel gives a speech after awarding ceremonies on December 11, 1986.

My Notes

_____

6   And now the boy is turning to me. "Tell me," he asks, "what have you done with my future, what have you done with your life?" And I tell him that I have tried. That I have tried to keep memory alive, that I have tried to fight those who would forget. Because if we forget, we are guilty, we are accomplices.

7   And then I explain to him how **naïve** we were, that the world did know and remained silent. And that is why I swore never to be silent whenever, wherever human beings endure suffering and humiliation. We must take sides. Neutrality helps the oppressor, never the victim. Silence encourages the tormentor, never the tormented. Sometimes we must interfere. When human lives are endangered, when human dignity is in **jeopardy**, national borders and sensitivities become irrelevant. Wherever men and women are persecuted because of their race, religion, or political views, that place must—at that moment—become the center of the universe.

8   There is so much injustice and suffering crying out for our attention: victims of hunger, of racism and political persecution—in Chile, for instance, or in Ethiopia—writers and poets, prisoners in so many lands governed by the Left and by the Right.

9   Human rights are being violated on every continent. More people are oppressed than free. How can one not be sensitive to their plight? Human suffering anywhere concerns men and women everywhere.

10   There is so much to be done, there is so much that can be done. One person—a Raoul Wallenberg, an Albert Schweitzer, Martin Luther King Jr.— one person of **integrity**, can make a difference, a difference of life and death. As long as one **dissident** is in prison, our freedom will not be true. As long as one child is hungry, our life will be filled with anguish and shame. What all these victims need above all is to know that they are not alone, that we are not forgetting them, that when their voices are stifled we shall lend them ours, that while their freedom depends on ours, the quality of our freedom depends on theirs.

11   This is what I say to the young Jewish boy wondering what I have done with his years. It is in his name that I speak to you and that I express to you my deepest gratitude as one who has emerged from the Kingdom of Night. We know that every moment is a moment of grace, every hour an offering; not to share them would mean to betray them.

12   Our lives no longer belong to us alone; they belong to all those who need us desperately.

Making Observations
- Which parts of the speech appeal to your emotions?
- What imagery could you picture in your mind?

naïve: simple; unsophisticated

jeopardy: peril; danger

integrity: adherence to an ethical code

dissident: one who disagrees

Returning to the Text

- Return to the text as you respond to the following questions. Use text evidence to support your responses.
- Write any additional questions you have about the speech in your Reader/Writer Notebook.

1. What can you infer about the meaning of *bestow* in paragraph 1?

_____

_____

_____

_____

2. In paragraphs 2–5, Elie Wiesel makes reference to, or alludes to, what central event? Why does he use fragments to evoke the memory?

_____

_____

_____

_____

3. In paragraphs 6 and 7, why does the author start multiple sentences with *and*?

_____

_____

_____

_____

4. Closely read paragraphs 6 and 7. What is Wiesel saying about memory and silence?

_____

_____

_____

_____

Working from the Text

5. The purpose of "a call to action" is to provide a concluding statement or section that supports the argument by making clear to the audience what the writer or speaker wants them to think or do. How is Wiesel's last sentence a "call to action"?

6. You will be assigned a specific element from the following SOAPSTone strategy. Reread the speech and annotate it for this element.

Introducing the Strategy: SOAPSTone

SOAPSTone stands for Speaker, Occasion, Audience, Purpose, Subject, and Tone. It is a reading and writing tool for analyzing the relationship among a writer, his or her purpose, and the target audience of the text. SOAPSTone guides you in asking questions to analyze a text or to plan for writing a composition.

- **Speaker:** The speaker is the voice that tells the story.
- **Occasion:** The occasion is the time and place of the story; it is the context that prompted the writing.
- **Audience:** The audience is the person or persons to whom the piece is directed.
- **Purpose:** The purpose is the reason behind the text or what the writer wants the audience to think as a result of reading the text.
- **Subject:** The subject is the focus of the text.
- **Tone:** Tone is the speaker's attitude toward the subject.

7. Use your annotations of the speech to take notes on analyzing the argument in a SOAPSTone graphic organizer like the one that follows. Refer to the Resources section of your book for a SOAPSTone graphic organizer that you can copy and use for your analysis. The questions in the Analysis column should help guide your analysis of the speech.

Element	Analysis	Textual Evidence
Speaker	Who is the speaker?	
Occasion	What event(s) or situation(s) prompted the creation of this text?	
Audience	Who is the intended audience?	
Purpose	What is the speaker's claim? What is the speaker's reason for creating this text? What is the speaker's call to action?	
Subject	How does the speaker appeal to *logos* (i.e., how does the speaker use facts, examples, statistics, research, and logical reasoning for effect)? How does the speaker use counterclaims or concession and rebuttal? How does the speaker appeal to *pathos* (emotion)?	
Tone	What is the speaker's attitude toward the subject? How does the speaker use connotative diction and/or imagery to create tone?	

8. Use the following graphic organizer to organize your argumentative speech.

Argument Feature	Wiesel's Speech	Your Speech
Claim *What is your claim?*	There is so much injustice and suffering crying out for our attention.	
Logical Reasons *What are the reasons for your claim?*	As long as one dissident is in prison, our freedom will not be true. As long as one child is hungry, our life will be filled with anguish and shame. What all these victims need above all is to know that they are not alone. The quality of our freedom depends on theirs. There is so much to be done, there is so much that can be done.	
Relevant Evidence *What evidence are you using to support your claim?*	Human rights are being violated on every continent. More people are oppressed than free. Human suffering anywhere concerns men and women everywhere.	
Counterclaim *What claim are you opposing?*	The world did know and remained silent. And that is why I swore never to be silent whenever, wherever human beings endure suffering and humiliation. Silence encourages the tormentor, never the tormented.	
Credible Sources *What sources are you relying on?*	Wiesel, Elie. The Nobel Acceptance Speech. Oslo, Norway. December 10, 1986.	
Concluding Statement *What is your call to action?*	Our lives no longer belong to us alone; they belong to all those who need us desperately. There is so much to be done, there is so much that can be done. One ... person of integrity, can make a difference, a difference of life and death.	

My Notes

___

LANGUAGE & WRITER'S CRAFT: Reviewing Clauses

A clause is a group of words with both a subject and a verb. Common clauses include adverbial and adjectival clauses.

Adverbial: An adverbial clause is a dependent clause that functions as an adverb. It modifies a verb, adjective, or adverb. The writer can place the adverbial clause in different parts of the sentence, depending on where it best adds to the desired effect. An adverbial clause begins with a subordinating conjunction (such as *if*, *when*, *although*, *because*, or *as*).

> **Example:** "Experience is what you get <u>when you didn't get what you wanted</u>." (Randy Pausch, "The Last Lecture," 2008)

Adjectival: An adjectival clause is a dependent clause that is used as an adjective in a sentence. Since the adjectival clause modifies a noun or pronoun, it cannot be moved around. It should stay close to the word it modifies. An adjectival clause generally begins with a relative pronoun (*that*, *which*, *who*, *whom*, or *whose*).

> **Example:** "He <u>who can no longer pause to wonder and stand rapt in awe</u> is as good as dead." (Albert Einstein)

PRACTICE Look over your response to the Writing Prompt from Activity 3.14. If you used an adverbial or adjectival clause in your writing, copy it in your Reader/Writer Notebook. If you didn't, add one to your writing.

9. A call to action attempts to persuade the reader to do something. It increases the effectiveness of your argument by encouraging your audience to act on whatever advice you have given them.

Topic	Sample Call to Action
texting and driving	*The next time your phone dings while you're driving, pull over before checking your messages.*
volunteering	*Find a cause that is important to you and make the call to volunteer today.*

☑ Check Your Understanding

Elie Wiesel says that if we forget that injustices are taking place, we become accomplices. How does he support this argument? Do you agree? Discuss with a partner.

📝 Argumentative Writing Prompt

Write a short argumentative speech about the issue you identified in Activity 3.14. Be sure to:

- Assert a clear claim and address a counterclaim.
- Support your claim using facts as evidence and rhetorical appeals.
- End your speech with a strong call to action.
- Use adverbial and adjectival clauses effectively.
- Use dashes appropriately to punctuate any abrupt pauses in thought.

📖 INDEPENDENT READING LINK

Reading Plan

Explain how the subject of your biography or autobiography has chosen an issue and hopes to make a difference in the lives of others who might be suffering.

Students Taking Action

Marking the Text
Summarizing
Brainstorming
Graphic Organizer
Note-taking

Learning Targets

- Analyze informational texts about taking action.
- Research and evaluate issues of personal significance.

Preview

In this activity, you will collaborate with group members to choose an issue and create an original PSA campaign.

Setting a Purpose for Reading

- As you read the excerpt, underline words and phrases that are targeted for a youthful audience.
- Underline the key details and write notes about any connections that you notice among them.
- Circle unknown words and phrases. Try to determine the meaning of the words by using context clues, word parts, or a dictionary.

My Notes

About the Author

Nancy Lublin (b. 1971) is an entrepreneur and world leader in youth global activism. Lublin holds degrees from Brown University, Oxford University, and New York University School of Law. Over her career she has founded and run several non-profit organizations, including Dress for Success, which provides women in need with professional suits to wear on interviews, and DoSomething.org, which gives grants to young leaders working for social change. Lublin is currently the CEO of Crisis Text Line, a free, 24/7 crisis intervention service offered to teens across the world.

WORD CONNECTIONS

Etymology
Campaign comes from a French word meaning "open country," and it referred to military engagement in open fields. It later came to denote any large-scale military operation, and now it is used to refer to a series of steps in pursuit of a goal. You may be familiar with its use in political campaigns and fundraising campaigns.

Informational Text

See It! Believe It! Do It!

from Do Something! A Handbook for Young Activists

By **Nancy Lublin**

See It

1   So, you want to change the world? That's great! Where do you start? Do you know what you want to fight for? Improve? Get rid of? Do those dying penguins in Antarctica bum you out? Do the classroom lights left on all night make you mad? Does the thought of peace in the Middle East get you pumped? In other words: What's your thing? What's the issue that gets you sad or mad or leaves you feeling overwhelmed?

2   Maybe there's some terrible problem you pass on your street or hear about in the news, and you think: I need to fix that. Or maybe you just want to make a difference and don't know where to start. You just need to see it.

Believe It

3   You've got a thing—a problem you want to solve. It makes your heart hurt. It makes you squirmy, like you want to jump up and do something right now! Awesome. The next step is figuring out how you can crush, erase, clean, save, or change that thing. Caring is good. Action is better. But before you can act, you've got to believe, you've got to understand. You've got to know your thing inside and outside. You've got to know more than anyone. ... Once you do, you'll own your thing. You'll really believe it.

Do It

4   Seeing a problem is great. Believing you can make a difference is really important. Building a rock-solid plan will help you be incredibly effective. But nothing matters more than actually getting out there and doing it.

5   You can read and write about riding a horse, but at some point you need to get on and actually ride. Right? Pulling off your action plan means spreading the word, getting more people to sign on to help, staying organized, focused, and inspired. It's not always going to be easy—you have to prepare for the unexpected! But you've come too far to stop now. It's time for you to do it.

Working from the Text

1. You have read texts about events when few people took action. What ideas in Nancy Lublin's text are meant to get young people to take action? Which actions in Lublin's text are most appealing to you? Why?

Young Activists

2. Mark the text of the following campaign summaries to identify the what, why, and how of each issue.

   • What is the issue or problem the student wanted to do something about?
   • Why did the student care about this issue?
   • How did the student make a difference?

Student 1: Sarah Cronk **State:** IA **Issue:** Disability Rights

Sarah watched her older brother, Charlie, struggle to fit in during high school because of his disabilities. He was depressed and anxious, until the captain of the swim team invited him to join. Suddenly the cool kids welcomed him, and he found a new group of friends. Inspired by Charlie, Sarah cofounded the first high school–based inclusive cheerleading squad in the nation. Today, the Sparkle Effect has generated 26 squads in 15 states and South Africa, encouraging a culture of acceptance in every community.

Student 2: Danny Mendoza **State:** CA **Issue:** Foster Care

While in college, Danny learned that his nine-year-old cousin, Roger, was living in a car. After lots of maneuvering, Danny helped him move from the Honda to a house, but he was deeply disturbed by how little control Roger had over his own situation. Danny took action and created Together We Rise, a youth-led organization dedicated to running programs that not only bring a sense of normalcy and stability to children in foster care, but also allow foster children to make their own choices. Through programs like music lessons, mentoring, sports and athletics, résumé building, and job readiness, Together We Rise provides the resources for foster kids to prepare for success at age 18, when they are kicked out of the foster care system and left to fend for themselves. Together, Danny and Together We Rise have reached 3,000 foster care youth through these programs, providing a better opportunity for long-term success.

Student 3: Jordan Coleman **State:** NJ **Issue:** Education

Jordan was angry when he learned that fewer than half of African American boys graduate from high school. He's an actor, so he decided to make a movie called *Say It Loud* (at age 13) to raise awareness about the importance of education. He toured with the film to spread his message to young people in community centers and schools around the country. He even got to speak at an education rally during the Presidential Inauguration in 2009!

Student 4: Evan Ducker **State:** NY **Issue:** Discrimination

Evan was born with a large birthmark on his face. At age 14, he decided to educate the public about the medical and psychological issues facing kids born with these kinds of birthmarks through his book *Buddy Booby' s Birthmark* and his annual International *Buddy Booby' s Birthmark* Read-Along for Tolerance and Awareness.

GRAMMAR & USAGE

Commas

A comma after an introductory element in a sentence indicates a pause before the main part of the sentence.

Look at these examples:

Introductory participial phrase: **Inspired by Charlie, ...**

Introductory prepositional phrase: **At age 14, ...**

Look for introductory elements like these as you read, and note how you pause after them.

3. In the My Notes section next to Young Activists, summarize the kinds of young people that are featured and how they have made a difference.

4. Form a personal response to connect to the text by answering these questions:

   • Which student do you relate to most? Why?

   • Which student do you respect the most? Why?

5. Create a word web to brainstorm issues of community, national, and global significance that you care about.

6. Choose a cause from the website your teacher assigns you to explore as a group.

   Our Cause: Examples:

7. As a group, discuss the issues related to your selected cause. Have each person in your group focus on a different issue related to your cause. For example, if your cause is Animals, you can have one person research animal testing, another animal cruelty, and a third animal homelessness. Before you split up to do your research, plan an agenda for your next meeting with clear goals and deadlines for the task. Decide on how you will share your research and set time limits for speakers.

8. Complete the first row of the following graphic organizer by taking notes on the what, why, and how of your issue. Add your own ideas as well as the ones you find on the website. Then present your issue to your group members. As group members present their issues, take notes in the graphic organizer.

WHAT is the issue or problem? List informative and compelling facts.	WHY should you care? Record appeals to *logos*, *pathos*, and *ethos*.	HOW can you make a difference? Record a clear and reasonable call to action.
Issue: _____		
Issue: _____		
Issue: _____		

Our cause:

9. Reflect on your research: Which issues stand out to your group as a potential subject for your multimedia campaign? Vote for one issue to focus on for your multimedia campaign. Then brainstorm where you can look for more information about it.

☑ **Check Your Understanding**

Brainstorm a list of organizations that support your group's cause and that you would like to volunteer with. Work in small groups to gather more information about some of these volunteer opportunities. You can use this information as part of your call to action.

10. Evaluate the details in your graphic organizer in step 8, and underline the ideas that would provide the strongest support for your issue. Share your notes from your graphic organizer, and advocate orally for the cause you chose with your group. Be sure to point out the cause you chose and why the audience should care. Also provide instructions on what the audience can do to support the cause. Remember to use rhetorical appeals such as anecdotes, analogies, and illustrations while employing eye contact, speaking rate, volume, enunciation, a variety of natural gestures, and conventions of language to communicate your ideas effectively.

☑ Focus on the Sentence

Use your research notes and discussions about your issue to write sentences that demonstrate your knowledge of the issue.

Write one statement about the issue: _____

_____

Write a question you still have about the issue:_____

_____

Write a command or call to action for your peers:_____

_____

From Vision to Action

Learning Strategies

Metacognitive Markers
Diffusing
Rereading
Summarizing
Discussion Groups
Graphic Organizer
Drafting

Learning Targets

- Analyze informational texts and discuss the global impact of their subjects.
- Create content for a web page to represent a campaign to make a difference.
- Integrate ideas from multiple texts to build knowledge and vocabulary about making a difference.

Preview

In this activity, you will read about two ways that people can make a difference in the world. Then you will think about how you can make a difference for an issue you care about.

Setting a Purpose for Reading

- As you read, underline the phrases that show how one person has or could make a difference with a global impact.
- Circle unknown words and phrases. Try to determine the meaning of the words by using context clues, word parts, or a dictionary.

Informational Text

Wangari Maathai

from **BBC News**

Wangari Maathai rose to prominence fighting for those most easily marginalized in Africa—poor women.

1   The first African woman to win the Nobel Peace Prize (2004) was praised by the awarding committee as "a source of inspiration for everyone in Africa fighting for **sustainable** development, democracy and peace."

2   A pioneering academic, her role as an environmental campaigner began after she planted some trees in her back garden.

3   This inspired her in 1977 to form an organization—primarily of women— known as the Green Belt Movement aiming to **curtail** the **devastating** effects of **deforestation** and **desertification**.

4   Her desire was to produce sustainable wood for fuel use as well as combating soil **erosion**.

5   Her campaign to mobilize poor women to plant some 30 million trees has been copied by other countries.

6   Speaking as recently as Wednesday on the BBC's Africa Live program, she said her tree planting campaign was not at all popular when it first began.

KNOWLEDGE QUEST

Knowledge Question:
How can one person make a difference?

In Activity 3.17, you will read an informational text, a speech, and a website on the topic of making a difference. While you read and build knowledge about the topic, think about your answer to the Knowledge Question.

sustainable: able to be maintained
curtail: to cut short
devastating: highly destructive
deforestation: large-scale removal of trees and forests
desertification: the transformation of habitable land to desert
erosion: the process of wearing away

7 "It took me a lot of days and nights to convince people that women could improve their environment without much technology or without much financial resources."

8 The Green Belt Movement went on to campaign on education, nutrition, and other issues important to women.

Political role

9 Mrs. Maathai has been arrested several times for campaigning against deforestation in Africa.

10 In the late 1980s, she became a prominent opponent of a skyscraper planned for the middle of the Kenyan capital's main park—Uhuru Park.

11 She was **vilified** by Kenyan President Daniel arap Moi's government but succeeded in **thwarting** the plans.

12 More recently, she evolved into a leading campaigner on social matters.

13 Once she was beaten unconscious by heavy-handed police. On another occasion she led a demonstration of naked women.

14 In 1997, she ran for president against Mr. Moi but made little impact.

Esteem

15 But in elections in 2002, she was elected as MP with 98% of the votes as part of an opposition **coalition** which swept to power after Mr. Moi stepped down.

16 She was appointed as a deputy environment minister in 2003.

17 Mrs. Maathai says she usually uses a biblical analogy of creation to stress the importance of the environment.

18 "God created the planet from Monday to Friday. On Saturday he created human beings.

19 "The truth of the matter is … if man was created on Tuesday, I usually say, he would have been dead on Wednesday, because there would not have been the essential elements that he needs to survive," she told the BBC.

20 The Nobel Peace Prize committee praised her for taking "a **holistic** approach to sustainable development that embraces democracy, human rights and women's rights in particular."

21 She thinks globally and acts locally, they said.

22 She was born in 1940 and has three children.

23 Her former husband, whom she divorced in the 1980s, was said to have remarked that she was "too educated, too strong, too successful, too stubborn and too hard to control."

vilified: subjected to vicious statements
thwarting: preventing
coalition: an alliance of people or groups
holistic: emphasizing the whole of something, as opposed to its parts

My Notes

◎ Knowledge Quest

- What have you learned so far about Wangari Maathai?
- What is sustainable development?

Setting a Purpose for Reading

- As you read, underline the phrases that show how one person can make a difference.
- Circle unknown words and phrases. Try to determine the meaning of the words by using context clues, word parts, or a dictionary.

About the Author

Wangari Maathai (1940–2011) was the founder of the Green Belt Movement, an international environmental movement focused on planting trees, conservation, and women's rights. She was born in a rural village in Kenya in 1940. After receiving degrees in biology from the United States, Maathai went on to receive her Ph.D in veterinary anatomy from the University of Nairobi, becoming the first woman in East and Central Africa to earn a doctorate degree. In 2004, she received the Nobel Peace Prize for her contribution to "sustainable development, democracy, and peace."

Speech

Nobel Lecture
by Wangari Maathai
Oslo, December 10, 2004

◎ KNOWLEDGE QUEST

Knowledge Question:
How can one person make a difference?

Excellencies, ladies and gentlemen,

1   In 1977, when we started the Green Belt Movement, I was partly responding to needs identified by rural women, namely lack of firewood, clean drinking water, balanced diets, shelter and income.

2   Throughout Africa, women are the primary caretakers, holding significant responsibility for tilling the land and feeding their families. As a result, they are often the first to become aware of environmental damage as resources become scarce and incapable of sustaining their families.

3 The women we worked with recounted that unlike in the past, they were unable to meet their basic needs. This was due to the **degradation** of their immediate environment as well as the introduction of commercial farming, which replaced the growing of household food crops. But international trade controlled the price of the exports from these small-scale farmers and a reasonable and just income could not be guaranteed. I came to understand that when the environment is destroyed, plundered or mismanaged, we **undermine** our quality of life and that of future generations.

4 Tree planting became a natural choice to address some of the initial basic needs identified by women. Also, tree planting is simple, attainable and guarantees quick, successful results within a reasonable amount of time. This sustains interest and commitment.

5 So, together, we have planted over 30 million trees that provide fuel, food, shelter, and income to support their children's education and household needs. The activity also creates employment and improves soils and watersheds. Through their involvement, women gain some degree of power over their lives, especially their social and economic position and relevance in the family. This work continues.

6 Initially, the work was difficult because historically our people have been persuaded to believe that because they are poor, they lack not only capital, but also knowledge and skills to address their challenges. Instead they are conditioned to believe that solutions to their problems must come from 'outside'. Further, women did not realize that meeting their needs depended on their environment being healthy and well managed. They were also unaware that a degraded environment leads to a scramble for scarce resources and may culminate in poverty and even conflict. They were also unaware of the injustices of international economic arrangements.

7 In order to assist communities to understand these linkages, we developed a citizen education program, during which people identify their problems, the causes and possible solutions. They then make connections between their own personal actions and the problems they witness in the environment and in society. They learn that our world is confronted with a **litany** of woes: corruption, violence against women and children, disruption and breakdown of families, and disintegration of cultures and communities. They also identify the abuse of drugs and chemical substances, especially among young people. There are also devastating diseases that are defying cures or occurring in epidemic proportions. Of particular concern are HIV/AIDS, malaria and diseases associated with malnutrition.

8 On the environment front, they are exposed to many human activities that are devastating to the environment and societies. These include widespread destruction of ecosystems, especially through deforestation, **climatic instability**, and **contamination** in the soils and waters that all contribute to excruciating poverty.

degradation: severe reduction of quality

undermine: to weaken

litany: repetitive series of requests (usually for help)

climatic instability: state of Earth's atmosphere when it is so unstable it causes severely varying weather

contamination: being made impure by pollution

9   In the process, the participants discover that they must be part of the solutions. They realize their hidden potential and are empowered to overcome inertia and take action. They come to recognize that they are the primary custodians and beneficiaries of the environment that sustains them.

10   Entire communities also come to understand that while it is necessary to hold their governments accountable, it is equally important that in their own relationships with each other, they exemplify the leadership values they wish to see in their own leaders, namely justice, integrity and trust.

11   Although initially the Green Belt Movement's tree planting activities did not address issues of democracy and peace, it soon became clear that responsible governance of the environment was impossible without democratic space. Therefore, the tree became a symbol for the democratic struggle in Kenya. Citizens were mobilized to challenge widespread abuses of power, corruption and environmental mismanagement. In Nairobi's Uhuru Park, at Freedom Corner, and in many parts of the country, trees of peace were planted to demand the release of prisoners of conscience and a peaceful transition to democracy.

12   Through the Green Belt Movement, thousands of ordinary citizens were mobilized and empowered to take action and effect change. They learned to overcome fear and a sense of helplessness and moved to defend democratic rights.

⊘ Knowledge Quest
- What words, phrases, or ideas from the speech stick out to you?
- What facts about the Green Belt Movement do you find most interesting?

My Notes

Returning to the Text

- Return to the texts as you respond to the following questions. Use evidence from the texts to support your responses.
- Write any additional questions you have about the texts in your Reader/Writer Notebook.

1. What were some of the obstacles Wangari Maathai struggled against in creating and campaigning for the Green Belt Movement?

2. How does the analogy in paragraphs 17–19 in the BBC article help Maathai make her point about the importance of the environment?

3. Why do you think the Nobel Peace Prize committee praised Wangari Maathai for thinking globally and acting locally?

4. KQ How does Maathai's choice of the word *custodian* in paragraph 9 of her Nobel Lecture help her emphasize her view of humanity's relationship to the environment?

5. KQ Based on your reading of the BBC article and Nobel Lecture, what was Maathai's biggest challenge in creating the Green Belt Movement?

Setting a Purpose for Reading

- As you read, underline phrases that show how one person, including yourself, could make a difference in the world.
- Circle unknown words and phrases. Try to determine the meaning of the words by using context clues, word parts, or a dictionary.

Informational Text

About Freerice.com

1   Freerice is a nonprofit website that is owned by and supports the United Nations World Food Programme. Freerice has two goals:

- Provide education to everyone for free.
- Help end world hunger by providing rice to hungry people for free.

2   Whether you are a CEO of a large corporation or a street child in a poor country, improving your education can improve your life. It is a great investment in yourself.

3   Perhaps even greater is the investment your donated rice makes in hungry human beings, enabling them to function and be productive. Somewhere in the world, a person is eating rice that you helped provide.

Informational Text

Free Rice Online Quiz Game

1   Freerice is an online internet game that donates 20 grains of rice to the World Food Programme (WFP) for every word that is correctly defined. WFP, the United Nations frontline organization fighting hunger, distributes the rice to the hungry. WFP uses the donations from the site to purchase rice locally, both feeding people in need and **stimulating** local economies.

2   Already, the site has raised enough rice to feed over 1.5 million people for a day. The game has been embraced by young and old alike, proving to be an excellent tool for prepping for the SATs or to brush up on vocabulary words. Teachers have been using the game to teach both vocabulary and the value of helping others in need.

KNOWLEDGE QUEST

Knowledge Question:

How can one person make a difference?

INDEPENDENT READING LINK

Read and Respond

Think about the cause or issue that the person is fighting for in your independent reading book. What personal, political, or social connections exist between that cause or issue and the person?

stimulating: causing increased activity in

Returning to the Text

- Return to the texts as you respond to the following questions. Use text evidence to support your responses.
- Write any additional questions you have about the informational texts in your Reader/Writer Notebook.

6. How does the game on Freerice.com achieve its two goals?

_____

_____

7. According to the article about Freerice.com, how is the benefit of education the same for both rich and poor people?

_____

_____

8. KQ In the article about Freerice.com, how does the author's use of the word *investment* in paragraphs 1 and 2 help persuade people to donate?

_____

_____

9. KQ Reread Freerice.com's two goals. Based on your reading of all the texts in this activity, how does this website allow individual people to make a difference?

_____

_____

INDEPENDENT READING LINK

You can continue to build your knowledge about how one person can make a difference by reading other articles at ZINC Reading Labs. Search for keywords such as *activists* or *social justice*.

ZINC

✐ Knowledge Quest

Use what you learned from the three texts to work collaboratively with two peers to record evidence of how one person can make a difference. Each of you can be the recorder for one text while you work together to complete an Idea or Argument Evaluator graphic organizer for it. Be sure to:

- Include a clear statement about each authors' ideas.
- Explain how the details in each text support and elaborate the author's central idea.
- Cite evidence from each text to support your ideas.

Working from the Text

10. Wangari Maathai and Freerice.com each made a difference on a global scale by organizing their goals around a specific mission and taking action. Use the following chart to evaluate different elements from the home pages of their websites.

	Wangari Maathai	World Food Programme
Organization Name	The Green Belt Movement	World Food Programme Freerice
Slogan		
Mission Statement		
Call to Action		

☑ Check Your Understanding

Create a small newspaper advertisement for Freerice.com. Include facts about the program as well as a slogan in the advertisement. Share your advertisement with a partner.

Examining Media Campaigns

Learning Strategies

Graphic Organizer
Note-taking
Discussion Groups
Sketching

WORD CONNECTIONS

Word Relationships
You can see that commercial derives from the word *commerce*, which is the buying and selling of goods. As a noun, a *commercial* refers to an advertisement on television or radio. As an adjective, it describes a business or enterprise where the main goal is to make money and earn profits.

Learning Targets

• Explain how specific media types appeal to different target audiences.
• Use rhetorical devices in different types of media to convince a target audience to take action.
• Integrate ideas from multiple texts to build knowledge and vocabulary about a theme.

Preview

In this activity, you will read about multimedia campaigns and think about how to create your own.

Setting a Purpose for Reading

• As you read, underline any rhetorical devices in the text that attempt to convince the reader to take action.
• Circle unknown words and phrases. Try to determine the meaning of the words by using context clues, word parts, or a dictionary.
• While you read, record any questions you have in the margin.

Informational Text

Public Service Announcements

1   Broadcast media—radio and television—are required by the Federal Communications Commission (FCC) to serve "in the public interest." Most stations use PSAs as one of the ways they meet this requirement. While they aren't required to donate a fixed percentage of air time per day to PSAs, stations do have to state in their licensing and renewal applications how much air time they plan to devote to PSAs. Most stations donate about a third of their commercial spots to non-commercial causes; in other words, if a station has 18 minutes of commercials in a given hour, six minutes of that will probably be devoted to PSAs.

2   Public service announcements, or PSAs, are short messages produced on film, videotape, DVD, CD, audiotape, or as a computer file and given to radio and television stations. Generally, PSAs are sent as ready-to-air audio or video tapes, although radio stations sometimes prefer a script that their announcers can read live on the air.

3   Since World War II, public service announcements (PSAs) have informed and attempted to persuade the public about a variety of issues.

4   If people find an ad or PSA entertaining enough, they might talk about it with a friend or share it online. When this happens, many more people will receive the intended message.

INDEPENDENT READING LINK

Read and Discuss

Suppose you were to help the subject of your independent reading narrative make a PSA to promote his or her cause. Discuss with a classmate who the target audience of the PSA would be. What words or phrases would you use to appeal to that audience?

Working from the Text

1. Brainstorm types of media you could use to raise awareness and encourage action about an issue of national or global significance.

2. What is meant by a target audience? How does identifying the target audience affect how an argument is developed and presented?

3. Research examples of public service announcements and campaigns. You might use the Internet, listen to radio, watch television, or look at newspaper or magazine ads to find examples. Find at least three examples that appeal to you, and evaluate them for the clarity of their messages, use of visuals and multimedia elements, and effectiveness.

Description of PSA	Clarity of Message	Use of Visuals/ Multimedia Elements	Effectiveness
Name: Purpose: Audience: Content:			
Name: Purpose: Audience: Content:			
Name: Purpose: Audience: Content:			

4. Analyze the campaigns' use of rhetorical devices and logical fallacies for effect. How did each campaign use the appeals *pathos*, *ethos*, and *logos* to convince the target audience to take action? Give examples from your research. Did any of the campaigns use faulty reasoning or logical fallacies such as bandwagon appeals or circular reasoning? Explain their purpose. For a quick review of rhetorical appeals, see Activity 2.12. Explain their purpose. For a quick review of logical fallacies, see Activity 2.13.

Pathos:

Ethos:

Logos:

Logical Fallacies:

5. Of the different media and devices used, which would you use in your own multimedia campaign? Who would be your target audience? Which type of media would appeal to them? What type of ads would you create (magazine, newspaper, poster, billboard, web banner), and where would you put them in order to reach your target audience?

6. Choose one of the public service campaigns you researched and identify the types of media it uses to get the word out. For each type of media used, analyze the rhetorical devices for effect. Do the various ads appeal to *pathos, ethos,* or *logos*? Are these appeals effective? Also, look for intended and unintended use of logical fallacies. What is their purpose? Is their reasoning sound or faulty?

Public Service Announcement Campaign:

Sponsor Organization:

Volunteer Agency:

Type of Media	Target Audience	Types of Devices and/or Fallacies Used/Effectiveness

7. Revisit the target audiences and types of media you are considering for your campaign. How can you use rhetorical devices in different types of media to convince your target audience to take action? Sketch a visual to show your thinking. Think about these guidelines for creating a PSA:

- Aim for a memorable slogan.
- Use one powerful image.
- Use one shocking statistic.
- Search for images by idea or create your own images.
- Include a Credits slide for images as well as content. Document with this text: "This image is used under a CC license from [insert URL for image]."

 Gaining Perspectives

You've been learning about media campaigns. With a partner, think about how advertisers can affect aspects of a person's life. Look online and in print materials for advertisements that support social issues that might not be in the best interest of consumer's health and well-being. Select one ad and role-play the advertiser and a concerned citizen seeing the ad. The concerned citizen should question the advertiser about any negative aspects in the ad, such as social acceptance of alcohol use, promotion of thinness as the best body type, sexual images to sell products, and the normalization of violence. The advertiser should address the concerned citizen and understand his or her point of view. When you are finished, summarize the outcome of the discussion in your Reader/Writer Notebook.

☑ Check Your Understanding

Quickwrite: Briefly write about two advertisements—one that you think positively influences people and one that you think negatively influences people. Why do you think advertisements have these effects on viewers?

Learning Strategies

Diffusing
Graphic Organizer
Note-taking
Collaborative Discussion

Learning Targets

- Analyze the parts of an effective argument in spoken texts.
- Evaluate the effectiveness of arguments in spoken texts.

Preview

In this activity, you will read part of a speech and think about how to create an effective argument.

Setting a Purpose for Reading

- As you read the speech, mark with *L* words and phrases that use *logos* (facts) to support the argument, and mark with *P* words and phrases that use *pathos* (emotion).
- Circle the unknown words and phrases. Try to determine the meaning of the words by using context clues, word parts, or a dictionary.

About the Author

Cesar Chavez (1927–1993) was a Mexican American union leader and organizer. In 1962, troubled by his difficult experiences as a migrant worker, Chavez founded the National Farm Workers Association (NFWA). This group led strikes, or work stoppages, throughout California to protest the practices of agricultural businesses. The NFWA joined forces with another prominent union to form the United Farm Workers. Chavez continued to campaign for fair labor practices and worker safety with nonviolent protests, boycotts, and hunger strikes. Through his efforts, he helped improve conditions for farm workers in several states.

My Notes

GRAMMAR & USAGE

Verb Tenses
The present-progressive verb tense describes an ongoing action that is happening at the same time the statement is written. This tense is formed by using *am*, *is*, or *are* with the verb form ending in *-ing*. For example, look at the first sentence in paragraph 10: "In McFarland ... **are being reported** ..." The words *are being reported* show that the action is happening as the writer is writing. Look for another example of present-progressive verb tense in the text.

Speech
address by

Cesar Chavez,

PRESIDENT, UNITED FARM WORKERS OF AMERICA, AFL-CIO
Pacific Lutheran University, March 1989, Tacoma, Washington

1   What is the worth of a man or a woman? What is the worth of a farm worker? How do you measure the value of a life?

2   Ask the parents of Johnnie Rodriguez.

3   Johnnie Rodriguez was not even a man; Johnnie was a five-year-old boy when he died after a painful two-year battle against cancer.

4   His parents, Juan and Elia, are farm workers. Like all grape workers, they are exposed to pesticides and other agricultural chemicals. Elia worked in the

table grapes around Delano, California until she was eight months pregnant with Johnnie.

5 Juan and Elia cannot say for certain if pesticides caused their son's cancer. But neuroblastoma is one of the cancers found in McFarland, a small farm town only a few miles from Delano, where the Rodriguezes live.

6 "Pesticides are always in the fields and around the towns," Johnnie's father told us. "The children get the chemicals when they play outside, drink the water, or when they hug you after you come home from working in fields that are sprayed.

7 "Once your son has cancer, it's pretty hard to take," Juan Rodriguez says. "You hope it's a mistake; you pray. He was a real nice boy. He took it strong and lived as long as he could."

8 I keep a picture of Johnnie Rodriguez. He is sitting on his bed, hugging his teddy bears. His sad eyes and cherubic face stare out at you. The photo was taken four days before he died.

9 Johnnie Rodriguez was one of 13 McFarland children diagnosed with cancer in recent years and one of six who have died from the disease. With only 6,000 residents, the rate of cancer in McFarland is 400 percent above normal.

10 In McFarland and in Fowler, childhood cancer cases are being reported in excess of expected rates. In Delano and other farming towns, questions are also being raised.

11 The chief source of **carcinogens** in these communities are **pesticides** from the vineyards and fields that encircle them. Health experts believe the high rate of cancer in McFarland is from pesticides and nitrate-containing fertilizers **leaching** into the water system from surrounding fields ...

12 Farm workers and their families are exposed to pesticides from the crops they work. The soil the crops are grown in. Drift from sprays applied to adjoining fields—and often to the very field where they are working.

13 The fields that surround their homes are heavily and repeatedly sprayed. Pesticides pollute irrigation water and groundwater.

14 Children are still a big part of the labor force. Or they are taken to the fields by their parents because there is no child care.

15 Pregnant women labor in the fields to help support their families. **Toxic** exposure begins at a very young age—often in the womb.

16 What does acute pesticide poisoning produce?

17 Eye and respiratory irritations. Skin rashes. Systemic poisoning.

18 Death.

19 What are the chronic effects of pesticide poisoning on people, including farm workers and their children, according to scientific studies?

20 Birth defects. Sterility. Still births. Miscarriages. Neurological and neuropsychological effects. Effects on child growth and development.

WORD CONNECTIONS

Content Connections
Neuroblastoma is a tumor that affects young children. It commonly begins in the abdomen and develops from tissues in the part of the nervous system that controls body functions.

GRAMMAR & USAGE

Sentence Fragments
In almost all cases, incomplete sentences are not proper grammar in the English language. There are instances, however, where they can be used for effect. For example, look at paragraphs 17 and 18. The elements in these paragraphs are sentence fragments because they have no verbs. The writer used these sentence fragments for effect. By following the question about the effects of pesticide with sentence fragments, the author emphasizes each danger more than it would be in a regular sentence separated by commas. Find more sentence fragments in the speech. Notice what effect they create.

carcinogens: substances that cause cancer
pesticides: chemicals used to kill insects
leaching: draining
toxic: poisonous

21 Cancer.

22 Do we feel deeply enough the pain of those who must work in the fields every day with these poisons? Or the anguish of the families that have lost loved ones to cancer? Or the heartache of the parents who fear for the lives of their children? Who are raising children with deformities? Who agonize the outcome of their pregnancies?

23 Who ask in fear, "where will this deadly **plague** strike next?"

24 Do we feel their pain deeply enough?

25 I didn't. And I was ashamed.

26 I studied this **wanton** abuse of nature. I read the literature, heard from the experts about what pesticides do to our land and our food.

27 I talked with farm workers, listened to their families, and shared their anguish and their fears. I spoke out against the cycle of death.

28 But sometimes words come too cheaply. And their meaning is lost in the clutter that so often fills our lives.

29 That is why, in July and August of last year, I embarked on a 36-day unconditional, water-only fast.

30 The fast was first and foremost directed at myself. It was something I felt compelled to do to purify my own body, mind, and soul.

31 The fast was an act of **penance** for our own members who, out of ignorance or need, cooperate with those who grow and sell food treated with toxins.

32 The fast was also for those who know what is right and just. It pains me that we continue to shop without protest at stores that offer grapes, that we eat in restaurants that display them, that we are too patient and understanding with those who serve them to us.

33 The fast, then, was for those who know that they could or should do more—for those who, by not acting, become bystanders in the poisoning of our food and the people who produce it.

34 The fast was, finally, a declaration of noncooperation with supermarkets that promote, sell, and profit from California table grapes. They are as culpable as those who manufacture the poisons and those who use them.

35 It is my hope that our friends everywhere will resist in many nonviolent ways the presence of grapes in the stores where they shop.

plague: a highly fatal epidemic affliction

wanton: immoral and excessive

penance: a punishment taken for an offense

Making Observations

- What emotions do you sense or feel while reading the speech?
- What additional questions do you have about Cesar Chavez and pesticides after reading this speech?

Returning to the Text

- Return to the text as you respond to the following questions. Use text evidence to support your responses.
- Write any additional questions you have about the speech in your Reader/Writer Notebook.

1. Reread the opening question of the speech. Is the question intended to appeal to *logos*, *pathos*, or *ethos*? Explain.

_____

_____

_____

_____

2. The speaker opens his speech with an anecdote. What kind of rhetorical device is he using, and what effect does it have?

_____

_____

_____

_____

3. What claim does Cesar Chavez make?

_____

_____

_____

_____

4. Think about the logic of Chavez's argument about the relationship between human health and pesticides. How does the author depend on logical reasoning and relevant evidence (*logos*)?

_____

_____

_____

_____

5. How does Cesar Chavez participate in his own call to action?

_____

_____

_____

_____

Working from the Text

6. Who is the speech's target audience? How do you know?

7. Based on the target audience, use your analysis to evaluate each element of the author's argument.

8. Overall, is the argument effective? Why or why not?

9. Find an online site (probably a site that ends in ".org") that advocates for the use of safe pesticides and the protection of the environment, for instance, http://www.beyondpesticides.org/. Use the following organizer to take notes on the website you find and the elements of a multimedia campaign to create change. Then find another site or an article to compare the facts and determine reliability. Ask yourself the questions in the site evaluation process that your teacher showed you.

   Next, use the organizer to take notes on how the website uses *logos* and *pathos* to relay its message to you. Evaluate how the site utilizes various multimedia elements to create a campaign for change.

Logos Facts used to help me understand the issue	Pathos Images used to create emotion and to convince me to act

☑ Check Your Understanding

Quickwrite: How does the text use *ethos* to raise awareness of the use of pesticides in farming? How can you use *ethos* in your own multimedia campaign?

🔲 Independent Reading Checkpoint

You are going to participate in book talks in small groups to share insights into the narratives you have each read. You should consider the challenge to society presented in your independent reading book and how that challenge was confronted. What did it take for one person to address that challenge, and how was that person successful? How has he or she left a positive impact on our society or on the world?

Learning Targets

- Understand how to use appropriate verb tenses in writing.
- Revise writing to correct inappropriate shifts in verb tense.

Preview

In this activity, you will write an introductory paragraph using correct and consistent verb tense.

Understanding Verb Tense

Verbs do more than express action or a state of being: they also tell *when* something happened—in the past, present, or future. The expression of a verb's time is called **verb tense**.

1. Read the following excerpt from Cesar Chavez's speech. Identify each verb.

   What is the worth of a man or a woman? What is the worth of a farm worker? How do you measure the value of a life?

2. With a partner, decide whether the verbs are in the past, present, or future tense. Why do you think Chavez uses this tense?

3. Look at the next passage from Chavez's address. Identify each verb.

   Johnnie Rodriguez was not even a man; Johnnie was a five year old boy when he died after a painful two year battle against cancer.

   His parents, Juan and Elia, are farm workers. Like all grape workers, they are exposed to pesticides and other agricultural chemicals. Elia worked in the table grapes around Delano, California, until she was eight months pregnant with Johnnie.

4. With a partner, look at the verbs and identify the verb tense or tenses. What does Chavez's use of verb tense tell you about the actions in this passage?

5. Look at this passage from Chavez's address. Identify the verbs.

   It is my hope that our friends everywhere will resist in many nonviolent ways the presence of grapes in the stores where they shop.

6. With a partner, look at the verbs and identify the tenses. Why do you think Chavez uses these tenses?

7. Look at this passage and underline the verbs.

   In McFarland and in Fowler, childhood cancer cases are being reported in excess of expected rates. In Delano and other farming towns, questions are also being raised.

8. What do the verbs in Step 7 tell you about the timing of the action?

Inappropriate Verb Tense Shifts

Chavez changes his verb tense throughout his address, sometimes even within the same sentence. He uses a variety of tenses to narrate details about events that have happened in the past, to describe realities of the moment, and to express his wishes for the future. Using a variety of tenses as Chavez does can be a powerful rhetorical tool. But switching tenses unintentionally can make writing unclear. In your writing, use tenses consistently unless you have a good reason to switch them.

9. Read the following sentences about Chavez's speech. Underline the verbs that incorrectly shift in tense. Write each sentence correctly in the space provided, and underline the correction you made.

a. During his talk at Pacific Lutheran University, Chavez was speaking about the difficult lives of farmworkers, and he <u>asks</u> the audience, "Do we feel their pain deeply enough?"

b. Chavez fought for the rights of farmworkers because he <u>believes</u> in the value of every human life.

c. Just because people who pick crops do not have as much money as other people, and some of them can't afford the same healthcare, it doesn't mean their lives <u>had</u> less value.

Revising

Read the following paragraph from a student's essay about Cesar Chavez's address. Work with a partner to check whether the verbs maintain an appropriate and consistent tense. Circle any mistakes you notice, and then mark the text to correct the mistakes.

[1] Cesar Chavez is the President of the United Farm Workers of America. [2] He was speaking to a group of people at a university when he tells the story of Johnnie Rodriguez, a young boy who is dying of cancer. [3] There were so many people dying of cancer in McFarland that Chavez says the disease must be linked to the pesticides the farmers use. [4] For instance, Johnnie's mother picked grapes while she was pregnant with Johnnie, so Chavez believes the pesticides are the cause of his illness. [5] Chavez decides that he must fight the unjust treatment of farm workers.

☑ Check Your Understanding

Imagine you are editing a classmate's writing and you notice incorrect shifts in verb tense. In your own words, write an explanation to help your classmate understand the mistakes and how to correct them. Then add an item to your Editor's Checklist to help you remember how to revise your writing to correct inappropriate shifts in verb tense.

Practice

Using what you have learned about verb tense, write an introductory paragraph to an essay about Cesar Chavez. The claim should address whether Cesar Chavez's argument for workers' rights is effective. Trade your work with a partner to:

• Underline verbs.

• Make sure your verbs are in appropriate tenses.

• Ensure that you do not shift verb tenses unnecessarily.

Presenting a Multimedia Campaign

ASSIGNMENT

Develop a multimedia presentation that informs your peers about an issue of national or global significance and convinces them to take action. Work collaboratively to conduct and synthesize research into an engaging campaign that challenges your audience to make a difference.

Planning and Researching: Collaborate with a group of peers to select and gather information on an issue for your campaign.	■ Which of the issues from the list your class has developed are of interest to you? ■ Where could you look online to find out about more issues of national or global significance? ■ How will you evaluate the credibility and timeliness of sources? ■ How will you investigate what others are doing about your issue in order to evaluate possible solutions to incorporate into your call to action? ■ How will you give credit for information found in your sources and prepare a Works Cited page or an Annotated Bibliography?
Drafting: Collaborate with your group to design a multimedia campaign.	■ How will you use rhetorical appeals (*pathos*, *logos*, and *ethos*) to persuade your audience to care? ■ How can you raise awareness by informing your peers about compelling facts related to your issue? ■ What will be your group's name, mission statement, logo, and/or slogan? ■ What media channels will you use in your presentation, such as presentation tools, audio/visual components, social media, or others? ■ How will you organize talking points to inform your audience about the issue, convince them to care, and provide a call to action (what, why, and how)?
Rehearsing and Presenting: Use effective speaking and listening to prepare, present, and observe.	■ How can you use feedback from a dress rehearsal to improve your presentation? ■ How will you use the scoring guide to provide feedback on your own and others' presentations? ■ How will you listen and take notes on the what, why, and how of each multimedia presentation? ■ How will you make sure to employ eye contact, speaking rate, volume, enunciation, a variety of natural gestures, and conventions of language to communicate ideas effectively?

Reflection

After completing this Embedded Assessment, think about how you went about accomplishing this task, and respond to the following:

• Which presentations were effective in convincing you to care about the issue and why?

• What were the most effective media channels you observed, and what were the strengths of each?

SCORING GUIDE

Scoring Criteria	Exemplary	Proficient	Emerging	Incomplete
Ideas	The presentation • supports a clear claim and addresses counterclaim(s) with relevant reasons and evidence from a variety of accurate sources • uses rhetorical devices effectively • integrates engaging multimedia and campaign features to clarify ideas.	The presentation • supports a claim and addresses counterclaim(s) with sufficient reasons and evidence from reliable sources • uses rhetorical devices • includes adequate multimedia and campaign features to clarify ideas.	The presentation • has an unclear or unsupported claim, addresses counterclaim(s) ineffectively, and/or uses research from insufficient or unreliable sources • uses rhetorical devices unevenly • includes inadequate multimedia and campaign features.	The presentation • has no claim or counterclaim, and/or shows little or no evidence of research • does not use rhetorical devices • lacks multimedia or campaign features.
Structure	The presentation • demonstrates extensive evidence of collaboration and preparation • has an introduction that engages and informs the audience • sequences ideas and quotations smoothly with transitions • concludes with a clear call to action.	The presentation • demonstrates adequate evidence of collaboration and preparation • has an introduction that informs and orients the audience • sequences ideas and embeds quotations with transitions • includes a conclusion with a call to action.	The presentation • demonstrates insufficient or uneven collaboration and/or preparation • has a weak introduction • uses flawed or illogical sequencing; quotations seem disconnected • includes a weak or partial conclusion.	The presentation • demonstrates a failure to collaborate or prepare • lacks an introduction • has little or no evidence of sequencing or transitions • lacks a conclusion.
Use of Language	The speaker • communicates to a target audience with a persuasive tone and precise diction • demonstrates command of the conventions of standard English grammar, usage, and language (including correct mood/voice) • cites and evaluates sources thoroughly in an annotated bibliography.	The speaker • communicates to a target audience with appropriate tone and some precise diction • demonstrates adequate command of the conventions of standard English grammar, usage, and language (including correct mood/voice) • cites and evaluates sources in an annotated bibliography.	The speaker • communicates to a target audience inappropriately; may use basic diction • demonstrates partial command of the conventions of standard English grammar, usage, and language • begins to cite and/or evaluate sources in an annotated bibliography; may use improper format.	The speaker • does not communicate clearly; uses vague or confusing diction • has frequent errors in standard English grammar, usage, and language • lacks an annotated bibliography.

VISUAL PROMPT
What makes people laugh? What do you find funny? How can laughter help people overcome challenges?

THE CHALLENGE OF COMEDY

If we shadows have offended,
Think but this, and all is mended:
That you have but slumb'red here,
While these visions did appear.
And this weak and idle theme,
No more yielding but a dream...

—from Puck's epilogue *A Midsummer Night's Dream*, by William Shakespeare

GOALS

- To use knowledge of genre characteristics and purposes to analyze texts
- To analyze how a variety of authors create humor in print and nonprint texts
- To analyze how humor is used to reveal a universal truth (theme)
- To write a well-developed analysis of a humorous text
- To analyze and perform a scene from a Shakespearean comedy
- To revise and edit drafts using standard English conventions

VOCABULARY

ACADEMIC
juxtaposition
derision
denounce
caricature

LITERARY
persona
voice
satire
irony
dialect
hyperbole
alliteration
pun
monologue
multiple points of view

CONTENTS

Texts not included in these materials.

My Independent Reading List

Learning Targets

- Preview the big ideas in the unit.
- Demonstrate an understanding of the skills and knowledge needed to complete Embedded Assessment 1 successfully.

Preview

In this activity, you will identify and understand the skills needed to complete Embedded Assessment 1

Making Connections

In the final unit you will encounter the challenging task of appreciating humorous texts and Shakespearean texts. You will use all your collaborative, speaking and listening, reading, and writing skills as you examine the ways in which authors create humor.

Essential Questions

Based on your current knowledge, respond to the following Essential Questions:

1. How do writers and speakers use humor to convey truth?

2. What makes an effective performance of a Shakespearean comedy?

Developing Vocabulary

Use a QHT chart to sort the terms on the Contents page. Remember, one academic goal is to move all words to the "T" column by the end of the unit.

Unpacking Embedded Assessment 1

Closely read the assignment for Embedded Assessment 1.

 Write an essay that explains how an author creates humor for effect and uses it to communicate a universal truth.

Then, find the Scoring Guide and work with your class to paraphrase the expectations. Create a graphic organizer to use as a visual reminder of the required concepts (what you need to know) and skills (what you need to do).

After each activity, use this graphic to guide reflection about what you have learned and what you still need to learn in order to be successful in the Embedded Assessment.

My Notes

INDEPENDENT READING LINK

Reading Plan

For your outside reading for this unit, choose texts by writers whom you find humorous. You might look for humorous short stories as well as narrative essays and poetry. Create a list of titles in your Independent Reading List of at least five texts based on recommendations from your teacher as well as your own research.

Understanding the Complexity of Humor

Learning Targets

- Write an objective summary of an informational text about a genre.
- Demonstrate understanding of the denotations and connotations of words related to humor.

Preview

In this activity, you will read an essay on the topic of humor. As you read, think about your own sense of humor and what makes you laugh.

Genre Study: Humor

In this unit, you will learn about the characteristics, structures, and purposes of humor writing. Humor is a literary tool whose purpose is to entertain readers, maintain their attention, and develop character and plot. Humor writers, whether in fiction or nonfiction, rely on several devices—including irony, hyperbole, understatement, sarcasm, slapstick, and puns—all of which you will learn about in this unit.

Setting a Purpose for Reading

- As you read, underline words that make you laugh.
- Circle unknown words and phrases. Try to determine the meaning of the words by using context clues, word parts, or a dictionary.

About the Author

Marc Tyler Nobleman (b. 1972) is a pop-culture archaeologist who has written more than 70 books. In *Bill the Boy Wonder: The Secret Co-Creator of Batman*, Nobleman exposes the real creator of *Batman* who, until this book, had never been credited before. Nobleman is also a cartoonist, whose work has been published in *The Wall Street Journal*, *Forbes*, *The Saturday Evening Post*, and *New York Daily News*.

My Notes

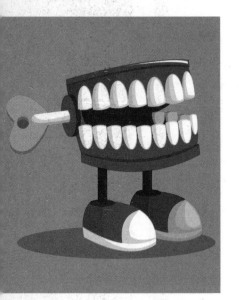

Essay

Made You Laugh

by **Marc Tyler Nobleman**

1 Would you like to know a language everyone in the world understands? You already do—because you laugh. Any two people from vastly different cultures who don't speak a word of the other's language still know exactly what is meant when the other person laughs.

2 Think of laughter as the unofficial language of Earth. Yet how much do any of us really understand about humor?

On the Laugh Track

3 What makes things funny? READ asked John Ficarra, the editor of MAD magazine. After all, he should know. Here's what he said: "Monkeys. They're unbeatable. For example, show a photo of a dentist—not funny. Show a photo of a dentist with a monkey in his chair, and it's comedy gold. Try this theory out on a few of your family photos, and you'll see." OK, so monkeys are funny. What else? How about this?

4 Two hunters were in the woods, when one collapsed. He didn't seem to be breathing. The other called the emergency number and said, "My friend is dead! What can I do?" The operator said, "Calm down, I can help. First, let's make sure he's dead." After a second of silence on the hunter's end, the operator heard a gunshot. The hunter came back on the phone and said, "OK, now what?"

5 If you laughed, you're not alone. In the year 2001, that joke was voted the funniest in the world as part of a project called LaughLab. Psychologist Richard Wiseman's goal was to determine what makes people laugh and what is found to be funny among men and women, older and younger people, and people from different countries. His research team tested people in person and asked others to submit opinions online using a "Giggleometer," which ranked jokes on a scale of 1–5. More than 40,000 jokes were tested.

6 You may be saying to yourself, "Studying jokes? Is that science?" But plenty of smart people say yes. Laughter is a biological function. It has a certain rhythm; laughter syllables build, then trail off, and they come out in a repetitive, not random, sequence. For example, "ha-ha-ho-ho-he" is typical, but "ha-ho-ha-ho-ha" or "he-ho-he" just doesn't happen.

7 Babies begin to laugh instinctively when they're about four months old, perhaps to form a connection with parents. Those born blind and deaf also laugh, so laughter is not dependent on sight and hearing. Other animals, notably chimps, exhibit laugh-like behavior when playing with one another.

GRAMMAR & USAGE

Pronoun-Antecedent Agreement

Just as subjects and verbs must agree in number, so must pronouns and their antecedents. Pronouns take the place of nouns or other pronouns. An antecedent, or the word the pronoun refers to or takes the place of, must agree in number with the pronoun. For example:

"Babies begin to laugh instinctively when they're about four months old ..." The word *babies* is plural, so the pronoun that replaces it (they) must also be plural.

"Ask an average person why humans laugh, and he or she would probably say, 'Because something was funny.'" The word *person* is singular, so the pronoun (he, she) must also be singular.

As you read "Made You Laugh," select three sentences that contain pronouns and antecedents. Underline these words and note whether they are singular or plural.

Even rats, when tickled, make high-pitched squeals that can be interpreted as laughter. (As you might guess, only a dedicated few know this firsthand.)

Comedy Is Serious Stuff

8 Comics know that the same jokes are not funny to everyone everywhere. Ed Hiestand, a writer for comedy great Johnny Carson, told READ, "Everyone who writes comedy needs to know the audience. On the Carson show, everybody would laugh on a Friday night. Nobody would laugh on a Monday." Even within one state or town or family, senses of humor are as varied as the people are. Professional comics do not assume a 10 p.m. audience will like a joke because a 7 p.m. audience did.

9 Comedians who test jokes for a living say it's hit or miss. "It's a tough gig, and you have to have a large threshold for pain," said stand-up Jay Nog. Performers whose jokes get a two-second laugh consider that a significant accomplishment.

10 Timing is critical. Starting stand-up Zubair Simonson said he's learning the hard way that "good timing can cause a weak joke to soar, while poor timing can cause a strong joke to falter." Authors and film actors do not often get immediate public feedback. But comics do.

11 What keeps the funny guys going? The laughs and after-effects. "The best humor has some sort of layer to it; it makes a statement of some kind or comment," said Margy Yuspa, a director at Comedy Central. "An example is [Dave] Chappelle. His comedy is funny on the surface and also often comments on race or social issues."

Funny You Said That

12 Comedians have their own theories about humor. "What makes us laugh is a surprise change in perspective that connects an unknown with a known idea in a unique manner," said Ronald P. Culberson, a humorist at FUNsulting.com. "For instance, a three-legged dog walks into an Old West saloon and says, "I'm looking for the man who shot my paw."

13 Ask an average person why humans laugh, and he or she would probably say, "Because something was funny." But comics need to know what gives the giggles; their livelihood depends on it.

14 Comedian Anthony DeVito told READ that "people tend to laugh at things that reinforce what they already believe. Comedy tells them they're right."

15 Gary Gulman, a finalist in Last Comic Standing, a reality TV show and comedy competition, gave specifics. "Sometimes it's a keen observation about something you thought you lived through. Sometimes it's a **juxtaposition** of words. Sometimes it's a gesture or a sound. An encyclopedia couldn't do this question justice."

My Notes

ACADEMIC VOCABULARY

Juxtaposition is a technique used by artists and writers, places normally unassociated ideas, words, and phrases next to one another for effect (e.g., surprise or wit).

_____

_____

_____

_____

_____

_____

_____

_____

_____

_____

_____

_____

_____

_____

_____

VOCABULARY

LITERARY

A **persona** is a character assumed by an author in a written work or by an actor in a performance.

The phrase *public persona* is used to describe how an individual presents him- or herself to other people.

WORD CONNECTIONS

Roots and Affixes

Superiority has the Latin root *super*, which means "placed above." This root is found in many English words, including *superb, superlative, supreme, supervise, superintendent,* and *supernatural.*

An **incongruity** happens when things do not match as they are expected to. The word *incongruity* has the Latin root *congru*, which means "to come together," "to agree," or "to coincide." The prefix *in-* means "not" or "without."

What Are You Laughing At?

16 Yet laughter is not always a planned response to a joke. One study found that 80 percent of the time, we laugh at something that just happens. People often laugh just because someone else does. Like a yawn, a laugh is contagious. That's why some sit-coms use laugh tracks.

17 Laughter is also social, a way to bond with others. After all, how often do you laugh alone? When two or more people laugh at the same thing, it is as if nature reminds them of what they have in common.

18 Behavioral neuroscientist Robert R. Provine conducted a 10-year experiment in which he eavesdropped on 2,000 conversations in malls, at parties, and on city sidewalks. He found that the greatest guffaws did not follow intentionally funny statements; people laughed hardest at everyday comments that seemed funny only in a certain social context.

19 "Do you have a rubber band?" is not in and of itself humorous, but it is if it's said in response to "I like Amelia so much. I wish I could get her attention."

Theories of Funniness

20 There are three main theories about humor.

21 Release theory—Humor gives a break from tension. In a horror movie, as a character creeps through a dark house (often idiotically) to follow an eerie noise, he might open a door to find a cat playing with a squeeze toy. The audience laughs in relief. Humor also lets us deal with unpleasant or forbidden issues, such as death and violence. People are often more comfortable laughing at something shocking said by someone else, though they would never say it themselves. Comedian Keenen Ivory Wayans once said, "Comedy is the flip side of pain. The worst things that happen to you are hysterical—in retrospect. But a comedian doesn't need retrospect; he realizes it's funny while he's in the eye of the storm."

22 Superiority theory—Audience members laugh at those who appear to be more stupid than they judge themselves to be. Slapstick humor, such as seeing a guy slip on a banana peel, often falls into this category. This theory dates back to Plato in ancient Greece and was prominent in the Middle Ages, when people with deformities were often employed as court jesters.

23 Some comedians exploited this theory by building a routine—or even a **persona**—around the idea that they were losers who couldn't catch a break. Larry David, David Letterman, and Woody Allen are comedians who have done this, each in his own way.

24 Incongruity theory—People laugh when things that are not normally associated with each other are put together. Many comedy duos, from Laurel and Hardy to David Spade and Chris Farley, feature a thin man and a fat man, a visual contrast.

25 People also laugh when there is a difference between what they expect to happen and what actually occurs. They are being led in a certain direction, and then that direction abruptly changes, and the unpredictability makes them laugh. Children see birds all the time without reaction, but if one flies into their classroom through an open window, they will probably explode in giggles.

Got Laughs?

26 What we laugh at changes as we age. Here are some examples.

Audience	Often Likes
Young children	Slapstick, or silly **physical humor**
Elementary-school children	**Puns,** simple jokes that play off the sound rather than the meaning of a word, such as "Lettuce all go to the salad bar"
Teens	**Jokes** about topics that authority figures would consider rebellious, a way to use humor to deal with nerve-racking subjects
Adults, particularly well-educated ones	**Satire,** which makes fun of the weaknesses of people and society

27 Generally, children laugh more than adults. One study found that adults laugh 20 times a day, while children laugh 200 times!

The Secrets of Humor

28 Certain comedic devices turn up again and again in jokes, comic strips, and filmed entertainment—because they succeed.

29 "There were tricks," said Hiestand of his days writing for *The Tonight Show* hosted by Johnny Carson, "things you would see, certain things always got laughs." One of the most popular is often called the rule of threes. That is a pattern in which two nonfunny elements are followed by a third that is funny (yet still makes sense within the context). Many jokes start off with a list of three, such as "A rabbi, a lawyer, and a duck walk into a bar." As the joke unfolds, the rabbi says something straightforward, then the lawyer does as well, but the duck finishes with something witty or absurd.

30 Three guys were stranded on an island. An antique lamp washed ashore. When the guys touched it, a genie came out. "I'll grant each of you one wish," the genie said. The first guy said, "I want to go home," then disappeared. The second guy said, "I also want to go home," and he too disappeared. The third man suddenly looked sad. He said, "I want my two friends back to keep me company."

31 Certain concepts seem to be more amusing than others. If you tell any joke involving an animal, and it doesn't matter which one you use, think Donald and Daffy. In the LaughLab experiment, scientists determined that the funniest animal is the duck. (It's not arbitrary that a duck was used in the rule-of-threes joke.)

My Notes

_____

_____

_____

_____

_____

_____

_____

_____

_____

_____

_____

_____

_____

_____

_____

_____

Do Tell—But Do It Right

32 There are also known techniques for telling jokes well.

- **Keep it short**—Don't include any details that are not necessary to bring you to the punch line. In the genie joke, there was no need to specify it was a tropical island or to name the castaways. The quicker you tell a joke, the funnier it will be.

- **Be specific**—Some comedians swear that a joke is funnier if you say "Aquafresh" instead of "toothpaste." The attention to detail makes the story seem more real.

- **Keep a straight face**—Deliver the joke deadpan, or without emotion. That way, any strangeness in the joke will seem even stranger because the person telling it doesn't seem to notice.

- **Don't laugh at your own joke**—Let your audience decide whether it is funny or foolish—or both.

33 Theories and techniques aside, much about humor remains a mystery. According to Hiestand, Carson many times said, "I don't understand what makes comedy a sure thing. There's no 100-percent surefire formula." Meanwhile, for most of us, laughter is never a problem. It does not need to be solved, just enjoyed.

Making Observations

- What details or ideas about humor stand out to you?
- What questions do you have after reading the essay?

☑ Focus on the Sentence

Write four different sentences about humor based on information in the essay "Made You Laugh."

Statement: _____

_____

Question: _____

_____

Exclamation: _____

_____

Command: _____

_____

Returning to the Text

- Return to the text as you respond to the following questions. Use text evidence to support your responses.
- Write any additional questions you have about the essay in your Reader/Writer Notebook.

   1. Why does laughter seem to qualify as a biological function? What might be the biological function of laughter?

   _____

   _____

   _____

   _____

2. In paragraph 7, what purpose does the sentence in parentheses serve?

_____

_____

_____

_____

3. As discussed in paragraphs 16–19, why is unplanned humor often funnier than planned humor?

_____

_____

_____

_____

4. What context clues in paragraph 21 help you understand the meaning of the word *retrospect*?

_____

_____

_____

_____

5. Based on paragraphs 26–27, what distinction can you make between what makes children laugh and what makes adults laugh? Why might children laugh more often than adults?

_____

_____

_____

_____

6. Reread each of the headings throughout the essay. Which heading is an example of juxtaposition? Explain your answer.

_____

_____

_____

_____

7. What is the author's thesis in this essay? Cite specific evidence from the text in your response.

_____

_____

_____

_____

Working from the Text

8. Referring to the words and phrases you've underlined, write an accurate summary of a section of the text by putting the main points into your own words. Remember that a summary is a broad overview of the text; stick to the main points by writing about big ideas and excluding smaller details.

9. To analyze a text carefully, one must use precise words to describe the humor and explain the intended effect. Work collaboratively to define terms and to understand the nuances of words with similar denotations (definitions). You have already encountered some of these words.

Words to Describe Humor	Denotation	Connotations
amusing		
cute		
facetious		
hysterical		
ironic		
irreverent		
laughable		
light-hearted		
ludicrous		
mocking		
sarcastic		
satirical		
witty		

Words in Response to Humor	Denotation	Connotations
chuckle		
giggle		
grin		
groan		
guffaw		
outburst		
snort		
scoff		
smile		
smirk		
snicker		

10. Listen as your teacher reads you a joke. Think about the type of humor that makes the joke funny (or attempts to). Explain your answer using vocabulary from the essay "What Makes Us Laugh."

LANGUAGE & WRITER'S CRAFT: Pronoun-Antecedent Agreement

Remember that pronouns and antecedents have to agree in number. Note that pronouns such as *everyone, either, no one,* and *everybody* are always singular, while pronouns such as *few, many,* and *all* are always plural. For example:

Would <u>everyone</u> in class please find <u>his</u> or <u>her</u> desk?

<u>Many</u> are going to <u>their</u> school's game on Friday.

<u>Jasper</u> and <u>Frederica</u> earned excellent scores at <u>their</u> piano recital this weekend.

Practice completing each sentence with the correct pronoun to match the antecedent.

1. According to the news, all eighth-grade students will help _____ city by participating in a cleanup project.

2. Either <u>Carla</u> or <u>Laura</u> has _____ grandmother's book.

3. The teacher announced, "Would everyone please find _____ seat?"

PRACTICE Now go back to your response to step 8 and revise your summary, using what you have learned about the agreement between pronouns and their antecedents.

☑ Focus on the Sentence

Writing complex sentences is one way to improve your writing. Complex sentences have two clauses, one main or independent and one subordinate or dependent. The essential ingredient in a complex sentence is the subordinate conjunction. The subordinate conjunction provides a necessary transition between the two ideas in a sentence. Take a look at the sample sentence that follows, and note the use of the comma after the subordinate clause that begins with a subordinating conjunction.

Because she was shivering, he gave her a blanket.

Write four complex sentences using the word *humor.* You may add suffixes.

Regardless _____

Although _____

Whenever _____

If _____

📝 Informational Writing Prompt

Create a detailed paragraph that uses precise diction to explain your sense of humor. Use what you learned about humor and at least two words each from the "Words to Describe Humor" and "Words in Response to Humor" charts. Explain what does and does not make you laugh and how you typically respond to humorous texts. Be sure to:

- Begin with a clear thesis statement explaining your sense of humor.
- Include some specific examples of things that make you laugh.
- Check your pronouns and their antecedents to ensure that they agree in number.
- Use complete, complex sentences with correctly placed commas.

Learning Strategies

Marking the Text
Graphic Organizer
Note-taking
Discussion Groups
Brainstorming
RAFT
Drafting

WORD CONNECTIONS

Cognates

The English word *comedy* comes from the Latin word *comoedia*, meaning "an amusing play or performance." It has the same meaning as the Spanish word *comedia*.

My Notes

Learning Targets
- Categorize humorous texts by levels of comedy.
- Analyze print and graphic features to explain how authors create humor.

Preview

In this activity, you will analyze the elements of humorous texts.

Understanding Levels of Comedy

Comedy occurs in different ways.

1. Read and mark the text to indicate information that is new to you.

Low comedy refers to the type of humor that is focused primarily on a situation or series of events. It includes such things as physical mishaps, humor concerning the human body and its functions, coincidences, and humorous situations. With low comedy, the humor is straightforward and generally easy to follow and understand.

Since the primary purpose of most low comedy is to entertain, the action is frequently seen as hilarious or hysterical and the effect is often side-splitting laughter and guffaws. Many times, the characters are exaggerated caricatures rather than fully developed characters. These caricatures are often caught in unlikely situations or they become victims of circumstances seemingly beyond their control. Thus, the plot takes priority over the characters. Examples of low comedy might include *Madea's Family Reunion, Meet the Parents,* and *America's Funniest Home Videos*. Shakespeare's comedies, such as *A Midsummer Night's Dream* and *Twelfth Night*, are full of low comedy.

High comedy refers to the type of humor that is focused primarily on characters, dialogue, or ideas. It includes such things as clever wordplay, wit, and pointed remarks regarding larger issues. Many times, high comedy takes an irreverent or unconventional look at serious issues.

Sometimes the humor of high comedy is not immediately obvious; it can take a bit of reflection in order to realize the humorous intent. Frequently, the purpose of high comedy is to express an opinion, to persuade, or to promote deeper consideration of an idea. Often described as amusing, clever, or witty, high comedy typically results in chuckles, grins, and smiles rather than loud laughter. Clever use of language and interesting characters receive more attention than the circumstances that surround them. Examples of high comedy include *Modern Family, The Middle,* and, at times, *The Simpsons*. Shakespeare's tragedies, such as *Hamlet* and *Romeo and Juliet*, also include instances of high comedy.

2. Why do we distinguish between different kinds of comedy?

3. With a partner, take notes to complete the two comedy charts that follow. Brainstorm a strong example at each level of comedy.

Low Comedy

Purpose	Common Subjects	Emphasis	Descriptions	Intended Responses

High Comedy

Purpose	Common Subjects	Emphasis	Descriptions	Intended Responses

4. Using the vocabulary you just learned, share with another pair of students the examples of high and low comedy you and your partner brainstormed.

My Notes

Analyzing Humorous Texts

5. Brainstorm what you already know about comic strips and political cartoons. Think about format, audience, topics, descriptions of humor, intended effects, etc.

Comic Strips:

Political Cartoons:

6. Read and mark the text of the following definitions for information that is new to you:

Comic strips are meant primarily to entertain. They have a beginning and middle that lead to a humorous ending. They tend to be low-level comedy that is easily understood by a wide audience.

Political cartoons deal with larger issues and are often meant to communicate a particular political or social message. They often have a single panel with a powerful statement to reinforce humor displayed through a picture (characters or symbols). They tend to be high-level comedy, appealing to a smaller population that is well-informed about a specific topic.

☑ Check Your Understanding

In order to compare and contrast comic strips and political cartoons, create a Venn diagram in your Reader/Writer Notebook that lists the characteristics of each. Are there any areas where they overlap? Continue to add to your diagram as you analyze examples of these two humorous texts.

Introducing the Strategy: RAFT

RAFT is an acronym that stands for role, audience, format, and topic. RAFT is a strategy that can be used for responding to and analyzing a text by identifying and examining its role, audience, format, and topic.

7. As you review a comic strip and a political cartoon, think about each author's purpose and how he or she achieves it. Think about the print elements, the graphic elements, and the dialogue. Use the graphic organizer and the RAFT strategy that follow to analyze the humor in the comic strip and the political cartoon based on the previous definitions.

🔲 INDEPENDENT READING LINK

Read and Respond

Analyze one of the humorous texts you are reading. Does the text reflect high comedy or low comedy? Cite specific examples from the text to support your answer, and record your responses in your Reader/ Writer Notebook.

Titles _____

	Comic Strip:	Political Cartoon:
Role Who is the author? Where is this comic strip or political cartoon found? What is the attitude (tone) of the author toward the topic? How can you tell?		
Audience Who does this comic strip or political cartoon target? How do you know?		
Format Describe the use of print and nonprint techniques (dialogue, narration frames, and angles) used for effect.		
Topic What is this comic/cartoon about? Who are the characters? What is happening? How would you describe the humor? What is the intended effect?		

✍ Writing to Sources: Informational Text

Compare and contrast the two humorous texts that you analyzed in this activity: the comic strip and the political cartoon. How does the author of each text create humor? Write a paragraph explaining your answer. Be sure to:

- Establish a controlling idea that explains the authors' purpose and describes how print or graphic features in the cartoon and comic strip help the authors achieve that purpose.
- Include specific details from the cartoon and comic strip to support your ideas.
- Explain whether the cartoon and comic strip are high or low humor and why.
- Use precise diction to describe the humor of the cartoon and comic strip.

Humorous Anecdotes

Learning Targets

- Analyze how authors convey humor in speech and writing.
- Write and present an oral reading of an original humorous anecdote.
- Integrate ideas from multiple texts to build knowledge and vocabulary about humor.

Preview

In this activity, you will read a humorous essay and think about any funny memories you've had related to a road trip or riding in a car.

Humorous Anecdotes

1. In Unit 2, you learned about how authors of argumentative essays use anecdotes to support their claims. Humor authors also rely on anecdotes. Read the following information to see how the use of anecdotes applies to a study of humor.

   An anecdote is a brief, entertaining account of an incident or event. Often, anecdotes are shared because of their humorous nature, but anecdotes can also help illustrate larger ideas and concepts. Families sometimes share anecdotes about the humorous things family members have done. Frequently, the stories become more and more absurd as the details are exaggerated with each retelling.

2. Do you or your family have a humorous anecdote that is shared over and over? What is it? Why is it retold? Who tells it? How does it change over time?

Viewing a Humorous Monologue

The following monologue provides humorous accounts of somewhat ordinary events. Finding and describing the humor in the people, places, and events you encounter can enrich your conversations as well as your writing.

3. As you watch the clip for the first time, listen for different topics in the monologue and take notes.

Comedian's Persona	People	Places	Events

4. The second time you view the clip, pay attention to how the comedian delivers the anecdote. Take notes on your assigned section.

1. Describe the comedian's delivery. What is the effect on the audience? Tone: Facial Expressions: Gestures: Volume: Pacing: Inflection (emphasis): Effect:	2. Record the comedian's transitions between topics within his anecdote. What words or phrasing does he use?
3. Describe the imagery the comedian uses. List details that describe a person, place, or event. Why does the comedian include these specific details? Topic: Descriptive Details: Figurative Language:	4. Does the speaker's tone shift? Record his attitude about the topic at the beginning of the monologue and if his attitude changes. How does he communicate this shift?

☑ Check Your Understanding

List three ways the comedian in the clip makes the audience laugh with a simple anecdote. Does he use his persona? people in the story? humorous events?

LITERARY

Voice is a writer's (or speaker's) distinctive use of language to express ideas as well as his or her persona.

An author's voice is conveyed by both their style and diction.

Setting a Purpose for Reading

- Underline words and phrases that show the author's personality and distinctive voice.
- As you read, underline any words or phrases that you find humorous.
- Circle unknown words and phrases. Try to determine the meaning of the words by using context clues, word parts, or a dictionary.

About the Author

Jon Scieszka (b. 1954) is the oldest of six brothers in his family. He became an elementary school teacher and found that his students liked the funny stories that he enjoyed telling. He has since published a number of children's books, which are illustrated by his friend Lane Smith. In 2008, the Library of Congress named him National Ambassador for Young People's Literature.

✎ KNOWLEDGE QUEST

Knowledge Question:

Why is humor an effective way to communicate wisdom?

Across Activities 4.4 and 4.5 you will read two essays on the topic of humor as a way to communicate wisdom. While you read and build knowledge about the topic, think about your answer to the Knowledge Question.

Essay

from  # Brothers

by **Jon Scieszka**

1   Brothers are the guys you stick with and stick up for.

2   The Scieszka brothers are scattered all over the country now, but we still get together once a year to play a family golf tournament. We named it after our dad, Lou, and his favorite car—his old Cadillac Coupe de Ville. It is the Coupe de Lou Classic. We all grew up playing golf, because Dad Lou, an elementary school principal, taught Junior Golf and gave us lessons during summers off. And I'm sure my brothers would want me to point out the amazing fact that I am the winner of both the very first Coupe de Lou 1983 and the latest Coupe de Lou 2004.

3   But of all the Scieszka brother memories, I believe it was a family car trip that gave us our finest moment of brotherhood. We were driving cross-country from Michigan to Florida, all of us, including the family cat (a guy cat, naturally), in the family station wagon. Somewhere mid-trip we stopped at one of those Stuckey's rest-stop restaurants to eat and load up on Stuckey's candy.

4 We ate lunch, ran around like maniacs in the warm sun, then packed back into the station wagon—Mom and Dad up front, Jim, Jon, Tom, Gregg, Brian, Jeff, and the cat in back. Somebody dropped his Stuckey's Pecan Log Roll® on the floor. The cat found it and must have scarfed every bit of it, because two minutes later we heard that awful ack ack ack sound of a cat getting ready to barf.

5 The cat puked up the pecan nut log. Jeff, the youngest and smallest (and closest to the floor) was the first to go. He got one look and whiff of the pecan nut cat yack and blew his own sticky lunch all over the cat. The puke-covered cat jumped on Brian, Brian barfed on Gregg. Gregg upchucked on Tom. Tom burped a bit of Stuckey lunch back on Gregg. Jim and I rolled down the windows and hung out as far as we could, yelling in group puke horror.

6 Dad Lou didn't know what had hit the back of the car. No time to ask questions. He just pulled off to the side of the road. All of the brothers—Jim, Jon, Tom, Gregg, Brian, and Jeff—spilled out of the puke wagon and fell in the grass, gagging and yelling and laughing until we couldn't laugh anymore.

7 What does it all mean? What essential guy wisdom did I learn from this?

8 Stick with your brothers. Stick up for your brothers. And if you ever drop a pecan nut log in a car with your five brothers and your cat … you will probably stick to your brothers.

Knowledge Quest
- What happens in the story?
- What parts of this essay made you laugh?

Focus on the Sentence
Complete the given sentences using the conjunctions because, *so*, and *but*.

The cat barfed because _____

_____

The cat barfed, so _____

_____

The cat barfed, but _____

_____

Returning to the Text
- Return to the text as you respond to the following questions. Use text evidence to support your responses.
- Write any additional questions you have about the essay in your Reader/Writer Notebook.

5. How does the author show that he and his brothers have close relationships?

_____
_____
_____
_____

6. What events happened during a family car trip to make it memorable?

_____

_____

_____

_____

7. **KQ** How does the author's use of the word *brotherhood* help you to understand this essay is about more than just a humorous anecdote?

_____

_____

_____

_____

8. How do the events in the story reveal a lesson the author learned?

_____

_____

_____

_____

9. Describe the author's voice. What language does he use to create his distinct voice and convey his personality in the text?

_____

_____

_____

_____

_____

10. **KQ** How does the author use humor to reveal a truth about life?

_____

_____

_____

_____

Working from the Text

11. Review the essay and make connections between the essay and your own experiences. Also think about other humorous texts—particularly your independent reading books—that you have read and how the essay connects to those texts. Finally, make connections between the essay and the world around you. Use the following symbols to mark the text.

   E/S = Essay to Self
   E/T = Essay to other Texts
   E/W = Essay to World

   Quickwrite: After marking the text, write a paragraph in your Reader/Writer Notebook exploring these text connections in detail. Compare your paragraph with a partner's to see how they differ.

Introducing the Strategy: TWIST

TWIST is an acronym for tone, word choice, imagery, style, and theme. This writing strategy helps a writer analyze each of these elements in a text in order to write a response to an analytical writing prompt about the text.

12. Reread the excerpt from "Brothers," and use the TWIST strategy to guide your analysis of the text.

Acronym	Text: "Brothers" by Jon Scieszka
Tone *What is the author's attitude about the topic?*	
Word choice *What specific diction does the author use for effect? How does the author's word choice contribute to their voice?*	
Imagery *What specific descriptive details and figurative language does the author use for effect?*	
Style *How does the author use language to create humor?* *What is the intended response the author hopes to achieve? How does the author's style contribute to their voice?*	
Theme *What is the central idea of this text? What idea about life is the author trying to convey through humor?* *What is the author's purpose?*	

13. Once you have found textual evidence from the text "Brothers" and made an inference about the theme, you are ready to write an analytical topic sentence. State the title, author, and genre (TAG) in your thesis or topic sentence.
For example:

Jon Scieszka's anecdote "Brothers" is a low-level comedy that uses a comic situation, exaggeration, and comic diction to reveal a universal truth about how brothers who laugh together stick together.

Practice writing a topic sentence about the comedic monologues you viewed in class using the TAG format.

Writing and Presenting Your Own Anecdote

14. Use the TWIST graphic organizer to plan your own anecdote.

Subject of Humorous Memory:	People/Places/Events:

Tone:

What is your attitude about the topic? How will you convey that attitude?

Word Choice:

What specific diction can you use for effect?

Imagery:

What specific descriptive and figurative language can you use for effect?

Style:

How can you use language (diction and syntax) to create humor?

What is the intended response you hope to achieve?

Theme:

What idea about life are you trying to convey through humor?

15. Draft your anecdote. Be sure to include a beginning, middle, and end. Think about who was involved, what happened, how you dealt with it, and what you learned about yourself or the world as a result.

16. Present an oral reading of your draft to a partner. After your partner presents, provide feedback relating to his or her ideas, organization, and language and the humorous effect.

LANGUAGE & WRITER'S CRAFT: Using Verbals

A verbal is a form of a verb that functions as something other than a verb. For example, a verbal might be used as a noun, an adjective, or an adverb. An infinitive is the *to* form of a verb, such as *to chuckle* or *to snort*. Infinitives are verbals that can be used as nouns, adjectives, or adverbs. A participle is a verbal that is used as an adjective. There are present and past participles.

Present: giggling, snickering
Past: raised, destroyed

A gerund is a verbal that acts as a noun and ends in *-ing*. It can sometimes be difficult to tell the difference between a gerund and a present participle because both end in *-ing*. The key is to determine whether the word acts as an adjective or a noun.

Participle: The giggling child made lots of noise.
Giggling is an adjective describing the noun *child*.

Gerund: His giggling was distracting.
Giggling is the subject of the sentence, so it is a noun.

Writers use verbals for variety and effect.

Look at these examples based on the essay:

Golfing was an activity that the Scieszka family enjoyed. (*Golfing* is a gerund because it acts as a noun. It is the subject of the sentence.)

"Jim and I rolled down the windows and hung out as far as we could, yelling in group puke horror." (*Yelling* is a present participle. It modifies Jim and I.)

"We still get together once a year to play a family golf tournament." (*To play* is an infinitive. It functions as an adverb, modifying the verb *get* by answering the question "why.")

PRACTICE In your Reader/Writer Notebook, write a brief summary of Jon Scieszka's anecdote using one infinitive, one gerund, and one participle.

Writing to Sources: Informational Text

Select an anecdote in audio or visual format. Write a paragraph explaining the humor the author creates and its intended response. Be sure to:

- Clearly state how the anecdote uses the elements of humor.
- Include examples from the text to support your analysis.
- Use precise diction.
- Use participles, gerunds, and infinitives in your writing.

My Notes

INDEPENDENT READING LINK

Read and Connect
Describe a personal connection to the text you are reading independently. Look for anecdotes like the one you read in this activity. What anecdotes in your independent reading text struck you? How do you connect to them?

Learning Strategies

Think-Pair-Share
Marking the Text
Questioning the Text
Discussion Groups
Socratic Seminar

Learning Targets

- Analyze a humorous essay by participating in a Socratic Seminar.
- Explain how an author conveys universal truths through humor.
- Integrate ideas from multiple texts to build knowledge and vocabulary about humor.

Preview

In this activity, you will read a humorous essay and explore how people use comedy to discuss serious topics.

KNOWLEDGE QUEST

Knowledge Question:
Why is humor an effective way to communicate wisdom?

Setting a Purpose for Reading

- As you read the essay, underline words and phrases that are intended to be humorous.
- Underscore the parts of the text that seem to reveal a truth about life.
- Circle unknown words and phrases. Try to determine the meaning of the words by using context clues, word parts, or a dictionary.

My Notes

About the Author

Dave Barry (b. 1947) was a humor columnist for the *Miami Herald* from 1983 to 2005, during which time he won a Pulitzer Prize for Commentary. Barry has written over 30 books, including two that were turned into a sitcom, *Dave's World*. Much of Barry's work provides humorous commentary on current social issues.

Essay

I've Got a Few Pet Peeves about Sea Creatures

by **Dave Barry**

1   Pets are good, because they teach children important lessons about life, the main one being that, sooner or later, life kicks the bucket.

2   With me, it was sooner. When I was a boy, my dad, who worked in New York City, would periodically bring home a turtle in a little plastic tank

that had a little plastic island with a little plastic palm tree, as is so often found in natural turtle habitats. I was excited about having a pet, and I'd give the turtle a fun pet name like Scooter. But my excitement was not shared by Scooter, who, despite residing in a tropical paradise, never did anything except mope around.

3   Actually, he didn't even mope "around": He moped in one place without moving, or even blinking, for days on end, displaying basically the same vital signs as an ashtray. Eventually I would realize—it wasn't easy to tell—that Scooter had passed on to that Big Pond in the Sky, and I'd bury him in the garden, where he'd decompose and become food for the zucchini, which in turn would be eaten by my dad, who would in turn go to New York City, where, compelled by powerful instincts that even he did not understand, he would buy me another moping death turtle. And so the cycle of life would repeat.

4   I say all this to explain why I recently bought fish for my 4-year-old daughter, Sophie. My wife and I realized how badly she wanted an animal when she found a beetle on the patio and declared that it was a pet, named Marvin. She put Marvin into a Tupperware container, where, under Sophie's loving care and feeding, he thrived for maybe nine seconds before expiring like a little six-legged parking meter. Fortunately, we have a beetle-intensive patio, so, **unbeknownst** to Sophie, we were able to replace Marvin with a parade of stand-ins of various sizes ("Look! Marvin has grown bigger!" "Wow! Today Marvin has grown smaller!"). But it gets to be **tedious**, going out early every morning to wrangle patio beetles. So we decided to go with fish.

5   I had fish of my own, years ago, and it did not go well. They got some disease like Mongolian Fin Rot, which left them basically just little pooping torsos. But I figured that today, with all the technological advances we have such as cellular phones and "digital" things and carbohydrate-free toothpaste, modern fish would be more reliable.

6   So we got an aquarium and prepared it with special water and special gravel and special fake plants and a special scenic rock so the fish would be intellectually stimulated and get into a decent college. When everything was ready I went to the aquarium store to buy fish, my only criteria being that they should be 1) hardy digital fish; and 2) fish that looked a LOT like other fish, in case God forbid we had to Marvinize them. This is when I discovered how complex fish society is. I'd point to some colorful fish and say, "What about these?" And the aquarium guy would say, "Those are great fish but they do get aggressive when they mate." And I'd say, "Like, how aggressive?" And he'd say, "They'll kill all the other fish."

7   This was a recurring theme. I'd point to some fish, and the aquarium guy would inform me that these fish could become aggressive if there were fewer than four of them, or an odd number of them, or it was a month containing the letter "R," or they heard the song "Who Let the Dogs Out." It turns out

My Notes

unbeknownst: without someone's knowledge

tedious: long and tiring

My Notes

_____
_____
_____
_____
_____
_____
_____
_____
_____
_____
_____
_____
_____
_____
_____
_____
_____
_____
_____
_____
_____
_____
_____
_____
_____
_____
_____
_____
_____
_____
_____
_____
_____
_____
_____
_____
_____
_____
_____
_____
_____

that an aquarium is a powder keg that can explode in deadly violence at any moment, just like the Middle East, or junior high school.

8   TRUE STORY: A friend of mine named David Shor told me that his kids had an aquarium containing a kind of fish called African cichlids, and one of them died. So David went to the aquarium store and picked out a replacement African cichlid, but the aquarium guy said he couldn't buy that one, and David asked why, and the guy said: "Because that one is from a different lake."

9   But getting back to my daughter's fish: After much thought, the aquarium guy was able to find me three totally **pacifist** fish—Barney Fife fish, fish so nonviolent that, in the wild, worms routinely beat them up and steal their lunch money. I brought these home, and so far they have not killed each other or died in any way. Plus, Sophie LOVES them. So everything is working out beautifully. I hope it stays that way, because I hate zucchini.

⊘ Knowledge Quest

- How and where did this essay make you laugh?
- Where did you find yourself agreeing with the author?

pacifist: opposed to violence

Returning to the Text

- Return to the text as you respond to the following questions. Use text evidence to support your responses.

- Write any additional questions you have about the essay in your Reader/Writer Notebook.

1. What is the effect of the repetition of "a little plastic" in paragraph 2?

_____

_____

_____

_____

2. What is the effect of the juxtaposed ideas "grown bigger" and "grown smaller" in paragraph 4?

_____

_____

_____

_____

3. How does the author use stories from his boyhood to support his feelings about pets?

_____

_____

_____

_____

4. **KQ** In paragraph 6, why is referring to a group of fish as being a "society" humorous? How does the author's humorous use of the term *fish society* help you understand his position about pet fish?

_____

_____

_____

_____

5. What specific details does the author include in paragraph 7 in order to have a comic effect?

_____

_____

_____

_____

My Notes

6. **KQ** In both "Brothers" and "I've Got a Few Pet Peeves About Sea Creatures," the authors relate a funny story about their boyhood. Why is the authors' use of these funny boyhood stories an effective way to make their statements about life? How does it help you understand their statements in a deeper way?

INDEPENDENT READING LINK

Read and Respond

You can continue to build your knowledge about the way authors use humor by reading other articles at ZINC Reading Labs. Search for keywords such as *comedy* or *humor*.

ZINC

⌀ Knowledge Quest

Use your knowledge about "Brothers" and "I've Got a Few Pet Peeves About Sea Creatures" to discuss with a partner why humor is an effective way to communicate universal truths about life. Talk about the ways the authors' use of humor made you pay attention to the life lessons they wrote about. Be sure to:

- Explain your answer to your partner, be specific and use as many details as possible.
- When your partner explains their answer, ask for clarification by posing follow-up questions as needed.
- After the discussion, write down the ideas you talked about.

Working from the Text

7. Create a Venn Diagram in your Reader/Writer Notebook to compare and contrast the two humorous essays, "Brothers" and "I've Got a Few Pet Peeves about Sea Creatures." Then, write a response that demonstrates your understanding of each text.

8. Read and respond to the following quote. Then find a quote from the essay that shows how Barry slipped in the truth after making you laugh.

Quote	Interpretation	Personal Commentary
"The power of comedy is to make people laugh, and when they have their mouths open and they least expect it—you slip in the truth."		

9. How would you classify this essay (high or low comedy)? Explain.

10. How does the author use language (diction, syntax, imagery, and figurative language) to create a humorous tone?

11. How does the author appeal to the audience's emotions, interests, values, and/or beliefs?

12. What is the universal truth (theme) of the text? How does the author develop the idea through humorous language?

My Notes

13. Develop Levels of Questions based on your analysis to prepare for a Socratic Seminar discussion. Remember to maintain a formal style in your speaking during the Socratic Seminar. Be sure to:

   - Use precise verbs such as *communicates, creates, emphasizes,* or *illustrates* when discussing the author's purpose.
   - Use the author's last name: "Barry creates humor by …"
   - Cite textual evidence to support your opinion.

Levels of Questioning	"I've got a few pet peeves about sea creatures"
Level 1: Literal	
Level 2: Interpretive	
Level 3: Universal (thematic)	

14. Use your analysis and questions to engage in a Socratic Seminar discussion.

☑ Check Your Understanding

In preparation for your Writing to Sources activity, think about a universal truth that Barry expresses in his essay. Then find one sentence from the essay that you think supports this truth. Share your sentence with a partner and explain how your quote from the essay supports a universal truth.

INDEPENDENT READING LINK

Read and Discuss

For independent practice, choose one of the humorous texts from your list and explain the theme using specific evidence for support. Write several Levels of Questions for a specific section of reading in your Reader/Writer Notebook. Use the Level 3 questions to have a discussion about themes with your peers.

 Writing to Sources: Informational Text

Write a paragraph that explains how Barry uses humor to convey a truth about life. Be sure to:

   - Establish a clear controlling idea about conveying a truth.
   - Cite specific evidence from the text.
   - Use precise diction to describe humorous effects.
   - Edit your draft to make sure you are using verb tenses correctly and consistently.

Satirical Humor

Learning Strategies

Marking the Text
Discussion Groups
Rereading
Revisiting
Adding
Substituting

Learning Targets

- Analyze how authors use satire to expose human folly.
- Write a paragraph using appropriate and varied transitions.

Preview

In this activity, you will read a satirical article and think about how the author uses satire to express disapproval on a particular topic.

Exploring Satire

1. You will next view a film clip your teacher shows and take notes on the **satire** you observe. How is the satirist using **derision** to **denounce** the subject?

This clip is from:

SUBJECT (vice or folly exposed)	SATIRE (examples of irony, sarcasm, or ridicule used)

Setting a Purpose for Reading

- As you read the article, underline words and phrases that make you laugh or that you recognize as humor.
- Circle unknown words and phrases. Try to determine the meaning of the words by using context clues, word parts, or a dictionary.

About the Author

The Onion is an American digital media company and news satire organization that publishes articles on international, national, and local news. Based in Chicago, the company originated as a weekly print publication on August 29, 1988, in Madison, Wisconsin. *The Onion*'s articles cover current events, both real and fictional, satirizing the tone and format of traditional news organizations with stories, editorials, op-ed pieces, and person-in-the-street interviews using a traditional news website layout and a formal editorial voice.

VOCABULARY

LITERARY

Satire is a form of comedy that uses humor, irony, or exaggeration to expose and criticize issues in society or people's weaknesses. Satirists are writers who rely on satire to deride (mock) a subject.

ACADEMIC

Derision is the strong disapproval or mocking of an attitude or topic.

To **denounce** something is to publicly declare something to be wrong.

My Notes

GRAMMAR & USAGE

Active and Passive Voice

Remember that writers use active and passive voice to emphasize different ideas in their writing. The active voice emphasizes who or what is doing the action. For example:

"The past tense provides students with a unique and consistent outlet for self-expression." In this example, *past tense* is the thing doing the providing.

On the other hand, passive voice emphasizes the person or thing being acted upon. Passive voice can be used effectively when the actor in the situation is unknown or not important. For example:

"School districts in California have been forced to cut addition and subtraction from their math departments." The emphasis is on the school districts, the things being acted upon. We don't need to know who forced them to cut addition and subtraction.

As you read, look for other examples of active and passive voice and notice the different effects they create.

Article

Underfunded Schools Forced to Cut Past Tense from Language Programs

from **The Onion**

1   WASHINGTON—Faced with ongoing budget crises, underfunded schools nationwide are increasingly left with no option but to cut the past tense—a grammatical construction traditionally used to relate all actions and states that have **transpired** at an earlier point in time—from their standard English and language arts programs.

2   A part of American school curricula for more than 200 years, the past tense was deemed by school administrators to be too expensive to keep in primary and secondary education.

3   "This was by no means an easy decision, but teaching our students how to conjugate verbs in a way that would allow them to describe events that have already occurred is a luxury that we can no longer afford," Phoenix-area high school principal Sam Pennock said.

4   "With our current budget, the past tense must unfortunately become a thing of the past."

5   In the most dramatic display of the new trend yet, the Tennessee Department of Education decided Monday to remove "-ed" endings from all of the state's English classrooms, saving struggling schools an estimated $3 million each year. Officials say they plan to slowly phase out the tense by first eliminating the past perfect; once students have adjusted to the change, the past progressive, the past continuous, the past perfect progressive, and the simple past will be cut. Hundreds of school districts across the country are expected to follow suit.

6   "This is the end of an era," said Alicia Reynolds, a school district director in Tuscaloosa, AL. "For some, reading and writing about things not immediately taking place was almost as much a part of school as history class and social studies."

7   "That is, until we were forced to drop history class and social studies a couple of months ago," Reynolds added.

8   Nevertheless, a number of educators are coming out against the cuts, claiming that the embattled verb tense, while **outmoded**, still plays an important role in the development of today's youth.

transpired: taken place
outmoded: out of style

9 "Much like art and music, the past tense provides students with a unique and consistent outlet for self-expression," South Boston English teacher David Floen said. "Without it I fear many of our students will lack a number of important creative skills. Like being able to describe anything that happened earlier in the day."

10 Despite concerns that cutting the past tense will prevent graduates from communicating effectively in the workplace, the home, the grocery store, church, and various other public spaces, a number of lawmakers, such as Utah Sen. Orrin Hatch, have welcomed the cuts as proof that the American school system is taking a more forward-thinking approach to education. "Our tax dollars should be spent preparing our children for the future, not for what has already happened," Hatch said at a recent press conference. "It's about time we stopped wasting everyone's time with who 'did' what or 'went' where. The past tense is, by definition, outdated." Said Hatch, "I can't even remember the last time I had to use it."

11 Past-tense instruction is only the latest school program to face the chopping block. School districts in California have been forced to cut addition and subtraction from their math departments, while nearly all high schools have reduced foreign language courses to only the most basic phrases, including "May I please use the bathroom?" and "No, I do not want to go to the beach with Maria and Juan." Some legislators are even calling for an end to teaching grammar itself, saying that in many inner-city school districts, where funding is most lacking, students rarely use grammar at all.

12 Regardless of the recent upheaval, students throughout the country are learning to accept, and even embrace, the change to their curriculum.

13 "At first I think the decision to drop the past tense from class is ridiculous, and I feel very upset by it," said David Keller, a seventh-grade student at Hampstead School in Fort Meyers, FL. "But now, it's almost like it never happens."

Making Observations
- What do you notice about the details in this essay?
- What do you notice in the essay that someone skimming over it might miss?

Returning to the Text

- Return to the text as you respond to the following questions. Use text evidence to support your responses.
- Write any additional questions you have about the article in your Reader/Writer Notebook.

2. What role does the first paragraph play in the structure of this article?

_____

_____

_____

_____

3. How do quotes from specific people throughout the article add to the development of ideas?

_____

_____

_____

_____

4. How does the use of present tense in the last quote in paragraph 13 emphasize the satire?

_____

_____

_____

_____

Working from the Text

5. Work collaboratively to diffuse and paraphrase the definition of satire.

Satire, a form of high comedy, is the use of irony, sarcasm, and/or ridicule in exposing, denouncing, and/or deriding human vice and folly.

Parody:

6. Highly connotative diction is language that contains a strong positive or negative meaning. For example, saying that you are angry has a negative connotation. However, saying you are livid has a much stronger connotation and effect. Reread the text and place an exclamation point by the highly connotative diction that stands out to you. Note the effect of those words in the My Notes space.

7. Circle and explain your response to this text. I think this text is:

hilarious   funny   clever   ridiculous   because ...

Discuss the parts of the text that made you laugh, and describe how the connotative words help create the humor.

8. Collaboratively, use the graphic organizer to explore the satire.

The vice or folly exposed in the text:	Textual Evidence: Irony: Sarcasm: Ridicule:

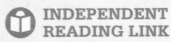
Writing an Analytical Paragraph

When writing about texts, use the "literary present" (e.g., "The article *states* … ,"not "The article *stated* …").

Maintain clarity and coherence in your writing. Scan your writing for the passive voice, and revise to the active voice to strengthen your work. Use well-chosen transition words or phrases to help show the relationship (connection) between the ideas in your writing. Refer to the following list of commonly used transitional words and phrases for help.

Purpose	Example
Add	*and, again, and then, besides, equally important, finally, further, furthermore, nor, too, next, lastly, what's more, moreover, in addition, first (second, etc.)*
Compare	*whereas, but, yet, on the other hand, however, nevertheless, on the contrary, by comparison, where, compared to, up against, balanced against, but, although, conversely, meanwhile, after all, in contrast, although this may be true*
Prove	*because, for, since, for the same reason, obviously, evidently, furthermore, moreover, besides, indeed, in fact, in addition, in any case, that is*
Show Exception	*yet, still, however, nevertheless, in spite of, despite, of course, once in a while, sometimes*
Show Time	*immediately, thereafter, soon, after a few hours, finally, then, later, previously, formerly, first (second, etc.), next, and then*
Repeat	*in brief, as I have said, as I have noted, as has been noted, to reiterate*
Emphasize	*definitely, extremely, obviously, in fact, indeed, in any case, absolutely, positively, naturally, surprisingly, always, forever, perennially, eternally, never, emphatically, unquestionably, without a doubt, certainly, undeniably, without reservation*
Show Sequence	*first, second, third, next, then, following this, at this time, now, at this point, after, afterward, subsequently, finally, consequently, previously, before this, simultaneously, concurrently, thus, therefore, hence, next, and then, soon*
Give an Example	*for example, for instance, in this case, in another case, on this occasion, in this situation, take the case of, to demonstrate, to illustrate, as an illustration, to illustrate*
Summarize or Conclude	*in brief, on the whole, summing up, to conclude, in conclusion, as I have shown, as I have said, hence, therefore, accordingly, thus, as a result, consequently*

LANGUAGE & WRITER'S CRAFT: Inappropriate Shifts in Verb Voice and Mood

As you've learned, there are two major **verb voices** in language (**active** and **passive**), and five major **verb moods** (**indicative, imperative, interrogative, conditional, subjunctive**). When writers shift voice and mood inappropriately, it can cause confusion for the reader.

For example, in this sentence from the Onion article:

Said Hatch, "<u>I can't</u> even <u>remember</u> the last time <u>I had</u> to use it."

The sentence is written completely in the active voice. The subject is doing the action of the verb. The subject ("I") is doing the action ("can't remember"; "had to use"). The sentence is also written in the indicative mood since it makes a direct statement about something.

If the sentence had an inappropriate shift in voice in mood it might look like this:

<u>Said Hatch, "I can't even remember</u> | <u>the last time it was used by me?"</u>

The sentence shifts from the active voice and indicative mood, to the passive voice and interrogative mood halfway through. These shifts create confusion for the reader!

Example: *We should spend our tax dollars preparing kids for the future, and you must get rid of the past tense.*

PRACTICE Examine the sentence above for inappropriate shifts in verb voice and mood. Revise the sentence to make the voice and mood the same throughout the sentence.

☑ Check Your Understanding

Which instances of satire in the article do you think went the furthest to make the author's point? Why? Discuss with a partner.

✏ Writing to Sources: Informational Text

Analyze how the text about underfunded schools uses satirical humor to expose human vice or folly. Be sure to:

- Establish and support a controlling idea.
- Use transitions to create cohesion and clarify the relationships among ideas and concepts.
- Use precise diction and maintain a formal style including a consistent and appropriate use of active voice.
- Support your analysis with evidence from the text.

Elements of Humor: Comic Characters and Caricatures

ACADEMIC VOCABULARY

To use a **caricature** or to caricaturize someone is to exaggerate or imitate certain characteristics to create a comic or distorted idea of a person. A caricature can just be funny or be used to insult someone.

Learning Targets

- Identify and define comic characters and caricatures.
- Analyze characters and caricatures in a literary text.

Preview

In this activity, you will read a short story and think about the author's use of characterization.

Comic Caricatures and Characters

Characterization is the way a writer reveals a character's personality through what the character says, thinks, and feels or through how the character looks, acts, or interacts with others.

A **caricature** is a pictorial, written, and/or acted representation of a person that exaggerates characteristics or traits for comic effect. Caricatures are often used in cartoon versions of people's faces and usually exaggerate features for comic effect.

1. You will next view some comic scenes. As you view the opening sequence, take notes in the graphic organizer.

Characters: Sketch the caricature.	Details: Describe the characterization.	Interpretation: What idea is conveyed through the characterization?
Bart	Bart is repetitively writing sentences on the board that say ...	He is the stereotype of the bad kid in the classroom.
Homer		
Marge		
Lisa		
Family		

My Notes

_____
_____
_____
_____
_____
_____
_____
_____
_____
_____
_____
_____
_____
_____
_____
_____
_____

2. With your discussion group, discuss what truth about life the cartoonist is conveying through humor. Cite specific examples from the graphic organizer.

Setting a Purpose for Reading

- As you read the short story, underline words and phrases that reveal something about Framton Nuttel and the niece.
- Circle unknown words and phrases. Try to determine the meaning by using context clues, word parts, or a dictionary.

About the Author

Hector Hugh Munro (1870–1916), better known by his pen name, Saki, was a British writer and satirist famous for his masterful short stories poking fun at Edwardian society. He frequently mocked the customs and manners popular at the time. His witty and intelligent stories are considered among the best the genre has to offer.

Short Story

The Open Window

by **Saki (H. H. Munro)**

1 "My aunt will be down presently, Mr. Nuttel," said a very self-possessed young lady of 15; "in the meantime you must try and put up with me."

2 Framton Nuttel endeavoured to say the correct something which should **duly** flatter the niece of the moment without unduly discounting the aunt that was to come. Privately he doubted more than ever whether these formal visits on a succession of total strangers would do much towards helping the nerve cure which he was supposed to be undergoing.

3 "I know how it will be," his sister had said when he was preparing to migrate to this rural retreat; "you will bury yourself down there and not speak to a living soul, and your nerves will be worse than ever from moping. I shall just give you letters of introduction to all the people I know there. Some of them, as far as I can remember, were quite nice."

4 Framton wondered whether Mrs. Sappleton, the lady to whom he was presenting one of the letters of introduction, came into the nice division.

5 "Do you know many of the people round here?" asked the niece, when she judged that they had had sufficient silent communion.

6 "Hardly a soul," said Framton. "My sister was staying here, at the **rectory**, you know, some four years ago, and she gave me letters of introduction to some of the people here."

duly: properly or fittingly
rectory: the house in which a parish priest or minister lives

My Notes

My Notes

7   He made the last statement in a tone of distinct regret.

8   "Then you know practically nothing about my aunt?" pursued the self-possessed young lady.

9   "Only her name and address," admitted the caller. He was wondering whether Mrs. Sappleton was in the married or widowed state. An undefinable something about the room seemed to suggest masculine habitation.

10   "Her great tragedy happened just three years ago," said the child; "that would be since your sister's time."

11   "Her tragedy?" asked Framton; somehow in this restful country spot tragedies seemed out of place.

12   "You may wonder why we keep that window wide open on an October afternoon," said the niece, indicating a large French window that opened on to a lawn.

13   "It is quite warm for the time of the year," said Framton; "but has that window got anything to do with the tragedy?"

14   "Out through that window, three years ago to a day, her husband and her two young brothers went off for their day's shooting. They never came back. In crossing the **moor** to their favourite snipe-shooting ground they were all three engulfed in a treacherous piece of bog. It had been that dreadful wet summer, you know, and places that were safe in other years gave way suddenly without warning. Their bodies were never recovered. That was the dreadful part of it." Here the child's voice lost its self-possessed note and became falteringly human. "Poor aunt always thinks that they will come back some day, they and the little brown spaniel that was lost with them, and walk in at that window just as they used to do. That is why the window is kept open every evening till it is quite dusk. Poor dear aunt, she has often told me how they went out, her husband with his white waterproof coat over his arm, and Ronnie, her youngest brother, singing 'Bertie, why do you bound?' as he always did to tease her, because she said it got on her nerves. Do you know, sometimes on still, quiet evenings like this, I almost get a creepy feeling that they will all walk in through that window—"

15   She broke off with a little shudder. It was a relief to Framton when the aunt bustled into the room with a whirl of apologies for being late in making her appearance.

16   "I hope Vera has been amusing you?" she said.

17   "She has been very interesting," said Framton.

18   "I hope you don't mind the open window," said Mrs. Sappleton briskly; "my husband and brothers will be home directly from shooting, and they always come in this way. They've been out for snipe in the marshes to-day, so they'll make a fine mess over my poor carpets. So like you men-folk, isn't it?"

19   She rattled on cheerfully about the shooting and the **scarcity** of birds, and the prospects for duck in the winter. To Framton it was all purely horrible. He made a desperate but only partially successful effort to turn the talk on to a less ghastly topic; he was conscious that his hostess was giving him only a fragment

moor: boggy grassland
scarcity: short supply

of her attention, and her eyes were constantly straying past him to the open window and the lawn beyond. It was certainly an unfortunate coincidence that he should have paid his visit on this tragic anniversary.

20 "The doctors agree in ordering me complete rest, an absence of mental excitement, and avoidance of anything in the nature of violent physical exercise," announced Framton, who **laboured under** the tolerably wide-spread **delusion** that total strangers and chance acquaintances are hungry for the least detail of one's ailments and infirmities, their cause and cure. "On the matter of diet they are not so much in agreement," he continued.

21 "No?" said Mrs. Sappleton, in a voice which only replaced a yawn at the last moment. Then she suddenly brightened into alert attention—but not to what Framton was saying.

22 "Here they are at last!" she cried. "Just in time for tea, and don't they look as if they were muddy up to the eyes!"

23 Framton shivered slightly and turned towards the niece with a look intended to convey sympathetic comprehension. The child was staring out through the open window with dazed horror in her eyes. In a chill shock of nameless fear Framton swung round in his seat and looked in the same direction.

24 In the deepening twilight three figures were walking across the lawn towards the window; they all carried guns under their arms, and one of them was additionally burdened with a white coat hung over his shoulders. A tired brown spaniel kept close at their heels. Noiselessly they neared the house, and then a hoarse young voice chanted out of the dusk: "I said, Bertie, why do you bound?"

25 Framton grabbed wildly at his stick and hat; the hall-door, the gravel-drive, and the front gate were dimly-noted stages in his headlong retreat. A cyclist coming along the road had to run into the hedge to avoid an imminent collision.

26 "Here we are, my dear," said the bearer of the white **mackintosh**, coming in through the window; "fairly muddy, but most of it's dry. Who was that who bolted out as we came up?"

27 "A most extraordinary man, a Mr. Nuttel," said Mrs. Sappleton; "could only talk about his illnesses, and dashed off without a word of good-bye or apology when you arrived. One would think he had seen a ghost."

28 "I expect it was the spaniel," said the niece calmly; "he told me he had a horror of dogs. He was once hunted into a cemetery somewhere on the banks of the Ganges by a pack of pariah dogs, and had to spend the night in a newly dug grave with the creatures snarling and grinning and foaming just above him. Enough to make anyone lose their nerve."

29 Romance at short notice was her speciality.

My Notes

Making Observations

- What characters do we meet in the story?
- What happens in the story?

---

laboured under: was misled by
delusion: persistent false belief
mackintosh: raincoat

Returning to the Text

- Return to the text as you respond to the following questions. Use text evidence to support your responses.
- Write any additional questions you have about the short story in your Reader/Writer Notebook.

3. Why is it significant that Framton Nuttel is described as undergoing a "nerve cure" in paragraph 2? How is this detail used for humorous effect?

_____

_____

_____

_____

4. What does Framton Nuttel's sister say will happen to Framton on his rural retreat? What does her prediction reveal about Framton's character? Cite evidence in your answer.

_____

_____

_____

_____

5. What is the meaning of the word *habitation* in paragraph 9? What clues in the text leading up to and including paragraph 9 support your response?

_____

_____

_____

_____

6. What tone does the niece convey with her description of the "tragedy" in paragraph 14? What effect might this precise detail have on her guest?

_____

_____

_____

_____

7. Now that you know the ending, go back and find any clues the author left the reader to hint that a joke was coming.

_____

_____

_____

_____

8. Why is it "horrible" for Framton to listen to Mrs. Sappleton as noted in paragraph 19?

_____

_____

_____

_____

9. What is the meaning of the word *ailments* in paragraph 20? What clues in the text support your response?

_____

_____

_____

_____

10. What can you conclude about Framton's character from paragraph 20? What details helped you to know?

_____

_____

_____

_____

11. Why is Framton's reaction to the return of the men in paragraph 25 comic rather than appropriate?

_____

_____

_____

_____

12. What aspects of the niece's character are revealed in her last line of dialogue in paragraph 28?

_____

_____

_____

_____

Working from the Text

13. For each unfamiliar word you circled, use a dictionary or thesaurus to write a synonym in My Notes.

14. **Quickwrite** using a 3–2–1 reflection. Write your response in your Reader/Writer Notebook.

  3 – Describe three things you notice about the author's use of humor in the story.

  2 – Describe two characters you can picture most vividly.

  1 – Share one question you have.

15. Use the graphic organizer to express ideas you have about the characters and humor in this text.

Details: How does the author develop the character? (actions, words, thoughts)	Characters: Describe the character using precise adjectives. Would any of them be considered a caricature?	Interpretation: What truth about life is revealed through the comic character?
Framton Nuttel		
Mrs. Sappleton		
The niece		

Elements of Humor

Explaining why something is funny can be a challenge, but there are some common things authors do that usually make people laugh. Writers create humor by focusing on descriptions and actions that make characters funny, comic situations, and comic language. Humor often depends on some combination of these three elements.

16. Preview the Elements of Humor graphic organizer in Activity 4.11 and add notes about the comic characters and caricatures you explored in this activity. After you explore each new element of humor in the upcoming activities, return to this graphic organizer to add notes about new learning.

☑ Check Your Understanding

Mr. Nuttel might be considered a caricature of a nervous person. Find examples in the story that support this idea and note them in your Reader/Writer Notebook.

Elements of Humor: Comic Situations

Learning Strategies

Graphic Organizer
Note-taking
Think-Pair-Share
Marking the Text
Discussion Groups

Learning Targets

- Analyze comic situations in a literary text collaboratively.
- Determine the impact of word choice on meaning and tone in a comic situation.

Preview

In this activity, you will read an excerpt from a novel and think about the author's use of irony to create comic situations.

Comic Situations

Comic situations can be created in many different ways:

- by placing a character in an unlikely situation in which he or she obviously does not belong.
- by portraying characters as victims of circumstances who are surprised by unusual events and react in a comical way.
- by creating situational **irony** where there is contrast between what characters or readers might reasonably expect to happen and what actually happens.

LITERARY

Irony is a literary device that plays on readers' expectations by portraying events in a way that is actually different from reality. Irony can make a situation seem funny to a reader or viewer.

VOCABULARY

1. While you watch a film clip, think about how the situation contributes to the humor.

2. As you view the clip a second time, take notes using the following graphic organizer.

Clip: Director:

Comic Character	Comic Situation	Film Techniques That Help Create Humor
Appearance and Facial Expressions:	Setting:	Framing:
Actions:	Situational Irony:	Angles:
Words:		Sound:

3. Use the information in your chart to explain how irony is used to create comedy.

My Notes

Setting a Purpose for Reading

- As you read the excerpt, underline any comic situations you find for further analysis later.
- Circle unknown words and phrases. Try to determine the meaning of the words by using context clues, word parts, or a dictionary.

About the Author

Born Samuel Langhorne Clemens, Mark Twain (1835–1910) was an American author and humorist. He adopted his pen name while writing stories, sketches, and editorials as a reporter. His style—often funny and satirical—made him famous. He is noted for his novels *The Adventures of Huckleberry Finn* (1885) and *The Adventures of Tom Sawyer* (1876). He has been lauded as the "greatest American humorist of his age."

Novel Excerpt

from
The Adventures of Tom Sawyer

by **Mark Twain**

"A Day's Work"

Chunk 1

1   SATURDAY morning was come, and all the summer world was bright and fresh, and brimming with life. There was a song in every heart; and if the heart was young the music issued at the lips. There was cheer in every face and a spring in every step. The locust-trees were in bloom and the fragrance of the blossoms filled the air. Cardiff Hill, beyond the village and above it, was green with vegetation and it lay just far enough away to seem a Delectable Land, dreamy, reposeful, and inviting.

Chunk 2

2   Tom appeared on the sidewalk with a bucket of whitewash and a long-handled brush. He surveyed the fence, and all gladness left him and a deep melancholy settled down upon his spirit. Thirty yards of board fence nine feet high. Life to him seemed hollow, and existence but a burden. Sighing, he dipped his brush and passed it along the topmost plank; repeated the operation; did it again; compared the insignificant whitewashed streak with the far-reaching continent of unwhitewashed fence, and sat down on a tree-box discouraged. Jim came skipping out at the gate with a tin pail, and singing Buffalo Gals. Bringing water from the town pump had always been hateful

WORD CONNECTIONS

Multiple Meaning Words
The word whitewash has come to have a second meaning. In this story, *whitewash* means "a whitening mixture used on fences and walls." The word has also come to mean "to conceal or cover up crimes, scandals, flaws, or failures." You can see how this usage comes from the idea of using whitewash to cover up something bad.

work in Tom's eyes, before, but now it did not strike him so. He remembered that there was company at the pump. White, mulatto, and negro boys and girls were always there waiting their turns, resting, trading playthings, quarrelling, fighting, skylarking. And he remembered that although the pump was only a hundred and fifty yards off, Jim never got back with a bucket of water under an hour—and even then somebody generally had to go after him. Tom said:

Chunk 3

3   "Say, Jim, I'll fetch the water if you'll whitewash some."

4   Jim shook his head and said:

5   "Can't, Mars Tom. Ole missis, she tole me I got to go an' git dis water an' not stop foolin' roun' wid anybody. She say she spec' Mars Tom gwine to ax me to whitewash, an' so she tole me go 'long an' 'tend to my own business—she 'lowed SHE'D 'tend to de whitewashin'."

6   "Oh, never you mind what she said, Jim. That's the way she always talks. Gimme the bucket—I won't be gone only a minute. SHE won't ever know."

7   "Oh, I dasn't, Mars Tom. Ole missis she'd take an' tar de head off'n me. 'Deed she would."

8   "SHE! She never licks anybody—whacks 'em over the head with her thimble—and who cares for that, I'd like to know. She talks awful, but talk don't hurt—anyways it don't if she don't cry. Jim, I'll give you a marvel. I'll give you a **white alley!**"

9   Jim began to waver.

10 "White alley, Jim! And it's a bully taw."

11 "My! Dat's a mighty gay marvel, I tell you! But Mars Tom I's powerful 'fraid ole missis—"

12 "And besides, if you will I'll show you my sore toe."

13 Jim was only human—this attraction was too much for him. He put down his pail, took the white alley, and bent over the toe with absorbing interest while the bandage was being unwound. In another moment he was flying down the street with his pail and a tingling rear, Tom was whitewashing with **vigor**, and Aunt Polly was retiring from the field with a slipper in her hand and triumph in her eye.

14 But Tom's energy did not last. He began to think of the fun he had planned for this day, and his sorrows multiplied. Soon the free boys would come tripping along on all sorts of delicious expeditions, and they would make a world of fun of him for having to work—the very thought of it burnt him like fire. He got out his worldly wealth and examined it—bits of toys, marbles, and trash; enough to buy an exchange of WORK, maybe, but not half enough to buy so much as half an hour of pure freedom. So he returned his **straitened** means to his pocket, and gave up the idea of trying to buy the boys. At this dark and hopeless moment an inspiration burst upon him! Nothing less than a great, magnificent inspiration.

My Notes

WORD CONNECTIONS

Word Relationships
The words **great** and **magnificent** may seem similar; however, Twain uses *magnificent* to mean "splendid; impressive," while *great*, in this context, means "important." Twain uses both words to inform the reader that a pivotal change is about to occur in the story because of Tom's idea.

white alley: a kind of marble
vigor: strength or force
straitened: characterized by poverty

Illustration of Mark Twain's character Tom Sawyer whitewashing a fence. This screen print was created in 1910.

My Notes

Chunk 4

15 He took up his brush and went tranquilly to work. Ben Rogers hove in sight presently—the very boy, of all boys, whose ridicule he had been dreading. Ben's gait was the hop-skip-and-jump—proof enough that his heart was light and his anticipations high. He was eating an apple, and giving a long, melodious whoop, at intervals, followed by a deep-toned ding-dong-dong, ding-dong-dong, for he was personating a steamboat. As he drew near, he slackened speed, took the middle of the street, leaned far over to starboard and rounded to ponderously and with laborious pomp and circumstance—for he was personating the *Big Missouri*, and considered himself to be drawing nine feet of water. He was boat and captain and engine-bells combined, so he had to imagine himself standing on his own hurricane-deck giving the orders and executing them:

16 "Stop her, sir! Ting-a-ling-ling!" The headway ran almost out, and he drew up slowly toward the sidewalk.

17 "Ship up to back! Ting-a-ling-ling!" His arms straightened and stiffened down his sides.

18 "Set her back on the stabboard! Ting-a-ling-ling! Chow! ch-chow-wow! Chow!" His right hand, mean-time, describing stately circles—for it was representing a forty-foot wheel.

19 "Let her go back on the labboard! Ting-a-ling-ling! Chow-ch-chow-chow!" The left hand began to describe circles.

20 "Stop the stabboard! Ting-a-ling-ling! Stop the labboard! Come ahead on the stabboard! Stop her! Let your outside turn over slow! Ting-a-ling-ling! Chow-ow-ow! Get out that head-line! LIVELY now! Come—out with your spring-line—what're you about there! Take a turn round that stump with the bight of it! Stand by that stage, now—let her go! Done with the engines, sir! Ting-a-ling-ling! SH'T! S'H'T! SH'T!" (trying the gauge-cocks).

21 Tom went on whitewashing—paid no attention to the steamboat. Ben stared a moment and then said: "Hi-YI! YOU'RE up a stump, ain't you!"

Chunk 5

22 No answer. Tom surveyed his last touch with the eye of an artist, then he gave his brush another gentle sweep and surveyed the result, as before. Ben ranged up alongside of him. Tom's mouth watered for the apple, but he stuck to his work. Ben said:

23 "Hello, old chap, you got to work, hey?"

24 Tom wheeled suddenly and said:

25 "Why, it's you, Ben! I warn't noticing."

26 "Say—I'm going in a-swimming, I am. Don't you wish you could? But of course you'd druther WORK—wouldn't you? Course you would!"

27 Tom contemplated the boy a bit, and said:

28 "What do you call work?"

29 "Why, ain't THAT work?"

30 Tom resumed his whitewashing, and answered carelessly:

31 "Well, maybe it is, and maybe it ain't. All I know, is, it suits Tom Sawyer."

32 "Oh come, now, you don't mean to let on that you LIKE it?"

33 The brush continued to move.

34 "Like it? Well, I don't see why I oughtn't to like it. Does a boy get a chance to whitewash a fence every day?"

35 That put the thing in a new light. Ben stopped nibbling his apple. Tom swept his brush daintily back and forth—stepped back to note the effect—added a touch here and there—criticized the effect again—Ben watching every move and getting more and more interested, more and more absorbed. Presently he said:

36 "Say, Tom, let ME whitewash a little."

37 Tom considered, was about to consent; but he altered his mind:

38 "No—no—I reckon it wouldn't hardly do, Ben. You see, Aunt Polly's awful particular about this fence—right here on the street, you know—but if it was the back fence I wouldn't mind and SHE wouldn't. Yes, she's awful particular about this fence; it's got to be done very careful; I reckon there ain't one boy in a thousand, maybe two thousand, that can do it the way it's got to be done."

39 "No—is that so? Oh come, now—lemme just try. Only just a little—I'd let YOU, if you was me, Tom."

40 "Ben, I'd like to, honest injun; but Aunt Polly—well, Jim wanted to do it, but she wouldn't let him; Sid wanted to do it, and she wouldn't let Sid. Now don't you see how I'm fixed? If you was to tackle this fence and anything was to happen to it—"

41 "Oh, shucks, I'll be just as careful. Now lemme try. Say—I'll give you the core of my apple."

42 "Well, here—No, Ben, now don't. I'm afeard—"

43 "I'll give you ALL of it!"

Chunk 6

44 Tom gave up the brush with reluctance in his face, but **alacrity** in his heart. And while the late steamer *Big Missouri* worked and sweated in the sun, the retired artist sat on a barrel in the shade close by, dangled his legs, munched his apple, and planned the slaughter of more innocents. There was no lack of material; boys happened along every little while; they came to jeer, but remained to whitewash. By the time Ben was fagged out, Tom had traded the next chance to Billy Fisher for a kite, in good repair; and when he played out, Johnny Miller bought in for a dead rat and a string to swing it with—and so on, and so on, hour after hour. And when the middle of the afternoon came, from being a poor poverty-stricken boy in the morning, Tom was literally rolling in wealth. He had besides the things before mentioned, twelve marbles, part of a jews-harp, a piece of blue bottle-glass to look through, a spool cannon, a key that wouldn't unlock anything, a fragment of chalk, a glass stopper of a decanter, a tin soldier, a couple of tadpoles, six fire-crackers, a kitten with only one eye, a brass door-knob, a dog-collar—but no dog—the handle of a knife, four pieces of orange-peel, and a **dilapidated** old window sash.

GRAMMAR & USAGE

Denotation and Connotation
Remember that a word's **denotation** is its actual meaning. Its **connotation** is the feeling or impression it gives the reader. When Ben enters the fence scene, he's described as "eating an apple." The connotation of this description is literal: He is actually eating an apple. But further along, he is described as "nibbling" the apple. The denotation of *nibbling* is "taking small bites." The use of *nibbling* implies that Ben has become too distracted to eat the apple, so he is taking tiny bites while he thinks. After Ben starts to paint and gives his apple to Tom, Tom "munched" his apple. The word *munched* carries a connotation of joy, so it helps show how happy Tom is with himself.

As you read, look for two more instances where the author has chosen words especially for their connotations.

alacrity: willingness
dilapidated: ruined

Making Observations
- What do you notice about the setting of the novel excerpt?
- What do you notice about the characters in the novel excerpt?

Returning to the Text

- Return to the text as you respond to the following questions. Use text evidence to support your responses.
- Write any additional questions you have about the novel excerpt in your Reader/Writer Notebook.

4. What does the word *reposeful* mean in paragraph 1? What clues in the text help you understand the meaning of the word?

5. What does the word *melancholy* mean in paragraph 2? What clues in the text help you understand the meaning of the word? Use a print or digital resource to determine the word origin of *melancholy*. How has the word's meaning changed over time?

6. One of the notable characteristics of Twain's style is his use of verbals. Examine paragraph 2 and highlight all the verbals.

7. How does Tom try to get Jim to help him in Chunk 3? Why does he fail?

8. How does Twain use steamboat jargon for effect in Chunk 4?

_____

_____

_____

_____

9. Tom tries to manipulate his friends into doing whitewashing for him. How does he change his plan in Chunk 5 after Jim's refusal to help?

_____

_____

_____

_____

10. What is ironic about Tom's plan to get out of whitewashing the fence?

_____

_____

_____

_____

11. What is the intended effect of listing Tom's "treasures" in such great detail in paragraph 44? What does the audience understand about the value of these things that is different from Tom's point of view?

_____

_____

_____

_____

Working from the Text

12. Review the definition of **dialect**. Return to the text and place a "D" by examples of dialect. Then try to paraphrase a few lines of dialogue in My Notes.

13. Look back at the examples of dialect that you marked and compare them to your paraphrases. Think about how the story would be different if the author had not used dialect for the character. Then explain the effect of dialect on the excerpt.

> **LITERARY**
>
> **Dialect** is a regional or social variety of a language distinguished by pronunciation, grammar, or vocabulary. This section of the story includes a depiction of Tom's and Jim's dialects.

VOCABULARY

14. Mark Twain used verbals throughout this excerpt to make his writing more interesting. Verbals are made from verbs, but function as nouns, adjectives, or adverbs. Study the chart, and then work with a partner to complete the sentence frames for each type of verbal. Work together to label two examples of each type of verbal in Twain's text.

About Verbals	Gerund	Participle	Infinitive
Made	by adding *-ing*	by adding *-ed*	up of *to* + verb
Function as...	noun	adjective	noun, adjective, or adverb
Example: *whitewash*	*whitewashing*	*whitewashed; whitewashing*	*to whitewash*

Infinitive: A verbal made up of *to* and the present form of a verb.

An infinitive can function as a noun, an adjective, or an adverb.

Examples: to skip, to sing, to wait, to rest, to remember, to swim

I like to_____. (noun) direct object of *like*

I can't wait to_____. (adverb) modifies *wait*

Examples: to describe, to notice, to watch

The person _____ is Taylor. (adjective) tells which person

Gerund: A verbal ending in *-ing*.

A gerund functions as a noun. In this case, the gerund tells what is fun.

Examples: Drawing, Singing, Eating, Swimming

_____ is fun.

Participle: A verbal ending in *-ed* or *-ing*.

A participle functions as an adjective. In this case, the participle tells about the friend.

Examples: discouraged, interested, singing, resting

My _____ friend is at home.

15. On a separate piece of paper or in your Reader/Writer Notebook, create a graphic organizer like the one that follows to answer comprehension questions about the story.

Tom is like a ... (create a simile)	It is ironic that ...
The part of the story that stands out to me is ... (draw a picture)	I wonder ...
This is a comedic situation because ...	

16. Prepare for a collaborative discussion by annotating and reviewing the text as follows:

    - Review what you have already underlined as the plot and make changes as needed. Be prepared to paraphrase (retell in your own words) the plot.
    - Place a question mark next to any word or idea you would like to clarify (discuss to remove confusion).
    - Place a star next to any part of the text you would like to analyze (discern meaning, ask a question, or share an inference based on the text).

17. What is the level of comedy of this text? What is a universal truth, or theme, of this text? Write a thematic statement. Be sure to support your ideas with textual evidence.

Twain – "All in a Day's Work"
Level of Comedy:
Theme subject(s):
Theme statement:

☑ Check Your Understanding

In your Reader/Writer Notebook, record three specific comic situations from the text. Share them with a partner.

✒ Writing to Sources: Informational Text

Write an essay explaining how Mark Twain uses comic characters and irony to convey a universal truth through humor. Be sure to:

- Establish a controlling idea and support it with textual evidence and commentary.
- Use transitions to create cohesion and clarify the relationships among ideas and concepts.
- Use precise diction and maintain a formal style.
- Use verbals.

Elements of Humor

Add your notes about comic situations to the Elements of Humor graphic organizer in Activity 4.11.

My Notes

📦 **INDEPENDENT READING LINK**

Read and Research

Research other humorous works by Mark Twain. Choose one of these works and create a one-paragraph summary of a comic situation in your Reader/Writer Notebook. Note the level of comedy and identify the theme statement.

Language Checkpoint: Recognizing Frequently Confused Words

- Differentiate between the frequently confused words its/it's, your/you're, and their/they're/there.
- Revise writing by using frequently confused words correctly.

Preview

In this activity, you will choose the correct form of commonly misspelled words.

Recognizing Frequently Confused Words

In English, some of the most frequently confused words are *its*, *your*, and *their* and *it's*, *you're*, and *they're*. The adverb *there* is also frequently misused.

Pieces of information that add extra (but unnecessary) detail to a sentence are called nonrestrictive (or nonessential) elements. Nonrestrictive elements need to be set off with punctuation. For example, *Logos, a term that comes from the ancient Greek language, names a rhetorical appeal that uses logical reasoning.*

1. **Quickwrite:** Why do you think a writer might confuse these words?

2. Read the following sentences from *The Adventures of Tom Sawyer:*
   He [Tom] remembered that there was company at the pump ... [B]oys and girls were always <u>there</u> waiting <u>their</u> turns, resting, trading playthings, quarrelling, fighting, skylarking. What does each underlined word refer to?
   there:
   their:

Understanding Possessive Determiners

Quick Guide to Possessive Determiners	
your	Thank you for letting me borrow <u>your</u> book about Mark Twain.
its	I didn't know the word *straitened*, so I read <u>its</u> meaning in the margin.
their	The characters give Tom <u>their</u> prized possessions for a chance to paint.

Possessive determiners are words that show to whom something belongs. Writers use possessive determiners—which include the words *my*, *your*, *his*, *her*, *its*, *our*, and *their*—to make sentences more cohesive and less repetitive. For this reason, the sentence "Tom worked very hard, so Tom's energy did not last" is not typical. The more typical version of the sentence would be "Tom worked very hard, so his energy did not last."

3. Work with a partner to revise the following sentences to include possessive determiners.

   a. Tom, give me Tom's paintbrush!
   Revised:
   b. The children shared the children's wealth.
   Revised:
   c. The fence got the fence's paint, and all was well.
   Revised:

4. Take turns with your partner to read each pair of sentences aloud. How do the two versions sound different? Which sounds clearer? Why?

Understanding Contractions

A contraction is a shortened word, or two words spliced together, with an apostrophe. Writers use contractions to add variety to their sentences, or to create more realistic dialogue.

Quick Guide to Contractions		
Phrase	**Contraction**	**Sample Sentence**
you are	you're	You're a clever boy, Tom Sawyer!
it is	it's	It's a nice summer day.
they are	they're	They're doing Tom's work for him.

5. Mark Twain uses several contractions in The Adventures of Tom Sawyer to show the dialect of the characters. With your partner, scan the passage in Activity 4.8 and find examples of the following contractions. The chunks have been provided to narrow your search. Write the quotes in the chart. Then rewrite each sentence to include both words in the contraction.

Contraction	Quote	Expanded Sentence
it's [Chunk 3]		
you're [Chunk 4]		

6. Take turns with your partner to read the sentences aloud. How do the two versions sound different? How does the character change when you change his or her speech?

Editing

Read the following paragraph from a student's essay. Choose the word that belongs in each sentence.

> The Adventures of Tom Sawyer is a hilarious story that [your/you're] bound to like. Even though [its/it's] old, I found it entertaining. [Its/It's] central character is, of course, Tom Sawyer. Tom is a young boy who has to whitewash his aunt's fence one beautiful summer morning. He hates doing that chore, and he worries about what his friends will say when they pass by on [their/they're/there] way to play and have fun. Tom thinks [its/it's] unfair that he has to do work while [their/they're/there] free to roam about, so he comes up with a plan. As they walk by, he pretends he is having a good time painting the fence, and [their/they're/there] missing out. This tactic gets them to give Tom [their/they're/there] possessions in exchange for a chance to paint. He doesn't have to do the work, and he gets a lot of stuff he likes. Tom might not be [your/you're] favorite person, but no one can deny that he is clever.

Compare your choices with a partner's. Did you make the same choices? Work together to resolve any differences.

☑ Check Your Understanding

What question(s) can you ask yourself whenever you write to be sure that you have used the word or contraction you meant to use? Add the question(s) to your Editor's Checklist.

Practice

Reread the informational essay you wrote in Activity 4.8. Highlight each instance where you wrote the following words and determine whether or not you selected the correct word in each case.
your, you're, its, it's, their, they're, there

Elements of Humor: Hyperbole

VOCABULARY

LITERARY

Hyperbole describes the literary technique of extreme exaggeration for emphasis, often used for comic effect.
Alliteration is the repetition of consonant sounds at the beginnings of words that are close together.

My Notes

Learning Targets

- Analyze the effect of hyperbole in poetry.
- Identify hyperbole in previously studied print and nonprint texts.

Preview

In this activity, you will read a poem and think about the author's use of hyperbole.

Understanding Hyperbole

1. Finish the lines using hyperbolic language. The first line is shown as an example.

   - My dog is so big, he beeps when he backs up.

   - I'm so hungry, I could eat a _____.

   - My cat is so smart that _____.

   - She was so funny that _____.

Setting a Purpose for Reading

- As you read the poem, put an exclamation point next to examples of **hyperbole** and underline examples of **alliteration**.
- Circle unknown words and phrases. Try to determine the meaning of the words using context clues, word parts, or a dictionary.

About the Author

Ted Hughes (1930–1998) is considered to be one of the 20th century's greatest poets. He wrote almost 90 books during his long career and won numerous prizes and fellowships. In 1984, he was appointed England's poet laureate. According to London *Times* contributor Thomas Nye, Hughes "wanted to capture not just live animals, but the aliveness of animals in their natural state: their wildness, their quiddity, the fox-ness of the fox and the crow-ness of the crow."

Poetry

Mooses

by **Ted Hughes**

The goofy Moose, the walking house frame,
Is lost
In the forest. He bumps, he blunders, he stands.

With massy bony thoughts sticking out near his ears—

5 Reaching out palm upwards, to catch whatever might be
falling from heaven—
He tries to think,
Leaning their huge weight
On the **lectern** of his front legs.

10 He can't find the world!

Where did it go? What
does a world look like?

The Moose
Crashes on, and crashes into a

15 lake, and stares at the
mountain and cries:

'Where do I belong? This is no place!'

He turns dragging half the lake out after him

And charges the crackling underbrush

20 He meets another Moose
He stares, he thinks: 'It's only a mirror!'

Where is the world?' he groans. 'O my lost world!

And why am I so ugly?

'And why am I so far away from my feet?'

25 He weeps.
Hopeless drops drip from his droopy lips.

The other Moose just stands there doing the same.
Two dopes of the deep woods.

My Notes

lectern: a stand with an angled top, often used by people delivering speeches

Making Observations
- What emotions does the poem trigger?
- What image stands out to you?

Returning to the Text

- Return to the text as you respond to the following questions. Use text evidence to support your responses.
- Write any additional questions you have about the poem in your Reader/Writer Notebook.

2. Line 2 has only two words. What effect does this short line have?

_____

_____

_____

3. Is this poem high or low comedy? How do you know?

_____

_____

_____

4. What is the purpose of alliteration in line 26 of the poem?

_____

_____

_____

5. How does hyperbole in line 18 create a humorous effect?

_____

_____

_____

6. What tone does the author create in the last stanza? Use words and phrases from the text to support your answer?

_____

_____

_____

Working from the Text

7. Return to the humorous texts you have read in this unit and identify a couple examples of hyperbole. Share your examples in a small group and discuss how hyperbole creates a humorous effect. Record examples shared by your peers in the graphic organizer.

Title:

Example:

Title:

Example:

Hyperbole

Title:

Example:

Title:

Example:

Elements of Humor

8. Add your notes about hyperbole to the Elements of Humor graphic organizer in Activity 4.11.

INDEPENDENT READING LINK

Read and Connect

Research humorous texts in which the author uses hyperbole for effect. Choose a text that exemplifies the use of hyperbole, tone, and verbals. Cite examples to support your choice in your Reader/ Writer Notebook. Include a brief summary explaining why this humorous text appeals to you. You will use your notes to recommend the text to your peers in a small group setting.

Elements of Humor: Comic Wordplay

Learning Strategies

Marking the Text
Discussion Groups
RAFT

VOCABULARY

LITERARY

A **pun** is a funny play on words. Puns are created by using words that suggest other words with the same sounds but different meanings.

My Notes

Learning Targets

- Interpret the use of wordplay in poetry, drama, and previously read texts.
- Write an original poem using puns.

Preview

In this activity, you will read a poem and think about the author's use of wordplay, specifically puns.

Comic Wordplay

Comic wordplay is a literary technique in which the words that are used become the main subject of the text, primarily for the intended effect of amusement. A **pun** is a form of wordplay that makes use of similar-sounding words to cause a comedic effect.

Setting a Purpose for Reading

- As you read the poem, underline words and phrases that demonstrate the author's use of puns.
- Circle unknown words and phrases. Try to determine the meaning of the words by using context clues, word parts, or a dictionary.

About the Author

Jack Prelutsky (b. 1940) says that he has always enjoyed playing with language, although he did not always like poetry. He rediscovered poetry in his twenties, when he began writing humorous verse for children. Since then, he has written more than 50 poetry collections. His poems are sometimes silly, sometimes playful, sometimes frightening—but always entertaining. In 2006, the Poetry Foundation named him the first-ever Children's Poet Laureate. Prelutsky also studied music, and he has set several of his poems to music for the audio versions of his poetry anthologies.

Poetry

Is Traffic Jam Delectable?

by **Jack Prelutsky**

Is traffic jam **delectable**,
does jelly fish in lakes,
does tree bark make a racket,
does the clamor rattle snakes?

5 Can salmon scale a mountain,
does a belly laugh a lot,
do carpets nap in flower beds
or on an apricot?
Around my handsome bottleneck,

10 I wear a railroad tie,
my treasure chest puffs up a bit,
I blink my private eye.
I like to use piano keys
to open locks of hair,

15 then put a pair of brake shoes on
and dance on **debonair**.
I hold up my electric shorts
with my banana belt,
then sit upon a toadstool

20 and watch a tuna melt.
I dive into a car pool,
where I take an onion dip,
then stand aboard the tape deck
and sail my penmanship.

25 I put my dimes in riverbanks
and take a quarterback,
and when I fix a nothing flat
I use a lumberjack.
I often wave my second hand

30 to tell the overtime,
before I take my bull pen up
to write a silly rhyme.

WORD CONNECTIONS

Roots and Affixes
The word *clamor* comes from a Latin word meaning "to call out." The root *clam*, also spelled *claim*, appears in *exclaim* and *exclamation*, *proclaim* and *proclamation*, and *acclaim* and *acclamation*.

My Notes

delectable: delicious
debonair: charming

Returning to the Text

- Return to the text as you respond to the following questions. Use text evidence to support your responses.
- Write any additional questions you have about the poem in your Reader/Writer Notebook.

1. How does Prelutsky's understanding of children influence his choice of words? What is the result for the reader? Cite examples from the text to support your answer.

_____

_____

_____

_____

2. Is this poem an example of low comedy or high comedy? Include details from the poem to support your answer.

_____

_____

_____

_____

3. What effect does the author's use of puns in each line have on the poem?

_____

_____

_____

_____

Working from the Text

4. Mark the text by highlighting at least three humorous puns that you can visualize.

5. Sketch at least one of the puns on a piece of paper.

6. In your discussion groups, share your sketches and read aloud the corresponding pun. Explain the two meanings of the word or phrase that creates the pun. Be sure to use precise diction and discuss how the author uses puns for humorous effect.

7. As a group, review the poem and discuss the puns that you notated with question marks. Try to collaborate to make meaning of these.

8. Referencing the text as an example, define *pun* and create some examples of your own puns. Then use those puns to create a short poem of your own.

Analyzing a Humorous Skit

You will next read and/or listen to the skit "Who's on First?" by Abbott and Costello.

9. Based on the title of the skit, what do you think is the subject?

10. Sketch a baseball diamond on a separate piece of paper. As you read the skit, try to fill in the names of each of the players mentioned.

11. Write answers to the following questions about "Who's on First?" and compare them with a peer.

   • Why are Abbott and Costello having difficulty understanding each other?
   • How does the wordplay create humor at a high level of comedy?

☑ Check Your Understanding

Choose one of the puns that you created for your poem and draw a picture to illustrate it in your Reader/Writer Notebook.

✎ Writing to Sources: Informational Text

Compare and contrast the two humorous poems, "Mooses" and "Is Traffic Jam Delectable?" Explain how each poet uses comedic language to express a universal truth. Be sure to:

   • Establish a controlling idea and support it with quotes from the texts and commentary explaining the humor.
   • Use the correct terms to refer to the elements of humor.
   • Use verbals and precise diction.
   • Check that frequently confused words are used correctly.

Analyzing a Humorous Skit

12. Add your notes about comic language (hyperbole and wordplay) to the Elements of Humor graphic organizer in Activity 4.11.

Planning and Revising an Analysis of a Humorous Text

Learning Strategies

Graphic Organizer
Marking the Text
Note-taking
Drafting
Discussion Groups

Learning Targets

- Analyze the effects of humorous elements in texts.
- Draft and revise an essay analyzing a humorous text.

Preview

In this activity, you will identify the parts of an essay and revise a sample student essay.

Identifying and Analyzing the Elements of Humor

1. Review the Elements of Humor graphic organizer, and rank how comfortable you are with understanding the elements (#1 being most comfortable, #2 being second most, etc.).

Elements of Humor			
Humorous Element	**Definition**	**Level of Comedy**	**Examples from Texts**
Comic Characters and Caricatures	A caricature is a pictorial, written, or acted representation of a person that exaggerates characteristics or traits for comic effect.		
Comic Situations and Situational Irony	Comic situations are when characters are in an unlikely situation or are victims of circumstances and react in a comical way. Situational irony involves a contrast between what characters or readers might reasonably expect to happen and what actually happens.		
Comic Language: Hyperbole	Hyperbole is extreme exaggeration used for emphasis, often used for comic effect.		
Comic Language: Wordplay • One-liners • Puns	A one-liner is a short joke or witticism expressed in a single sentence. A pun is the humorous use of a word or words to suggest another word with the same sound or different meaning.		

2. Your teacher will assign a text for you to analyze.

   - Closely read (or reread) the text.
   - Mark the text by highlighting evidence of humorous elements.
   - Annotate the text using precise diction to describe the intended humor and humorous effect.

3. Collaborate with your group to complete the graphic organizers here and following.

Title: _____   Author: _____

Humorous Element	Examples from Text	Comedic Effect
Comic Characters and Caricatures		
Comic Situations and Situational Irony		
Comic Language: Hyperbole		
Comic Language: Wordplay • One-liners • Puns		

Level of Comedy	Explanation	Evidence

Description of Humor and Intended Effect	Examples from Text	Explanation (Commentary)

Universal Truth (Theme)	Evidence from Text

Reading and Analyzing a Sample Essay

An effective essay includes a clear introduction to the topic, body paragraphs that expand on the thesis and provide evidence and commentary to support it, and a conclusion that provides closure for the topic.

Introduction
- Begin with a **hook.**
- Set the **context** for the essay.
- Establish a **controlling idea** (**thesis** statement) that directly responds to the prompt.

Body Paragraphs
- Begin with a **topic sentence** related to the thesis.
- Include **evidence** from the text (paraphrased and directly quoted).
- Provide **commentary** that uses precise diction to describe humor and the intended effect.
- Use a variety of **transitions** to connect ideas and create coherence.

Concluding Paragraph
- Discuss the universal truth revealed through the text.
- Evaluate the effectiveness of the author's use of humor to communicate this truth.

Setting a Purpose for Reading
- As you read the sample student essay, draw two lines under commentary that uses precise diction and academic vocabulary, especially humorous vocabulary.
- Draw a rectangle around the hook in the first paragraph.
- Highlight in different colors the topic sentence, evidence, commentary, and transitional phrases in each body paragraph.
- Place a question mark by any sentences or sections that you think need to be revised.
- Circle the thesis statement in the first paragraph.
- Circle unknown words and phrases. Try to determine the meaning of the words by using context clues, word parts, or a dictionary.

My Notes

The Power of Pets

by **Isha Sharma (an eighth-grade student)**

1   Every child has gone through a phase in life when they have a sudden fixation with getting a pet, and parents often have to go through a lot of trouble in order to appease the child, at least until the obsession is replaced with another. In the light-hearted essay, "I've Got a Few Pet Peeves about Sea Creatures," Dave Barry uses hyperbole and verbal irony to show how a parent will often go through great lengths to satisfy his child, often hoping that the child will learn something in the process.

2   To point out the often ridiculous experiences parents go through for their children, Barry uses hyperbole to emphasize how complicated getting a pet fish can be. For example, he explains first how a "pet" beetle under his daughter's "loving care and feeding ... thrived for maybe nine seconds before expiring like a little six-legged parking meter." [1] The additional use of simile and the exaggerated amount of time adds to the humor, as in any case, one's "loving care and feeding" should not cause the death of anything so quickly, no matter how terrible the "care" could actually be. The explanation of the parents replacing each beetle with another shows how willing parents are to support their children no matter how ridiculous the circumstances. Furthermore, Barry calls the fish he bought "so nonviolent that, in the wild, worms routinely beat them up and steal their lunch money." As known to all people, it is fish that eat worms and not the other way around. This is hyperbolic because worms are not known for "beating fish up" and animals do not have money, lunch money included. This also ties back to a metaphor/analogy Barry made that "an aquarium is a powder keg that can explode in deadly violence at any moment, just like ... junior high." Both of these situations are highly exaggerated. Through the use of hyperbole, Barry is able to convey how parents often feel about their struggle even in simple situations, to which a child might react to them as being overdramatic.

3   Also, Barry uses verbal irony/sarcasm to vent and display his frustration, which proves furthermore the lengths he is going to help his daughter. For instance, when complaining about the aggressive nature of fish, he says they could become aggressive if "it was a month containing the letter 'R', or they heard the song 'Who Let the Dogs Out.'" Months and songs are all aspects of human life, it is unlikely that fish will ever have fish months or fish songs. This adds to the sarcastic tone of the writer, which shows that even through

My Notes

his frustrations, he is struggling to find the right choice for his daughter, no matter how much of a nuisance it is to make it. Also, Barry uses sarcasm when explaining the variety of needs for a fish tank so that "the fish would be intellectually stimulated and get into a decent college." The author, as with most intellectual people, knows that fish do not have colleges, and seeing that their intelligence capacity is smaller than a human's, they cannot be "intellectually stimulated." The author uses this verbal irony to point out that even though the needs of a fish are not as significant as the needs of a human, caring for them still requires a lot of effort. Clearly, the author chooses to go through this effort for his daughter. The usage of verbal irony in this piece further points out the "struggles" of a father to appease his child.

4   Even in the most trivial instances, the parent will go though many obstacles to help his child, often in the hope that the child will learn something along the way. Whether or not the child actually learns this is questionable, yet the parent's effort should not go unnoticed.

Working from the Text

4. Using your annotations of the text, identify the main points of the essay by completing the following outline. As you reread the essay, ask yourself: What is the author's thesis statement? How does the author support that thesis statement? What universal truth does the author reveal?

Outline

  I. Introductory Paragraph
      A. Hook:

      B. Thesis:

 II. Body Paragraphs
      A. Topic Sentence:

      B. Topic Sentence:

III. Concluding Paragraph
      A. Universal Truth:

5. Use your outline to write a one-paragraph summary of the essay. Be sure to include the central idea identified in the thesis, the main ideas identified in the two topic sentences, and the universal truth in the conclusion in order to summarize the essay. Then improve your paragraph by including transitions among the main points.

6. Referring to the question marks you notated in the text, create revision suggestions for each. Write your responses in the My Notes space next to the text.

7. Work with your writing group to revise the student essay. You may want to review the roles and responsibilities of writing group members in Activity 1.9. Select one or more of the following:
   - Write a new introduction.
   - Write a third support paragraph.
   - Write a new conclusion.

8. Work with your writing group to see where you might be able to add the following features for increased understanding and effect:
   - Headings
   - Graphics (charts, tables, etc.)
   - Multimedia (such as photos or drawings)

9. After you have revised the ideas in the essay, revise sentence-level errors. Be sure to:
   - Create variety in your sentences by using verbals.
   - Make sure your verb tense is consistent.
   - Maintain subject-verb and pronoun-antecedent agreement.
   - Punctuate clauses appropriately.

☑ Check Your Understanding

Working with a partner, evaluate the revised student essay and briefly discuss any further revisions you think would improve it. Consult the steps in this activity to guide your discussion.

🎁 Independent Reading Checkpoint

Consider the connections you made while reading humorous texts. In one paragraph, summarize one message (theme) a particular author tried to convey to the reader through humor. Briefly describe the level of comedy and the elements of humor used by the author.

Writing an Analysis of a Humorous Text

 ## ASSIGNMENT

Write an essay that explains how an author creates humor for effect and uses it to communicate a universal truth.

Planning and Prewriting: Take time to make a plan for your essay.	▪ What reading strategies (such as marking or diffusing the text) will help you take notes on the author's use of humor as you read the text? ▪ How can you demonstrate your knowledge of the humor genre by correctly identifying the level of comedy, elements of humor, and intended comedic effect on the reader? ▪ What prewriting strategies (such as outlining or graphic organizers) could help you explore, focus, and organize your ideas?
Drafting: Write a multiparagraph essay that effectively organizes your ideas.	▪ What elements of an effective introductory paragraph will you use in your writing? ▪ How will you develop support paragraphs with well-chosen examples (evidence) and thoughtful analysis (commentary) about at least two elements of humor? ▪ How will you use transitions to create cohesion? ▪ How will your conclusion support your ideas, identify and analyze the level(s) of comedy, and evaluate the author's effectiveness at communicating a universal truth?
Evaluating and Revising the Draft: Create opportunities to review and revise your work.	▪ During the process of writing, when can you pause to share and respond with others in order to elicit suggestions and ideas for revision? ▪ How can the Scoring Guide help you evaluate how well your draft meets the requirements of the assignment? ▪ How can you use a precise vocabulary of humor to enhance your critical analysis?
Checking and Editing for Publication: Confirm your final draft is ready for publication.	▪ How will you proofread and edit your draft to demonstrate command of the conventions of standard English capitalization, punctuation, spelling, grammar, and usage? ▪ Did you effectively use verbals? ▪ Did you establish and maintain a formal style?

Reflection

After completing this Embedded Assessment, think about how you went about accomplishing this task, and respond to the following:

- How has your understanding of how humor is created developed during this unit?
- Do you think your sense of humor will change as you mature? Explain.

SCORING GUIDE

Scoring Criteria	Exemplary	Proficient	Emerging	Incomplete
Ideas	The essay • establishes and fully maintains a clearly focused controlling idea about the use of humor to convey a universal truth • develops the topic with relevant details, examples, and textual evidence • uses insightful commentary to analyze the effect of humorous elements.	The essay • establishes and maintains a controlling idea about the use of humor to convey a universal truth • develops the topic with adequate details, examples, and textual evidence • uses sufficient commentary to analyze the effect of humorous elements.	The essay • establishes and unevenly maintains a controlling idea that may be unclear or unrelated to the use of humor to convey a universal truth • develops the topic with inadequate details, examples, and textual evidence • uses insufficient commentary to analyze the humor.	The essay • lacks a controlling idea • fails to develop the topic with details, examples, and textual evidence • does not provide commentary or analysis.
Structure	The essay • introduces the topic and context in an engaging manner • uses a well-chosen organizational structure that progresses smoothly to connect ideas • uses a variety of effective transitional strategies • provides a satisfying conclusion.	The essay • introduces the topic and context clearly • uses an organizational structure that progresses logically to connect ideas • uses appropriate transitions to create cohesion and link ideas • provides a logical conclusion.	The essay • provides a weak or partial introduction • uses a flawed or inconsistent organizational structure • uses inappropriate, repetitive, or basic transitions • provides a weak or disconnected conclusion.	The essay • lacks an introduction • has little or no obvious organizational structure • uses few or no transitions • lacks a conclusion.
Use of Language	The essay • uses precise diction and language to maintain an academic voice and formal style • demonstrates command of the conventions of standard English capitalization, punctuation, spelling, grammar, and usage.	The essay • uses some precise diction to maintain a generally appropriate voice and style • demonstrates adequate command of the conventions of standard English capitalization, punctuation, spelling, grammar, and usage.	The essay • uses diction that creates an inappropriate voice and style • demonstrates partial or inconsistent command of the conventions of standard English capitalization, punctuation, spelling, grammar, and usage.	The essay • uses vague or confusing language • lacks command of the conventions of standard English capitalization, punctuation, spelling, grammar, and usage.

Unpacking Embedded Assessment 2

Learning Targets

* Reflect on prior learning and make connections.
* Demonstrate an understanding of the skills and knowledge needed to complete Embedded Assessment 2 successfully

Preview

In this activity, you will begin to explore performing a scene from Shakespeare.

Making Connections

You have written an analysis of a humorous text, which required you to know and understand how a writer uses words, characters, and situations to create a humorous effect. Now you will have an opportunity to understand humor from a different perspective—that of a performer.

Essential Questions

Reflect on your understanding of Essential Question 1 from Activity 4.1: How do writers and speakers use humor to convey truth? Then respond to Essential Question 2: What makes an effective performance of a Shakespearean comedy?

Developing Vocabulary

Including the humor-related vocabulary from the first half of the unit, sort the unit Academic Vocabulary and Literary Terms by parts of speech using a dictionary.

Then re-sort the vocabulary from the first half of the unit using the QHT strategy. Compare the new sort with your original QHT sort. How has your understanding changed? Select one word and write a concise statement about how your understanding of the word has changed over the course of this unit.

Unpacking Embedded Assessment 2

Closely read the Embedded Assessment 2 assignment:

 Present your assigned scene in front of your peers to demonstrate your understanding of Shakespeare's text, elements of comedy, and performance.

Then, using the Scoring Guide, work with your class to paraphrase the expectations and create a graphic organizer to use as a visual reminder of the required concepts and skills. Copy the graphic organizer for future reference.

After each activity, use this graphic to guide reflection about what you have learned and what you still need to learn in order to be successful in completing the Embedded Assessment.

My Notes

 INDEPENDENT READING LINK

Reading Plan

In this half of the unit, you will prepare to perform a scene from one of Shakespeare's plays. You will have the chance to read other humorous texts independently. Gather in a small group and discuss other humor writers you know about and other comedies by Shakespeare. Add the titles you choose to read to the My Independent Reading List on the Contents page of this unit.

Analyzing Multiple Points of View

Learning Strategies

Activating Prior Knowledge
Collaborative Discussion
RAFT

VOCABULARY

LITERARY
A **monologue** is a speech or written expression of thoughts by a character and is always written from the first-person point of view. Monologues have a certain structure: a beginning that hooks the reader, a middle that sequences and develops ideas, and an end that offers a conclusion. Content is tailored to the purpose and audience.

Learning Targets
- Identify and analyze an author's use of multiple points of view in a novel excerpt.
- Transform a narrative into a monologue and deliver it as an oral performance.

Preview

In this activity, you will analyze how Paul Fleischman uses multiple points of view to create one interconnected narrative in *Seedfolks*. Then you will practice oral performance by adopting one point of view to write a **monologue** and present it in class.

Multiple Points of View

During the course of this year, you read and analyzed narratives that tell the story from different points of view. Turn to a partner and discuss the types of points of view you have encountered: first-person, second-person, third-person limited, and third-person omniscient. Try to identify at least one narrative that you have read this year that tells the story from each of these points of view. In your discussion, consider who is the narrator of the story. Consider also how the narrator's use of personal pronouns, such as *I*, *you*, or *he/she* provides a clue about the point of view. After the discussion, make notes about what you recalled about each point of view.

First Person	Second Person

Third Person Omniscient	Third Person Limited

Writers sometimes use **multiple points of view** when writing a single narrative. This literary device provides the reader with multiple perspectives on the conflict of the story, often resulting in the reader having more knowledge about the conflict than each character has individually.

Setting a Purpose for Reading

- As you read the novel excerpt, place a star near clues that help you identify the conflict in the narrative.
- Circle unknown words and phrases. Try to determine the meaning of the words by using context clues, word parts, or a dictionary.

About the Author

Paul Fleischman (1952–) writes fiction, non-fiction, drama, and poetry. Many of his works use multiple points of view to tell a story. He won the Newbery Medal in 1989 for *Joyful Noise: Poems for Two Voices*. His novel *Seedfolks* has won a number of awards and was chosen by Vermont as its One-State One-Book selection. It has also been adapted into a play.

Novel

from
Seedfolks

by **Paul Fleischman**

Kim

1   I stood before our family altar. It was dawn. No one else in the apartment was awake. I stared at my father's photograph—his thin face stern, lips latched tight, his eyes peering permanently to the right. I was nine years old and still hoped that perhaps his eyes might move. Might notice me.

2   The candles and the incense sticks, lit the day before to mark his death anniversary, had burned out. The rice and meat offered him were gone. After the evening feast, past midnight, I'd been wakened by my mother's crying. My oldest sister had joined in. My own tears had then come as well, but for a different reason.

3   I turned from the altar, tiptoed to the kitchen, and quietly drew a spoon from a drawer. I filled my lunch thermos with water and reached into our jar of dried lima beans. Then I walked outside to the street.

4   The sidewalk was completely empty. It was Sunday, early in April. An icy wind teetered trash cans and turned my cheeks to marble. In Vietnam we had no weather like that. Here in Cleveland people call it spring. I walked half a block, then crossed the street and reached the vacant lot.

5   I stood tall and scouted. No one was sleeping on the old couch in the middle. I'd never entered the lot before, or wanted to. I did so now, picking

When writers use more than one point of view to tell a story, they are using a literary device called **multiple points of view**. For example, a writer may tell a story from more than one character's point of view all in first-person. This gives each lead character a chance to tell the story from their own perspective. It also gives the reader a direct experience of each character's feelings and emotions. At other times, a writer may mix first-person and third-person point of view to transfer back and forth from a narrator who participates in the story and an outside narrator. This provides both subjective and objective points of view.

VOCABULARY

My Notes

_____
_____
_____
_____
_____
_____
_____
_____
_____
_____
_____
_____
_____
_____
_____
_____

my way between tires and trash bags. I nearly stepped on two rats gnawing and froze. Then I told myself that I must show my bravery. I continued farther and chose a spot far from the sidewalk and hidden from view by a rusty refrigerator. I had to keep my project safe.

6   I took out my spoon and began to dig. The snow had melted, but the ground was hard. After much work, I finished one hole, then a second, then a third. I thought about how my mother and sisters remembered my father, how they knew his face from every angle and held in their fingers the feel of his hands. I had no such memories to cry over. I'd been born eight months after he'd died. Worse, he had no memories of me. When his spirit hovered over our altar, did it even know who I was?

7   I dug six holes. All his life in Vietnam my father had been a farmer. Here our apartment house had no yard. But in that vacant lot he would see me. He would watch my beans break ground and spread, and would notice with pleasure their pods growing plump. He would see my patience and my hard work. I would show him that I could raise plants, as he had. I would show him that I was his daughter.

8   My class had sprouted lima beans in paper cups the year before. I now placed a bean in each of the holes. I covered them up, pressing the soil down firmly with my fingertips. I opened my thermos and watered them all. And I vowed to myself that those beans would thrive.

Ana

9   I do love to sit and look out the window. Why do I need TV when I have forty-eight apartment windows to watch across the vacant lot, and a sliver of Lake Erie? I've seen history out this window. So much. I was four when we moved here in 1919. The fruit-sellers' carts and coal wagons were pulled down the street by horses back then. I used to stand just here and watch the coal brought up by the handsome lad from Groza, the village my parents were born in. Gibb Street was mainly Rumanians back then. It was "Adio"—"Good-bye"—in all the shops when you left. Then the Rumanians started leaving. They weren't the first, or the last. This has always been a working-class neighborhood. It's like a cheap hotel—you stay until you've got enough money to leave… I watched it happen, through this very window.

10   I lived over in Cleveland Heights for eighteen years, then I moved back in to take care of my parents.… Then steel mills and factories closed and *everybody* left, like rats. Buildings abandoned. Men with no work drinking from nine to five instead, down there in the lot.… Now I see families…from countries I don't know.…New languages in the shops and on the street. These new people leave when they can, like the others. I'm the only one staying. It's so. Staying and staring out this same window.

11   This spring I looked out and I saw something strange. Down in the lot, a little black-haired girl, hiding behind that refrigerator. She was working at the dirt and looking around suspiciously all the time. Then I realized. She was burying something. I never had children of my own, but I've seen enough

in that lot to know she was mixed up in something she shouldn't be. And after twenty years typing for the Parole department, I just about knew what she'd buried. Drugs most likely, or money, or a gun. The next moment, she disappeared like a rabbit.

12 I thought of calling up the police. Then I saw her there the next morning, and I decided I'd solve this case myself. We had a long spell of rain then. I didn't set eyes on her once. Then the weather turned warm and I saw her twice more, always in the morning, on her way to school. She was crouched down with her back to me so I couldn't see just what she was doing. My curiosity was like a fever inside me. Then one morning she was there, glancing about, and she looked straight up at the window. I pulled my head back behind the curtain. I wasn't sure if she'd seen me. If she had, she wouldn't leave her treasure buried long. Then I knew I'd have to dig it up before she did.

13 I waited an hour after she left. Then I took and old butter knife and my cane and hobbled down all three flights of stairs. I worked my way through that awful jungle of junk and finally came to her spot. I stooped down. It was wet there and easy digging. I hacked and dug, but didn't find anything, except for a large white bean. I tried a new spot and found another, then a third. Then the truth of it slapped me full in the face. I said to myself, "What have you *done*?" Two beans had roots. I knew I'd done them harm. I felt like I'd read through her secret diary and had ripped out a page without meaning to. I laid those beans right back in the ground, as gently as sleeping babies. Then I patted the soil as smooth as could be.

14 The next morning she was back. I peeked around the curtain. She didn't look up here or give any sign that she noticed something wrong. I could see her clearly this time. She reached a hand down into her schoolbag. Then she pulled out a jar, unscrewed the lid, and poured out water onto the ground.

15 That afternoon I bought some binoculars.

Wendell

16 My phone doesn't ring much, which suits me fine. That's how I got the news about our boy, shot dead like a dog in the street. And the word, last year, about my wife's car wreck. I can't hear a phone and not jerk inside. When Ana called I was still asleep. Phone calls that wake me up are the worst.

17 "Get up here quick!" she says. I live on the ground floor and watch out for her a little....I ran up the stairs. I could tell it was serious. I prayed I wouldn't find her dead. When I got there, she looked perfectly fine. She dragged me over to the window. "Look down there!" she says. "They're dying!"

18 "What?" I yelled back.

19 "The plants!" she says.

20 I was mad. She gave me some binoculars and told me all about the Chinese girl. I found the plants and got them in focus. There were four of them in a row, still little. They were wilted. Leaves flopped flat on the ground.

21 "What are they?" she asked.

22 "Some kind of beans." I grew up on a little farm in Kentucky. "But she planted 'em way too early. She's lucky those seeds even came up."

23 "But they did," said Ana. "And it's up to us to save them."

24 It was a weekend in May and hot. You'd have thought that those beans were hers. They needed water, especially in that heat. She said the girl hadn't come in four days—sick, probably, or gone out of town. Ana had twisted her ankle and couldn't manage the stairs. She pointed to a pitcher. "Fill that up and soak them good. Quick now."

25 School janitors take too much bossing all week to listen to an extra helping on weekends. I stared at her one long moment, then took my time filling the pitcher.

26 I walked down the stairs and into the lot and found the girl's plants. You don't plant beans till the weather's hot. Then I saw what had kept her seeds from freezing. The refrigerator in front of them had bounced the sunlight back on the soil, heating it up like an oven. I bent down and gave the dirt a feel. It was hard packed and light colored. I studied the plants. Leaves shaped like spades in a deck of cards. Definitely beans. I scraped up a ring of dirt around the first plant, to hold the water and any rain that fell. I picked up the pitcher and poured the water slowly. Then I heard something move and spun around. The girl was there, stone-still, ten feet away, holding her own water jar.

27 She hadn't seen me behind the refrigerator. She looked afraid for her life. Maybe she thought I'd jump up and grab her. I gave her a smile and showed her that I was just giving her plants some water. This made her eyes go even bigger. I stood up slowly and backed away. I smiled again. She watched me leave. We never spoke one word.

28 I walked back there that evening and checked on the beans. They'd picked themselves up and were looking fine. I saw that she'd made a circle of dirt around the other three plants. Out of nowhere the words from the Bible came into my head: "And a little child shall lead them." I didn't know why at first. Then I did. There's plenty about my life I can't change. Can't bring the dead back to life on this earth. Can't make the world loving and kind. Can't change myself into a millionaire. But a patch of ground in this trashy lot—I *can* change that. Can change it big. Better to put my time into that than moaning about the other all day. That little grammar-school girl showed me that.

29 The lot had buildings on three sides. I walked around and picked myself out a spot that wouldn't be shaded too much. I dragged the garbage off to the side and tossed out the biggest pieces of broken glass. I looked over my plot, squatted down, and fingered the soil awhile.

30 That Monday I brought a shovel home from work.

Gonzalo

31 The older you are, the younger you get when you move to the United States.

32 They don't teach you that equation in school. Big Brain, Mr. Smoltz, my eighth-grade math teacher, hasn't even heard of it. It's not in *Gateway* to *Algebra*. It's Garcia's Equation. I'm the Garcia.

33   Two years after my father and I moved here from Guatemala I could speak English. I learned it on the playground and watching lots of TV. Don't believe what people say—cartoons make you *smart*. But my father, he worked all day in a kitchen with Mexicans and Salvadorans. His English was worse than a kindergartener's. He would only buy food at the *bodega* down the block. Outside of there he lowered his eyes and tried to get by on mumbles and smiles. He didn't want strangers to hear his mistakes. So he used me to make phone calls and to talk to the landlady and to buy things in stores where you had to use English. He got younger. I got older.

34   Then my younger brothers and mother and Tío Juan, her uncle, came north and joined us. Tío Juan was the oldest man in his *pueblo*[1]. But here he became a little baby. He'd been a farmer, but here he couldn't work. He couldn't sit out in the plaza and talk—there aren't any plazas here, and if you sit out in public some gang driving by might use you for target practice. He couldn't understand TV. So he wandered around the apartment all day, in and out of rooms, talking to himself, just like a kid in diapers.

35   One morning he wandered outside and down the street. My mother practically fainted. He doesn't speak Spanish, just an Indian language. I finally found him standing in front of the beauty parlor, staring through the glass at a woman with a drier over her head. He must have wondered what weird planet he'd moved to. I led him home, holding his hand, the way you would a three-year-old. Since then I'm supposed to baby-sit him after school.

36   One afternoon I was watching TV, getting smart on *The Brady Bunch*. Suddenly I looked up. He was gone. I checked the halls on all five floors of the apartment house. I ran to the street. He wasn't in the *bodega* or the pawnshop. I called his name, imagining my mother's face when she found out he'd fallen through a manhole or been run over. I turned the corner, looking for the white straw hat he always wore. Two blocks down I spotted it. I flew down the sidewalk and found him standing in front of the vacant lot, making gestures to a man with a shovel.

37   I took his hand, but he pulled me through the trash and into the lot. I recognized the man with the shovel—he was the janitor at my school. He had a little garden planted. Different shades of green leaves were coming up in rows. Tío Juan was smiling and trying to tell him something. The man couldn't understand him and finally went back to digging. I turned Tío Juan around and led him home.

38   That night he told my mother all about it. She was the only one who could understand him. When she got home from work the next day she asked me to take him back there. I did. He studied the sun. Then the soil. He felt it, then smelled it, then actually tasted it. He chose a spot not too far from the sidewalk. Where my mother changed busses she'd gone into a store and bought him a trowel and four packets of seeds. I cleared the trash, he turned the soil. I wished we were farther from the street and I was praying that none of my

---

[1] **pueblo:** village, town

friends or girlfriends or enemies saw me. Tío Juan didn't even notice people—he was totally wrapped up in the work.

39 He showed me exactly how far apart the rows should be and how deep. He couldn't read the words on the seed packets, but he knew from the pictures what seeds were inside. He poured them into his hand and smiled. He seemed to recognize them, like old friends. Watching him carefully sprinkling them into the troughs he'd made, I realized that I didn't know anything about growing food and that he knew everything. I stared at his busy fingers, then his eyes. They were focused, not far away or confused. He'd changed from a baby back into a man.

Making Observations
- Who do we meet in each chapter?
- What do you notice about the setting of the novel?

Returning to the Text
- Return to the text as you respond to the following questions. Use text evidence to support your responses.

- Write any additional questions you have about the novel excerpt in your Reader/Writer Notebook.

1. How does Ana's description of the neighborhood introduce the conflict in the excerpt?

_____

_____

_____

_____

2. How does the setting influence what Ana believes about her neighbors, specifically about Kim?

_____

_____

_____

_____

3. Use text evidence to describe how Kim's planting of the seeds influences the plot.

_____

_____

_____

_____

_____

_____

_____

4. Identify the points of view that are used in this excerpt. How does the author create the points of view?

_____

_____

_____

_____

5. What effect does the point of view of the narrative have on the reader?

_____

_____

_____

_____

_____

_____

_____

_____

_____

Working from the Text

6. Work with your group to identify the sequence of events in your assigned character's chapter. What events do you learn about from that character's point of view? Then as a class, you will work together to combine each character's sequence of events into one main time line.

☑ Focus on the Sentence

Choose one character from *Seedfolks* and write four different sentence types from the point of view of that character. Use information from the story to write the sentences.

Statement:

_____

_____

Question:

_____

_____

Exclamation:

_____

_____

Command:

_____

_____

7. RAFT is a strategy that is primarily used to create new texts by manipulating elements of a text during prewriting and drafting. This strategy helps you create or substitute various roles, audiences, formats, and topics as a way to focus your thinking about a new text. In preparation for writing a monologue from the point of view of a character from the novel excerpt, complete the following RAFT table using the prompts to guide your thinking.

Role	From whose perspective will you write? How does that character function in the narrative? What are their motivations?
Audience	To whom are you writing or speaking (the audience, yourself, one or more characters)?
Format	What format would be appropriate for your audience?
Topic	What is the subject of your writing? What points do you want to make?

 **Narrative Writing Prompt**

Use the RAFT strategy to create a monologue from the point of view of one of the characters from *Seedfolks*. Imagine what he or she might say about the conflict. Be sure to:

- Use narrative techniques to express a point of view and create interest.
- Use a consistent point of view.
- Use diction, syntax, and punctuation to create a persona and a dramatic effect.
- Check your dramatic performance for frequently confused words and other misspellings.

Presenting Your Monologue

8. Once you have written your monologue, prepare to perform it as an oral interpretation.

- Mark the text to indicate effective volume, rate (speed), pitch (high or low), inflection (emphasis on specific words for effect), and tone (speaker's attitude toward the subject) throughout the monologue. Remember: these elements should shift if the ideas or speaker shifts.
- Mark the text to indicate appropriate eye contact, facial expressions, and movement. These elements should support your tone.
- Brainstorm creative yet simple ideas for pantomime and props, recording your ideas next to appropriate sections in the monologue.
- Remember: when you are delivering a monologue from someone else's point of view, you are adopting a persona. Become that person!
- Rehearse.
- Practice adapting your speech and tone to be more formal, as if presenting it to the whole school, and less formal, as if presenting it to a small group of your peers.
- Practice delivering your lines fluently.
- Practice delivering your lines with an effective volume, rate, pitch, inflection, and tone.
- Practice using eye contact, facial expressions, and movement appropriate for your lines.
- Deliver your oral performance of the monologue.
- As part of the audience, listen to other students' performances. Use the Scoring Guide Criteria to compare and contrast the most effective elements of an oral performance.

Gaining Perspectives

Being healthy is a frequent topic of conversation among friends and family. People often ask each other how they are feeling and sometimes give each other advice, but this advice might conflict with the perspectives of healthcare professionals. You have just read a work using multiple perspectives. Now work with a partner to gather reliable health information. Search websites of renowned healthcare facilities, such as mayoclinic.org and ucsfhealth.org. Use what you learn to complete the graphic organizer. Carefully record the Internet address or the name of the cellphone app in the graphic organizer. Then work with your partner to use what you learn about these health-related technologies to write a monologue. Then take turns using video or audio technology to record your monologue. You can share the recorded monologue with family members, friends, and peers at school.

Define the Technology	Internet Address

Where to Find or Use an App	Cell phone or Internet App

Creating Context for Shakespearean Comedy

Learning Strategies

Note-taking
Marking the Text
Skimming/Scanning
Discussion Groups

Learning Targets

- Research topics to build knowledge about Shakespeare.
- Gather relevant information to understand the context of the play *A Midsummer Night's Dream*.

Preview

In this activity, you will build background knowledge about William Shakespeare and his play *A Midsummer Night's Dream*.

Genre Study: Shakespearean Drama

1. Complete the sentence starters about William Shakespeare in the first column of the following graphic organizer. Support your responses to the statements, and note any questions you have about him.

Who Is Shakespeare?	How Do I Know This?	Questions I Have
Shakespeare was an author of plays and poetry.	I have seen a movie based on one of his plays, called *Romeo and Juliet*.	How many of his other works have been made into movies?
Shakespeare lived ...		
Shakespeare accomplished ...		
Shakespeare ...		

2. Pick a question that you identified in the third column of your chart about Shakespeare. With guidance from your teacher, do research to answer that question. Use at least 3 different sources (the Internet, books, and other resources you have available). Identify at least 2 follow-up questions that occur to you based on what you learned in your research. Record the questions and answers in your Reader/Writer Notebook. Then share the results of your research with your group.

☑ Focus on the Sentence

Expand the brief sentence that follows by answering the questions and then combining them into a complete sentence.

He lived.

Who? _____

Where? _____

When? _____

Expanded Sentence:

_____

_____

Returning to the Text

3. Read these scenarios to determine how you would respond. Make notes about your reactions in the My Notes space.

The person you are in love with has invited you to your high school dance. Your parents, who disapprove of this person, lay down the law, saying, "You are absolutely not allowed to attend the dance with this person. If you wish to attend, you may go with *X*. Your choices are to go to the dance with *X* or not go at all." You are now faced with a dilemma. You are forbidden to go to the dance with the person you love, but you are permitted to attend with *X*, who has been in love with you forever and whom your parents adore.

Consider this: Would you still go to the dance under these conditions? Why or why not?

Since you were forbidden by your parents to attend the dance with the person you love, the two of you devise a plan to sneak out and attend the dance anyway. All of a sudden you notice that your love is nowhere in sight. You begin to search the room for her/him. Eventually, you find her/him in the corner of the room talking with your best friend. You happily interrupt the conversation only to be horrified to discover that your love is confessing her/his love to your best friend.

Consider this: What would you do if you saw your girlfriend/boyfriend confessing her/his love to your best friend? How would you feel?

You confront your love after seeing her/him kiss your best friend. Your girlfriend/boyfriend loudly announces that she/he is no longer interested in you and no longer wants anything to do with you. Your best friend seems confused about the situation as she/he has always been in love with your boyfriend or girlfriend, but the feeling was never shared.

Consider this: What would you do if your girlfriend/boyfriend treated you this way? Would you be mad at your best friend?

Connection to the Play

In Shakespeare's comedy *A Midsummer Night's Dream*, four characters—Lysander, Hermia, Helena, and Demetrius—are entangled in a very complicated love relationship that leaves them open to all sorts of comical mishaps.

Using the following information about the key characters from the play, create a visual that shows the relationship among the listed characters. Consult appropriate print or digital resources to find the pronunciations of character names. Add these to the chart and practice pronouncing them. Remember to note the long and short vowel sounds and silent letters as a guide to facilitate your pronunciation.

Character's Name	Pronunciation	I am ...	I love ...
Hermia		The daughter of a wealthy nobleman	Lysander
Lysander		A prominent businessman	Hermia
Demetrius		Hermia's father's choice for her husband	Hermia too!
Helena		Hermia's best friend	Demetrius

Visual Representation of Characters' Relationships

Narrative Writing Prompt

Using the information from the three scenarios, write your own scenarios for the four key characters described above. Be sure to:

- Incorporate genre characteristics of comedy examined earlier in this unit.
- Provide detail about the situation described in your scenario.
- Use precise diction.
- Use an online or print dictionary to check the definitions and spellings of any words that are frequently confused with similar words. Also check and practice the pronunciation of the word.

Insulting Language

- Read closely to interpret the meaning of Shakespeare's language.
- Deliver a line with proper inflection, tone, gestures, and movement.

Preview

In this activity, you will create a Shakespearean insult and deliver it aloud.

Decoding Shakespeare's Language

Note that punctuation marks signal tone of voice and timing, crucial elements of performance. Read the two lines that follow, pausing briefly for commas and longer for end punctuation. Practice until you achieve a flow that sounds authentic.

"Hang off, thou cat, thou burr! Vile thing, let loose,
Or I will shake thee from me like a serpent."

1. As you complete the chart, think about how punctuation affects the meaning of each line. What impact does it have on the tone of the speaker?

Character	Quote/Insult	Paraphrase (Modern English)
Helena says to Hermia ...	"I will not trust you, Nor longer stay in your *curst* company."	
Lysander says to Hermia ...	"Out, *tawny Tartar*, out! Out, *loathed medicine*! O, *hated, potion*, hence!"	
Hermia says to Helena ...	"You *juggler*, you *canker-blossom*! You *thief of love*! What, have you come by night And stol'n my love's heart from him?"	
Helena says to Hermia ...	"Fie, fie! You *counterfeit, you puppet, you*!"	

2. Once you have determined the meaning of the lines, select one and complete the chart that follows. Rehearse your line in preparation for a performance. Then, role-play by becoming that character and feeling that emotion. Move throughout the room and deliver your insult with flair. Be sure to allow time for peers to react to your delivery.

Record your chosen insult.	What inflection will you use? What words will you stress when you speak your lines?	How will you alter your tone when you deliver your line?	What gestures/ movements will you use to enhance your line?

3. What tone of voice do people usually use when delivering an insult? What emotions might someone be feeling when they insult another person, and why?

☑ Check Your Understanding

Reflect on your understanding of Shakespeare's language. What resources did you use to help you interpret his words? Were they useful? What would you do differently the next time you have to read his words? Discuss with a partner.

Close Reading of a Scene

Learning Targets

- Analyze graphical elements in drama.
- Summarize text to maintain meaning.

Preview

In this activity, you will read a scene from a Shakespearean play and think about its meaning.

Setting a Purpose for Reading

- As you read the scene, underline words and phrases that are meant to be insults.
- Circle unknown words and phrases. Try to determine the meaning of the words by using context clues, word parts, or a dictionary.

About the Author

Little is known about the early life of William Shakespeare (1564–1616), except that he was born and grew up in Stratford-on-Avon in England. As a young man, he went to London and became an actor and playwright. He wrote at least 37 plays (comedies, tragedies, and histories) and is considered one of the greatest playwrights who ever lived. *A Midsummer Night's Dream* was written around the same time as *Romeo and Juliet* and marks an increasing depth and maturity in Shakespeare's work.

My Notes

Drama

from A Midsummer Night's Dream

Act 3, Scene 2, Lines 282–305

by **William Shakespeare**

> **HERMIA:** Oh me! you juggler! you canker-blossom!
> You thief of love! What, have you come by night
> And stolen my love's heart from him?
>
> **HELENA:** Fine, i'faith!
>
> 285 Have you no modesty, no maiden shame,
> No touch of bashfulness? What, will you tear

GRAMMAR & USAGE

Punctuation

Punctuation gives clear cues as to how lines should be performed, particularly in poetry and plays.

An **exclamation mark** shows surprise, extreme happiness, or anger: *Oh me! you juggler! you canker-blossom!*

A **question mark** indicates a question or confusion on the part of the speaker: *Puppet? Why so?*

A **comma** indicates a pause, usually for dramatic effect: *Fie, fie! you counterfeit, you puppet, you!*

A **semicolon** marks a pause that is longer than that for a comma but not as long as that for a period: *And are you grown so high in his esteem;/Because I am so dwarfish and so low?*

As you prepare to read a piece out loud, highlight the different forms of punctuation and think about how they will affect your reading.

INDEPENDENT READING LINK

Read and Connect

Read an excerpt from another Shakespearean play classified as a comedy. Compare and contrast the use of punctuation in your reading to the excerpt from *A Midsummer Night's Dream*. Note the similarities and differences in your Reader/Writer Notebook.

forsooth: indeed; used to express surprise or indignation

Impatient answers from my gentle tongue?
Fie, fie! you counterfeit, you puppet, you!

HERMIA: Puppet? Why so? Ay, that way goes the game.

290 Now, I perceive that she hath made compare
Between our statures; she hath urged her height;
And with her personage, her tall personage,
Her height, **forsooth**, she hath prevail'd with him.
And are you grown so high in his esteem;
295 Because I am so dwarfish and so low?
How low am I, thou painted maypole? speak;
How low am I? I am not yet so low
But that my nails can reach unto thine eyes.

HELENA: I pray you, though you mock me, gentlemen,

300 Let her not hurt me: I was never curst;
I have no gift at all in shrewishness;
I am a right maid for my cowardice:
Let her not strike me. You perhaps may think,
Because she is something lower than myself,
305 That I can match her.

HERMIA: Lower! hark, again.

Making Observations

- What do you notice about the characters?
- How do the characters speak to each other?

Illustration from an 1895 edition of *A Midsummer Night's Dream* by William Shakespeare, published in London by J. M. Dent.

☑ Focus on the Sentence

Complete the given sentences using *because, but,* and *so.*

Hermia insults Helena because _____

Hermia insults Helena, but _____

Hermia insults Helena, so _____

Returning to the Text

- Return to the text as you respond to the following questions. Use text evidence to support your responses.
- Write any additional questions you have about the drama excerpt in your Reader/Writer Notebook.

1. What details in the text should a director consider when casting Helena and Hermia?

_____

_____

_____

2. Which details in Hermia's opening statement reveal her emotions? How does this set the tone of the scene?

_____

_____

_____

3. How does the use of apostrophes affect the meaning of lines in this excerpt?

_____

_____

_____

Working from the Text

4. Reread the text orally with your group. Use print or digital resources to determine the pronunciation of unfamiliar or archaic words.

5. As you listen to the text being read a third time, visualize how the characters would be moving, gesturing, and speaking. Write comments, draw pictures, or stand to act out what you are visualizing.

Check Your Understanding

Explain how this scene is intended to be comical onstage. What elements of comedy are represented?

Acting Companies and Collaborative Close Reading

Learning Strategies

Close Reading
Skimming/Scanning
Rereading
Paraphrasing
Summarizing
Marking the Text
Rehearsing

Learning Targets

- Collaborate to annotate a dramatic scene.
- Analyze the elements of a dramatic scene and rehearse it collaboratively.

Preview

In this activity, you will rehearse a dramatic scene.

My Notes

Preparing for a Dramatic Scene

1. **Quickwrite:** Describe the attitudes and behaviors (norms) of a positive and productive member of an acting group.

2. In the spaces that follow, write the names of the members of your acting company for the roles they will play. Write the scene you will perform, the names of the characters, and who will play each character.

   Acting Company Members

   Director:

   Actors:

   Scene:

   Characters:

Analyzing a Dramatic Scene

3. You will next be assigned a scene from *A Midsummer Night's Dream* that your acting group will perform. Work collaboratively in your acting group to make meaning of the text. Follow these steps to guide your close reading and annotation of the text. You will be responsible for taking notes on your script and for using this script and notes as you plan and rehearse your scene.

- Skim/scan the text and circle unfamiliar words. Use a dictionary or thesaurus to replace each unfamiliar word with a synonym.

- Reread the scene and paraphrase the lines in modern English.

- Summarize the action. What is happening in the scene?

- Reread the scene and mark the text to indicate elements of humor (caricature, situation, irony, wordplay, hyperbole).

- Mark the punctuation and determine how the punctuation affects the spoken lines. Look up the pronunciation and syllable breakdown of words in a print or digital resource as needed. Discuss tone of voice and inflection.

- Analyze the movement in your scene:

  What is each character doing?

  When should characters enter and exit?

  How should characters enter and exit?

  What could you do to exaggerate the humor or create a humorous spin?

- Analyze the blocking in your scene, that is, the movement and placement of characters as they speak:

  Where is each character standing?

  To whom is each spoken line addressed?

- Analyze your scene in the context of the play:

  What has happened in the play before this scene? What happens after this scene?

  How does this scene affect the dramatic action of the play?

Rehearsing a Dramatic Scene

4. Divide lines equally between group members. You may have to be more than one character. One person in your group will be both a player (actor) and the director.

Player (student's name)	Acting As (character's name)
Director:	

My Notes

5. Rehearse your scene. To accurately portray your character and achieve your intended comic effect, be sure to focus on the following:

- tone and inflection
- correct pronunciation of words
- facial expression and gesture

Check Your Understanding

Reflect on the process of reading your scene and determining the meaning of the text, as well as your preparation for and rehearsal of the scene.

- What went well? What will you want to replicate in future rehearsals and in your performance?
- What is a revision or something new you plan to do as you continue to rehearse?

Facing the Challenge of Performance

Learning Targets

- Recognize the controlling idea and supporting details of an informational text.
- Make connections to an informational text by identifying tips to help your dramatic performance.
- Memorize and rehearse lines for a performance.
- Integrate ideas from multiple texts to build knowledge and vocabulary about a topic.

Preview

In this activity, you will read two informational texts about performing and think about how these tips can help you prepare for your performance.

Setting a Purpose for Reading

- Underscore the main ideas and supporting details about how to overcome stage fright.
- Circle unknown words and phrases. Try to determine the meaning of the words by using context clues, word parts, or a dictionary.

About the Author

Gary Guwe is an award-winning speaker and authority in the areas of delivering presentations, influencing others, and impromptu (improvised) speaking. Using his unique methods and curriculum, he has coached many students to impromptu speech championships. Guwe has trained and helped more than 12,500 people.

Informational Text

Adapted from

Fear Busters
10 Tips to Overcome Stage Fright!

by **Gary Guwe**

F – Focus on Your Most Powerful Experience

1   Think about your most memorable and powerful experience when you accomplished a goal—maybe a time you worked extremely hard on a project or did well on a test. Reflect on your most powerful experience and remember the feeling of confidence; think about everything you did to create that feeling and how proud you felt after doing something challenging.

Learning Strategies

Marking the Text
Discussion Groups
Note-taking
Rehearsal

My Notes

KNOWLEDGE QUEST

Knowledge Question:

What are effective ways to overcome stage fright?

In Activity 4.18, you will read an informational text and an article on the topic of stage fright. While you read and build knowledge about the topic, think about your answer to the Knowledge Question.

My Notes

_____

_____

_____

_____

_____

_____

_____

_____

_____

_____

_____

_____

_____

_____

_____

_____

_____

_____

_____

_____

_____

_____

_____

_____

_____

_____

dissipate: lessen

regulate: adjust to a standard

sabotage: destroy or interfere
with your task

E – Energize Yourself

2   You have adrenaline pumping through your veins. Your heart is racing and your muscles are all tensed up. Your eyes are shifty and you are unsettled. You are ready to bolt for the door ... or are you?

3   An adrenaline rush is a built-in defense mechanism for human beings. It is a natural response mechanism that allows us to fight or take flight in the event of danger. That explains the heightened sensitivity we have when we are nervous and excited.

4   Harness this nervous energy and make it work for you! One way we harness this nervous energy is to move around. Your character will at some point move and gesture. Use the times when your character can move and react as opportunities to **dissipate** your nervous energy.

A – Acknowledge Your Fears

5   It is said that fear is here to protect us, not paralyze us. Don't run away from being afraid. Acknowledge it as being part of you ... use it to identify the possible pitfalls, then work to think about how you can avoid the pitfalls or how you can adjust or adapt if something goes wrong during your performance.

R – Relax ... Breathe!

6   Take deep breaths and **regulate** your breathing. Let the breathing regulate and calm your heart rate. Practice breathing when you rehearse.

B – Believe in Yourself

7   Know that your performance has the potential for being a powerful and memorable moment in your life. You will feel a huge sense of accomplishment and pride when you successfully perform your scene. Be knowledgeable about your part and prepared with your lines, and you will be ready to execute with confidence.

U – Understand the Audience

8   Understand that the audience is here to see you succeed. They know how it feels to perform, and they're not here to **sabotage** you, or poke fun at you ... they're here to learn from you, to laugh, and to be entertained.

S – Smile!

9   Changing one's physiology can impact one's mental state.

10   Before your performance, when your character allows, and immediately afterwards—smile. Soon enough, your body will tell your brain that you're happy ... and before you know it, any fear you have will melt away.

T – Talk to Yourself

11 Many people will begin telling themselves various reasons why they will not be able to perform well. Counter that.

12 Tell yourself that you will be able to do a good job and remind yourself of the reasons why you can ("I am prepared." "I will have fun." "I know my peers will laugh when ... ").

E – Enjoy Yourself

13 Get out on the stage and seek to have fun!

R – Rejoice!

14 Many people begin visualizing their worst case scenario as they ready themselves to perform.

15 Visualize yourself victorious at the end of the performance. Think of the amount of effort you will have put into preparing and think about the smiles and laughter which you will create and the skills and concepts you will have practiced and mastered.

⊘ Knowledge Quest

- What word is created when you put together the first letters in the magenta headings of the text?
- Which tip in "Fear Buster" did you find most useful? Explain why.

Working from the Text

1. **Quickwrite:** What is the biggest challenge you face when it comes to performing your comic scene?

2. Refer to the text and write your personal response to each tip in the My Notes space. Use them as a guide for a collaborative discussion.

3. Discuss the ten tips with your acting group. Which tips did you notate as applying most to you? How will you use this advice?

My Notes

4. Refer to the words and phrases you underlined and summarize the main idea of each section. Then discuss the overall controlling idea of the informational text with your acting group.

5. How is the text structured? Why do you think the author structured the text in this way? How does the structure support the controlling idea of the text?

Memorization Tips

Memorizing lines is a key part of delivering a good performance. Think about school plays you may have seen. Characters who deliver their lines clearly and without hesitation perform well.

Tip 1: Repeat, Repeat, Repeat, Repeat

Say the line over and over, but do it one word at a time, returning to the beginning of the line each time.

Example: Line 108 from Scene 5: "If we offend, it is with our good will."

"If." "If we." "If we offend." "If we offend, it." "If we offend, it is." "If we offend, it is with." "If we offend, it is with our." "If we offend, it is with our good." "If we offend, it is with our good will."

Tip 2: Recite and Erase

Write your line(s) on a whiteboard, and then practice the words.

• Recite the line.

• Erase a word or phrase, and recite the missing piece from memory.

• Repeat the process until all the words have disappeared and you are saying the line(s) from memory.

6. Discuss other tips your peers may have for memorizing lines. Then, select your hardest line to memorize and use the memorization tips to work on it.

Setting a Purpose for Reading

- Underscore the main ideas and supporting details about how to overcome stage fright.
- Circle unknown words and phrases. Try to determine the meaning of the words by using context clues, word parts, or a dictionary.

About the Author

Emma Sarran Webster is a Chicago-based freelance writer, editor, and journalist. She covers a range of lifestyle topics like home, fashion, and relationships for publications like *WIRED*, *The Muse*, *Babble*, and *Made Man*. She is currently a regular contributor to *Teen Vogue*.

Article

Adapted from

9 Public Speaking Tips to Get Over Stage Fright

by **Emma Sarran Webster**

You can do this.

1 Ugh, public speaking. That's generally how most people feel about the topic—90% of us, in fact. According to *Forbes*, only about 10 percent of the population actually loves public speaking. "The fear of public speaking really comes down to a fear of rejection, humiliation, and isolation," Josephine Lee, an entrepreneur and seasoned public speaker who placed third in the 2016 Toastmasters World Championship of Public Speaking competition, tells *Teen Vogue*.

2 The good news? Even though that fear may be biologically ingrained in us, it's one we can overcome—and it's worth it to try doing so. So how do you get to that point? Heed this expert advice.

1. Know that anyone can become a good public speaker.

3 You could just say, "I'm not good at public speaking, so I'm not going to do it," but that's neither beneficial (remember: it's tough to avoid) nor the truth. You may not have been born a proficient **orator**, but you can certainly get there. "Just like any other skill, some may naturally have more confidence than others, but anyone can learn to become a better public speaker," Josephine says. That said, it won't happen overnight. Manage your expectations, and know that your first attempt may not be the best presentation you've ever given. That's okay: Just start small and give it time.

KNOWLEDGE QUEST

Knowledge Question:
What are effective ways to overcome stage fright?

---

orator: person who is skilled in giving speeches

2. Practice, practice, practice.

4 Of course, the best way to get better is through repetition. "It's just like learning how to play the violin," Josephine says. "Practice, practice, practice!" For her part, Josephine joined Toastmasters International, a nonprofit devoted to helping members with public speaking, communication, and leadership in what she says is a "supportive setting," with chapters all over the world.

5 Outside of groups like Toastmasters, you can practice on your own in front of a mirror, as well as friends and family. Before each presentation, prepare thoroughly so you're as comfortable as possible going into it.

3. Visualize your success.

6 In whatever you do, visualizing your success beforehand can be a powerful tool. Before your next presentation, try closing your eyes and mentally taking yourself through the entire thing beforehand, like Josephine does. "The day of the speech, I start to **envision** myself onstage and the audience members," she says. "I envision how I will deliver my lines, how the audience will respond, and how I will feel giving a great speech. Doing this gives me confidence to deliver just as I envisioned."

4. Be aware of your body language.

7 The way you present yourself, physically, can have a real effect on your presentation—both in the way the audience perceives you and the way you feel about yourself. Body language and image expert Yana German points out a few key things to remember when you're standing in front of the crowd. First, stand in a solid position with your feet shoulder-width apart and facing the audience; avoid crossing your legs or standing in a way that makes you unsteady. Keep your hands in front of you and your palms up, above your waistline for as much of your speech as you can. Don't cross your arms, in front of you or behind your back, the latter of which Yana says sends the signal that you don't want to be noticed and you lack confidence.

5. Pass on the podium, and keep moving.

8 A **podium** certainly looks official, but using one may do you a disservice. "Podiums can act as barriers from the audience, not allowing you to connect with them," Yana says. Instead, pass on the podium (if you have notes, try holding small note cards so they're more manageable) and move around the stage or floor every so often. "If you are able to walk around and even make eye contact with the audience, not only does it allow you to relate more to [them], but it [also] shows you are grounded and firm in what you are saying."

6. Consider the audience.

9 Most of us go into public speaking situations focused almost completely on ourselves. But remember: Speeches are given for the benefit of the audience rather than the speaker. You're providing information, insight, or entertainment that they want (or need) to hear; so they're going to be more focused on what they're getting out of it than anything else. Keep that in mind when you're up there.

envision: make a picture of in one's head

podium: a stand at which a person gives a speech

7. Smile and make eye contact.

10 It's easy to build up the people in the audience as scary and judgmental in your mind, particularly if you've never met or talked to them. If you have time, chat with a few people before you get started so you'll have some friendly faces you can look to when you get nervous. And while you're giving your speech, smile, look at your audience, and make eye contact.

8. Project your voice.

11 Not everyone has a naturally booming voice; but Yana notes that it's important to project as much as you can (without yelling or straining your vocal chords, of course) to give yourself more presence and authority onstage—aside from the whole practical aspect of making it so the audience can hear you, of course. "The best way to project your voice is by taking relaxed deep breaths before you speak," she says.

9. Know that nerves are okay.

12 Here's the thing: Regardless of how much you practice and how many times you do this, the nerves may never *fully* go away. But that's okay. In fact, it's probably more natural than you think. "Even after 5 years of public speaking, I still get nervous," Josephine says. "But it's not about getting rid of your nerves; it's about learning how to convert [them] to excitement and using the **adrenaline** to your advantage." And *that's* where all of these tips and all of your practice come in. The more of this you do, the more likely it is that you'll be able to harness your nerves for good, rather than letting them derail you.

13 And when all else fails, remember that challenging yourself to do something you're scared of comes with its own benefits, regardless of how well you "perform." "So many of us don't pursue things that are scary to us," Josephine says. "But it is precisely at those moments that we grow the most."

Ⓞ Knowledge Quest
- What details in this article are similar to ideas in the previous one?
- What details surprised you?
- What questions will you ask yourself as you reread this article?

Returning to the Text
- Return to the text as you respond to the following questions. Use evidence from the text to support your responses.
- Write any additional questions you have about the excerpt in your Reader/Writer Notebook.

---

adrenaline: a substance in the body triggered by stress, increasing heart rate and sweating

7. According to "Fear Busters," what is the purpose of fear? What does the second article say is the cause of fear of public speaking?

_____

_____

_____

_____

8. According to the authors, why is moving around while public speaking important?

_____

_____

_____

_____

9. What is Emma Sarran Webster's opinion on public speaking? Why does she think it is worthwhile? How does she support her idea?

_____

_____

_____

_____

10. KQ How does the word *adrenaline* play a role in these two texts? Why does each author mention adrenaline?

_____

_____

_____

_____

11. KQ How does knowing the biological reasons for the fear of speaking in front of an audience help a fearful public speaker? Use evidence from the two texts to support your answer.

_____

_____

_____

_____

Knowledge Quest

Use your knowledge of the two articles to consider how you can use what you learned to overcome stage fright. Work with a partner. Together choose a word from the text and make up your own acronym that responds to the question: What are effective ways to overcome stage fright? Be sure to:

- Include a clear statement about each author's ideas.
- Explain how the details in each text support the author's central idea.
- Cite evidence from the text to support your ideas.

 INDEPENDENT READING LINK

You can continue to build your knowledge about public speaking by reading other articles and speeches at ZINC Reading Labs. Search for keywords such as *public speaking* or *speech*.

 ZINC

Working from the Text

12. Refer to the text and write your personal response to each tip in the My Notes space.

☑ **Check Your Understanding**

Describe at least three strategies you can use to overcome stage fright. How will you remind yourself of those strategies on the day of the performance?

 Gaining Perspectives

You have been reading about stage fright when communicating to a group. But communicating well with friends and family is also important. Work with a partner to look up the communication skills in the graphic organizer. Together read the articles. Then communicate about what you learned. When you are finished, summarize the articles and your conversation in your Reader/Writer Notebook.

Communication Skills	My Notes
How to Set Boundaries http://www.rookiemag.com/2018/02/how-to-set-boundaries/	
How to Give a Real Apology http://www.rookiemag.com/2018/02/give-real-apology/	
How to Ask for Help http://www.rookiemag.com/2018/04/how-to-ask-for-help/	

Working with Acting Companies and Focus Groups

Learning Strategies

Rereading
Close reading
Note-taking
Discussion Groups
Rehearsal

Learning Targets

- Use evidence to support understanding of a character.
- Synthesize information to create a performance plan.

Preview

In this activity, you will work in focus groups to deepen your understanding of your character(s) before returning to your acting company to rehearse.

Character Focus Groups

1. **Players:** Reread your lines, using the graphic organizer to guide a close reading and analysis of your character.

   Meet in a focus group whose members are all acting as the same character, and work collaboratively to interpret what the lines reveal about your character. Take turns sharing your individual analysis, and add new insights to the graphic organizer.

I am playing:

Aspects of Characterization	Detail from Text	Interpretation *What does this reveal about the character?*
Appearance		
Actions		
Words		

Aspects of Characterization	Detail from Text	Interpretation *What does this reveal about the character?*
Thoughts/Feelings/Motivations		
Others' Reactions		
Comedic Actions/Words		

2. Take turns reading your character's lines. Practice making the analysis of your character come to life through your tone, inflection, facial expression, and gestures.

3. **Directors:** Select key action sequences and consider possible stage directions to determine how these scenes might be performed onstage.

Key Action Sequences	Stage Directions and Movement Onstage	What This Reveals About the Overall Scene (Comedic Effect)
Thoughts/Feelings/Motivations		
Others' Reactions		
Comedic Actions/Words		

Acting Groups

4. Return to your acting group and share your analysis in the order that your character speaks during your scene. Discuss the implications of each character's words and actions.

5. Develop a detailed performance plan by consulting the Scoring Guide.

   After reviewing the Scoring Guide criteria, I need to ...

6. Work with your acting company to complete this chart, and outline your performance plan.

Performance Plan				
Character	Played By	Contribution to Set Design	Prop(s)	Costume

7. Individually, synthesize all the details of your performance plan.

Element of Performance	Ideas for Character	Explanation
Blocking		
Movements Enter/Exit		
Gestures		
Facial Expression(s)		
Emotion		
Comedic Emphasis		

8. Complete this section if you are the director. Share your plan with the members of your acting company.

We want to create a _____ mood. To accomplish this goal, we will ...

I will introduce the acting company and scene by ...

The scene will end when _____ so the audience will be left with a feeling of ...

We will focus on the comic effects listed below (create the list) to ensure that ...

9. Use your performance plan to rehearse your scene to accurately portray your character and achieve your intended comic effect. Be sure to focus on the following:
- tone and inflection
- correct pronunciation of words
- gestures and movement

☑ Check Your Understanding

Reflect on the process of planning for and rehearsing your scene. Think about what went well and what you will want to improve in future performances. In your Reader/Writer Notebook, write one improvement you would like to make on your own part, and one suggestion for improvement you can offer the group as a whole.

Same Text, Different Text

Learning Strategies

Discussion Groups
Note-taking
Brainstorming
Rehearsal

Learning Targets

- Compare and contrast scenes in different media.
- Evaluate the effects of directors' choices in film.

Preview

In this activity, you will learn why a director might change a script and how a director's choices create a comedic effect.

Viewing Shakespeare on Film

1. Unlike comparing novels to film versions, turning a play script into a movie allows the viewer to make a close comparison. Think about the extent to which the film scripts adhere to or stray from the original Shakespeare scene and how the actors make the lines come alive through their voices, expressions, and movements.

2. As you view the film or a scene from *A Midsummer Night's Dream*, take notes on what you observe about your assigned scene. Use the graphic organizer for either "Actors" or "Directors."

Actors:

Version of *A Midsummer Night's Dream* (Director/Year)	Physical Gestures and Movements	Costume and Makeup	Interpretive Choices in the Delivery of Lines
Film 1:			
Film 2:			

Actors' Questions

3. To what extent do these films stay faithful to or depart from the original script? Why might these particular choices have been made, and what effect do these choices have on the viewers' understanding of the scene?

4. How do your character's gestures, movements, and language achieve a comical effect? What elements of humor did you see?

Directors:

Version of *A Midsummer Night's Dream* (Director/Year)	Placement of Actors in Relationship to Props, Scenery, Each Other	Music or Other Sound Effects	Set Design, Lighting, Props
Film 1:			
Film 2:			

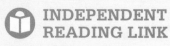

INDEPENDENT READING LINK

Read and Research

See if there is a modern-day retelling of the play you are reading independently. Watch it and fill out a similar graphic organizer for it.

My Notes

Directors' Questions

5. How has the director stayed faithful to or departed from the scene as written by Shakespeare? What effects do certain staging and technical choices have on the viewers' understanding of the scene?

6. How do the staging, set design, lighting, sound, and props achieve a comical effect? What elements of humor did you see?

☑ Check Your Understanding

Why would a film director choose to portray a scene differently than the way the author wrote it? What effects might the director be trying to achieve?

Directors' Questions

7. Collaborative Discussion: Now that you have seen the play in its entirety, analyze how Shakespeare uses the structure of the play, acts and scenes, to develop dramatic action.

Dress Rehearsal

Learning Targets

- Demonstrate understanding of the characteristics of drama by rehearsing a dramatic scene.
- Reflect on performance strengths and challenges and use this information to refine a performance.

Preview

In this activity, you will participate in a dress rehearsal and reflect on your performance.

My Notes

Dress Rehearsal

1. Participate in a dress rehearsal in which you perform your scene in front of another group. This rehearsal will help you determine what works well in your performance and what does not.

2. When you are in the role of a small group audience, use the Scoring Guide criteria to provide constructive feedback to enable the acting company to adjust its performance.

3. Consider using these questions to start your feedback conversation:

- What elements of humor do you think you were most successful at using? Least successful?
- Can you explain why you made the choice to ...
- When did you feel the audience was most with you?
- When did you feel the audience was least connected to your performance?
- Did you ever have to adapt or adjust differently than you had planned? Explain. How did it work out?

Dress Rehearsal Reflection

4. What went well? What will you want to replicate in your performance?

5. What is the most significant thing you are going to do differently? How will you prepare?

🎭 Independent Reading Checkpoint

Write a paragraph in which you analyze how the playwright of the play you have been reading independently develops dramatic action through the use of acts and scenes.

Performing Shakespearean Comedy

 ASSIGNMENT

Present your assigned scene in front of your peers to demonstrate your understanding of Shakespeare's text, elements of comedy, and performance.

Planning: As an acting company, prepare to perform your scene.	▪ How will you collaborate as a group on a performance plan that demonstrates an understanding of Shakespeare's humor? ▪ Does each member of the acting company understand the scene's meaning, as well as his or her role? ▪ What elements of humor will your company focus on in performance? ▪ How will you emphasize these elements through the delivery of lines, characterization, gestures, movements, props, and/or setting? ▪ How will you mark your script to help you pronounce words correctly, emphasize words appropriately, and remember your lines and deliver them smoothly? ▪ How will you use blocking and movement to interact onstage and emphasize elements of humor?
Rehearsing: Rehearse and revise your performance with your acting company.	▪ How will you show how characters, conflicts, and events contribute to a universal idea? ▪ How will you introduce and conclude the scene? ▪ How can the Scoring Guide help you evaluate how well your performance meets the requirements of the assignment? ▪ How can you give and receive feedback about your use of eye contact, volume, and inflection in order to improve your own and others' performances?
Performing and Listening: Perform your scene and participate as an audience member.	▪ How will you convey ideas and emotions through your performance? ▪ How will you take notes on the elements of humor emphasized in other performances?

Reflection

After completing this Embedded Assessment, think about how you went about accomplishing this task, and respond to the following:

- How did different performers emphasize the elements of humor in their scenes?
- Which performances were successful in eliciting a humorous response from the audience, and what made them effective?

SCORING GUIDE

Scoring Criteria	Exemplary	Proficient	Emerging	Incomplete
Ideas	The performance • demonstrates a deep understanding of Shakespeare's intended humor • uses a variety of effective performance elements (staging, set design, lighting, sound, props) for comic effect • shows evidence of extensive planning, rehearsal, and reflection.	The performance • demonstrates an adequate understanding of Shakespeare's intended humor • uses some performance elements (staging, set design, lighting, sound, props) for comic effect • shows evidence of sufficient planning, rehearsal, and reflection.	The performance • demonstrates a partial or uneven understanding of Shakespeare's intended humor • uses disconnected or basic performance elements (staging, set design, lighting, sound, props) • shows evidence of ineffective or insufficient planning, rehearsal, and reflection.	The performance • demonstrates little or no understanding of Shakespeare's intended humor • lacks performance elements • does not show evidence of planning, rehearsal, and reflection.
Structure	The performance • demonstrates extensive evidence of collaboration • provides context in an engaging introduction • communicates a satisfying ending to the audience.	The performance • demonstrates adequate evidence of collaboration • provides context in an appropriate introduction • communicates an ending to the audience.	The performance • demonstrates uneven or ineffective collaboration • provides a partial or weak introduction • communicates an abrupt or illogical ending to the audience.	The performance • demonstrates a failure to collaborate • provides no introduction • does not communicate an ending to the audience.
Use of Language	The performer • makes effective interpretive choices to deliver lines for comic effect and to convey meaning (including tone, pronunciation, inflection, facial expressions, gestures, movement, and blocking) • uses punctuation cues consistently and naturally to inform vocal delivery • memorizes lines fully and accurately.	The performer • makes appropriate interpretive choices to deliver lines for comic effect and to convey meaning (including tone, pronunciation, inflection, facial expressions, gestures, movement, and blocking) • uses some punctuation cues to inform vocal delivery • demonstrates an adequate ability to memorize lines.	The performer • makes undeveloped or inappropriate interpretive choices to deliver lines (including tone, pronunciation, inflection, facial expressions, gestures, movement, and blocking) • uses punctuation cues unevenly or inconsistently • demonstrates insufficient ability to memorize lines.	The performer • makes undeveloped or inappropriate interpretive choices to deliver lines • does not recognize punctuation cues or use them incorrectly • does not have any lines memorized.

Resources

Independent Reading

Learning Strategies

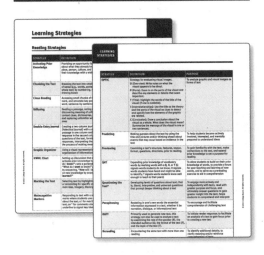

Graphic Organizers

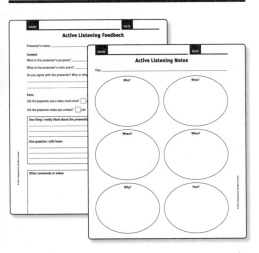

English-Spanish Glossary

Index of Skills

Index of Authors and Titles

Suggestions for Independent Reading

This list, divided into the categories of **Literature** and **Nonfiction/Informational Text**, comprises titles related to the themes and content of the unit. For your independent reading, you can select from this wide array of titles, which have been chosen based on complexity and interest. You can do your own research and select titles that intrigue you.

Unit 1 Independent Reading List: The Challenge of Heroism

Literature		
Author	Title	Lexile
Alvarez, Julia	*Antes de ser libres*	N/A
Alvarez, Julia	*Before We Were Free*	890L
Anderson, Laurie Halse	*Fever 1793*	580L
Avi	*Crispin: The Cross of Lead*	780L
Butler, Octavia	*The Parable of the Sower*	710L
Coelho, Paul	*The Alchemist*	910L
Crew, Linda	*Children of the River*	700L
Crutcher, Chris	*Whale Talk*	1000L
Dashner, James	*The Maze Runner*	770L
Dashner, James	*Maze Runner: Correr o morir*	HL710L
Hinton, S.E.	*The Outsiders*	750L
Johnston, E.K.	*The Story of Owen: Dragon Slayer of Trondheim*	1020L
Jones, Diana Wynne	*Howl's Moving Castle*	800L
L'Engle, Madeline	*A Wrinkle in Time*	740L
Lewis, C.S.	*The Chronicles of Narnia* series	N/A
Lewis, Richard	*The Killing Sea*	760L
Lupica, Mike	*Hero*	730L
O'Connor, George	*Athena: Grey-Eyed Goddess*	720L
Paolini, Christopher	*Eragon*	710L
Park, Linda Sue	*When My Name Was Keoko*	610L
Paulsen, Gary	*Soldier's Heart*	1000L
Pierce, Tamora	*Alanna: The First Adventure*	690L
Riordan, Rick	*Heroes of Olympus* series	N/A
Robbins, Trina	*Freedom Songs: A Tale of the Underground Railroad*	580L
Robbins, Trina	*Lily Renee, Escape Artist: From Holocaust Survivor to Comic Book Pioneer*	510L
Selznick, Brian	*The Invention of Hugo Cabret* (Graphic Novel)	820L
Sepetys, Ruta	*Between Shades of Gray*	490L
Storrie, Paul	*Hercules: The 12 Labors*	N/A
White, T.H.	*The Once and Future King*	1080L

Nonfiction/Informational Text		
Author	**Title**	**Lexile**
Bardhan-Quallen, Sudipta	*Up-Close: Jane Goodall*	1140L
Beales, Melba Pattilo	*Warriors Don't Cry*	1000L
Bradley, James	*Flags of Our Fathers*	950L
Chin-Lee, Cynthia	*Akira to Zoltan: 26 Men Who Changed the World*	1060L
Chin-Lee, Cynthia	*Amelia to Zora: 26 Women Who Changed the World*	1040L
Collier, Peter	*Choosing Courage: Inspiring Stories of What It Means to Be a Hero*	1150L
Cooper, Michael L	*Fighting for Honor: Japanese Americans and World War II*	1040L
Freedman, Russell	*Kids at Work: Lewis Hine and the Crusade Against Child Labor*	1140L
Ganges, Montse	*Viajeros intrépidos*	970L
Hillenbrand, Laura	*Unbroken: An Olympian's Journey from Airman to Castaway to Captive*	850L
Hurley, Michael	*World's Greatest Olympians*	960L
Krull, Kathleen	*Lives of Extraordinary Women: Rulers, Rebels (and What the Neighbors Thought)*	1150L
Meltzer, Milton	*Lincoln: In His Own Words*	1140L
Myers, Walter Dean	*The Greatest: Muhammad Ali*	1030L
Peet, Mal	*The Keeper*	780L
Wells, Susan	*Amelia Earhart: The Thrill of It All*	N/A
Yousafzai, Malala	*I Am Malala*	830L

Unit 2 Independent Reading List: The Challenge of Utopia

Literature		
Author	**Title**	**Lexile**
Ada, Alma	*Love, Amalia*	940L
Asimov, Isaac	*I, Robot*	820L
Bradbury, Ray	*The Martian Chronicles: Something Wicked This Way Comes*	820L
Budhos, Marina	*Ask Me No Questions*	790L
Burg, Ann	*All the Broken Pieces*	680L
Borges, Jorge Luis	*El aleph*	940L
Carlson, Lori Marie	*Red Hot Salsa*	N/A
Cisneros, Sandra	*The House on Mango Street*	870L
Collins, Suzanne	*The Hunger Games*	810L
Dayton, Arwen Elys	*Seeker*	800L
Farmer, Nancy	*The House of the Scorpion*	660L
Frank, Pat	*Alas, Babylon*	870L
Heinlein, Robert	*Stranger in a Strange Land*	940L
Huxley, Aldous	*Brave New World*	870L
LeGuin, Ursula	*The Left Hand of Darkness*	970L
Lu, Marie	*Legend*	710L
Meyer, Marissa	*Cinder*	790L
More, Thomas	*Utopia*	1370L
Orwell, George	*1984*	1090L
Orwell, George	*Animal Farm*	1170L
Reinhardt, Dana	*A Brief Chapter in My Impossible Life*	910L
Roth, Veronica	*Divergent*	700L
Salisbury, Graham	*House of the Red Fish*	610L
Verne, Jules	*Twenty Thousand Leagues Under the Sea*	1030L
Wells, H.G.	*The Time Machine*	1070L
Wells, H.G.	*The War of the Worlds*	1040L
Westerfield, Scott	*Uglies*	770L
Yancey, Rick	*The Fifth Wave*	N/A
Yang, Dori Jones	*Daughter of Xanadu*	780L

Nonfiction/Informational Text

Author	Title	Lexile
Bausum, Ann	Denied, Detained, Deported: Stories from the Dark Side of American Immigration	1170L
Carson, Rachel	Silent Spring	1340L
Carson, Rachel	The Sea Around Us	1340L
Corey, Shana	Es horado actuar: El gran discurso de John F. Kennedy	870L
D'Aluisio, Faith and Peter Menzel	What the World Eats	1150L
Engle, Margarita	The Lightening Dreamer: Cuba's Greatest Abolitionists	N/A
Fallon, Michael	Self-Driving Cars	1200L
Gore, Al	Global Warming Is an Immediate Crisis	N/A
Hatkoff, Juliana and Isabella Hatkoff	Winter's Tail: How One Little Dolphin Learned to Swim Again	930L
Hesse, Karen	Aleutian Sparrow	N/A
Hoose, Philip	The Race to Save the Lord God Bird	1150L
Kalan, Robert	We Are Not Beasts of Burden	1150L
Lasky, Kathryn	John Muir: America's First Environmentalist	1050L
Markle, Sandra	How Many Baby Pandas?	N/A
Pollan, Michael	In Defense of Food: An Eater's Manifesto	1390L
Schlosser, Eric	Fast Food Nation	1240L
Scholsser, Eric and Wilson, Charles,	Chew on This: Everything You Don't Want to Know About Fast Food	1110L
Sivertsen, Linda and Josh Sivertsen	Generation Green: The Ultimate Teen Guide to Living an Eco-Friendly Life	N/A
Somervill, Barbara	Animal Survivors of the Wetlands	1060L
Stearman, Kaye	Taking Action Against Homelessness	N/A
Waters, Alice	Edible Schoolyard: A Universal Idea	N/A
Welsbacher, Anne	Earth-Friendly Design	N/A

Unit 3 Independent Reading List: The Challenge to Make a Difference

Literature		
Author	**Title**	**Lexile**
Adlington, L. J.	The Diary of Pelly D.	770L
Arato, Rona	The Last Train: A Holocaust Story	580L
Bergman, Tamar	Along the Tracks	650L
Boom, Corrie Ten	The Hiding Place	900L
Boyne, John	El nino con el pijama de rayas	880L
Bradley, Kimberly Brubaker	La guerra que salvó mi vida	580L
Chotjewitz, David	Daniel Half Human: And the Good Nazi	740L
Drucker, Malka and Michael Halperin	Jacob's Rescue	680L
Gratz, Alan and Gruener, Ruth	Prisoner B-3087	760L
Hesse, Karen	The Cats in Krasinski Square	990L
Hoestlandt, Jo	Star of Fear, Star of Hope	490L
Isaacs, Anne	Torn Thread	880L
Lowry, Lois	Number the Stars	670L
Matas, Carol	Daniel's Story	720L
Matas, Carol	The Garden	810L
Mazer, Norma Fox	Good Night, Maman	510L
Meminger, Neesha	Shine, Coconut Moon	740L
Morpurgo, Michael	Waiting for Anya	770L
Na, An	The Fold	700L
Napoli, Donna Jo	Stones in Water	630L
Nye, Naomi Shihab	19 Varieties of Gazelle: Poems of the Middle East	970L
Orgel, Doris	The Devil in Vienna	700L
Orlev, Uri	Run, Boy, Run	570L
Orlev, Uri	The Island on Bird Street	690L
Peacock, Carol Antoinette	Red Thread Sisters	700L
Polacco, Patricia	The Butterfly	430L
Radin, Ruth Yaffe	Escape to the Forest: Based on a True Story of the Holocaust	660L
Spinelli, Jerry	Milkweed	510L
Venkatraman, Padma	Climbing the Stairs	750L
Yep, Laurence	Golden Mountain Chronicles: Child of the Owl	920L
Yolen, Jane	The Devil's Arithmetic	730L
Zullo, Allan	We Fought Back: Teen Resisters of the Holocaust	1070L
Zusak, Markus	The Book Thief	730L

Nonfiction/Informational Text		
Author	Title	Lexile
Bachrach, Susan D.	*Tell Them We Remember: The Story of the Holocaust*	1190L
Bitton-Jackson, Livia	*I Have Lived a Thousand Years: Growing Up in the Holocaust*	720L
Boas, Jacob	*We Are Witnesses: Five Diaries of Teenagers Who Died in the Holocaust*	970L
Deedy, Carmen Agra	*The Yellow Star: The Legend of King Christian X of Denmark*	550L
Frank, Anne	*The Diary of a Young Girl*	1080L
Freedman, Russell	*Kids at Work: Lewis Hine and the Crusade Against Child Labor*	1140L
Gregory, Josh	*Cesar Chavez*	930L
Herman, Gail	*Who Was Jackie Robinson?*	670L
Hoose, Philip	*The Race to Save the Lord God Bird*	1150L
Lobel, Anita	*No Pretty Pictures: A Child of War*	750L
Meltzer, Milton	*Rescue: The Story of How Gentiles Saved Jews in the Holocaust*	1020L
Millman, Isaac	*Hidden Child*	860L
Nir, Yehuda	*The Lost Childhood: A World War II Memoir*	920L
Opdyke, Irene Gut	*In My Hands: Memories of a Holocaust Rescuer*	890L
Perl, Lila and Lazan, Marion Blumenthal	*Four Perfect Pebbles: A Holocaust Story*	1080L
Sender, Ruth Minsky	*The Cage*	500L
Siegal, Aranka	*Upon the Head of the Goat: A Childhood in Hungary 1939–1944*	830L
Swanson, Jennifer	*Environmental Activist Wangari Maathai*	880L
Thompson, Laurie Ann	*Be a Changemaker: How to Start Something That Matters*	1130L
van de Rol, Rudd and Verhoeven, Rian	*Anne Frank: Beyond the Diary: A Photographic Remembrance*	1030L
Warren, Andrea	*Charles Dickens and the Street Children of London*	1160L
Wiesel, Elie	*Night*	570L

Unit 4 Independent Reading List: The Challenge of Comedy

Literature

Author	Title	Lexile
Adams, Douglas	*The Hitchhiker's Guide to the Galaxy*	1000L
Alexie, Sherman	*The Absolutely True Diary of a Part-Time Indian*	600L
Allison, Jennifer	*Gilda Joyce, Psychic Investigator: A Mystery*	1000L
Cofer, Judith Ortiz	*Una isla como tú*	830L
Dahl, Roald	*The Wonderful Story of Henry Sugar: And Six More*	850L
Eliott, Rob	*Laugh Out Loud Jokes for Kids*	N/A
Healey, Christopher	*Hero's Guide to Saving Your Kingdom Series*	750L
Kindl, Patrice	*Keeping the Castle*	1050L
Kinney, Jeff	*Diary of a Wimpy Kid*	900L
Kinney, Jeff	*El Diario de Greg, un renacuajo*	880L
Kipling, Rudyard	*Just So Stories*	1190L
Korman, Gordon	*Don't Care High*	920L
Leavitt, Lindsey	*Princess for Hire*	670L
McAlpine, Gordon	*The Tell-Tale Start: The Misadventures of Edgar & Allan Poe (series)*	850L
McCloskey, Robert	*Homer Price*	1000L
Paulsen, Gary	*Molly McGinty Has a Really Good Day*	960L
Pilkey, Dav	*Captain Underpants Collection*	800L
Scieszka, Jon	*Frank Einstein and the Antimatter Motor*	730L
Snicket, Lemony	*The Bad Beginning*	1010L
Snicket, Lemony	*The Grim Grotto*	1120L
Sparknotes	*No Fear Shakespeare Graphic Novels*	N/A
Swift, Jonathan	*A Modest Proposal*	1520L
Twain, Mark	*The Celebrated Jumping Frog and Other Stories*	1000L
Vonnegut, Kurt	*Cat's Cradle*	790L

Nonfiction/Informational Text

Author	Title	Lexile
Cameron, W. Bruce	*A Dog's Purpose*	970L
Crutcher, Chris	*King of the Mild Frontier: An Ill-Advised Autobiography*	1180L
Dahl, Roald	*Boy*	1090L
Fey, Tina	*Bossypants*	950L
Jackson, Donna	*What's So Funny? Making Sense of Humor*	1060L
Kimmel, Haven	*A Girl Named Zippy*	1010L
Marcus, Leonard S	*Funny Business*	920L
Martin, Steve	*Born Standing Up: A Comic's Life*	N/A
Mayfield, Katherine	*Acting A to Z: The Young Person's Guide to a Stage or Screen Career*	1030L
Wilson, Daniel H.	*How to Survive a Robot Uprising*	1140L

Independent Reading Log

Directions: This log is a place to record your progress and thinking about your independent reading during each unit. Add your log pages to your Reader/Writer Notebook or keep them as a separate place to record your reading insights.

Unit _____

Independent Reading Title _____

Author(s) _____ Text Type _____

Pages read: from _____ to _____

_____

_____

_____

_____

_____

_____

Independent Reading Title _____

Author(s) _____ Text Type _____

Pages read: from _____ to _____

_____

_____

_____

_____

_____

_____

_____

Independent Reading Title _____

Author(s) _____ Text Type _____

Pages read: from _____ to _____

_____

_____

_____

_____

_____

_____

_____

Unit _____

Independent Reading Title _____

Author(s) _____ Text Type _____

Pages read: from _____ to _____

_____

_____

_____

_____

Independent Reading Title _____

Author(s) _____ Text Type _____

Pages read: from _____ to _____

_____

_____

_____

_____

Independent Reading Title _____

Author(s) _____ Text Type _____

Pages read: from _____ to _____

_____

_____

_____

_____

_____

Independent Reading Title _____

Author(s) _____ Text Type _____

Pages read: from _____ to _____

_____

_____

_____

_____

Learning Strategies

Reading Strategies

STRATEGY	DEFINITION	PURPOSE
Activating Prior Knowledge	Providing an opportunity for students to think about what they already know about a concept, place, person, culture, and so on, and share their knowledge with a wider audience	To prepare students to encounter new concepts, places, persons, cultures, and so on, prior to reading a text; an Anticipation Guide and a Quickwrite can be used to activate and assess prior knowledge
Chunking the Text	Breaking the text into smaller, manageable units of sense (e.g., words, sentences, paragraphs, whole text) by numbering, separating phrases, drawing boxes	To reduce the intimidation factor when encountering long words, sentences, or whole texts; to increase comprehension of difficult or challenging text
Close Reading	Accessing small chunks of text to read, reread, mark, and annotate key passages, word-for-word, sentence-by-sentence, and line-by-line	To develop comprehensive understanding by engaging in one or more focused readings of a text
Diffusing	Reading a passage, noting unfamiliar words, discovering meaning of unfamiliar words using context clues, dictionaries, and/or thesauruses, and replacing unfamiliar words with familiar ones	To facilitate a close reading of text, the use of resources, an understanding of synonyms, and increased comprehension of text
Double-Entry Journal	Creating a two-column journal (also called Dialectical Journal) with a student-selected passage in one column and the student's response in the second column (e.g., asking questions of the text, forming personal responses, interpreting the text, reflecting on the process of making meaning of the text)	To assist in note-taking and organizing key textual elements and responses noted during reading in order to generate textual support that can be incorporated into a piece of writing at a later time
Graphic Organizer	Using a visual representation for the organization of information from the text	To facilitate increased comprehension and discussion
KWHL Chart	Setting up discussion that allows students to activate prior knowledge by answering, "What do I **know**?"; sets a purpose by answering, "What do I **want** to know?"; helps preview a task by answering, **"How** will I learn it?"; and reflects on new knowledge by answering, "What have I **learned**?"	To organize thinking, access prior knowledge, and reflect on learning to increase comprehension and engagement
Marking the Text	Selecting text by highlighting, underlining, and/or annotating for specific components, such as main idea, imagery, literary devices, and so on	To focus reading for specific purposes, such as author's craft, and to organize information from selections; to facilitate reexamination of a text
Metacognitive Markers	Responding to text with a system of cueing marks where students use a ? for questions about the text; a ! for reactions related to the text; an * for comments about the text; and an underline to signal key ideas	To track responses to texts and use those responses as a point of departure for talking or writing about texts

STRATEGY	DEFINITION	PURPOSE
OPTIC	Strategy for evaluating visual images. **O** (Overview): Write notes on what the visual appears to be about. **P** (Parts): Zoom in on the parts of the visual and describe any elements or details that seem important. **T** (Title): Highlight the words of the title of the visual (if one is available). **I** (Interrelationships): Use the title as the theory and the parts of the visual as clues to detect and specify how the elements of the graphic are related. **C** (Conclusion); Draw a conclusion about the visual as a whole. What does the visual mean? Summarize the message of the visual in one or two sentences.	To analyze graphic and visual images as forms of text
Predicting	Making guesses about the text by using the title and pictures and/or thinking ahead about events that may occur based on evidence in the text	To help students become actively involved, interested, and mentally prepared to understand ideas
Previewing	Examining a text's structure, features, layout, format, questions, directions, prior to reading	To gain familiarity with the text, make connections to the text, and extend prior knowledge to set a purpose for reading
QHT	Expanding prior knowledge of vocabulary words by marking words with a **Q**, **H**, or **T** (Q signals words students do not know; H signals words students have heard and might be able to identify; T signals words students know well enough to teach to their peers)	To allow students to build on their prior knowledge of words, to provide a forum for peer teaching and learning of new words, and to serve as a prereading exercise to aid in comprehension
Questioning the Text*	Developing levels of questions about text; that is, literal, interpretive, and universal questions that prompt deeper thinking about a text	To engage more actively and independently with texts, read with greater purpose and focus, and ultimately answer questions to gain greater insight into the text; helps students to comprehend and interpret
Paraphrasing	Restating in one's own words the essential information expressed in a text, whether it be narration, dialogue, or informational text	To encourage and facilitate comprehension of challenging text
RAFT	Primarily used to generate new text, this strategy can also be used to analyze a text by examining the role of the speaker (R), the intended audience (A), the format of the text (F), and the topic of the text (T).	To initiate reader response; to facilitate an analysis of a text to gain focus prior to creating a new text
Rereading	Encountering the same text with more than one reading	To identify additional details; to clarify meaning and/or reinforce comprehension of texts

STRATEGY	DEFINITION	PURPOSE
SIFT*	Analyzing a fictional text by examining stylistic elements, especially symbol, imagery, and figures of speech in order to show how all work together to reveal tone and theme	To focus and facilitate an analysis of a fictional text by examining the title and text for symbolism, identifying images and sensory details, analyzing figurative language and identifying how all these elements reveal tone and theme
Skimming/Scanning	Skimming by rapid or superficial reading of a text to form an overall impression or to obtain a general understanding of the material; scanning focuses on key words, phrases, or specific details and provides speedy recognition of information	To quickly form an overall impression prior to an in-depth study of a text; to answer specific questions or quickly locate targeted information or detail in a text
SMELL*	Analyzing a persuasive speech or essay by asking five essential questions: • **S**ender-receiver relationship—What is the sender-receiver relationship? Who are the images and language meant to attract? Describe the speaker of the text. • **M**essage—What is the message? Summarize the statement made in the text. • **E**motional Strategies—What is the desired effect? • **L**ogical Strategies—What logic is operating? How does it (or its absence) affect the message? Consider the logic of the images as well as the words. • **L**anguage—What does the language of the text describe? How does it affect the meaning and effectiveness of the writing? Consider the language of the images as well as the words.	To analyze a persuasive speech or essay by focusing on five essential questions
SOAPSTone*	Analyzing text by discussing and identifying **S**peaker, **O**ccasion, **A**udience, **P**urpose, **S**ubject, and **Tone**	To facilitate the analysis of specific elements of nonfiction, literary, and informational texts, and show the relationship among the elements to an understanding of the whole
Summarizing	Giving a brief statement of the main points or essential information expressed in a text, whether it be narration, dialogue, or informational text	To facilitate comprehension and recall of a text
Think Aloud	Talking through a difficult passage or task by using a form of metacognition whereby the reader expresses how he/she has made sense of the text	To reflect on how readers make meaning of challenging texts and to facilitate discussion

STRATEGY	DEFINITION	PURPOSE
TP-CASTT*	Analyzing a poetic text by identifying and discussing **T**itle, **P**araphrase, **C**onnotation, **A**ttitude, **S**hift, **T**heme, and **T**itle again	To facilitate the analysis of specific elements of a literary text, especially poetry. To show how the elements work together to create meaning
Visualizing	Forming a picture (mentally and/or literally) while reading a text	To increase reading comprehension and promote active engagement with text
Word Maps	Using a clearly defined graphic organizer such as concept circles or word webs to identify and reinforce word meanings	To provide a visual tool for identifying and remembering multiple aspects of words and word meanings

Writing Strategies

STRATEGY	DEFINITION	PURPOSE
Adding	Making conscious choices to enhance a text by adding additional words, phrases, sentences, or ideas	To refine and clarify the writer's thoughts during revision and/or drafting
Brainstorming	Using a flexible but deliberate process of listing multiple ideas in a short period of time without excluding any idea from the preliminary list	To generate ideas, concepts, or key words that provide a focus and/or establish organization as part of the prewriting or revision process
Deleting	Providing clarity and cohesiveness for a text by eliminating words, phrases, sentences, or ideas	To refine and clarify the writer's thoughts during revision and/or drafting
Drafting	Composing a text in its initial form	To incorporate brainstormed or initial ideas into a written format
Freewriting	Writing freely without constraints in order to capture thinking and convey the writer's purpose	To refine and clarify the writer's thoughts, spark new ideas, and/or generate content during revision and/or drafting
Generating Questions	Clarifying and developing ideas by asking questions of the draft. May be part of self-editing or peer editing	To clarify and develop ideas in a draft; used during drafting and as part of writer response
Graphic Organizer	Organizing ideas and information visually (e.g., Venn diagrams, flowcharts, cluster maps)	To provide a visual system for organizing multiple ideas, details, and/or textual support to be included in a piece of writing
Looping	After freewriting, one section of a text is circled to promote elaboration or the generation of new ideas for that section. This process is repeated to further develop ideas from the newly generated segments.	To refine and clarify the writer's thoughts, spark new ideas, and/or generate new content during revision and/or drafting

STRATEGY	DEFINITION	PURPOSE
Mapping	Creating a graphic organizer that serves as a visual representation of the organizational plan for a written text	To generate ideas, concepts, or key words that provide a focus and/or establish organization during the prewriting, drafting, or revision process
Marking the Draft	Interacting with the draft version of a piece of writing by highlighting, underlining, color-coding, and annotating to indicate revision ideas	To encourage focused, reflective thinking about revising drafts
Note-taking	Making notes about ideas in response to text or discussions; one form is the double-entry journal in which textual evidence is recorded on the left side and personal commentary about the meaning of the evidence on the other side	To assist in organizing key textual elements and responses noted during reading in order to generate textual support that can be incorporated into a piece of writing at a later time. Note-taking is also a reading and listening strategy.
Outlining	Using a system of numerals and letters in order to identify topics and supporting details and ensure an appropriate balance of ideas	To generate ideas, concepts, or key words that provide a focus and/or establish organization prior to writing an initial draft and/or during the revision process
Quickwrite	Writing for a short, specific amount of time in response to a prompt provided	To generate multiple ideas in a quick fashion that could be turned into longer pieces of writing at a later time (may be considered as part of the drafting process)
RAFT	Generating a new text and/or transforming a text by identifying and manipulating its component parts of Role, Audience, Format, and Topic	To generate a new text by identifying the main elements of a text during the prewriting and drafting stages of the writing process
Rearranging	Selecting components of a text and moving them to another place within the text and/or modifying the order in which the author's ideas are presented	To refine and clarify the writer's thoughts during revision and/or drafting
Self-Editing/Peer Editing	Working individually or with a partner to examine a text closely in order to identify areas that might need to be corrected for grammar, punctuation, spelling	To provide a systematic process for editing a written text to ensure correctness of identified components such as conventions of standard English
Sharing and Responding	Communicating with another person or a small group of peers who respond to a piece of writing as focused readers (not necessarily as evaluators)	To make suggestions for improvement to the work of others and/or to receive appropriate and relevant feedback on the writer's own work, used during the drafting and revision process
Sketching	Drawing or sketching ideas or ordering of ideas (includes storyboarding, visualizing)	To generate and/or clarify ideas by visualizing them (may be part of prewriting)
Substituting/ Replacing	Replacing original words or phrases in a text with new words or phrases that achieve the desired effect	To refine and clarify the writer's thoughts during revision and/or drafting

STRATEGY	DEFINITION	PURPOSE
TWIST*	Arriving at a thesis statement that incorporates the following literary elements: **T**one, **W**ord choice (diction), **I**magery, **S**tyle, and **T**heme	To craft an interpretive thesis in response to a prompt about a text
Webbing	Developing a graphic organizer that consists of a series of circles connected with lines to indicate relationships among ideas	To generate ideas, concepts, or key words that provide a focus and/or establish organization prior to writing an initial draft and/or during the revision process
Writer's Checklist	Using a co-constructed checklist (that could be written on a bookmark and/or displayed on the wall) in order to look for specific features of a writing text and check for accuracy	To focus on key areas of the writing process so that the writer can effectively revise a draft and correct mistakes
Writing Groups	A type of discussion group devoted to sharing and responding to student work	To facilitate a collaborative approach to generating ideas for and revising writing

Speaking and Listening Strategies

STRATEGY	DEFINITION	PURPOSE
Choral Reading	Reading text lines aloud in student groups and/or individually to present an interpretation	To develop fluency; differentiate between the reading of statements and questions; practice phrasing, pacing, and reading dialogue; show how a character's emotions are captured through vocal stress and intonation
Note-taking	Creating a record of information while listening to a speaker or reading a text	To facilitate active listening or close reading; to record and organize ideas that assist in processing information
Oral Reading	Reading aloud one's own text or the texts of others (e.g., echo reading, choral reading, paired readings)	To share one's own work or the work of others; build fluency and increase confidence in presenting to a group
Rehearsal	Encouraging multiple practices of a piece of text prior to a performance	To provide students with an opportunity to clarify the meaning of a text prior to a performance as they refine the use of dramatic conventions (e.g., gestures, vocal interpretations, facial expressions)
Role-Playing	Assuming the role or persona of a character	To develop the voice, emotions, and mannerisms of a character to facilitate improved comprehension of a text

Collaborative Strategies

STRATEGY	DEFINITION	PURPOSE
Discussion Groups	Engaging in an interactive, small-group discussion, often with an assigned role; to consider a topic, text, or question	To gain new understanding of or insight into a text from multiple perspectives
Think-Pair-Share	Pairing with a peer to share ideas before sharing ideas and discussion with a larger group	To construct meaning about a topic or question; to test thinking in relation to the ideas of others; to prepare for a discussion with a larger group

Graphic Organizer Directory

Contents

Active Listening Feedback

Presenter's name: _____

Content

What is the presenter's purpose? _____

What is the presenter's main point? _____

Do you agree with the presenter? Why or why not? _____

_____

_____

Form

Did the presenter use a clear, loud voice? ☐ yes ☐ no

Did the presenter make eye contact? ☐ yes ☐ no

One thing I really liked about the presentation:
_____
_____
_____
One question I still have:
_____
_____
_____

Other comments or notes:

Active Listening Notes

Title: _____

Who?

What?

Where?

When?

Why?

How?

Audience Notes and Feedback

Scoring Criteria	Notes/Feedback
Introduction/ Conclusion	
Timing	
Voice	
Eye Contact/ Gestures	
Use of Media, Visuals, Props	
Audience Engagement	

Cause and Effect

Title: _____

Cause: What happened?	→	Effect: An effect of this is

Cause: What happened?	→	Effect: An effect of this is

Cause: What happened?	→	Effect: An effect of this is

Cause: What happened?	→	Effect: An effect of this is

Character Map

Character name: _____

What does the character look like?

How does the character act and feel?

What do other characters say or think about the character?

Collaborative Dialogue

Topic: _____

Use the space below to record ideas.

| **"Wh-" Prompts** |
| Who?   What?   Where?   When?   Why? |

Speaker 1

Speaker 2

Conclusion Builder

Evidence

Evidence

Evidence

Based on this evidence, I can conclude

Conflict Map

Title: _____

What is the main conflict in this story?

What causes this conflict?

How is the conflict resolved?

What are some other ways the conflict could have been resolved?

Conversation for Quickwrite

1. Turn to a partner and restate the prompt in your own words.

2. Brainstorm key words to use in your quickwrite response.

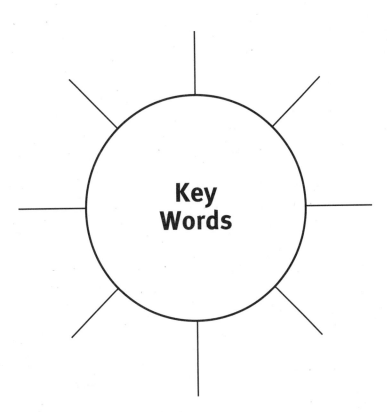

Key Words

3. Take turns explaining your ideas to your partner. Try using some of the key words you brainstormed.

4. On your own, write a response to the quickwrite.

Definition and Reflection

Academic Vocabulary Word
Definition in own words
Illustration (literal or symbolic)

My experiences with this concept:

- I haven't really thought about this concept.

_____

- I have only thought about this concept in English Language Arts class.

_____

- I have applied this concept in other classes.

_____

- I have applied this concept outside of school.

_____

My level of understanding:

- I am still trying to understand this concept.

_____

- I am familiar with this concept, but I am not comfortable applying it.

_____

- I am very comfortable with this concept and I know how to apply it.

_____

- I could teach this concept to another classmate.

_____

Discourse Starters

Questioning and Discussing a Text

One question I have is _____.

Could this mean _____?

Why do you think the author _____?

I understand _____, but I wonder _____.

I notice that _____.

I think this (word/sentence/paragraph) means _____.

I think _____ because the text says _____.

In paragraph _____, the author says _____.

According to the text, _____.

One way to interpret _____ is _____.

Summarizing

The main events that take place are _____.

The major points of the text are _____.

The main idea of _____ is _____.

One central idea of this text is _____.

Another central idea is _____.

All in all, the message is _____.

The author's main purpose is to _____.

Basically, the author is saying that _____.

Comparing and Contrasting

_____ and _____ are similar because _____.

_____ and _____ are similar in that they both _____.

_____ is _____. Similarly, _____ is _____.

One thing _____ and _____ have in common is _____.

_____ and _____ are different because _____.

_____ and _____ are different in that _____.

_____ is _____. On the other hand, _____ is _____.

One difference between _____ and _____ is _____.

Clarifying

I'm not sure I understand the instructions.

Could you repeat that please?

I have a question about _____.

I am having trouble with _____.

Will you explain that again?

Could you clarify _____?

Would you mind helping me with _____?

Which (page/paragraph/section) are we reading?

How do you spell/pronounce _____?

Discourse Starters

Agreeing and Disagreeing

I agree with the idea that _____ because _____.

I share your point of view because _____.

You made a good point when you said _____.

I agree with (a person) that _____.

Although I agree that _____, I also think _____.

I understand where you're coming from, but _____.

I disagree with the idea that _____ because _____.

I see it a different way because _____.

You have a point, but the evidence suggests _____.

Arguing and Persuading with Evidence

I believe that _____ because _____.

It is clear that _____ because _____.

One reason I think _____ is _____.

Based on evidence in the text, I think _____.

Evidence such as _____ suggests that _____.

An example to support my position is _____.

This is evident because _____.

What evidence supports the idea that _____?

Can you explain why you think _____?

Evaluating

This is effective because _____.

The evidence _____ is strong because _____.

This is convincing because _____.

I see why the author _____, but I think _____.

This is not very effective because _____.

The evidence _____ is weak because _____.

This would have been better if _____.

What do you think about the writer's choice to _____?

Why do you think _____ (is/isn't) effective?

Giving Feedback and Suggesting

The part where you _____ is strong because _____.

What impressed me the most is how you _____.

This is a good start. Maybe you should add _____.

I like how you _____, but I would try _____.

You might consider changing _____.

I would suggest revising _____ so that _____.

One suggestion would be to _____.

Why did you choose _____?

A better choice might be _____.

This would be clearer if _____.

Editor's Checklist

Over the course of the year with SpringBoard, customize this Editor's Checklist as your knowledge of language conventions grows. The three examples below show you how to write a good checklist item.

	Are all the sentences complete?
	Do the subject and verb of each sentence agree?
	Do all the sentences have correct punctuation?

Writer's Checklist

Ideas

	Does your first paragraph hook the reader?
	Is the purpose of your writing clear (to inform, to make an argument, etc.)?
	Is the genre of writing appropriate for your purpose?
	Is your main idea clear and easy to summarize?
	Does your text contain details and information that support your main idea?
	Are the ideas in the text well organized?
	Do you connect your ideas by using transitions?
	Do you use parallel structure to keep your ideas clear?
	Does each paragraph have a conclusion that transitions to the next paragraph?
	Does your writing end with a strong conclusion that restates the original purpose of the text

Language

	Do you keep a consistent point of view throughout?
	Do you use the present tense when writing about a text?
	Are any shifts in verb tense easy to follow and necessary?
	Have you removed unnecessary or confusing words?
	Do you use vivid verbs and descriptive adjectives when appropriate?
	Do you use different styles of language (like figurative or sensory) when appropriate?
	Do you use a variety of sentence types?
	Do you vary the way you begin your sentences?
	Did you split up run-on sentences?
	Are your pronoun references clear?

Evaluating Online Sources

The URL
 • What is its domain?
   • .com = a for-profit organization
   • .gov, .mil, .us (or other country code) = a government site
   • .edu = affiliated with an educational institution
   • .org = a nonprofit organization
 • Is this URL someone's personal page?
 • Do you recognize who is publishing this page?	

Sponsor: • Does the website give information about the organization or group that sponsors it? • Does it have a link (often called "About Us") that leads you to that information? • What do you learn?	
Timeliness: • When was the page last updated (usually this is posted at the top or bottom of the page)? • Is the topic something that changes frequently, like current events or technology?	
Purpose: • What is the purpose of the page? • What is its target audience? • Does it present information, opinion, or both? • Is it primarily objective or subjective? • How do you know?	
Author: • What credentials does the author have? • Is this person or group considered an authority on the topic?	
Links • Does the page provide links? • Do they work? • Are they helpful? • Are they objective or subjective?	

Idea and Argument Evaluator

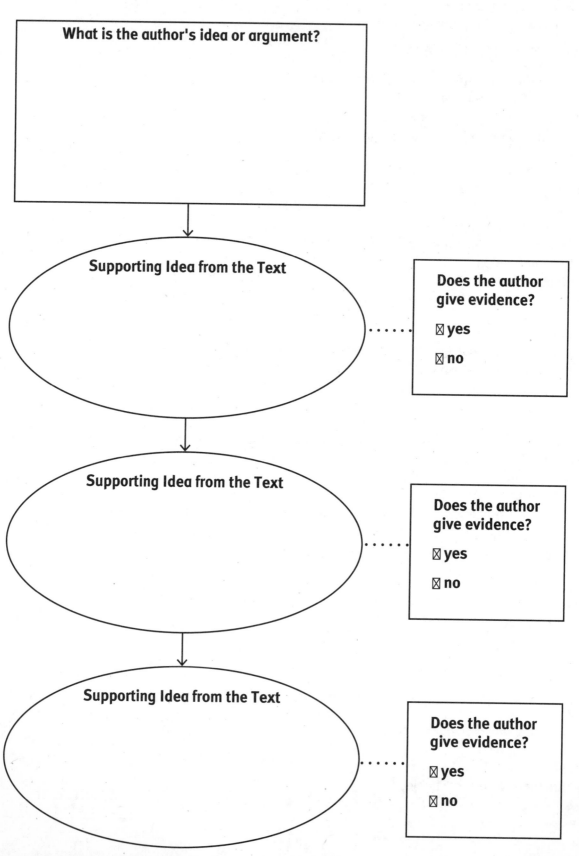

What is the author's idea or argument?

Supporting Idea from the Text

Does the author
give evidence?

☒ yes

☒ no

Supporting Idea from the Text

Does the author
give evidence?

☒ yes

☒ no

Supporting Idea from the Text

Does the author
give evidence?

☒ yes

☒ no

Idea Connector

Directions: Write two simple sentences about the same topic. Next, write transition words around the Idea Connector. Then, choose an appropriate word to connect ideas in the two sentences. Write your combined sentence in the space below.

Sentence One

Sentence Two

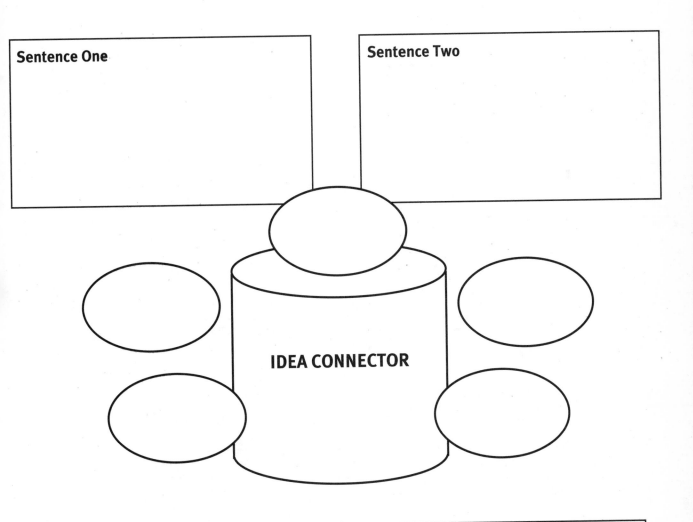

IDEA CONNECTOR

Combined Sentence

Key Idea and Details Chart

Title/Topic _____

Key Idea _____
_____
_____

Supporting detail 1 _____
_____
_____

Supporting detail 2 _____
_____
_____

Supporting detail 3 _____
_____
_____

Supporting detail 4 _____
_____
_____

Restate topic sentence: _____
_____

Concluding sentence: _____
_____
_____

Narrative Analysis and Writing

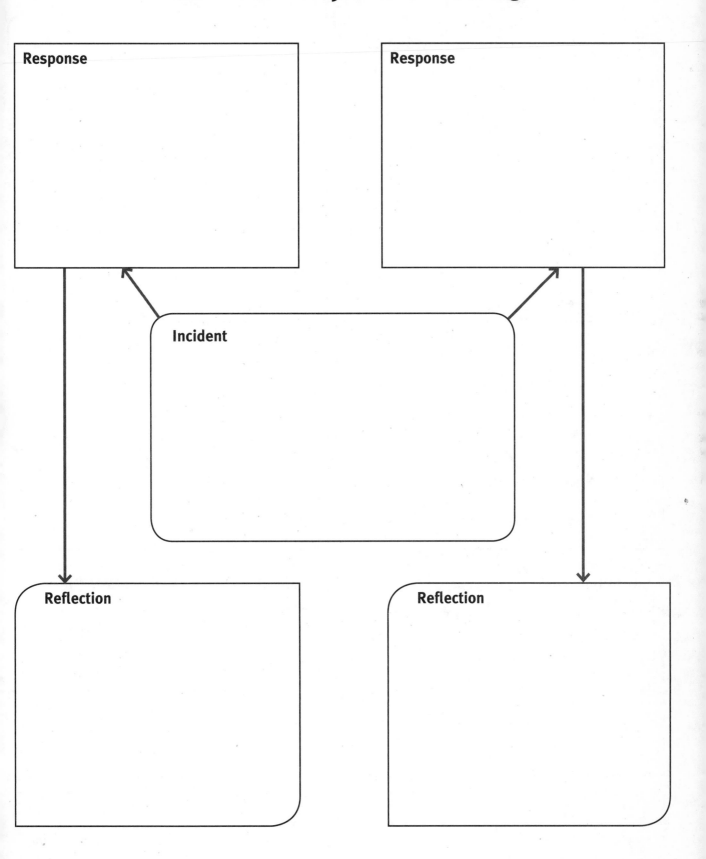

Response

Response

Incident

Reflection

Reflection

Notes for Reading Independently
Fiction

Title: _____

Author: _____

Something interesting I noticed:

A question I have:

Summary:

Illustration:

Connections to my life/other texts I've read:

How challenging this text was:

| Easy | 1 | 2 | 3 | 4 | 5 | 6 | 7 | 8 | 9 | 10 | Challenging |

Notes for Reading Independently
Nonfiction

Title: _____

Author: _____

Main idea:

Facts I learned:

Summary:

Questions I still have:

Connections to my life/other texts I've read:

How challenging this text was:

Easy   1   2   3   4   5   6   7   8   9   10   *Challenging*

Opinion Builder

| Reason | Reason |

Based on these reasons, my opinion is

| Reason | Reason |

Paragraph Frame for Conclusions

Conclusion Words and Phrases

shows that

based on

suggests that

leads to

indicates that

influences

The _____ (story, poem, play, passage, etc.)

shows that (helps us to conclude that) _____

_____

_____

There are several reasons why. First, _____

_____

_____

_____

_____

A second reason is _____

_____

_____

_____

_____

Finally, _____

_____

_____

_____

In conclusion, _____

_____

_____

_____

_____

Paragraph Frame for Sequencing

Sequence Words and Phrases

at the beginning

in the first place

as a result

later

eventually

in the end

lastly

In the _____ (story, poem, play, passage, etc.)

there are three important _____

(events, steps, directions, etc.)

First, _____

_____

_____

_____

_____

Second, _____

_____

_____

_____

_____

Third, _____

_____

_____

_____

_____

Finally, _____

_____

_____

_____

_____

Paraphrasing and Summarizing Map

What does the text say?	How can I say it in my own words?

How can I use my own words to summarize the text?

Peer Editing

Writer's name: _____

Did the writer answer the prompt? ☐ yes ☐ no

Did the writer use appropriate details or evidence to develop their writing? ☐ yes ☐ no

Is the writing organized in a way that makes sense? ☐ yes ☐ no

Did the writer use a variety of sentence types to make the writing more interesting? ☐ yes ☐ no

Are there any spelling or punctuation mistakes? ☐ yes ☐ no

Are there any grammar errors? ☐ yes ☐ no

Two things I really liked about the writer's story:

1. _____
   _____
   _____

2. _____
   _____
   _____

One thing I think the writer could do to improve the writing:

1. _____
   _____
   _____

Other comments or notes:

Persuasive/Argument Writing Map

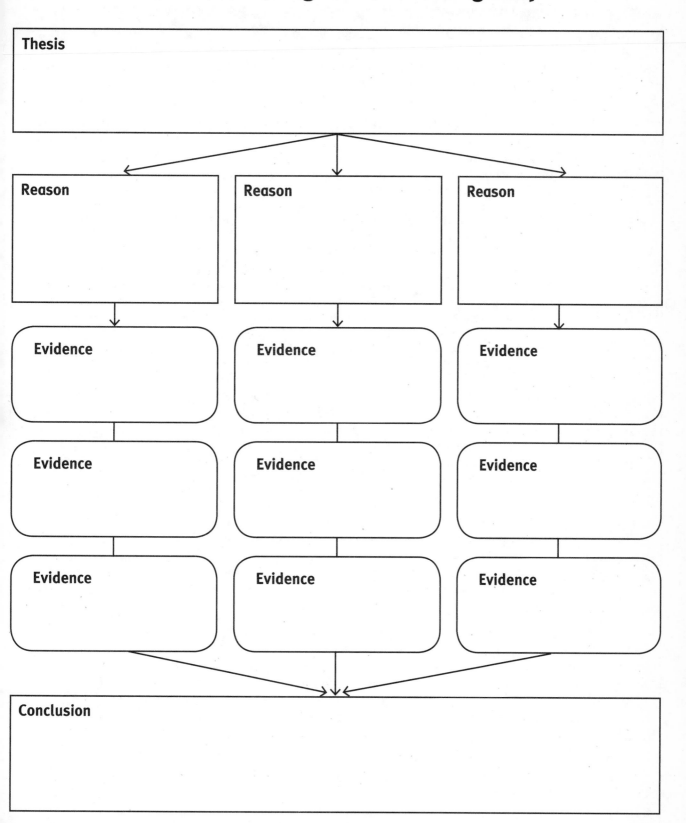

Thesis

Reason

Reason

Reason

Evidence

Evidence

Evidence

Evidence

Evidence

Evidence

Evidence

Evidence

Evidence

Conclusion

Presenting Scoring Guide

Scoring Criteria	Exemplary	Proficient	Emerging	Incomplete
Introduction / Conclusion	The presentation • provides a clear, engaging, and appropriate introduction to the topic or performance • provides a clear, engaging, and appropriate conclusion that closes, summarizes, draws connections to broader themes, or supports the ideas presented.	The presentation • provides a clear and appropriate introduction to the topic or performance • provides a clear and appropriate conclusion that closes, summarizes, draws connections to broader themes, or supports the ideas presented.	The presentation • provides an adequate introduction to the topic or performance • provides an adequate conclusion that closes, summarizes, draws connections to broader themes, or supports the ideas presented.	The presentation • does not provide an introduction to the topic or performance • does not provide a conclusion that closes, summarizes, draws connections to broader themes, or supports the ideas presented.
Timing	The presentation • thoroughly delivers its intended message within the allotted time • is thoughtfully and appropriately paced throughout.	The presentation • mostly delivers its intended message within the allotted time • is appropriately paced most of the time.	The presentation • delivers some of its intended message within the allotted time • is sometimes not paced appropriately.	The presentation • does not deliver its intended message within the allotted time • is not paced appropriately.
Voice (Volume, Enunciation, Rate)	The presentation • is delivered with adequate volume enabling audience members to fully comprehend what is said • is delivered with clear enunciation.	The presentation • is delivered with adequate volume enabling audience members to mostly comprehend what is said • is delivered with mostly clear enunciation.	The presentation • is delivered with somewhat adequate volume enabling audience members to comprehend some of what is said • is delivered with somewhat clear enunciation.	The presentation • is not delivered with adequate volume, so that audience members are unable to comprehend what is said • is delivered with unclear enunciation.
Eye Contact/ Gestures	The presentation • is delivered with appropriate eye contact that helps engage audience members • makes use of natural gestures and/or body language to convey meaning.	The presentation • is delivered with some appropriate eye contact that helps engage audience members • makes use of gestures and/or body language to convey meaning.	The presentation • is delivered with occasional eye contact that sometimes engages audience members • makes some use of gestures and/or body language to convey meaning.	The presentation • is not delivered with eye contact to engage audience members • makes little or no use of gestures and/or body language to convey meaning.
Use of Media, Visuals, Props	The presentation • makes use of highly engaging visuals, multimedia, and/or props that enhance delivery.	The presentation • makes use of visuals, multimedia, and/or props that enhance delivery.	The presentation • makes use of some visuals, multimedia, and/or props that somewhat enhance delivery.	The presentation • makes use of few or no visuals, multimedia, and/or props that enhance delivery.
Audience Engagement	The presentation • includes thoughtful and appropriate interactions with and responses to audience members.	The presentation • includes appropriate interactions with and responses to audience members.	The presentation • includes a few interactions with and responses to audience members.	The presentation • does not include interactions with and responses to audience members.

RAFT

Role	Who or what are you as a writer?
Audience	As a writer, to whom are you writing?
Format	As a writer, what format would be appropriate for your audience (essay, letter, speech, poem, etc.)?
Topic	As a writer, what is the subject of your writing? What points do you want to make?

Roots and Affixes Brainstorm

Directions: Write the root or affix in the circle. Brainstorm or use a dictionary to find the meaning of the root or affix and add it to the circle. Then, find words that use that root or affix. Write one word in each box. Write a sentence for each word.

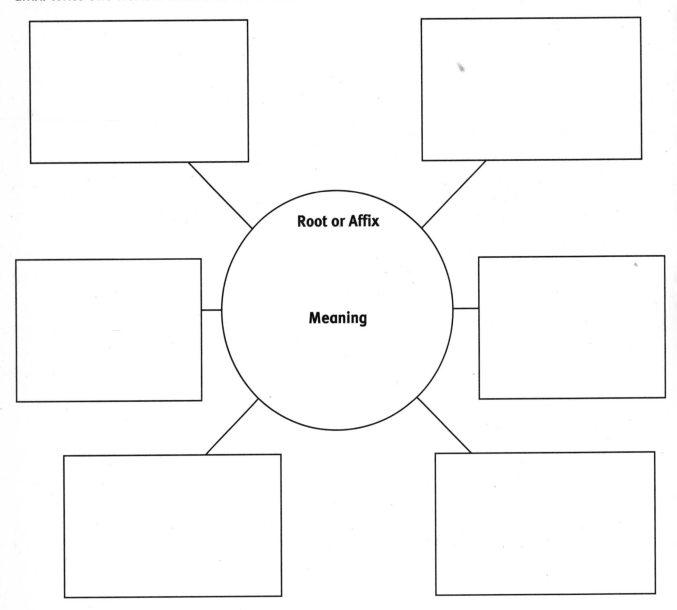

Round Table Discussion

Directions: Write the topic in the center box. One student begins by stating his or her ideas while the student to the left takes notes. Then the next student speaks while the student to his or her left takes notes, and so on.

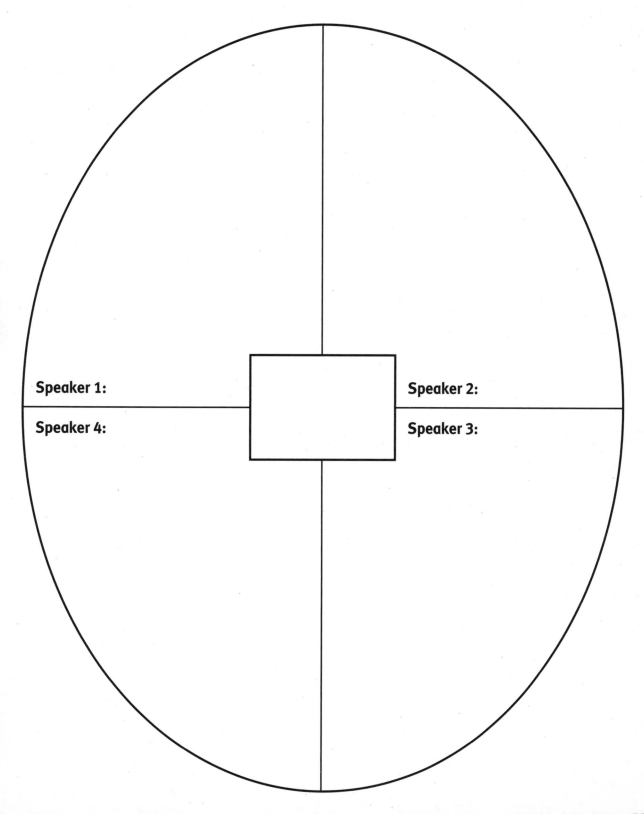

Speaker 1:

Speaker 2:

Speaker 4:

Speaker 3:

Sequence of Events Time Line

Title: _____

What happened first?

Next?

Beginning   Middle   End

Then?

Finally?

SMELL

Sender-Receiver Relationship—Who are the senders and receivers of the message, and what is their relationship (consider what different audiences the text may be addressing)?

Message—What is a literal summary of the content? What is the meaning/significance of this information?

Emotional Strategies—What emotional appeals (*pathos*) are included? What seems to be their desired effect?

Logical Strategies—What logical arguments/appeals (*logos*) are included? What is their effect?

Language—What specific language is used to support the message? How does it affect the text's effectiveness? Consider both images and actual words.

SOAPSTone

SOAPSTone	Analysis	Textual Support
Subject What does the reader know about the writer?		
Occasion What are the circumstances surrounding this text?		
Audience Who is the target audience?		
Purpose Why did the author write this text?		
Subject What is the topic?		
Tone What is the author's tone, or attitude?		

Text Structure Stairs

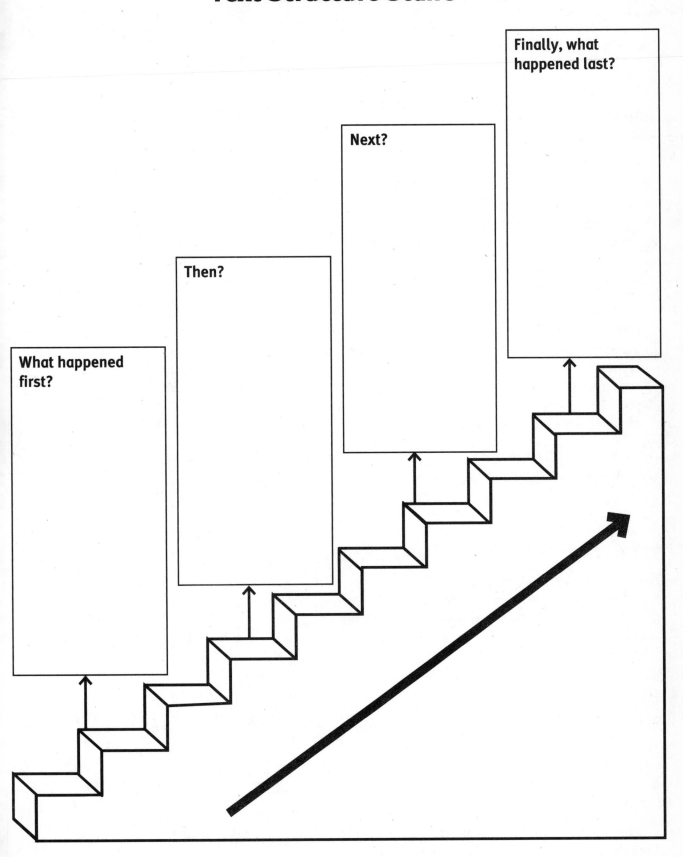

Finally, what happened last?

Next?

Then?

What happened first?

TP-CASTT Analysis

Poem Title:

Author:

Title: Make a Prediction. What do you think the title means before you read the poem?

Paraphrase: Translate the poem in your own words. What is the poem about? Rephrase difficult sections word for word.

Connotation: Look beyond the literal meaning of key words and images to their associations.

Attitude: What is the speaker's attitude? What is the author's attitude? How does the author feel about the speaker, about other characters, about the subject?

Shifts: Where do the shifts in tone, setting, voice, etc., occur? Look for time and place, keywords, punctuation, stanza divisions, changes in length or rhyme, and sentence structure. What is the purpose of each shift? How do they contribute to effect and meaning?

Title: Reexamine the title. What do you think it means now in the context of the poem?

Theme: Think of the literal and metaphorical layers of the poem. Then determine the overall theme. The theme must be written in a complete sentence.

TP-CASTT

Poem Title:

Author:

Title		
Paraphrase		
Connotation		
Attitude		
Shifts		
Title		
Theme		

Unknown Word Solver

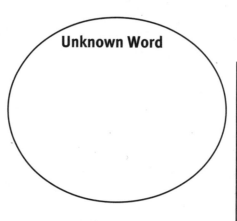

Unknown Word

Can you find any context clues? List them.

Do you recognize any word parts?

Prefix:

Root Word:

Suffix:

Do you know another meaning of this word that does not make sense in this context?

Does it look or sound like a word in another language?

What is the dictionary definition?

How can you define the word in your own words?

Venn Diagram for Writing a Comparison

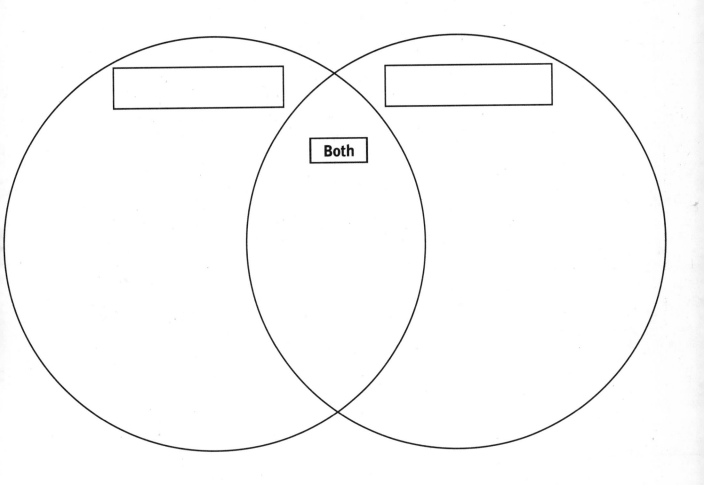

Both

They are similar in that _____

_____

_____

_____

_____

_____

They are different in that _____

_____

_____

_____

_____

_____

Verbal & Visual Word Association

Definition in Your Own Words	Important Elements

Academic Vocabulary Word

Visual Representation	Personal Association

Web Organizer

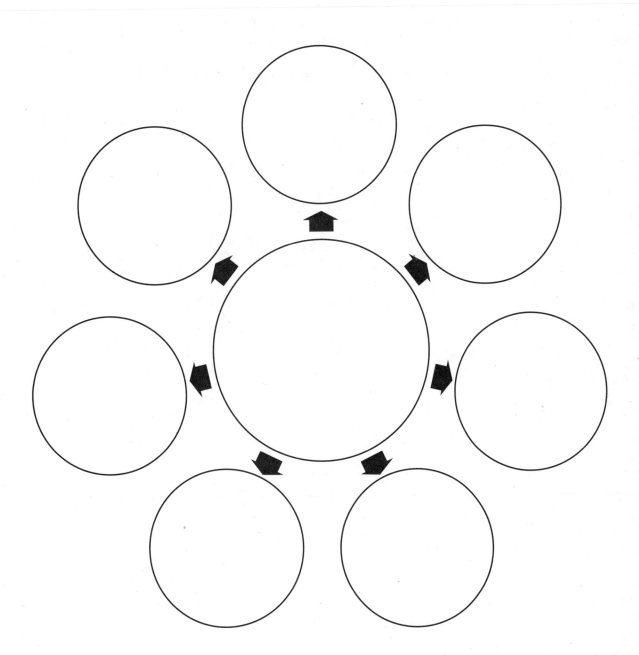

Word Choice Analyzer

Word or phrase from the text	Definition of word or phrase	How can I restate the definition in my own words?	What effect did the author produce by choosing these words?

Explain Your Analysis

The author uses the word or phrase _____ , which means

_____

Another way to say this is _____

_____

I think the author chose these words to _____

_____

_____

One way I can modify this sentence to add detail is to _____

_____

Word Map

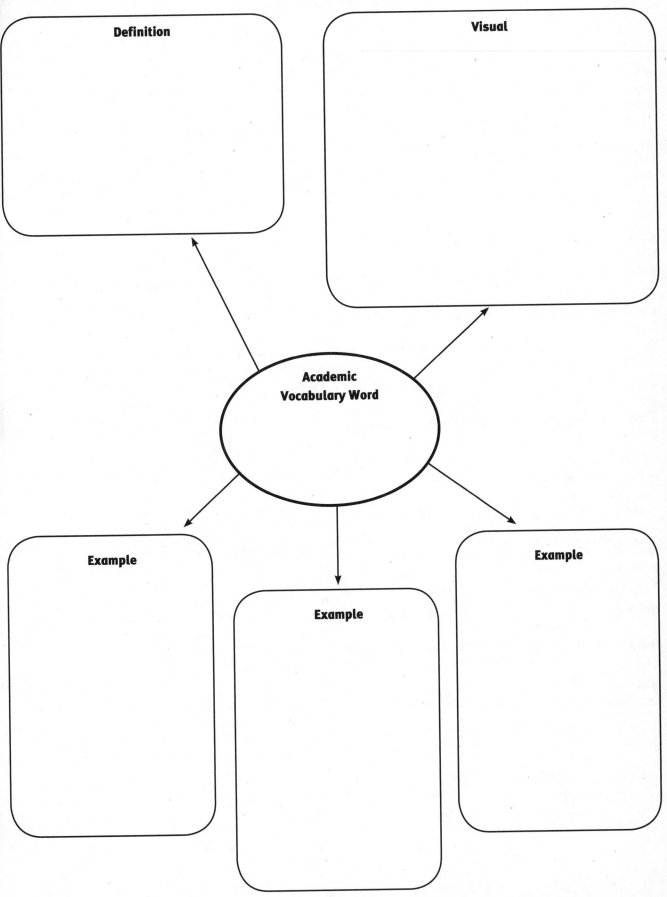

Definition

Visual

Academic Vocabulary Word

Example

Example

Example

Glossary/Glosario

A

advertising: the use of print, graphics, or videos to persuade people to buy a product or use a service
publicidad: uso de impresos, gráfica o videos para persuadir a las personas a comprar un producto o usar un servicio

allegory: a story in which the characters, objects, or actions have a meaning beyond the surface of the story
alegoría: cuento en el que los personajes, objetos o acciones tienen un significado que va más allá de la superficie de la historia

alliteration: the repetition of consonant sounds at the beginnings of words that are close together
aliteración: repetición de sonidos consonánticos al comienzo de palabras que están cercanas

allusion: a reference to a well-known person, place, event, literary work, or work of art
alusión: referencia a una persona, lugar, obra literaria u obra de arte muy conocidos

analogy: a comparison of the similarity of two things; for example, comparing a *part to a whole* or the *whole to a part*
analogía: comparación de la semejanza de dos cosas; por ejemplo, comparar una *parte con un todo* o el *todo con una parte*

analyze (literary): study the details of a work to identify essential features or meaning
analizar (literario): estudiar los detalles de una obra para identificar características o significados esenciales

anecdote: a brief, entertaining account of an incident or event
anécdota: breve relato entretenido de un incidente o suceso

annotate: write notes to explain or present ideas that help you analyze and understand a text
anotar: tomar notas para explicar o presentar las ideas que te ayuden a analizar y a entender un texto

antonyms: words with opposite meanings
antónimos: palabras con significados opuestos

archetype: a character, symbol, story pattern, or other element that is common to human experience across cultures and that occurs frequently in literature, myth, and folklore
arquetipo: personaje, símbolo, patrón de un cuento u otro elemento que es común a la experiencia humana a través de diversas culturas y que aparece con frecuencia en literatura, mitos y folclor

argument: facts or reasoning offered to support a position as being true
argumento: hechos o razonamiento entregados para apoyar una posición como verdadera

artifact: an object made by a human being, typically an item that has cultural or historical significance
artefacto: objeto hecho por un ser humano, habitualmente un objeto que tiene significación cultural o histórica

atmosphere: the feeling created by a literary work or passage
atmósfera: sentimiento creado por una obra o pasaje literario

audience: the intended readers of specific types of texts or the viewers of a program or performance
público: lectores objetivo de tipos específicos de textos o espectadores de un programa o actuación

B

balanced sentence: a sentence that presents ideas of equal weight in similar grammatical form to emphasize the similarity or difference between the ideas
oración balanceada: oración que presenta ideas de igual peso en forma gramatical similar para enfatizar la semejanza o diferencia entre las ideas

bibliography: a list of source materials used to prepare a research paper or presentation
bibliografía: lista de las fuentes utilizadas para preparar una investigación o una presentación

body paragraph: a paragraph that contains a topic sentence, supporting details and commentary, and a concluding sentence and that is usually part of a longer text
párrafo representativo: párrafo que contiene una oración principal, detalles de apoyo y comentarios, y una oración concluyente que normalmente forma parte de un texto más extenso

C

caricature: a visual or verbal representation in which characteristics or traits are distorted for emphasis
caricatura: representación visual o verbal en la que las características o rasgos son distorsionados para dar énfasis

cause: an initial action; an event that makes something else happen
causa: acción inicial; suceso que hace que otra cosa ocurra

character: a person or animal that takes part in the action of a literary work
personaje: persona o animal que participa en la acción de una obra literaria

characterization: the methods a writer uses to develop characters; for example, through description, actions, and dialogue
caracterización: métodos que usa un escritor para desarrollar personajes; por ejemplo, a través de descripción, acciones y diálogo

citation: giving credit to the authors of source information
cita: dar crédito a los autores de información usada como fuente

claim: a writer's statement of a position or opinion about a topic
afirmación: declaración de un escritor acerca de una posición u opinión sobre un tema

cliché: an overused expression or idea
cliché: expresión o idea usada en exceso

climax: the turning point or the high point of a story
clímax: punto de inflexión o momento culminante de un cuento

coherence: the clear and orderly presentation of ideas in a paragraph or essay
coherencia: presentación clara y ordenada de las ideas en un párrafo o ensayo

collaborate: work together with other members of a group
colaborar: trabajar en conjunto con otros miembros de un grupo

comedy: an entertainment that is amusing or humorous
comedia: espectáculo que es divertido o cómico

commentary: explanation of the way the facts, details, and/or examples in a paragraph or essay support the topic sentence
comentario: explicación de la manera en que los hechos, detalles y ejemplos de un párrafo o ensayo apoyan la oración principal

commercialism: an emphasis on gaining profits through advertising or sponsorship
mercantilismo: énfasis en obtener utilidades por medio de la publicidad o el auspicio

communication: the process of giving or exchanging information. **Verbal communication** involves the written or spoken word. **Nonverbal communication** involves movement, gestures, or facial expressions.
comunicación: proceso de dar o intercambiar información. La **comunicación verbal** involucra palabras escritas o habladas. La **comunicación no verbal** involucra movimientos, gestos o expresiones faciales.

compare: to identify similarities in two or more items; *see also* contrast
comparar: identificar semejanzas entre dos o más elementos; *ver también*, contrastar

concluding sentence: a final sentence that pulls together the ideas in a paragraph by restating the main idea or by summarizing or commenting on the ideas in the paragraph
oración concluyente: oración final que reúne las ideas de un párrafo, reformulando la idea principal o resumiendo o comentando las ideas del párrafo

conclusion: the ending of a paragraph or essay, which brings it to a close and leaves an impression with the reader
conclusión: fin de un párrafo o ensayo, que lo lleva a su término y deja una impresión en el lector

conflict: a struggle between opposing forces. In an **external conflict**, a character struggles with an outside force, such as another character or something in nature. In an **internal conflict**, the character struggles with his or her own needs, desires, or emotions.
conflicto: lucha entre fuerzas opuestas. En un **conflicto externo**, un personaje lucha contra una fuerza externa, como por ejemplo otro personaje o algo de la naturaleza. En un **conflicto interno**, el personaje lucha contra sus propias necesidades, deseos o emociones.

connotation: the suggested or implied meaning or emotion associated with a word—beyond its literal definition
connotación: significado o emoción sugerida o implícita que se asocia con una palabra—más allá de su definición literal

consumer: a buyer; a person who acquires goods and services
consumidor: comprador, persona que adquiere bienes y servicios

consumerism: the buying and consuming of goods and products; the belief that it is good to buy and consume goods and services
consumismo: compra y consumo de bienes y productos; creencia de que es bueno comprar y consumir bienes y servicios

context clue: information in words and phrases surrounding an unfamiliar word that hint at the meaning of the unfamiliar word.
clave de contexto: información en las palabras y frases que rodean una palabra no conocida y que dan una pista acerca del significado de esa palabra.

contrast: to identify differences in two or more items; *see also* compare
contrastar: identificar diferencias entre dos o más elementos; *ver también*, comparar

controversy: a public debate or dispute concerning a matter of opinion
controversia: debate público o disputa sobre una cuestión sujeta a opinión

copy: the actual text in an advertisement
texto publicitario: información actual en un anuncio publicitario

counter-argument: reasoning or facts given in opposition to an argument
contraargumento: razonamiento o hechos dados en oposición a un argumento

credible: to be trusted or believed
creíble: ser confiable o creíble

criteria: the facts, rules, or standards on which judgments are based.
criterios: hechos, reglas o estándares sobre las cuales están basadas las opiniones.

D

debate: *n.* a discussion involving opposing points of view; *v.* to present the sides of an argument by discussing opposing points
debate: *s.* discusión que involucra puntos de vista opuestos; *v.* presentar los lados de un argumento discutiendo puntos opuestos

definition: the process of making clear the meaning or nature of something
definición: proceso de aclarar el significado o naturaleza de algo

denotation: the exact, literal meaning of a word
denotación: significado exacto y literal de una palabra

detail: in writing, evidence (facts, statistics, examples) that supports the topic sentence
detalle: en la escritura, evidencia (hechos, estadística, ejemplos) que apoya la oracón principal

dialogue: conversation between characters
diálogo: conversación entre personajes

diction: a writer's or speaker's choice of words
dicción: selección de palabras por parte del escritor u orador

dissolve: the slow fading away of one image in a film as another fades in to take its place
desvanecimiento: desaparición lenta de una imagen en una película a medida que otra aparece progresivamente para tomar su lugar

drama: a genre of literature that is intended to be performed before an audience; a play
drama: género literario destinado a ser representado ante un público; obra teatral

dystopia: an imagined place or state in which the condition of life is imperfect or bad
distopía: lugar o estado imaginario en el que las condiciones de vida son imperfectas o malas

E

editorial: a short essay in which a publication, or someone speaking for a publication, expresses an opinion or takes a stand on an issue
editorial: ensayo corto en el que una publicación, o alguien que representa una publicación, expresa una opinión o toma partido acerca de un tema

effect: the result of an event or action
efecto: resultado de un suceso o acción

epic: a long narrative poem about the deeds of heroes or gods
épica: poema narrativo largo acerca de las proezas de héroes o dioses

epilogue: a section at the end of a book or play that extends or comments on the ending
epílogo: sección al final de un libro u obra teatral, que extiende o comenta el final

essay: a short literary composition on a single subject
ensayo: composición literaria corta acerca de un único tema

ethos: a rhetorical appeal that focuses on the character or qualifications of the speaker
ethos: recurso retórico centrado en el carácter o las capacidades del orador

euphemism: an inoffensive expression that is used in place of one that is considered harsh or blunt
eufemismo: expresión inofensiva usada en lugar de una considerada cruel o ruda

evaluate: to examine and judge carefully to determine the value of something, such as an idea, a comment, or a source
evaluar: estudiar y juzgar cuidadosamente para determinar el valor de algo, tal como una idea, un comentario, o una fuente

evidence: the information that supports or proves an idea or claim; forms of evidence include facts, statistics (numerical facts), expert opinions, examples, and anecdotes; see also, anecdotal, empirical, and logical evidence
evidencia: información que apoya o prueba una idea o afirmación; algunas formas de evidencia incluyen hechos, estadísticas (datos numéricos), opiniones de expertos, ejemplos y anécdotas; ver también evidencia anecdótica, empírica y lógica

explanatory essay: an essay that makes an assertion and explains it with details, reasons, textual evidence, and commentary
ensayo explicativo: ensayo que hace una afirmación y la explica con detalles, razones, evidencia textual y comentarios

explanatory paragraph: a paragraph that makes an assertion and supports it with details and commentary
párrafo explicativo: párrafo que hace una afirmación y la apoya con detalles y comentarios

exposition: events that give a reader background information needed to understand a story
exposición: sucesos que entregan al lector los antecedentes necesarios para comprender un cuento

F

fable: a brief story that teaches a lesson or moral, usually through animal characters that take on human qualities
fábula: cuento breve que enseña una lección o moraleja, normalmente por medio de personajes animales que asumen cualidades humanas

fact: a statement that can be proven
hecho: enunciado que puede demostrarse

fairy tale: a story that involves fantasy elements such as witches, goblins, and elves. These stories often involve princes and princesses and today are generally told to entertain children.
cuento de hadas: cuento que involucra elementos fantásticos como brujas, duendes y elfos. A menudo, estos cuentos involucran a príncipes y princesas y hoy se cuentan generalmente para entretener a los niños.

falling action: events after the climax of a story but before the resolution
acción descendente: sucesos posteriores al clímax de un cuento, pero antes de la resolución

fantasy: a story based on things that could not happen in real life
fantasía: cuento basado en cosas que no podrían ocurrir en la vida real

fiction: writing that consists of imagined events
ficción: escritura que consiste en acontecimientos imaginados

figurative language: imaginative language that is not meant to be interpreted literally
lenguaje figurativo: lenguaje imaginativo que no pretende ser interpretado literalmente

flashback: a sudden and vivid memory of an event in the past; also, an interruption in the sequence of events in the plot of a story to relate events that occurred in the past
narración retrospectiva: recuerdo repentino y vívido de un suceso del pasado; además, interrupción en la secuencia de los sucesos del argumento de un cuento para relatar sucesos ocurridos en el pasado

fluency: the ability to use language clearly and easily
fluidez: capacidad de usar el lenguaje fácilmente y de manera clara

folk literature: the traditional literature of a culture, consisting of a variety of myths and folk tales
literatura folclórica: literatura tradicional de una cultura, consistente en una variedad de mitos y cuentos folclóricos

folk tale: an anonymous traditional story passed on orally from one generation to another
cuento folclórico: cuento tradicional anónimo pasada oralmente de generación en generación

folklore: the stories, traditions, sayings, and customs of a culture or a society
folclor: historias, tradiciones, dichos y costumbres de una cultura o sociedad

foreshadowing: clues or hints signaling events that will occur later in the plot
presagio: claves o pistas que señalan sucesos que ocurrirán mas adelante en el argumento

formal style: a style of writing or speaking that is appropriate for formal communication such as in academics or business
estilo formal: estilo de escribir o hablar adecuado para la comunicación formal como la académica o comercial

free verse: a kind of poetry that does not follow any regular pattern, rhythm, or rhyme
verso libre: tipo de poesía que no sigue ningún patrón, ritmo o rima regular

G

genre: a category or type of literature, such as short story, folk tale, poem, novel, play
género: categoría o tipo de literatura, como el cuento corto, cuento folclórico, poema, novela, obra teatral

global revision: the process of deeply revising a text to improve organization, development of ideas, focus, and voice
revisión global: proceso de revisar en profundidad un texto para mejorar su organización, desarrollo de ideas, enfoque y voz

graphic novel: a narrative told through visuals and captions
novela gráfica: narrativa que se cuenta por medio de efectos visuales y leyendas

H

headline: a short piece of text at the top of an article, usually in larger type, designed to be the first words the audience reads
titular: trozo corto de texto en la parte superior de un artículo, habitualmente en letra más grande, diseñado para ser las primeras palabras que el público lear

humor: the quality of being comical or amusing
humor: cualidad de ser cómico o divertido

hook: *n.* a compelling idea or statement designed to get readers' attention in an introduction
gancho: *n.* idea o afirmación atractiva diseñada para captar la atención del lector en una introducción

hyperbole: extreme exaggeration used for emphasis, often used for comic effect
hypérbole: exageración extrema usada para dar énfasis, habitualmente usada para dar efecto cómico

I

iamb: a metrical foot that consists of an unstressed syllable followed by a stressed syllable
yambo: pie métrico que consta de una sílaba átona seguida de una sílaba tónica

iambic pentameter: a rhythmic pattern of five feet (or units) of one unstressed syllable followed by a stressed syllable
pentámetro yámbico: patrón rítmico de cinco pies (o unidades) de una sílaba átona seguida de una sílaba tónica

idiom: a figure of speech that cannot be defined literally
expresión idiomatica: figura del discurso que no puede definirse literalmente

image: a picture, drawing, photograph, illustration, chart, or other graphic that is designed to affect the audience in some purposeful way
imagen: pintura, dibujo, fotografía, ilustración, cuadro u otra gráfica diseñada para producir algún efecto intencional sobre el público

imagery: descriptive or figurative language used to create word pictures; imagery is created by details that appeal to one or more of the five senses
imaginería: lenguaje descriptivo o figurativo utilizado para crear imágenes verbales; la imaginería es creada por detalles que apelan a uno o más de los cinco sentidos

improvise: to respond or perform on the spur of the moment
improvisar: reaccionar o representar impulsivamente

incident: a distinct piece of action as in an episode in a story or a play. More than one incident may make up an event.
incidente: trozo de acción distintivo como un episodio de un cuento o de una obra teatral. Más de un incidente puede conformar un suceso.

inference: a logical guess or conclusion based on observation, prior experience, or textual evidence
inferencia: conjetura o conclusión lógica basada en la observación, experiencias anteriores o evidencia textual

inflection: the emphasis a speaker places on words through change in pitch or volume
inflexión: énfasis que pone un orador en las palabras por medio del cambio de tono o volumen

interpretation: a writer's or artist's representation of the meaning of a story or idea
interpretación: representación que hace un escritor o artista del significado de un cuento o idea

interview: a meeting between two people in which one, usually a reporter, asks the other questions to get that person's views on a subject
entrevista: reunión entre dos personas, en la que una, normalmente un reportero, hace preguntas a la otra para conocer sus opiniones acerca de un tema

introduction: the opening paragraph of an essay, which must get the reader's attention and indicate the topic
introducción: párrafo inicial de un ensayo, que debe captar la atención del lector e indicar el tema

L

legend: a traditional story believed to be based on actual people and events. Legends, which typically celebrate heroic individuals or significant achievements, tend to express the values of a culture.
leyenda: cuento tradicional que se considera basado en personas y sucesos reales. Las leyendas, que típicamente celebran a individuos heroicos o logros importantes, tienden a expresar los valores de una cultura.

limerick: a light, humorous, nonsensical verse of few lines, usually with a rhyme scheme of a-a-b-b-a
quintilla: verso liviano, humorístico, disparatado y de pocas líneas, normalmente con un esquema a-a-b-b-a

listening: the process of receiving a message and making meaning of it from verbal and nonverbal cues
escuchar: proceso de recibir el mensaje y comprender su significado a partir de claves verbales y no verbales

literary analysis: the process of examining closely and commenting on the elements of a literary work
análisis literario: proceso de examinar atentamente y comentar los elementos de una obra literaria

local revision: revising a text on a word or sentence level
revisión local: revisar un texto a nivel de palabras o de oraciones

logo: a unique design symbol used to identify a company visually
logotipo: símbolo único de diseño, utilizado para identificar visualmente una empresa

logos: a rhetorical appeal to reason or logic through statistics, facts, and reasonable examples
logos: apelación retórica a la razón o la lógica por medio de estadísticas, hechos y ejemplos razonables

M

media: the various means of mass communication, such as radio, television, newspapers, and magazines
medios de comunicación: los diversos medios de comunicación masiva, como radio, televisión, periódicos y revistas

media channel: a type of media, such as television or newspaper
canal mediático: tipo de medios de comunicación, como televisión o periódicos

metaphor: a comparison between two unlike things in which one thing becomes another
metáfora: comparación entre dos cosas diferentes en la que una cosa se convierte en otra

monologue: a speech or written expression of thoughts by a character
monólogo: discurso o expresión escrita de pensamientos por parte de un personaje

mood: the overall emotional quality of a work, which is created by the author's language and tone and the subject matter
carácter: la calidad emocional general de una obra, que es creada por el lenguaje y tono del autor y por el tema

motif: a recurring element, image, or idea in a work of literature
motivo: elemento, imagen o idea recurrente en una obra literaria

multimedia: the use of several media (for example, print, film, audio, and video) to communicate ideas
multimedia: uso de varios medios de comunicación (por ejemplo: impresos, cine, audio y video) para comunicar ideas

multiple intelligences: the variety of learning styles that everyone has in varying degrees. In each individual, different intelligences predominate.
inteligencias múltiples: diversidad de estilos de aprendizaje que todos tienen en diversos grados. En cada individuo predominan diferentes inteligencias.

myth: a traditional story that explains the actions of gods or heroes or the origins of the elements of nature
mito: cuento tradicional que explica las acciones de dioses o héroes o los orígenes de los elementos de la naturaleza

N

narrative: a type of writing that tells a story or describes a sequence of events in an incident
narrativa: tipo de escritura que cuenta un cuento o describe una secuencia de sucesos de un incidente

narrative poem: a story told in verse
poema narrativo: historia contada en verso

news article: an article in a news publication that objectively presents both sides of an issue
artículo noticioso: artículo de una publicación noticiosa que presenta objetivamente ambos lados de un asunto

nonfiction: writing that is based on facts and actual events
no ficción: escritura que se basa en hechos o acontecimientos reales

nonprint text: a text, such as film or graphics, that communicates ideas without print
texto no impreso: texto, como una película o gráfica, que comunica ideas sin imprimir

nonverbal communication: gestures, facial expressions, and inflection that form unspoken communication
comunicación no verbal: gestos, expresiones faciales e inflexión que forman la comunicación no hablada

novel: a type of literary genre that tells a fictional story
novela: tipo de género literario que cuenta una historia ficticia

O

objective: supported by facts and not influenced by personal opinion
objetivo: apoyado por hechos y no influenciado por la opinión personal

objective camera view: in film, when the camera takes a neutral point of view
visión objetiva de la cámara: en el cine, cuando la cámara toma un punto de vista neutro

omniscient: a third-person point of view in which the narrator is all-knowing
omnisciente: punto de vista de una tercera persona, en la que el narador lo sabe todo

onomatopoeia: the use of words that imitate the sounds of what they describe
onomatopeya: el uso de palabras que imitan los sonidos de lo que describen

one-liner: a short joke or witticism expressed in a single sentence
agudeza: chiste u comentario ingenioso que se expresa en una sola oración.

opinion: a perspective that can be debated
opinión: perspectiva que es debatible

oral interpretation: reading aloud a literary text with expression
interpretación oral: leer en voz alta un texto literario con expresión

oxymoron: a figure of speech in which the words seem to contradict each other; for example, "jumbo shrimp"
oxímoron: figura del discurso en la que las palabras parecen contradecirse mutuamente; por ejemplo, "audaz cobardía"

P

pantomime: a form of acting without words, in which motions, gestures, and expressions convey emotions or situations
pantomima: forma de actuación sin palabras, en la que los movimientos, gestos y expresiones transmiten emociones o situationes

paraphrase: to restate in one's own words
parafrasear: reformular en nuestras propias palabras

parody: a humorous imitation of a literary work
parodia: imitación humorística de una obra literaria

pathos: a rhetorical appeal to the reader's or listener's senses or emotions through connotative language and imagery
pathos: apelación retórica a los sentidos o emociones del lector u oyente por medio de un lenguaje connotativo y figurado

performance: presenting or staging a play
actuación: presentar o poner en escena una obra teatral

persona: the voice or character speaking or narrating a story
persona: voz o personaje que habla o narra una historia

personal letter: a written communication between friends, relatives, or acquaintances that shares news, thoughts, or feelings
carta personal: comunicación escrita entre amigos, parientes o conocidos, que comparte noticias, pensamientos o sentimientos

personal narrative: a piece of writing that describes an incident and includes a personal response to and reflection on the incident

narrativa personal: texto escrito que describe un incidente e incluye una reacción personal ante el incidente y una reflexión acerca de él

personification: a kind of metaphor that gives objects or abstract ideas human characteristics

personificación: tipo de metáfora que da características humanas a los objetos o ideas abstractas

perspective: the way a specific character views a situation or other characters

perspectiva: manera en que un personaje específico visualiza una situación o a otros personajes

persuasion: the act or skill of causing someone to do or believe something

persuasión: acto o destreza de hacer que alguien haga o crea algo

persuasive essay: an essay that attempts to convince the reader to take an action or believe an idea

ensayo persuasivo: ensayo que intenta convencer al lector de que realice una acción o crea una idea

phrasing: dividing a speech into smaller parts, adding pauses for emphasis

frasear: dividir un discurso en partes más pequeñas, añadiendo pausas para dar énfasis

pitch: the highness or lowness of a sound, particularly the voice in speaking

tono: altura de un sonido, especialmente de la voz al hablar

plagiarism: taking and using as your own the words and ideas of another

plagio: tomar y usar como propias las palabras e ideas de otro

plot: the sequence of related events that make up a story or novel

trama: secuencia de sucesos relacionados, que conforman un cuento o novela

point of view: the perspective from which a story is told. In **first-person** point of view, the teller is a character in the story telling what he or she sees or knows. In **third-person** point of view, the narrator is someone outside of the story.

punto de vista: perspectiva desde la cual se cuenta una historia. En el punto de vista de la **primera persona**, el relator es un personaje del cuento que narra lo que ve o sabe. En el punto de vista de la **tercera persona**, el narrador es alguien que está fuera del cuento.

prediction: a logical guess or assumption about something that has not yet happened

predicción: conjetura lógica o suposición acerca de algo que aún no ha ocurrido

presentation: delivery of a formal reading, talk, or performance

presentación: entrega de una lectura, charla o representación formal

prose: the ordinary form of written language, using sentences and paragraphs; writing that is not poetry, drama, or song

prosa: forma común del lenguaje escrito, usando oraciones y párrafos; escritura que no es poesía, drama ni canción

pun: the humorous use of a word or words to suggest another word with the same sound or a different meaning

retruécano: uso humorístico de una o varias palabras para sugerir otra palabra que tiene el mismo sonido o un significado diferente

purpose: the reason for writing; what the writer hopes to accomplish

propósito: razón para escribir; lo que el escritor espera lograr

Q

quatrain: a four-line stanza in poetry
cuarteta: en poesía, estrofa de cuatro versos

R

rate: the speed at which a speaker delivers words
rapidez: velocidad a la que el orador pronuncia las palabras

reasons: the points that explain why the author is making a certain claim
razones: los puntos que explican por qué un autor propone cierta afirmacón

reflection: a kind of thinking and writing that seriously explores the significance of an experience, idea, or observation
reflexión: tipo de pensamiento y escritura que explora seriamente la importancia de una experiencia, idea u observación

reflective essay: an essay in which the writer explores the significance of an experience or observation
ensayo reflexivo: ensayo en que el autor explora la importancia de una experiencia u observación

refrain: a regularly repeated word, phrase, line, or group of lines in a poem or song
estribillo: palabra, frase, verso o grupo de versos de un poema o canción que se repite con regularidad

relevant: closely connected to the matter at hand (for example, evidence supporting a claim)
relevante: relacionado estrechamente con el asunto en cuestión (por ejemplo, la evidencia que apoya una afirmación)

repetition: the use of the same words or structure over again
repetición: uso de las mismas palabras o estructura una y otra vez

research: (v.) to locate information from a variety of sources; (n.) the information found from investigating a variety of sources
investigar: (v.) proceso de buscar información en una variedad de fuentes; *también*, **investigación** (n.) información que se halla al investigar una variedad de fuentes

resolution: the outcome of the conflict of a story, when loose ends are wrapped up
resolución: resultado del conflicto de un cuento, cuando se atan los cabos sueltos

revision: a process of evaluating a written piece to improve coherence and use of language; *see also* local revision, global revision
revisión: proceso de evaluar un texto escrito para mejorar la coherencia y el uso del lenguaje; *ver también*, revisión local, revisión global

rhetorical appeals: the use of emotional, ethical, and logical arguments to persuade in writing or speaking
recursos retóricos: uso de argumentos emotivos, éticos y lógicos para persuadir al escribir o hablar

rhetorical question: a question asked to emphasize a point or create an effect; no answer is expected
pregunta retórica: pregunta que se hace para enfatizar un punto o crear un efecto; no se espera una respuesta

rhyme: the repetition of sounds at the ends of words
rima: repetición de sonidos al final de las palabras

rhyme scheme: a consistent pattern of end rhyme throughout a poem
esquema de la rima: patrón consistente de una rima final a lo largo de un poema

rhythm: the pattern of stressed and unstressed syllables in spoken or written language, especially in poetry
ritmo: patrón de sílabas acentuadas y no acentuadas en lenguaje hablado o escrito, especialmente en poesía

rising action: major events that develop the plot of a story and lead to the climax
acción ascendente: sucesos importantes que desarrollan la trama de un cuento y conducen al clímax

S

science fiction: a genre in which the imaginary elements of the story could be scientifically possible
ciencia ficción: género en que los elementos imaginarios del cuento podrían ser científicamente posibles

sensory language: words or information that appeal to the five senses
lenguaje sensorial: palabras o información que apelan a los cinco sentidos

sequence: the order in which events happen
secuencia: orden en que ocurren los sucesos

setting: the time and the place in which a narrative occurs
ambiente: tiempo y lugar en que ocurre un relato

short story: a work of fiction that presents a sequence of events, or plot, that deals with a conflict
cuento corto: obra de ficción que presenta una secuencia de sucesos, o trama, que tratan de un conflicto

simile: a comparison between two unlike things, using the words *like* or *as*
símil: comparación entre dos cosas diferentes usando las palabras como o *tan*

slogan: a catchphrase that evokes a particular feeling about a company and its product
eslogan: frase o consigna publicitaria que evoca un sentimiento en particular acerca de una empresa y su producto

source: a place from which information comes or is obtained
fuente: lugar de donde surge o se obtiene la información

speaker: the voice that communicates with the reader of a poem
hablante: la voz que se comunica con el lector de un poema

speaking: the process of sharing information, ideas, and emotions using verbal and nonverbal means communication
hablar: proceso de compartir información, ideas y emociones usando medios de comunicación verbales y no verbales

stanza: a group of lines, usually similar in length and pattern, that form a unit within a poem
estrofa: grupo de versos, normalmente similares en longitud y patrón, que forman una unidad dentro de un poema

stereotype: a fixed, oversimplified image of a person, group, or idea; something conforming to that image
estereotipo: imagen fija y demasiado simplificada de una persona, grupo o idea; algo que cumple esa imagen

subjective: influenced by personal opinions or ideas
subjectivo: influenciado por opiniones o ideas personales

subjective camera view: in film, when the camera seems to show the events through a character's eyes
visión subjetiva de la cámara: en el cine, cuando la cámara parece mostrar los sucesos a través de los ojos de un personaje

subplot: a secondary plot that occurs along with a main plot
trama secundaria: argumento secundario que ocurre conjuntamente con un argumento principal

sufficient: adequate for the purpose of supporting a claim or reason
suficiente: adecuado para cumplir con el propósito de apoyar una afirmación o razón

summarize: to briefly restate the main ideas of a piece of writing
resumir: reformular brevemente las ideas principales de un texto escrito

supporting details: in writing, evidence (facts, statistics, examples) that supports the topic sentence
detalles de apoyo: en la escritura, evidencia (hechos, estadísticas ejemplos) que apoya la oracon principal

symbol: an object, a person, or a place that stands for something else
símbolo: objeto, persona o lugar que representa otra cosa

symbolism: the use of symbols
simbolismo: el uso de símbolos

synonyms: words with similar meanings
sinónimos: palabras con significados semejantes

synthesize: to combine elements from different sources to create, express, or support a new idea
sintetizar: combinar elementos de diferentes fuentes para crear, expresar o apoyar una idea nueva

T

tableau: a purposeful arrangement of characters frozen as if in a painting or a photograph
cuadro: disposición intencional de personajes que permanecen inmóviles como en una pintura o foto

talking points: important points or concepts to be included in a presentation
puntos centrales: puntos o conceptos importantes a incluirse en una presentación

tall tale: a highly exaggerated and often humorous story about folk heroes in local settings
cuento increíble: cuento muy exagerado y normalmente humorístico acerca de héroes folclóricos en ambientes locales

target audience: the specific group of people that advertisers aim to persuade to buy
público objetivo: grupo específico de personas a quienes los publicistas desean persuadir de comprar

tempo: the speed or rate of speaking
ritmo: velocidad o rapidez al hablar

textual evidence: quotations, summaries, or paraphrases from text passages to support a position
evidencia textual: citas, resúmenes o paráfrasis de pasajes de texto para apoyar una position

theme: the central idea, message, or purpose of a literary work
tema: idea, mensaje o propósito central de una obra literaria

thesis statement: a sentence, in the introduction of an essay, that states the writer's position or opinion on the topic of the essay
enunciado de tesis: oración, en la introducción de un ensayo, que plantea el punto de vista u opinión del autor acerca del tema del ensayo

tone: a writer's or speaker's attitude toward a subject
tono: actitud de un escritor u orador hacia un tema

topic sentence: a sentence that states the main idea of a paragraph; in an essay, it also makes a point that supports the thesis statement
oración principal: oración que plantea la idea principal de un párrafo; en un ensayo, también plantea un punto que apoya el enunciado de tesis

transitions: words or phrases that connect ideas, details, or events in writing
transiciones: palabras o frases que conectan ideas, detalles o sucesos de un escrito

TV news story: a report on a news program about a specific event
documental de televisión: reportaje en un programa noticioso acerca de un suceso específico

U

utopia: an ideal or perfect place
utopía: lugar ideal o perfecto

V

verse: a unit of poetry, such as a line or a stanza
verso: unidad de la poesía, como un verso o una estrofa

voice: a writer's distinctive use of language
voz: uso distintivo del lenguaje por parte de un escritor

voice-over: the voice of an unseen character in film
expressing his or her thoughts
voz en off: voz de un personaje de una película, que no se ve
pero que expresa sus pensamientos

volume: the degree of loudness of a speaker's voice or
other sound
volumen: grado de intensidad sonora de la voz de un orador
o de otro sonido

W

wordplay: a witty or clever verbal exchange or a play
on words
juego de palabras: intercambio verbal ingenioso u
ocurrente o un juego con palabras

Index of Skills

Literary Skills

Acts, 257, 452
Allegory, 91–93, 241–244
Alliteration, 398, 400
Allusion, 307
Analogy, 176, 177, 198, 322
Anecdote, 333, 363–364
Archetype, 4, 7, 10, 17, 27, 41, 161, 168
Argument, 172, 326, 330, 333
Argumentative essay, 173
Article, 84, 89, 154–155, 177, 184–185, 195–197, 202–207, 373–375
Attitude (Tone), 77
Audience, 80, 174, 207, 308, 334, 356, 357, 370, 424
Author's purpose, 72, 80, 130, 174, 207, 228, 302, 308, 350, 354, 355, 373
Autobiography, 95–97, 99, 232–234, 239–240
Bandwagon appeals, 189, 193
Call to action, 302, 307, 333
Caption, 50
Caricature, 354, 380–386, 386, 406, 407, 435
Characterization, 40, 76, 149, 228, 267, 380, 446–449, 454
    actions, 34, 35, 36, 160, 163, 228, 354, 380, 386, 387, 446, 447
    appearance, 36, 380, 387, 446
    feelings, 35, 36, 163, 277, 447
    others' reactions, 35, 36, 447
    thoughts, 35, 36, 48, 163, 386, 447
    words, 34, 35, 36, 48, 163, 262, 263, 271, 385, 386, 387, 397, 446, 447
Character(s), 10, 11, 24, 25, 26, 151, 152, 228, 254, 255, 256, 262, 273, 274, 280, 424, 454
    analysis, 40, 93, 251
    antagonist, 148, 164
    comic/humorous, 354, 355, 370, 380–386, 387, 434, 435
    protagonist (main character), 122, 148, 149, 150, 160, 161–156, 163, 164, 165, 168
    relationships among, 428
    types, 7, 148
Children's book, 230, 241
Circular reasoning, 189
Claim, 333
Close-up, 50

Comedic skit, 405
Comedy, 72
    elements of, 405, 433
    high, 354, 355, 356, 357, 370, 373–379, 400, 404, 406, 407
    low, 354, 355, 356, 357, 370, 400, 404, 406, 407
    satirical humor, 373–379
    Shakespearean, 429, 454
    universal truth in, 366, 371, 372, 405
Comic situations, 354, 355, 387, 406, 407, 435
Comic strips, 356, 357
Comic wordplay, 402–405, 406, 407, 435
Commentary, 273, 369
Conflict, 10, 24, 129, 141, 144, 149, 151, 163, 164, 165, 254, 263, 422, 454
    external, 228
    internal, 24, 228
Connotation, 61, 72, 73, 77, 245
Context, 15, 253, 409, 411, 426
Contrast, 93, 129, 165
Definition essay, 106–117
Definition strategies, 82–88, 98
    by example, 83–84, 87, 98
    by function, 83–84, 87
    by negation, 83–84, 87, 106–107
Denotation, 72, 245, 351
Details, 22, 23, 34, 47, 48, 61, 76, 80, 86, 93, 97, 99, 129, 137, 140, 174, 235–236, 238, 262, 263, 271, 273, 278, 307, 308, 322, 325, 333, 350, 361–362, 369, 376, 380, 384, 385, 393, 394, 400, 405, 411, 433, 440
Dialect, 393, 394
Dialogue balloon, 50
Diary, 275–276
Diction (word choice), 72, 80, 140, 228, 235–236, 362, 370, 404
    connotation, 61, 73, 245–246, 263, 351–352, 377
    denotation, 351–352
    humorous, 351, 354, 387, 404
Digital text, 149, 152, 162, 164, 165, 245, 402
Drama, 257, 279, 426
Dystopia, 122, 133, 141, 144
Effect, 24, 34, 47, 50, 61, 80, 140, 163, 228, 235–236, 252, 302, 356, 358, 369, 380, 384, 385, 394, 405, 409
Epic, 27

Epic poem, 27
Essay
    analyzation of, 409
    argumentative, 179
    humorous, 360–362, 366, 370, 409
    informational text, 343–348, 410–411
Essential questions, 4, 71, 122, 171, 222, 300, 342, 415
Euphemism, 182, 245–246
Evidence, 149, 174, 182, 198
Extreme close-up, 50
Extreme long shot, 50
Fantasy, 148
Fiction, 133, 148, 254, 268–270
Figurative language, 22, 186
Figurative meaning, 76
Flashback, 160–161, 237
Folklore, 103
Foreshadowing, 160–161, 232, 236, 237
Format, 356, 357, 424
Full-length story, 11
Graphic novel, 50, 61
Gutter, 50
Hero's Journey, 4, 10, 11, 17, 27, 41, 160, 161–156, 163, 165
    film, 7
    illustrated, 38, 41
    nonfiction, 124–127, 225, 228, 247, 251
Humor, 342, 354, 358
    analyze, 356, 366, 387, 394, 405, 406, 413
    anecdotes, 358–365
    comic characters and caricatures, 380–386, 406, 407, 435
    comic situations, 387–395, 406, 407, 435
    comic wordplay, 402–405, 406, 407, 435
    complexity of, 343
    elements of, 357, 365, 380, 386, 387, 395, 398, 401, 402, 406, 407
    essay, 360–361, 366, 370, 410–411
    hyperbole, 398–401, 405, 406, 407, 435
    planned vs. unplanned, 350
    satirical, 373–379
    universal truth in, 366, 371, 372, 405
    words to describe, 72, 356
Humorous skit, 405
Hyperbole, 398–401, 405, 406, 407, 435

Reading Skills

Analyzing the text, 5–6, 17, 27, 37, 61, 74, 78, 89, 238, 241, 308, 317, 356, 388

Annotating the text, 61, 263, 308, 317, 395, 407, 411, 435, 437

Big ideas, 4, 122, 222, 342

Close reading, 4, 7, 17, 41, 74, 89, 109, 122, 123, 133, 160, 163, 165, 171, 179, 407, 431, 434–436, 446

Compare, 74, 78, 80–81, 89, 95, 99, 115, 154, 238, 405

Compare and contrast, 123, 124, 155–156, 186, 239–240, 356

Connecting to the text, 342, 361–362, 426, 428
    text-to-self, 228, 280, 314, 361–362
    text-to text, 228, 244, 280, 361–362
    text-to-world, 228, 280, 361–362

Context, 16, 179

Context clues, 7, 13, 27, 41, 74, 77, 78, 84, 89, 94, 106, 124, 154, 155, 174, 184, 198, 207, 232, 237, 241, 258, 267, 275, 277, 305, 311, 317, 324, 326, 330, 343, 350, 360, 366, 373, 381, 384, 385, 388, 392, 398, 402, 409, 417, 437

Contrast, 23

Essays, humorous, 360–361, 366–368

Independent Reading Checkpoint, 68, 115, 168, 215, 279, 334, 412, 453

Independent Reading Link, 16, 26, 27, 71, 87, 108, 115, 122, 150, 166, 171, 176, 179, 190, 201, 222, 237, 251, 258, 278, 300, 310, 324, 326, 342, 356, 365, 370, 372, 378, 395, 401, 415, 432, 440, 445, 452

Independent Reading Log, 12

Independent Reading Plan, 11, 222

Inferring, 15, 27, 47, 128, 140–142, 149, 160, 183, 271, 307, 363–364

Informational text, 74, 78, 194, 307, 437–439

Levels of questions, 149–150, 152, 156, 228, 372
    develop, 372
    interpretive, 372
    literal, 372
    universal (thematic), 372

Marking the text, 4, 7, 13, 16, 41, 74, 77, 78, 84, 89, 94, 103, 106, 124, 133, 154, 164, 174, 179, 184, 202, 232, 237, 258, 267, 275, 279, 305, 311, 313, 317, 324, 326, 330, 335, 336, 343, 354, 360, 366, 373, 377, 381, 388, 398, 402, 405, 407, 409, 417, 431, 437

Metacognitive markers, 7, 317

Note-taking, 4, 5, 27, 72, 77, 124, 148, 156, 163, 166, 167, 168, 201, 242–243, 247, 308, 313, 355, 361–362, 370–371, 376, 377, 380, 384, 394, 395, 401, 404, 411, 415, 426, 427, 435

Observation, 27

Paraphrase, 4, 6, 77, 89, 122, 140, 141, 171, 215, 300, 376, 435

Predicting, 12, 41, 148, 179, 182, 254, 267, 342

Previewing, 7, 11, 17, 41, 74, 78, 89, 106, 124, 133, 149, 154, 173, 179, 223, 225, 232, 241, 258, 267, 275, 305, 311, 317, 324, 326, 330, 342, 343, 360, 373, 381, 388, 398, 402, 431, 437

Questioning the text, 149–144, 156, 201

Read aloud, 66, 223, 405

Reader/Writer Notebook, 4, 6, 15, 16, 22, 34, 47, 76, 80, 93, 97, 108, 128, 140, 149, 152, 164, 178, 182, 186, 198, 207, 222, 238, 242, 262, 271, 277, 307, 322, 333, 350, 361–362, 369, 376, 384, 392, 395, 400, 401, 404, 422, 427, 433, 443

Rereading, 15, 22, 34, 47, 76, 80, 86, 93, 97, 128, 140, 160, 163, 174, 179, 182, 186, 198, 207, 235–236, 238, 242, 262, 271–272, 277, 279, 307, 322, 333, 350, 353, 361–362, 369, 376, 377, 384, 392–393, 397, 400, 404, 405, 411, 422–423, 433, 435, 439

Rhetorical device, 325, 326, 329

Scanning, 27, 162, 192, 194, 263, 435

Scenes, 37, 40, 47, 50, 61, 255, 256, 258, 262, 263, 264, 265, 266, 380, 391, 415, 431–432, 435, 450, 451, 452

Setting a purpose, 7, 17, 27, 41, 50, 74, 77, 78, 84, 89, 94, 106, 124, 133, 154, 173, 179, 184, 195, 202, 232, 237, 241, 258, 267, 275, 305, 311, 317, 326, 330, 343, 360, 366, 373, 381, 388, 398, 402, 409, 417, 431, 437

Sketching, 13, 229, 380, 404, 405

Skimming, 27, 41, 162, 192, 194, 263, 435

SOAPSTone strategy, 308

Stage directions, 257, 262

Summarizing, 13, 17, 34, 37, 74, 89, 144, 160, 247, 334, 431, 435, 440

Text features, 194

Text organization, 194

Textual evidence, 22, 23, 34, 37, 39, 47, 48, 86, 130, 140, 141, 148, 164, 174, 186, 207, 235–236, 277, 308, 314, 322, 325, 351, 363–364, 371, 372, 377, 384, 392, 400, 404, 407–409, 422, 444

TP-CASTT strategy, 74, 76–77, 89

TWIST strategy, 363–364

Visualizing, 16, 27, 41, 148, 176, 405, 431

Working from text, 16, 23, 35, 48, 61, 76, 80–81, 86–87, 93, 98, 108, 129–130, 141–142, 155, 174, 183, 187, 198, 209, 238, 262–264, 272–274, 277–279, 307–310, 314, 323, 325, 327–329, 334, 351–352, 362–363, 370–373, 376–377, 385–386, 393–395, 404–405, 411–412, 423, 433, 439–440, 443–444

Writing Skills

Advertisements, 323

Analytical paragraph, 378

Anecdote, 109, 358–365

AQQS strategy, 109–110

Argument, 172, 173, 176, 178, 190, 202, 211
    effectiveness of, 326, 330, 334
    validity of, 182, 188, 189, 190, 192

Argumentative writing, 171, 172, 173, 199–200, 210, 216, 309–310

Audience, 172, 191, 207, 216, 244, 327, 357

Background information, 110, 115, 213

Bibliography, 201, 216
    annotated, 201
    note (research) cards for, 201, 209

Big idea, 351

Body (supporting) paragraph, 102, 110, 112–114, 115, 213, 409, 411

Book preview, 225

Brainstorming, 5, 25, 82, 123, 174, 190, 192, 327

Bridge, 104, 110, 115, 116

Call to action, 213, 309–310, 323, 329, 337

Characters, 69, 98, 141

Media Skills

Speaking and Listening Skills

Index of Authors and Titles

Credits

Courtesy Games for Change, http://www.gamesforchange.org. KU Work Group for Community Health and Development. (2010). Chapter 3, Section 10: Conducting Concerns Surveys. Lawrence, KS: University of Kansas. Retrieved January 2, 2011, from the Community Tool Box: http://ctb.ku.edu/ en/tablecontents/section_1045.htm. Reprinted by permission.

Address by Cesar Chavez, President United Farm Workers of America, AFL-CIO, at Pacific Lutheran University, March 1989, Tacoma, Washington.

Excerpt from The Devil's Arithmetic, copyright © 1998 Jane Yolen, published by Puffin Books, a division of Penguin Young Reader's Group.

Unit 4
From "Made You Laugh" by Marc Tyler Nobleman. Published in *READ*, April 1, 2005. Copyright © 2005 by Weekly Reader Corporation. Reprinted by permission of Scholastic Inc.

From "Brothers" by Jon Scieszka from *Guys Write for Guys Read*. Copyright © 2005. Reprinted by permission of the author.

"Take a Walk on the Wild Side" by Dave Barry, *The Miami Herald*, July 11, 2004. Copyright © 2004 by Dave Barry, Herald columnist. Reprinted by permission of Dave Barry.

"Underfunded Schools Forced To Cut Past Tense From Language Programs," November 30, 2007. Reprinted by permission of The Onion. Copyright © 2014, by Onion, Inc., www.theonion.com.

"Mooses" from *Collected Poems* for Children © 2007 by Ted Hughes. Reprinted by permission of Farrar, Straus, and Giroux, LLC and Faber and Faber Ltd. All rights reserved.

"Is Traffic Jam Delectable?" from *It's Raining Pigs & Noodles* by Jack Prelutsky. Text copyright © 2000 by Jack Prelutsky. Used by permission of HarperCollins Publishers.

Excerpt from *Seedfolks* by Paul Fleischman. Text copyright © 2004 by Paul Fleischman. Used by permission of HarperCollins Publishers.

From "Fear Busters – 10 Tips to Overcome Stage Fright!" by Gary Guwe, August 9, 2007, http://garyguwe.wordpress.com. Reprinted by permission of the author.

Adapted from "9 Public Speaking Tips to Get Over Stage Fright" by Emma Sarran Webster, copyright © August 22, 2017, TeenVogue.com.

Image Credits
1 U.S. Air Force photo/Samuel King Jr.; 13 Granger Historical Picture Archive/Alamy Stock Photo; 14 Claude Lorrain (Claude Gellee) (1600-82) / Louvre, Paris, France / Bridgeman Images; 17 Everett Collection Inc/Alamy Stock Photo 20 Groome, William Henry Charles (1881-1914) / Private Collection / Bridgeman Images; 28 Marie-Lan Nguyen, via Wikimedia Commons; 38 As the Cyclops lay sleeping, Ulysses and his men blinded him (colour litho), English School, (20th century) / Private Collection / © Look and Learn / Bridgeman Images; 38 Polyphemus, from 'The Children's Hour: Stories from the Classics', published by the Waverley Book Company (colour litho), Brock, Charles Edmund (1870-1938) / Private Collection / Bridgeman Images; 38 Art and Picture Collection, Th e New York Public Library. "Th e Cyclops Polyphemus tosses rocks at the fl eeing Odysseus and his crew." New York Public Library Digital Collections. Accessed October 27, 2016. http://digitalcollections. nypl.org/items/510d4 41 Copyright ⌧ 2017 Allison Adams; 50 Larry D. Moore [CC BY-SA 3.0 (http://creativecommons.org/licenses/by-sa/3.0) or GFDL (http://www.gnu.org/copyleft/fdl.html)], via Wikimedia Commons; 74 Victor Grigore / webphoto.ro; 78 Copyright © 2017 Gale Fiege; 79 Tom Antos/Shutterstock; 84 Photo 12/Alamy Photo; 85 Illustration Works / Alamy Stock Photo; 89 By

Internet Archive Book Images [No restrictions], via Wikimedia Commons; 90 By Currier & Ives [Public domain], via Wikimedia Commons; 91 Stocktrek Images, Inc. / Alamy Stock Photo; 92 Pobytov/iStock; 94 Oscar White/Contributor/Pach Brothers/CORBIS/Getty Images; 95 Sarin Images / GRANGER — All rights reserved.; 100 Scott, William Edouard (1884-1964) / Private Collection / The Stapleton Collection / Bridgeman Images; 106 William Charles Ross [Public domain], via Wikimedia Commons; 107 lynea/Shutterstock; 119 WIN-Initiative/Neleman; 125 LIONSGATE Album / Alamy Stock Photo; 127 The Print Collector / Alamy Stock Photo; 134 Andersen/Contributor/Getty Images; 142 liuzishan/iStock; 142 Bertrand Benoit/Shutterstock; 154 Diego Schtutman / Alamy Stock Photo; 179 Ken Lubas/Los Angeles Times via Getty Images; 180 chombosan/Shutterstock; 184 NetPhotos / Alamy Stock Photo; 185 Illustration by Anita DuFalla for PublicSource, www.publicsource.org; 195 Copyright © 2017 Alex Davies; 196 chombosan/Shutterstock; 203 Illustration © James Provost 204 Illustration © James Provost 204 Illustration © James Provost 205 Illustration © James Provost 206 Illustration © James Provost 219 Young Women at the Memorial to the Murdered Jews of Europe, Berlin, Germany (photo) / Peter Langer/Design Pics/UIG / Bridgeman Images; 232 Agence Opale / Alamy Stock Photo; 234 Mantvydas Drevinskas/Shutterstock; 237 dpa picture alliance / Alamy Stock Photo; 237 Hopper, Edward (1882-1967) / San Diego Museum of Art, USA / Museum purchase through the Edwin S. and Carol Dempster Larsen Memorial Fund / Bridgeman Images; 251 Bill O'Leary/The Washington Post/Getty Images; 254 AF archive / Alamy Stock Photo; 256 Moviestore collection Ltd / Alamy Stock Photo; 257 Anne Frank Fonds Basel / Contributor/Getty Images; 258 Bettmann/Contributor/Getty Images;